THE
Second
Fifty

✳

THE
Second
Fifty

*

ANSWERS TO THE
7 BIG QUESTIONS OF
MIDLIFE AND BEYOND

DEBRA WHITMAN

W. W. NORTON & COMPANY
Independent Publishers Since 1923

For Grace and Owen

CONTENTS

INTRODUCTION

Compared to our ancestors of just a hundred years ago, we are living so much longer that we have gained almost a whole second life—a second fifty. In 1900 the average life expectancy for Americans was around forty-seven years. But thanks to the medical and public health revolutions of the twentieth century, by its high-water mark in 2016, average American life expectancy stood at eighty-one years for women and seventy-six for men. Despite the slight drop in U.S. life expectancy since then, children today have a 50 percent chance of living to a hundred. The number of American centenarians is expected to quadruple by 2054.

This is an astonishing achievement, and our increased lifespans have brought abundant opportunities. I meet people living active, fulfilling lives into their eighties, nineties, and beyond. My husband's Uncle Barry and Aunt Shelia have spent their retirement traveling the country, volunteering for Habitat for Humanity. Barry is now eighty-nine, but he still grabs a hammer twice a week to help his local Habitat. I read stories all the time about how older people are pushing the boundaries of what's possible. Liana Munro was a ballroom dance champion at seventy-seven. Fauja Singh, who took up running at age eighty-nine to cope with grief, completed a full marathon when he was a hundred. Businesswoman and designer Iris Apfel signed a modeling contract at ninety-seven. Tattooist Apo Whang-Od graced the cover of *Vogue Philippines* at age 106. It isn't that these people have all lived trouble-free lives. Retired nurse Barbara Hillary had survived two cancers by the time she became—in her late seventies—the first Black woman to reach both the North and South poles.

These are extraordinary feats, and I am not for a minute suggesting that we need to aspire to marathon running or intrepid travel for our later decades to be meaningful. Many of us will feel our lives are rich if we can keep enjoying the pastimes we always have, contribute to our communities, and relish time with loved ones.

Some of us will struggle. My own grandmother comes to mind. I grew up in a multigenerational household, a loving but complicated one. When my mother was young, my grandmother had been diagnosed with a serious mental illness and put into an institution, but after Mom grew up and got settled, she brought my grandmother to live with us. Grandma Pfeifer was soft-spoken and incredibly sweet. She cared for me, and I cared for her. She made the best cinnamon rolls I've ever tasted. In turn, I tried to teach her 1980s-style aerobics, in an effort to get both of us fit.

On the days when it was my job to make sure Grandma took her medicine, I'd keep an eye on the clock and bring her a glass of water and her pills at just the right time. These medications mostly managed her illness, but occasionally she would suffer from distressing hallucinations and have to be hospitalized for a short period. Eventually, between her mental illness and her decreasing mobility, my parents could no longer care for her on their own. Grandma Pfeifer moved to a nursing home when she was eighty-nine, where Mom visited her nearly every day until her death at ninety-six.

Growing up with my grandma taught me a lot—about mental illness and the emotional, logistical, and financial demands of caregiving; about how vulnerable aging and ill health can leave us; and about how reliant we can become on others. I saw that older people have value no matter their health. I later came to understand that the policies and programs we have in this country determine our options, which affect successive generations. Because of her disability, my grandmother received a small Supplemental Security Income check each month, enabling her to purchase her own clothes at the thrift shop (she loved polyester pastel suits) and take my brother and me to the candy store on special occasions. She also had Medicaid, which allowed her to see the doctors she needed and eventually covered the nursing home. If my grandmother had not had her Social Security and Medicaid, my parents likely would have struggled to send my brother and me to college.

As a specialist on the challenges facing an aging society, I've thought about these sorts of issues every day for the last twenty-five years. I am an economist and what's known as a policy wonk. I love diving into the details to figure out how existing policies are or aren't serving us and how we can develop better strategies to meet our needs. What is the state of Social Security, Medicare, and Medicaid? Can people afford retirement, or the care and support many will need as they age? I'm not a doctor or famous TV personality. You may never have heard of me before you picked up this book. But I've spent the last twenty-five years trying to fix these problems, and I know about the challenges you and your family are likely to encounter as you face your second fifty.

I started my career as a researcher at the Social Security Administration, exploring ways to improve the program for the millions who needed it. Then, for about a decade in the early 2000s, I worked on Capitol Hill, helping to pass legislation in the Senate on health programs, such as the expansion of Medicare to cover prescription drugs, and conducting research on aging for the Library of Congress. I also helped lead the Senate Committee on Aging, then a rare bastion of bipartisanship in Congress, where senators from both sides of the aisle teamed up on nearly every key hearing and piece of legislation.

For the past decade, I've been chief public policy officer at AARP, the nation's largest nonprofit, nonpartisan organization dedicated to empowering people to choose how they live as they age. We use policy development, research, and analysis to push and prod our government to better serve Americans over fifty. These are the people I answer to, including the millions of AARP members, a fact I remember whenever I get on a plane. If my seatmate is over a certain age, as soon as they find out what I do, they will invariably share with me what's going on in their lives: the challenges they faced getting home care for their father, the kind woman at the bank who'd saved their mother from being defrauded of all her savings, how dizzy they feel navigating Medicare, how they rely on that Social Security check to get by every month. Is there a way of knowing how much money they'll need? they ask. And what is my view, by the way, of those brain-boosting supplements?

As I approached my own fiftieth birthday in 2020, these concerns became much more personal. Despite the years I'd spent fighting for a better future for all Americans, I realized I hadn't given much thought to my own aging. It was as though my work had been about things that happened only to other people. I started to ask myself the questions I had spent my career studying and encouraging others to think about. How long will I live? Will I remain physically healthy and mentally sharp? How long will I be able to keep working? I knew what it was like to take care of others as they got older, but what if one day I needed long-term care? Would I be able to stay in my own home? Could I afford that? I'd saved for retirement my whole working life, but if I lived into my nineties, would I run out of money?

My desire to answer these questions, not just for myself but for everyone, led me to write this book. I had a fair idea of what the experts thought, but I wanted to understand what ordinary people were feeling about their lives as they aged. What were their priorities? What did they look forward to? What were their biggest fears, and what made them feel optimistic?

In search of clearer answers to these questions, I did what all good wonks do: I conducted a survey. In the spring of 2022, I led AARP in collaborating with *National Geographic* on a research initiative, the Second Half of Life Study (SHOL), which explored attitudes about aging across the country. The participants represented the full range of backgrounds, demographics, races and ethnicities, and levels of education. Our questions covered the gamut: health, finances, levels of happiness and optimism, relationships, retirement, housing, life expectancy, and thoughts about end-of-life care and dying. Because we wanted to understand the issues and concerns *and* how they shifted over the course of people's lives, we didn't interview just older people. We posed the same questions to more than twenty-five hundred respondents ranging in age from eighteen to ninety and above.

Some of what we saw in the results tracked with conventional views of aging. People worry about finances and about physical and brain health. The desire to retain mobility and independence is very strong. Relationships become even more important as we age, not only because we tend to rely more on others but because these connections bring meaning and joy to our lives. We want to be geographically close to those we love while minimizing the burden we place on them.

But some of our findings surprised me. While younger people often equate aging with reduced capacities and increased worries, people in their seventies and eighties reported a significant uptick in happiness: they were almost twice as happy as people in their forties and fifties. Even as people aged and the likelihood of a serious medical condition increased, their perception of their own well-being tended to improve. Among those seventy and older, a higher percentage rated their health excellent or very good than did those aged eighteen to thirty-nine. Most said they didn't want to live the longest possible life at all costs. They valued *quality* of health over *quantity* of years. And the older people got, the less they feared death.

The message our survey results drove home was that aging is a holistic process, involving our physical, spiritual, psychological, social, and emotional selves. While we experience more health conditions as we

age, other facets of our lives can flourish. "Aging is aging," as one partic-
ipant said. "It can be good if you have a right attitude. It can be terrible
if you resent it and think of all the aches and pains you acquire [that]
you didn't used to have. But you can accept them and still cherish each
day and the people you know, the experiences you have, things to do in
the world you look out at."

To write this book, I took everything I learned from the survey and
did a deep dive into how we are doing as a country addressing the issues
people are most concerned about, and what we have to do better if we're
going to ensure that the growing number of older Americans can have
a second half of life that is healthy and financially secure. My research
connected me with people from all over the world and in all walks of
life. I talked to ordinary people who are navigating the difficulties
and enjoying the rewards of life after fifty. I also talked to experts—
including demographers, neuroscientists, geriatricians, and advocates
for the paid and unpaid caregivers of our country. And I thought about
what I'd seen in my own family, because like most people, when I think
about what my future might hold, I consider what I've seen in the lives
of my parents, grandparents, and in-laws.

As I did this work, a few things were really brought home. First, all
the issues we navigate as we age are interconnected. So while each chapter of this book poses a different question, the answers depend on what
is happening in those other areas of our lives. How much money and
care we will need depends on how long we are going to live, but how
long we live—and how healthy we'll be—is determined by everything
from our level of education to the kind of neighborhood we grew up
in to whether our jobs take a physical toll on us. (Genes, it turns out,
have a lot less to do with it, while relationships have a lot more than
we'd realized. Chronic loneliness and isolation are deadlier than obesity, linked to weakened immune functioning, higher blood pressure,
and other health problems.) The state of our health can affect how long
we're able to work, when we'll need to claim that first Social Security
check (and thus how big it will be), and the kind of housing we'll need

as we age. How much we rely on those checks to get by will depend partly on whether we had a good job with a pension plan that made it easy to save for retirement.

All of which brings me to another fact that became more starkly clear as I wrote this book: We cannot talk about "aging in America" as though it's a single story. When it comes to growing older, there are many different Americas. The financial struggles some older people have are often in the news. What is less talked about are inequities in healthspan—the period of life we spend free of serious illness, pain, or disability—which varies widely from state to state, and between richer and poorer Americans. When it comes to lifespan, the wealthiest 1 percent of men live *nearly fifteen years longer* than the poorest 1 percent, while wealthier women live ten years longer than poorer women.

These disparities are shocking, especially in a country with the means to close those gaps, and they are part of the reason the United States underperforms in virtually every health metric. Americans can expect, on average, to live about seventy-six years, near the bottom of the list of wealthy countries. Our average healthspan is just sixty-six, on par not with our wealthy peers in Europe but with El Salvador and Barbados.

Fortunately, we, as individuals, are not helpless, and I'll reflect throughout the book on positive changes we can make in our own lives. Some have to do with brain health. We now know that cognitive decline is not inevitable. An estimated 40 percent of dementias could be prevented or delayed by modifying certain risk factors over which we have some control, and modifiable habits and choices play a role in 20 to 40 percent of annual deaths in the United States. In fact, while the sheer number of people with dementia is increasing—because more people are living longer—our chance of getting dementia is actually declining, a drop likely due to improvements in nutrition, health care, education, and lifestyle.

We can also push back against the stigma attached to aging—and we have evidence that doing so actually benefits our health. Studies by Becca Levy at Yale have shown that those who view aging positively live several years longer than those who hold the most negative attitudes. Internalized ageism is associated with more strokes and heart attacks, a higher risk of Alzheimer's disease, and longer recovery times after disabling illnesses or events.

We can push back against the claims of an entire self-help industry that encourages us to view aging as some kind of unnatural disaster—one we can head off if we simply take the right vitamins and count our steps. Some days it seems like every other product I see is "anti-aging" or "age-defying," from fatigue-fighting copper-infused socks to anti-wrinkle "bra pillows" to drinking straws shaped to prevent the creases that come from pursing our lips. Of course we should look after our health and well-being, but we can do that while accepting the inevitability of aging and even embracing what it offers.

Having a better second half of life, though, is going to take more than our individual efforts. That's because our healthspans and lifespans are impacted by what we call the "social drivers of health"—factors such as our zip code, level of education, income, and access to health care. Race and ethnicity intersect with these factors and are therefore linked to health outcomes and longevity. However those social drivers affect us, most of us will need some kind of support if we live long enough—whether medical, caregiving, housing, or financial. The beloved American myth of rugged individualism serves us only to a point—all well and good if we are young and healthy, but less helpful when we are old, ill, or physically or cognitively impaired.

Aging has its challenges, but many of the difficulties could be eased. They arise out of faulty, shortsighted approaches to the needs and wishes of older people, and just as we have created those conditions, we can change them. We need big-picture reforms. Our social and medical infrastructure is woefully unprepared for our increased longevity. Health care, housing, retirement plans, and programs such as Social Security and Medicare weren't designed for the twenty-first century. If *all* Americans are going to enjoy a healthier and more financially secure second half of life—regardless of where we live or how much money we make—these systems are going to have to be updated and also work together much better. We can't talk about housing for older people without talking about disability and long-term care needs, or about family caregivers without talking about work leave policies and affordable childcare. No one can save for retirement if their wages are so low they barely cover monthly expenses. The advice to exercise regularly and eat well is good, but it assumes we all have ready access to safe outdoor spaces, affordable gyms, and healthy food nearby that is within our budget. It all connects.

I've been working on these issues for half my life, and despite the obstacles I've talked about, I'm optimistic. Change is going to take all of us working together—policymakers from across the country, the people doing deep research and a lot of lobbying and legwork, and active and engaged citizens. But transformation is possible. In the final chapter, I map out what a better future would look like and how we can get there. The more we invest in health, education, and income security across all populations, the better off individuals and communities will be. So while this book is called *The Second Fifty*, I show how things like early education and safe neighborhoods help to set the stage for later life, and why policies to support older people can't be divorced from those supporting younger people.

In states and communities across the United States, forward-looking leaders are stepping up, supporting older adults to live long, healthy, and secure lives, whether through creating age-friendly environments that make it easier for people of all ages to get out and stay engaged, developing inclusive care models that allow us to age in our homes, or devising schemes to ensure that long-term care is actually affordable. Scientists who study aging, meanwhile, are building on what they've learned from modifying the rate of aging in animals (the hairless naked mole rat plays a surprising role) to develop geroprotectors, medications they hope will slow aging in humans, delaying the onset of age-related diseases such as cancer and dementia and allowing us to enjoy not just more years but more *healthy* years.

I'm not a fortune teller. And no book can tell you *exactly* how long you're going to live or how much money you'll need as you age, because we all arrive at our fiftieth birthday in different states of health, wealth, and well-being, and life will keep taking unexpected turns. But I hope my book will help you to think more clearly about what you'd like your life to look like as you get older and how you might plan for that. Writing it certainly nudged me in that direction. Thinking about the seven questions at the heart of the book opened up new conversations with my husband about both our dreams for the future and the realities we'll face. Interviewing my parents, who are in their eighties, allowed me to know them better. I hadn't fully appreciated all the love and sacrifice it took for my mother to care for her own mother for more than fifty years. I also have a clearer understanding of what is most important to them going forward, like remaining in their own home at all costs. I hope this book serves as inspiration for similar conversations with your family. Consider it your guidebook to the second fifty.

THE
Second
Fifty

✳

1

How Long Will I Live?

In the summer of 2017, my husband was hiking alone in the mountains of Colorado. He was fit and trim, a lifelong athlete, but as Glenn ascended the trail, he felt an unfamiliar tightness in his chest. A high school history teacher who gets CPR training each year, Glenn knew the signs of a heart attack. Surely it couldn't be that? He was only forty-six and had zero history of heart problems. He pushed on, hoping the sensation in his chest would go away. But it persisted.

At some point, two other hikers appeared on the trail, a father and daughter. It wasn't like Glenn to ask for help, but for once, he did. They immediately sat him down and called 911. Soon six members of Boulder Mountain Rescue, an elite group of volunteers who perform alpine search and rescue, came sprinting up the mountain. They strapped Glenn to a gurney and raced him down to a waiting ambulance.

I got a phone call from one of the helpful hikers while I was out running errands at home in Maryland. He was a little vague at first, but eventually I understood that things were serious, and I was soon speeding to the airport to catch a flight to Denver.

I couldn't believe this was happening. The vow Glenn and I had exchanged at our wedding in 1999 was "I will love you until I am 103." We come from different faiths, so we wrote our own ceremony and found saying "103" funnier than "forever." As the years passed, the line had become a running joke between us. It might seem strange that we assumed we could live that long. But the odds were in our favor. We were healthy, well educated, and financially secure—all factors that boost life expectancy. Not only had we promised to love each other beyond the age of one hundred, we had used that horizon to calculate how long we'd need to work and how much we would need to save for our retirement.

Suddenly, I realized that all our planning, all our optimistic assumptions, might be for nothing.

In the end, we were incredibly lucky: Glenn's heart didn't stop on that mountain. He reached the emergency room before he flatlined. The hospital staff flew into action and started chest compressions, breaking several ribs in the process. The cardiologist diagnosed a blockage in Glenn's left anterior descending artery. I didn't know it at the time, thankfully, but this vital blood vessel is known as the "widow-maker." When this kind of a heart attack occurs outside a hospital or advanced care center, the survival rate is only 12 percent. Until the 1980s, even patients who were hospitalized fared little better. But then coronary stents were developed. These tiny metal structures hold the artery open to prevent it from narrowing again and can save a patient even in the middle of a heart attack.

In a matter of minutes, Glenn's brilliant cardiologist had placed four stents in three arteries near Glenn's heart. My flight was about to take off when the doctor called to say the procedure had gone well. Glenn was already recovering in the ICU.

By the time I arrived, my husband was out of danger.

Glenn's general fitness and healthy habits have supported his recovery. His doctors say that, with the stents and proper medications, he can expect many more fully active years. He is now back to hiking regularly. But my own heart beats faster retelling the story here. I had a glimpse into the true complexity of this thing called longevity, and I was shocked to discover just how much I *didn't* know. Until Glenn's heart attack, he and I had assumed we held the most important pieces of the puzzle. Yet no one had ever detected that heart condition. Nor had we given much thought to the critical roles that geography, government, and community might play. So much of Glenn's survival had come down to luck. We were lucky that those other hikers had come along and that they had cell phones and reception. We were lucky he'd had a heart attack in a county with a well-equipped rescue team, and that they'd been able to get him to the hospital so quickly. We were lucky that stents existed, that a qualified cardiologist was available, and that we had the health insurance to cover everything. In a literal heartbeat, my husband's fate had depended on people, programs, policies, and circumstances that I'd never imagined would factor into his life expectancy. And I work in the field of aging!

Glenn's heart attack forced me to confront the fact that even when the odds are in our favor, longevity is an uncertain business. We may live to 103, or we may not make it past fifty. There are no guarantees.

The close call didn't turn me into a fatalist, though. Instead, it set me on a mission. I wanted to know what determines how long we live, and why some of us live much longer and healthier lives than others. How much of a role do genes play? What factors are within our control, and which ones are beyond it? And how do governmental priorities, like the support for health care in Colorado that helped save Glenn's life, shrink or extend life expectancy? Might there be a way to ensure that we *all* live to 103?

It didn't take long to realize that . . . it's complicated. For all the factors that push life expectancy upward, including incredible medical and technological advances, our society also faces a lot of challenges that can press life expectancy downward. And these upward and downward pressures are different for different people. Typical lifespans in the United States vary widely among different income and racial groups, from county to county, and even within individual cities. The life expectancy of Asian Americans, the longest-living group in the United States, is *eighteen years longer* than that of Native Americans, who have the shortest lives. This is a shocking gap. It is also an average across a population. When we talk about "life expectancy," we mean a prediction of the age at which a person is expected to die. Very few of us will die precisely at the age indicated by our life expectancy. Some of us will die sooner, and some will live much longer. I can't reveal exactly the age at which *you* will die, but I can tell you what we know about how long, on average, people in your demographic live.

Over the last century, U.S. life expectancy at birth has increased dramatically, from forty-eight years in 1900 to 77.3 years by 2020. We owe a lot of the progress to scientific advances that have reduced death in early life. Before 1900, it was tragically common for women and babies to die during childbirth, and diseases such as diphtheria, cholera, typhus, and polio carried off thousands of children every year. But increases in life expectancy have also resulted from public health research and policy changes. Clean drinking water, antibiotics, and vaccines have extended millions of lives around the world. Improved access to maternal and child health care caused the infant mortality rate to plummet. Medications to fight hypertension and blood glucose made dramatic gains on conditions such as heart disease and diabetes. By the end of the twentieth century, previously unthinkable lifesaving procedures like kidney, liver, heart, and lung transplants were being performed by the tens of thousands.

Meanwhile, U.S. agencies such as the Food and Drug Administration, the Environmental Protection Agency, and the Occupational Safety and Health Administration have helped to ensure that the air we breathe is cleaner, our food and medications are safer, and we are less likely to get injured on the job. With improved automotive safety and emergency medical technology, as well as changes in driving laws and driver behaviors, the motor vehicle death rate has fallen almost 60 percent since its peak in 1937.

The remarkable increase in the number of years Americans can expect to live is wonderful news. The not-so-good news is that for the last couple of decades, the United States has lagged behind most other high-income countries in boosting life expectancy. Countries with the highest life expectancies added almost two and a half years of life each decade, roughly six hours per day, while here it rose at half that rate. By the late 2010s, life expectancy was 78.8 years in the United States, while in Japan it was 84.4 years. By 2019, the United States ranked fortieth in the world on this measure, below Turkey and just ahead of Ecuador. Even more troubling is the fact that since the mid-2010s, well before the dip caused by the Covid-19 pandemic, life expectancy in the United States had begun to fall for the first time since 1918—when World War I was still dragging on and a global influenza pandemic was raging. Between 2014 and 2016, it dropped from 78.8 years to 78.5 years. The decline didn't hold true for all Americans. In certain groups, it is still rising, but many more people, especially those who had dropped out of high school, were dying at younger ages than in the previous decade.

One big reason was a spike in deaths from suicide, alcoholism, and drug overdoses, especially among people in their late forties and early fifties who were without a bachelor's degree. People in this group were four times more likely than college graduates to die by suicide or from substance abuse. Economists Anne Case and Angus Deaton coined the term *deaths of despair* to describe these losses. They counted 158,000 such deaths in 2017 alone, attributing many to America's opioid epidemic and, for those without a college degree, to the "long-term drip of losing opportunities and losing meaning and structure in life."

Then in 2020 the pandemic hit, worsening social isolation and the physical, mental, and financial health of many people; the pandemic made it harder for people to access support and compounded the tragedy of deaths of despair. In 2021, more than 107,000 people died from drug overdoses, up almost 15 percent from the previous year. The combination of lethal overdoses and over one million deaths from Covid-19 sent life expectancy spiraling downward. By 2021, Americans could expect to live for 76.1 years—a nearly three-year drop from 2015 that erased a generation's worth of gains.

The pandemic shone a light on weaknesses in our public health system and on the powerful connections between economic status, education, race and ethnicity, geography, and health. Counties that had the highest household incomes had fewer Covid-19 deaths than lower-income counties. People who never graduated from high school had significantly higher death rates than did graduates. Deaths varied significantly from state to state, with Arizona having a death rate three and a half times that of Hawaii, which had the lowest rate. People of color had the highest rates of infection, hospitalization, and death, far out of proportion to their numbers in the general population, while infection and death rates on reservations across the country were much greater than in nearby non-native communities. Even the horrific death toll in nursing homes was highest among Black and Hispanic residents.

Some of the causes for these disparities echo the reasons for longevity discrepancies generally.

What Determines How Long We Live?

My mom and dad are both in their eighties. Theoretically, if I nurture my health as they have, I should have a good run. The fact that my grandmothers lived to ninety-six and eighty-one supports this theory. But what about my grandfathers, who died in their forties and seventies?

Many of us assume that genes play a much larger role in longevity than they actually do. In fact, they account for as little as 10 to 20 percent of the variation between one person's lifespan and another's. The health care we receive is another 10 to 20 percent.* The rest is attributed to what we call the social drivers of health—our social and physical environment, as well as our behavior. (Social drivers were

---

* I use these estimates as an illustration while acknowledging that the contribution of each factor varies depending on methodology. Robert M. Kaplan and Arnold Milstein, "Contributions of Health Care to Longevity: A Review of 4 Estimation Methods," *Annals of Family Medicine* 17, no. 3 (2019): 267–72. Experts also point out that components affecting our life expectancy overlap and can't be neatly separated out from each other: Nancy Krieger, "Health Equity and the Fallacy of Treating Causes of Population Health as If They Sum to 100%," *American Journal of Public Health* 107, no. 4 (April 2017): 541–49.

often called social "determinants" in the past, but "drivers" more accurately reflects the fact that neither the conditions nor the health outcomes are set in stone; policymakers, communities, and individuals can make changes that will influence health outcomes.) These social drivers are estimated to account for about 60 percent of what determines how long we live.

Genes do play a role, though, and to help me understand the balance between genes and social drivers, I invited Thomas Perls out to breakfast one morning while we were both attending a gerontology conference. Tall and wiry, with a full head of curly gray hair, Tom is one of the world's leading experts on centenarians. Since 1995, he's been collecting information on nearly every resident over one hundred in eight towns surrounding Boston. So far, he's studied over two thousand centenarians and nearly two hundred "super-centenarians," people over 110. Tom also leads the Long Life Family Study, which is following multigenerational families from the United States and Denmark to learn why some people live and maintain their health to a very old age. If anyone knows about the genetics of aging, it's Tom.

Tom gave me some good news: exceptional genes likely do play a role in making it into those "super" old ages, but good behaviors and the right environment are really important. While eating his own healthy breakfast, Tom told me that "good behavior" means having a nutritious diet, exercising regularly, and not smoking or drinking too much alcohol. "Right environment" means clean air and water, good sanitation, physical and emotional safety, and social support. He mentioned Seventh-day Adventists, a Christian denomination who practice a healthy lifestyle, including exercise and a diet that avoids meat and is heavy on plants, nuts, fruits, vegetables, and grains. Members of this group have very low rates of smoking and alcohol consumption and strong networks of community support. Several studies have found that Seventh-day Adventists have lower rates of several kinds of cancer, cardiovascular disease, and diabetes, and a higher life expectancy than the general population.

We're seeing more centenarians than ever, Tom explained, not because some new superlongevity gene has come along but because fewer people today die earlier in life, which allows more people to live up to their genetic potential.

While Tom told me that how life treats us and how we treat ourselves make the biggest difference in how long we live, he acknowledged that genes matter more as we approach one hundred. At that point, the relative importance of genes and behavior reverses, and genes play a bigger role. Which is why you often see older siblings celebrating major birthday milestones together. But while decoding centenarians' genes is still a work in progress, Tom said, one variable spans as well as challenges the so-called nature-nurture divide: gender. "Women are much stronger when it comes to aging than men," he told me.

The comment brought me back to the day my widowed father-in-law moved into his assisted living community. The first thing I noticed was that most of the residents were female. Garrett, at eighty-five, was tall, suave, and able to get around without a walker, and he received considerable attention from the ladies. Eventually, an elegant woman five years his senior caught his eye and his heart. Garrett and Flo became constant companions, until he passed a few years later, leaving Flo—who had previously survived a husband and another boyfriend—alone again.

Garrett and Flo's story is not unusual. For every one hundred centenarians, about fifteen are male and eighty-five are female. Although men, as a rule, are physically stronger, have fewer disabilities, and are more likely to claim that they're in good health, women outlive them by three to seven years. Researchers call this the gender paradox, and it is one of the most robust features of human biology because it holds true around the globe, regardless of nation or culture.

There are a number of reasons for the paradox, having to do with both "sex" and "gender." While the two terms are often used interchangeably, *sex* technically refers to biological attributes, while *gender* reflects self-identity, presentation, and behaviors. Both play critical roles in differentiating male and female characteristics.

Sex hormones such as estrogen, progesterone, and testosterone—which account for many of the biological differences between men and women—are one factor that influences lifespan disparities. In general, women have more estrogen and progesterone, while men have more testosterone, but the amounts of them in our bodies vary with age. These hormones have been an important evolutionary tool in ensuring our species' survival by preparing the human body for conception, helping a mother survive pregnancy and childbirth to raise her offspring, and nudging a male to compete with his rivals over a fertile female. But sex hormones also affect our defenses against infection, disease, and injury—all of which impact how long we live. Estrogen, for example, ramps up immune responses, which may help women fight off viruses. It can give women a stronger defense against hypertension, high cholesterol, stroke, and heart failure. On the downside, it is linked to women's higher rates of breast cancer and may contribute to more autoimmune diseases, such as rheumatoid arthritis or lupus.

The primary male sex hormone, testosterone, actively suppresses several of the same immune responses that estrogen boosts, leaving men more susceptible to viruses, parasites, and bacterial and fungal infections.

Men and women do experience many of the same health conditions, but they tend to develop them at different rates and ages. A study found that although heart disease accounted for a similar proportion of all deaths in men and women, men tended to be a decade younger than women when first diagnosed. Men are also between two and four times more likely than women to develop most types of nonreproductive cancer, and their cancer survival rates are lower. These disparities hold true around the world, across all societies and at all ages.

Interestingly, not all the differences in life expectancy between men and women can be traced to biology. A study published in 2023 looking at 156 countries showed that *both* men and women live longer in countries with fewer gender inequities: as women achieve political, economic, and educational equality, overall life expectancy increases, and the gender gap narrows.

Individual behavior, environment, and cultural attitudes related to gender also contribute. To understand the interplay, it may help to take a quick trip back to the Middle Ages—when men typically lived *longer* than women. Medieval women had the same biological advantages as women today, but with poor sanitation, no birth control, and few medical remedies, they were much more likely to die during pregnancy and childbirth. This continued into the first decades of the twentieth century, when maternal mortality remained high in industrialized countries. The odds of surviving childbirth didn't improve until the advent of modern obstetrics, improved nutrition, and a reduction in poverty. And as more women survived childbirth, their overall life expectancy soared. (The rise in maternal deaths over the last several decades, especially among Black women and women over forty, may threaten this trend.)

Meanwhile, throughout history and around the globe, masculinity has been associated with risky behavior, from exploring new territories to dueling, brawling, and waging war. It's hardly surprising, then, that men are more likely than women to die prematurely as a result of physical injury. In the United States, high levels of gun violence, car crashes, and drug overdoses have shortened life expectancy for men by at least a year over men in other high-income countries—more than double the toll these injuries have taken on women's life expectancy. Violence does cross the gender barrier in one respect: every day almost three women are killed by an intimate partner or former partner.

I found exceptions to one aspect of the gender gap. In a few small corners of the world, men and women enjoy equally peaceable lifestyles. Throughout the twentieth century in Germany, for example, while the rest of the population struggled through two world wars, more than eleven thousand cloistered Catholic nuns and monks kept largely to themselves. Researchers analyzed a century of records for these Bavarian orders and found that, with gendered behavior equalized, the cloistered nuns lived *just one year* longer than the monks—even as the male-female longevity gap had widened in the rest of the country. This slim gap remained unchanged over the entire century.

Not all the risks men take involve reckless behavior or violence. More subtle behavioral tendencies can also shorten their lives. A national survey by Cleveland Clinic showed the extent to which men avoid going to the doctor. Only half engage in preventive care (while almost three-quarters would rather do household chores than see their physician). The reasons ranged from inconvenience to learning as boys that men don't complain about their health. The survey also found that men were often not honest with their doctors when they did visit, because they felt embarrassed, didn't want to change their lifestyles, or were unready to face a diagnosis despite knowing that something was wrong. Thank goodness my own husband asked for help when he needed it.

Glenn's survival depended on quality health care, and our access to such care clearly impacts our lifespan. If I'm not correctly diagnosed, or can't get the surgery, treatment, or medications I need when I need them, I may die. Surprisingly, then, only about five of the thirty years we gained in life expectancy during the twentieth century were due to improved medical care. As technology advanced, the contribution of medical care to extending our lives increased in the latter part of the century, and it is likely to increase more in the future. But the fact is that in the United States, between 20 and 40 percent of early deaths from the five leading causes (heart disease, cancer, chronic lower respiratory diseases, stroke, and unintentional injuries) could be averted through primary preventions such as exercising, wearing seat belts, not smoking, or other lifestyle changes. And yet of the trillions spent annually on health ($4.3 trillion in 2021), only 5 percent of it typically goes to public health and prevention. Because health care, use of preventive strategies, and disparities in access and insurance have such an effect on our health—perhaps even more than they do on our longevity—I'll talk about those in Chapter 2.

In his book *The Political Determinants of Health*, Daniel Dawes likens the social drivers of health and the political forces and policies that shape them to the conditions that surround a seedling from the moment it's planted until it dies. A seedling that is carefully nurtured and takes root in ideal conditions has a good chance of thriving, Dawes explains. But if that same seedling lands in the wrong kind of soil and is deprived of water, fertilizer, or care, it will likely wither and die prematurely. Some rare, extraordinarily hardy varieties can endure neglect and harsh treatment, but most of these plants will perish through no fault of their own. Nature may provide the seed with all the internal structures it needs, but its survival ultimately depends on how it is nurtured by its environment.

The same is true of people, says Dawes. If society fails to give us all an equal shot at long life, many who were born to live long will die prematurely. In a nutshell, those who bear the brunt of social, economic, and environmental inequity tend to live disproportionately shorter lives than those with more advantages. This may be because their daily struggles are more stressful or because they can't afford the latest medical and technological miracles. They may not receive their fair share of education, housing, and employment opportunities, or they may lack access to basic infrastructure and government services. All these factors affect our longevity.

The social drivers of health tend to intersect with income. And because so much of what we all need to stay healthy and survive carries a price tag, income influences our lifespan. But even I didn't realize just how big its impact is. Here are some shocking numbers: In the United States, the richest women live ten years longer than the poorest women. Men in the top 1 percent outlive men in the bottom 1 percent by *fifteen years*. Low-income American men have life expectancies comparable to those of men in Sudan and Pakistan.

Income is strongly correlated with education, another factor in life expectancy. I certainly wasn't thinking about extending my longevity when I entered college, but it turns out that's exactly what I was doing. Better education sets us up for more job opportunities and more successful careers, which leads to higher income and benefits, including greater pensions and Social Security contributions. These, in turn, lead to more financial security and better health care in later life. Over the course of their working lives, people with bachelor's degrees will earn over $1 million more than high school graduates, while an associate degree (a two-year degree from a community college, junior college, online university, or four-year institution) has a lifetime value of about $325,000 more than a high school degree.

The rise in U.S. life expectancy in the twentieth century tracks with the expansion of education. In 1869 only 1 percent of Americans between eighteen and twenty-four years old were enrolled in college, and virtually all those students were upper-class white men. By 1960, 10 percent of men and about 6 percent of women had completed four years of college. Today more than one in three Americans has a bachelor's degree, and since the mid-1980s, more women than men have been earning a degree. These college graduates have reaped the lion's share of life expectancy gains over the last thirty years; they now live about seven years longer than those who have only a high school education, and the gap is widening.

Earning power isn't the only explanation for the difference, though. Jobs with higher pay often come with benefits such as health insurance. Affluent people generally live in healthier and safer neighborhoods. They face less crime and pollution and enjoy better infrastructure and more public services. Even if they suffer major setbacks, wealthier people tend to fare better in old age than people who grew up poor, because *dis*advantages also multiply over time. People who are poor when they're young tend to struggle at every stage of life and are more likely to face later poverty and early death.

Over the last few decades, income inequality in the United States has increased dramatically. Households today with incomes in the top 20 percent earn fourteen times what those in the bottom 20 percent earn, a gap that has *doubled* in the last fifty years. At the same time, the longevity gap has widened, with nearly all the gains in years of life going to those at the top. Between 2001 and 2014, people in the top 5 percent of income distribution gained around three years of life expectancy, while the lifetimes of Americans in the bottom 5 percent barely increased at all. The saying that "time is money" may need to become "money is time."

Perhaps more important to your longevity than your income, education, gender, or genes is where you live. I first met Brian Smedley in the mid-2010s when he was giving a talk about the importance of geography to health. Brian is now an equity scholar and senior fellow at the Urban Institute, but at that time he was working on an initiative called Place Matters, which was creating maps to highlight the relationship between where people live and outcomes such as life expectancy. That research revealed dramatic, decades-wide differences between the most and least healthy communities within the same area.

At one point in Brian's presentation, he showed a map of the Washington, D.C., subway, with life expectancies superimposed on different areas of the city. I had known there were disparities in lifetimes from one city or area of the country to another, but the map showed a difference between where I lived and where I worked that stunned me. Only seven miles separate my home from my office at AARP, but across this short distance there was a five-year difference in life expectancy.

As I began to write this book, I wanted to understand more about why geography is such a strong predictor of life expectancy. I called on Brian because he is one of the smartest and most committed people I know working in this field. He's also from Detroit, a city that barely had a major grocery store left by the early 2000s, and he has seen firsthand how a lack of basic services affects a community's health.

Place, Brian told me, is a powerful shaper of virtually everything in our lives. It influences whether we have access to healthy foods, affordable housing, health services, and good schools. A healthy community includes everything from physical infrastructure—sidewalks, street lighting, public transportation—to environmental factors such as clean air, water, and soil. "What happens with a concentration of poverty," Brian said, "is that people tend to be exposed to higher health risks and have lower geographic and financial access to health-enhancing resources."

As with other disparities that are on the rise, we are now seeing the greatest gap in life expectancy by region in forty years. The country's lowest life expectancy is in South Dakota's Oglala Lakota County, home to the Oglala Sioux tribe and the Pine Ridge Reservation. Insufficient funding for the Indian Health Service often leaves tribal members' access to health care spotty. Average life expectancy there is just 66.8 years, on par with Sudan and far from the 86.9 years that residents of Colorado's Summit County, who have the highest average, can expect to live. Not surprisingly, the median income in Summit is $93,505, three times that of Oglala Lakota County, and the difference in levels of education is huge.

Bev Warne, an Oglala elder, was born on the Pine Ridge Reservation in 1939. Bev told me both she and her mother attended boarding schools. The schools were set up in the late 1860s for Native American children, many of whom suffered both physical and mental abuse while attending. While treatment of Native children was better at some schools than others, the ultimate goal of the institutions was to strip the children of their traditions, beliefs, and language, ultimately eradicating Native culture. The last of the schools closed in the 1960s, but the legacy of educational inequality lives on. Only about 21 percent of Native Americans over twenty-five have a bachelor's degree or higher.

As an adult, Bev became a nurse and lived around the world, but she came back in 2015 when South Dakota State University asked her to serve as coordinator of the Native American Nursing Education Center and improve its retention rates. Bev quickly discovered that students were dropping out not because of academic inability but because of poverty: having to choose between attending class and working more hours to pay an electricity bill or buy food. When she set up a fund to help her students in such emergencies, retention rates shot up from 64 to 96 percent.

"I see efforts that are superhuman from individuals in Pine Ridge, including young, educated indigenous people," Bev told me when we spoke in early 2023. "I'm hopeful today. The nursing students want to stay home and give back. How wonderful is that? That's what keeps me going at my age, and that part is sometimes not explored enough, the resiliency of the people. As leaders, we remind younger people that we're doing this in honor of our ancestors who went through so much so that we could be here today. To remember them with respect and prayer, and always acknowledge the future. We're doing this for future generations."

The differences in life expectancy between low- and high-income communities have grown rapidly—much faster, in fact, than has income inequality. People living in the most impoverished communities in the early 1980s were 9 percent more likely to die in a given year than those in affluent communities. By 2015, they were 49 percent more likely to die. When the pandemic struck, that gap increased to 61 percent.

When I compared cities that appear in some respects to be similar—say, big urban centers—I saw that location may play an even more important role than education or income in determining how long people will live. Low-income New Yorkers, for example, live five years longer on average than low-income residents of Detroit. Some of this can be explained by differences in behavior, such as smoking (more common in Detroit) and walking (more common in New York). But poor people live longest in cities like New York and San Francisco, where local government invests in services that encourage education and healthy behaviors. These cities have also shown the largest gains in life expectancy since 2000. For decades, Americans with the shortest life expectancies have been located in the South, the Mississippi basin, West Virginia, Kentucky, and selected counties with large Native American populations. These areas also happen to have some of the lowest expenditures on education in the country.

The good news is that state and local governments can increase life expectancy by prioritizing key services—education, health care and emergency services, affordable housing, public transportation, safe green spaces—and ensuring that all residents have access to them. Preparation for disaster can save lives, too, especially in an era of climate change, when wildfires, heat waves, hurricanes, and tornadoes are becoming more frequent and dangerous.

Philadelphia is a case in point. At the end of the twentieth century, as summer temperatures began to rise, concern grew for the city's most vulnerable residents, who were often elderly and poor, living alone with no air conditioning. Officials responded by mapping heat levels across Philadelphia's neighborhoods, then cross-referencing these maps with the locations of the most vulnerable, a lot of whom lived in the hottest areas. City leaders consulted with community leaders to devise a plan to help those people in the event of a heat wave. Solutions included creating cooling centers in houses of worship; establishing media alert systems to warn people when the heat index was expected to spike; doing outreach to the homeless; and recruiting block captains who would ensure that the most vulnerable were checked on. When researchers looked back over Philadelphia's heat response between 2001 and 2006, they estimated that this plan saved approximately forty-five lives every year. There were no miraculous medical interventions here, just data gathering, common sense policymaking, and implementing the plan.

Racial Differences in Longevity

In the summer of 2010, when Ron Howell attended his fortieth Yale College reunion, he found himself scrolling through the death notices for the class of 1970 and spotted something. There were a lot of Black men on the list. "It was very clear to me that the numbers were disproportionate," Ron told me when we spoke by phone. But it really hit home several weeks later when his close friend Clyde Murphy died at sixty-two of a pulmonary embolism. Clyde had been in Ron's class at Yale and was a fraternity brother and the best man at Ron's wedding. Clyde had gone on to Columbia Law School and, as a prominent civil rights lawyer, had argued successfully before the Supreme Court. "I was jogging in Prospect Park with my cell phone," Ron said, "and got a call from my son, who told me that Clyde had died. I was all but speechless."

By the time Ron went back to those death notices a few months later, two other Black classmates had died. Ron did the math and realized that almost one-third of his Black classmates—nine out of about thirty—had died by their early sixties. Black men made up only 3 percent of the class of 1970 but more than 10 percent of the deaths. (Yale did not open to female undergraduates until 1969.)

Ron was a journalism professor at Brooklyn College, so he was naturally inclined to dig into the reasons for this disparity. Shouldn't Black men who had made it to the highest echelon of American education enjoy lifespans similar to those of their white peers? It seemed not. There is some evidence that Black men who ascend the socioeconomic ladder may face a number of chronic medical conditions, including hypertension and cardiovascular disease, linked to the intensive stress of achieving in a context of racial barriers.

Ron told me he had felt the same pressures that many Black people did, highly educated or not. "When I say racial disparities," he explained, "it's not only in treatment and perceived treatment when dealing with others, but in expectations and feelings about yourself. But I've also felt very grateful for the opportunities I've had in life, and I think that counts for a lot."

Ron published an article about the disparities in the *Yale Alumni Magazine*. The piece generated a big response. One day he was at a luncheon of Yale Black alumni and noticed the young man next to him was a vegan. When Ron said he was vegan too, the man told him he'd "converted" after reading an article in *Yale Alumni Magazine* about the early deaths of Black graduates. "Well," Ron said, "you're talking to the guy who wrote the article."

While the overall disparities in life expectancy between people of different races or ethnicities have remained fairly constant, in the last decade the number of years different groups can expect to live has changed dramatically. Most opioid victims were white, which decreased the life expectancy gap between whites and other races—and nearly closed it between Black men and white men. Then Covid-19 hit, causing total U.S. life expectancy to drop by nearly three years between 2019 and 2021. But while white Americans lost about two and a half years of life expectancy between 2019 and 2021, Hispanic and Black people lost four years, and American Indians and Alaska Natives lost an astonishing 6.6 years.

In 2021, U.S. life expectancy by race showed concerning disparities, including a huge gap between the longest- and shortest-lived groups.

- Asian Americans: 83.5 years
- Hispanic Americans: 77.6 years
- White Americans: 76.4 years
- African Americans: 70.8 years
- Native Americans: 65.2 years

Asian Americans live the longest of all the racial groups studied, and Hispanic men and women live more than one year longer than non-Hispanic whites. Given what we know about the social drivers of health, these figures might seem paradoxical. Researchers don't agree on the reasons for longer life expectancy for Asian and Hispanic Americans. Some speculate that both groups live longer because of lower levels of smoking or drinking. Others believe it may be due to immigration patterns that self-select for healthier people, U.S. policies that favor skilled or educated immigrants, or the different psychological and social contexts in which immigrants live. Coming to this country by choice to pursue opportunity or seek safety, even with all the accompanying stresses, is different from the historical experiences of African Americans whose ancestors were enslaved. Another possible explanation is that these numbers combine people from very different countries into single racial and ethnic groups, which conceals wide variations in health and longevity outcomes between distinct groups.

In the late 1950s and early '60s, a study of Roseto, Pennsylvania— where a large community of immigrants from the same village in Italy lived—found that the residents were living much longer than those of neighboring towns. Researchers proposed that family traditions, including living in three-generation households, and a strong sense of community and mutual aid helped drive lower rates of cardiovascular disease among these recent immigrants. Over time, though, as the social structure of Roseto grew more typical of American society, life expectancy among its inhabitants became more like that of neighboring communities.

In any case, the disparities are not explained by differences in biology. What causes one racial group to live longer than another is largely about environment, behavior, and the social drivers of health that I've been talking about: income, education, and zip code. The question is how these factors interact with other aspects of ethnicity and race to produce such startling disparities. The explanations are neither simple nor obvious. When it comes to where we live, for instance, the factors that go into how healthy or unhealthy a particular location is often have deep historical roots. When Brian and the Place Matters team focused on Baltimore, they saw a nearly *thirty-year difference* between highest and lowest life expectancies across different parts of the city. To identify historical factors that might help to explain this huge gap, the team retrieved old redlining maps from the now-defunct Federal Home Owners' Loan Corporation. Dating back to the 1930s, redlining was the formal federal policy that assigned different levels of risk to different neighborhoods—color-coding them—to determine whether the government would back home mortgage loans in those areas. Whole neighborhoods were excluded from investment for generations.

The government stopped using the redlining maps in 1977, but when the Place Matters team compared the old maps with the neighborhoods that have seen persistent intergenerational poverty and poor health, they found a great deal of overlap between the two. In other words, Brian told me, "Those communities that were redlined, economically disenfranchised eighty years ago, still struggle today. And those are, by and large, neighborhoods where people of color live."

It wasn't only Black Americans who experienced historical segregation. Native Americans were relocated from traditional homelands and placed on federally designated reservations, and Chinese laborers were shunted to inferior real estate. Redlined neighborhoods, reservations, and "Chinatowns" were often located in undesirable areas with limited resources and numerous environmental hazards. As the United States industrialized, these neighborhoods frequently bordered factories, highways, and toxic dumps that raised the likelihood of air and water pollution. Funds and political will have often been lacking when it comes to providing services for these communities. As I write this, the years-long water crisis in Jackson, Mississippi, persists. Jackson, whose population is 83 percent Black, has one of the oldest water systems in the country. Its residents have routinely been directed to boil their water, and they often report leaking sewage. It is astonishing that in 2023, in the wealthiest country in the world, a whole city lacks drinkable water, a fundamental requirement for good health.

Racial discrimination itself can take a cumulative toll that leads to both physical and psychological health problems in midlife. The story of Ron Howell's Yale classmates illustrates that lifelong experiences of discrimination affect even the well-educated. The concept of "weathering" has gained traction in the years since it was coined in 1992 by Arline Geronimus, a public health researcher at the University of Michigan. It posits that chronic exposure to economic and social disadvantage and exclusion—all of which go hand in hand with discrimination—leads to early declines in health and even premature death, particularly in the lives of Black Americans. Weathering may help to explain racial disparities in a range of health conditions, as the high levels of stress hormones associated with coping with discrimination and marginalization can contribute to poor health outcomes. Because the effects are cumulative, health gaps between Black people and white people widen over time, Geronimus says, "producing ever-greater racial inequality in health with age." One study looking at 2,500 people showed that by the time Black Americans enter their second fifty, weathering has created a difference of six years between their biological age and that of their white peers. The majority of research on weathering has focused on

Black communities, but discrimination appears to have similar effects on the mental and physical health of certain LGBTQ+, Latino, Asian American, and American Indian populations.

These effects of discrimination may not be confined to a single generation. Over time, environmental stressors and deprivation—lack of access to affordable housing, quality health care and education, a clean environment, and healthy food—can shape gene expression (the process by which information from a gene is used) in ways that lead to genetic changes across generations. In this sense, good health is another asset that is passed on to successive generations. But poor health is passed on too.

Many of the conditions I've been talking about are the result of decisions made by those in government, dating back hundreds of years and continuing right up to the present. We can make different decisions in pursuit of better outcomes. We have the power as a society to change social circumstances and create healthier environments.

Healthy Eating—and Thinking— for a Longer Life

If you're like me, you've probably been keeping score for yourself as we've run through these longevity factors, imagining how your genes, gender, health care, income, education, zip code, and race might be mapping how long you'll live. Many of these circumstances are beyond our control, but healthy behaviors also make a real difference in our longevity. We are so used to hearing healthy behavior recommendations that it's tempting to tune them out. We shouldn't. A 2012 review of several international studies found that over half of premature deaths were caused by unhealthy behaviors such as poor diet and smoking. A more recent study published by Harvard found that five healthy habits—a good diet, exercise, a healthy body weight, no smoking, and very limited alcohol intake—helped people add years to their lives, and that those years were far more likely to be free of diabetes, cardiovascular diseases, and cancer. Healthy habits, in other words, also increase our "healthspan," which I'll talk about in the next chapter. Researchers followed more than 100,000 people over about three decades and found that those who practiced even one healthy habit lived two years longer. Women who practiced all five by age fifty lived an additional fourteen years, while men lived an added twelve years.

Another powerful driver of longevity is the views we hold about aging. A positive attitude can't solve everything, but it actually does boost health, while ageism can have the opposite effect. Ageism is unlike other forms of discrimination in that all of us, if we live long enough, are likely to face it. And we may be just as likely to hold negative ageist stereotypes about ourselves as we are to experience them from others.

Pushing back against ageist attitudes is critical, for when we internalize ageism, we lose years of our own lives. Becca Levy at Yale University reported in her 2022 book, *Breaking the Age Code: How Your Beliefs About Aging Determine How Long and Well You Live*, that psychosocial factors affect our cognitive and physical health as we age. In one study, her team tracked 660 older individuals who'd completed a survey up to twenty-three years earlier about their perceptions of aging. They found that those with positive views lived *7.5 years longer* than their peers who held the most negative attitudes. Levy and her team have shown that ageism is associated with more strokes and heart attacks, increased risk of Alzheimer's disease, and decline in physical functioning such as strength and balance. Older people with positive age stereotypes were more likely to fully recover from severe disability than those who held negative views. I'll talk more about ageism throughout this book and how it affects everything from brain health to our chances of finding a job in the second fifty.

Many people find it difficult to view aging positively. They see nothing but illness and decline. But as Louise Aronson writes in her book *Elderhood*, looking at old age and seeing *only* those things is like looking at parenthood and seeing only the months of sleepless nights with a screeching baby or the midnights waiting up for a reckless teenager. Those concerns are real, but they are part of a much bigger picture. In fact, as Louise points out, several studies have shown that midlife is the time of greatest anxiety and lowest satisfaction. Our happiness starts ticking up again in our early fifties—in the so-called U-curve—and continues upward into our eighties. It isn't growing old that brings suffering, Louise argues, but the circumstances that often accompany aging, such as poverty, isolation, and lack of purpose.

Having a sense of purpose doesn't just make us happier; it may actually help us live longer. The word *purpose,* as researchers use it, refers to the degree to which we feel our lives have goals and direction. It means contributing in whatever meaningful way we can to our friends, families, or communities, or finding hobbies or learning new skills that bring us joy. Taking care of a pet or a plant or performing small acts of kindness for others can help us feel a sense of purpose. Regardless of gender, race, or ethnicity, people with the strongest sense of purpose have been found to be at a measurably lower risk of dying from any cause than those with the lowest sense of purpose. Purpose has been shown to improve our health and cognitive abilities, and it could even increase our income. People with purpose may be less reactive to daily stresses and more inclined to focus on the bigger picture; they may also be more likely to practice health-promoting behaviors such as exercise and preventive medical care. All these benefits, in turn, help us live longer.

While working on this chapter, I sat down with Richard Leider, a life coach and author of numerous books on finding purpose. I had heard him give an inspiring presentation, in which he stressed that purpose is fundamental to our well-being throughout our entire lives. I mentioned that my own sense of purpose had recently changed, as my kids had left for college and no longer needed me to take care of them every day. He said that what I described was similar to what many people who had found meaning and purpose in their work felt after retiring. My role had changed. These shifts happen throughout our lives, he explained, whether we're becoming empty-nesters or retirees or adjusting to the loss of a loved one, a friend, or someone we've been caring for. "What doesn't change," he said, "is the need to have a purpose beyond yourself. You don't have to go work for the Red Cross or be Mother Teresa, but you need to figure out your next purpose in life."

Richard told me he had been a student of one of my favorite advocates of the importance of a sense of purpose, the Austrian psychiatrist and philosopher Viktor Frankl. Every year my husband Glenn rereads Frankl's Holocaust memoir *Man's Search for Meaning*, in which Frankl describes the difference in beliefs and attitudes between those who survived the camps and those who perished. A sense of meaning, Frankl found, was perhaps the most important key to survival, even in such extreme circumstances. "Those who have a 'why' to live," he wrote, "can bear with almost any 'how.'"

Frankl's book inspired Glenn to become a history teacher, a profession that gives him a great sense of purpose. With each reading, he feels challenged to reflect on what is most meaningful in his life at that moment. After his heart attack, he focused on sharing gratitude by writing thank you letters to the doctors and rescue workers, as well as to the friends, family members, teachers, coaches, and mentors who have played a role in his life. Glenn has a strong appreciation of community, which is something else that adds purpose and years to our lives. The risk of becoming isolated increases as we grow older. Social isolation and loneliness may shorten our survival by up to fifteen years, while being with others through shared hobbies or projects, or even connecting virtually or by phone, not only lifts our spirits but likely helps us to live longer.

The United States has a life expectancy problem. The scale of this problem, according to Steven Woolf, is "bigger than we ever thought." Woolf is director emeritus of the Center on Society and Health at Virginia Commonwealth University. In 2023 he published a study showing that the American disadvantage in life expectancy dates to the 1950s, further back than was believed—and that the United States is being outperformed by more countries than researchers previously realized. By enlarging the pool for comparison beyond the usual small group of wealthy peers, Woolf found that since the 1930s, fifty-six globally diverse countries—many without the infrastructure and support systems of the United States—surpassed the growth in life expectancy in the United States in at least one of those years. In 1950 Americans on average lived three and a half fewer years than people in the longest-lived country, but by 2020 we lived nearly eight fewer years. We haven't been keeping up with the growth in longevity that other countries have seen, and we are falling further and further behind.

Within this overall picture, there are big regional disparities. Some states, such as Hawaii and New York, performed nearly as well as the world's healthiest countries, while states in the Midwest and South Central region had much slower growth in life expectancy, skewing the national average downward. In the next chapter, I'll look at why health outcomes—which have a direct relation to longevity—differ so much from state to state. But this problem belongs to the whole country. When some of us suffer poorer health, we all pay a price, whether through government spending being channeled elsewhere, higher insurance premiums, or greater difficulty accessing the limited resources of care.

In 2018 a bill was introduced in Congress titled the National Strategy to Increase Life Expectancy Act. That bill, one of many thousands that went nowhere in Congress, would have required the Department of Health and Human Services to develop a nationwide strategy for increasing Americans' life expectancy to at least that of the average in countries similar to ours in terms of income and democracy. Legislation to help us live longer might seem pie-in-the-sky, but so many of the tools for extending our lives are within our grasp—not medical miracles or high-tech wizardry, but individual behavior changes and national and local policies that support us in living healthier lives.

2

Will I Be Healthy?

In the future, aging may look very different than it does today. Up to now, most of the medical research and treatments that have helped us live longer have targeted individual diseases such as cancer, heart disease, and dementia. These all have different causes, but the fact that we are more likely to develop them the older we get indicates that the biological processes that underpin aging are a common factor. What if, instead of treating each disease, we slowed down the aging in our cells and tissues? This is the goal of geroscience, a growing field of research that aims to extend our healthspans—the period of life spent in good health without serious disease, pain, or disability. Instead of waiting for a disease to develop and then treating it, geroscience focuses on developing geroprotectors. These medications and strategies won't stop us from aging, but they help our bodies to age more slowly, so that a disease we would otherwise have developed in our sixties may not appear until our seventies or eighties. This isn't science fiction. Many studies have shown that the rate of aging can be modified in animals, and geroscientists hope that human aging can be delayed as well, allowing us to remain healthier longer.

Compressing illnesses or disabilities into a shorter time frame when we are older, rather than having them stretch over years or decades of our lives, could have enormous benefits for both individuals and society. What most of us want, after all, is not just longer lives but longer *healthy* lives. Some of the factors that determine health are well known—cigarette smoking doesn't contribute to a long healthspan. But other factors are less obvious. In order to better understand why some people enjoy a lengthy healthspan and others don't, I traveled back to the campus of my alma mater, Syracuse University, to meet with Jennifer Karas Montez, the director of the Center for Aging and Policy Studies.

As I sat in Jennifer's office, she showed me a charted history of health policies by state, based on studies she and her colleagues have conducted looking at eighteen different policy areas.* Until the 1970s, she said, most states had similar laws around health, education, employment, immigration, housing, transportation, and voting. But over the last few decades, there has been a sharp split, followed by a divergence in health outcomes and life expectancy. As an example, she compared Connecticut and Oklahoma, two states that, in 1959, had the same life expectancy: seventy-one years. "Boy, did they pull apart," she said. By 2017, people in Connecticut could expect to live, on average, eighty-one years. Those in Oklahoma had a life expectancy of seventy-six. This difference tracked with changes in policies. It wasn't any one policy—Connecticut's higher minimum wage or cigarette tax, for instance, or its expansion of Medicaid—but rather the combined effect of these laws

---

* The eighteen policy areas tracked were: abortion, campaign finance, civil rights and liberties, criminal justice, education, environment, gun laws, health and welfare, housing and transportation, immigration, private and public sector labor, LGBTQ+ rights, marijuana, taxes, tax on tobacco, voting, and the overall level of policymaking activity. Jennifer Karas Montez et al., "U.S. State Policies, Politics, and Life Expectancy," *Milbank Quarterly* 98, no. 3 (2020): 668–99.

that made the big difference. Now 13 percent of people born in Connecticut will die by age sixty-five. In Oklahoma, 21 percent of people will die by that age.

Jennifer also showed me her research on how these policies impact health. Comparing when residents of various states develop health problems and disabilities, she found that there can be a gap of as much as *twenty years* from one state to another. She discovered the gap was correlated with the policies and laws that the state legislators had decided to enact.

On the one hand, I was gratified to hear what Jennifer said. I've spent my career pushing for better policies, such as expanded access to affordable, quality health care, and Jennifer's work was a reminder that policy really does have the power to improve health outcomes. But it was also disappointing, because it showed that in many parts of the country, we are still falling short in creating healthy communities.

Throughout the country, Americans are living shorter and less healthy lives than they could be, and it isn't all due to our individual choices. The same social drivers (described in Chapter 1) that influence how long we live—income, education, and the conditions in our neighborhoods and communities—play a big part in how healthy we are as we age. They also point to what needs to change if we are to increase healthspans for everyone.

Our Lagging Healthspans

It might seem natural to assume that as our lifespans increase, our healthspans keep pace. But that isn't what has happened. Between 2000 and 2015, life expectancy in the United States rose by nearly two years, but our healthspan increased by only four months—and even *began to decline*. In other words, most of the years we have been gaining haven't been healthy but have meant more time spent with disease or disability. As with other health indicators, the United States performs worse on this measure than other wealthy countries. The World Health Organization publishes healthy life expectancy—what I'm calling healthspan—numbers for each country. In 2019, while the average life expectancy for Americans was 78.5, we could expect just sixty-six years of *healthy* living, which put our healthspans below those of people in Albania and Costa Rica, and on par with residents of Jamaica and Belarus.

Healthspan, like lifespan, varies according to socioeconomic conditions. People who live in poverty are far more likely to report poor health than those with higher incomes; they develop high blood pressure, high cholesterol, obesity, and other conditions at much younger ages. Over the long haul, financial hardships can aggravate conditions such as diabetes, making them more life-threatening. Meanwhile racial disparities in health insurance coverage, treatment, and health outcomes persist.

One reason our healthspans rose was advances in medical treatment for specific diseases, but the impact of those advances seems to have leveled off. (Meanwhile the rise of obesity and diabetes among younger people may cause future generations to have shorter healthspans than their parents and grandparents.) The older we get, the more likely we are to suffer from multiple serious illnesses, so treating a single disease is like playing whack-a-mole. Often, we are cured of one condition only for another to develop in its place, and the first illness may have left us with lingering problems.

Given this reality, I was surprised to see that in AARP's SHOL study, as well as in other research looking at health and aging, older people often report being very satisfied with their health. In the AARP survey, over eight in ten people aged seventy and above said they were living with at least one serious health condition, yet just under half reported their health as excellent or very good. The same figure held even when people got into their eighties. Their satisfaction may be related to the fact that our expectations of how healthy we *should* be changes as we grow older, but medical support and technology have no doubt played a big role. Replacement surgeries, implantable devices, and other technical fixes reduce pain and improve mobility for millions. My father-in-law's license plate read 2HIPS to express his pride in his two titanium hip replacements. If there had been room on the plate, he would have added 2SHLDRS and 1KN, because he also had artificial shoulders and a new right knee. Without those fantastic technical advances, his later years would have been far more challenging and painful.

None of this is to sugarcoat the real challenges to our health and physical functioning that many of us face as we grow older (or the fact that we need resources and good health care for the kind of surgeries my father-in-law had). Often we can't easily do many of the things that we did unthinkingly when we were younger. Four in ten Americans over sixty-five have difficulty walking or climbing stairs, and ten million of those can't perform these basic movements at all. Around one in ten have trouble doing housework and need help bathing.

While I believe that extending our healthspan is an important goal, I am not so fond of the term *successful aging*. In the academic literature, successful aging usually refers to someone who is growing old with high physical, psychological, and social functioning and without major disease or disability. The concept was developed to increase awareness that contrary to the prevailing assumption that aging is solely a process of decline, a large portion of older people are active, healthy, and engaged. But applied to individuals, the term suggests that aging is a competition, and that some people are really good at it while others somehow "fail." There is also a school of thought that says that the less visibly we're aging, the more we are succeeding. We might refuse hearing aids and canes, for instance, even when both would help us engage with others or get out of the house. These measures of "success" are based in ageism as well as ableism, which undervalues those with disabilities.

Moreover the concept of successful aging doesn't always capture the complex environmental, cultural, and structural factors that go into how we age. Many of us won't actually "succeed" at aging, if that means being unaffected by it: 95 percent of American adults sixty years and older have at least one chronic health condition like depression, heart disease, or diabetes, and nearly 80 percent have two or more. But having a meaningful life of purpose and enjoyment doesn't require being completely able-bodied and disease-free. Even with a chronic condition, people can thrive, provided their environments and the health care system support them in living with their illnesses or disabilities.

Edmundo is a great example. Born in El Paso to parents who immigrated from Spain, Edmundo, sixty-eight, now lives in Dallas. When I spoke to him in the spring of 2023, he told me he was a widower and had retired from a forty-year career in IT. He has lived with congestive heart failure for more than twenty years. "It was a bit of a shock when I got diagnosed," he said. "But I started doing research and said, *Hey, this is livable.* You either come to terms with it and try to live your best possible life or you don't. I wasn't going to live my life terrified. So it doesn't stop me from enjoying life, getting up in the morning, getting dressed, going out, doing what I need to do, enjoying my retirement, and, more importantly, enjoying my family."

It is a tough disease, Edmundo said, and he knows it's progressing. He is now on his fifth pacemaker. But he continues to be proactive about his own health. He has a fitness tracker, is still increasing his steps, and has lost a lot of weight. Fortunately, he's had very good insurance, first through work and now with Medicare, so he doesn't have the added stress of worrying about uncovered medical bills. But what's really important is that he has things in life he treasures doing. When I asked about a poster behind him with guitars on it, he told me he's an avid music lover with a home studio and a collection of guitars and keyboards. He sometimes DJs for facilities where older people live. "It gives me an opportunity to meet people," he said, "and it's a lot of fun being able to make somebody smile."

Edmundo is someone who is making the most of his life, as much as or even more than many people without a chronic condition. "I've outlived two of my cardiologists," he said, smiling. "And when my time comes, I'll have no regrets because I've lived a good life." That good life is unfolding in tandem with serious health challenges. The two can coexist.

The Biology of Aging

Our bodies age at different rates. I bet that like me, you know people in their seventies and eighties who are still active, engaged, and even working, and others in their fifties or sixties whose lives are curtailed by poor health. These biological changes often track more closely with how old we feel than with the age on our ID cards.

There are many theories about how and why our bodies age, but there is no clear consensus on the subject. No single process causes or controls biological aging. Instead, multiple overlapping and interacting processes occurring in our cells and tissues seem to give rise to the changes we see and feel.

We begin to age the moment we're born, but like a lot of people, one of the first intimations I had of my own aging was when I noticed a wrinkle—one of the earliest visible signs of aging, because as we age, our bodies produce less collagen, the rejuvenating protein that keeps our skin plump and firm. Gray hairs are another sign (though some people get them quite young), as the melanocytes that give hair its color decrease over time. Many of us who never needed glasses or hearing aids will need them as we age. We may find that we're sleeping more fitfully, waking up several times each night. As we move out of the optimal years for procreation, both men and women might need help with sexual intimacy (though it is a myth that older people stop having sex: one in six adults aged seventy and over say they have sex weekly). Women have the added challenges that come with menopause. Decreases in estrogen and progesterone may result in symptoms such as hot flashes, difficulty sleeping, discomfort during sex, and even memory problems. The good news is that some symptoms often improve on their own over time, even "brain fog," and there are treatments for many others.

Some changes are less visible, but we can feel their effects. Our blood pressure tends to rise with age because our arteries gradually stiffen. As our metabolism naturally slows down and we expend less energy, we may be more likely to put on weight, even if we eat less than we used to. Or we may lose weight and become more easily fatigued, as cells require more energy to compensate for less efficient energy production. We begin to lose muscle mass from about age thirty, which means we have less strength and flexibility and a slower gait. Even the fittest among us move more slowly over time. While the fastest marathon ever officially clocked was just over two hours, run by twenty-three-year-old Kelvin Kiptum in 2023, Irish marathoner Tommy Hughes's over-sixty world record is a half hour slower. At eighty-five, Canadian Ed Whitlock made history by becoming the oldest person to run a marathon in under four hours.

Nature marks our biological age in several ways. For some time, researchers have regarded telomeres as a strong biomarker. Telomeres are the caps at the end of each strand of DNA that protect our chromosomes, a little like the plastic tips at the end of shoelaces. Whenever cells divide, as they do throughout our lives, our telomeres get shorter. Telomeres also shorten in response to stress, pollution, poor diet, and other lifestyle factors, including smoking and lack of exercise. As the DNA wears down, genetic mutations increase. And when these genetic strands are damaged or get too short, the cell can no longer divide; it becomes inactive or dies. Recently, scientists have begun to question the reliance on telomeres alone as an accurate indication of aging, particularly the belief that longer telomeres protect against aging. Other ways of calculating biological age—such as the "epigenetic clock," a method that measures the aging of blood and other tissues—are giving researchers new insights into the processes of aging.

When immune cells die, the body loses some of its ability to fight infection. A compromised immune system can also lead to inflammation. This may help to explain why chronic inflammatory conditions and diseases such as atherosclerosis, Alzheimer's disease, osteoporosis, and diabetes become more common with age. Some researchers have coined the term *inflamm-aging* to describe this syndrome. When the cells that are dying are stem cells, the body loses its ability to replace other damaged cells. Healthy stem cells normally develop into other types of cells, as needed, but as they age, their ability to distinguish and replace those other cells fades. Over time, as more and more stem cells die off, our bodies become progressively slower to heal. Even minor bruises and paper cuts last longer than they did when we were young.

A big reason some of us age faster than others at the cellular level involves the body's stress mechanisms. Evolution programmed these chemical responses to help us navigate danger. In a crisis, stress "turns on" our fight-or-flight reaction. Our muscles tense reflexively in preparation for action. Our heart races, and our breathing quickens. Stress hormones such as adrenaline and cortisol flood our bodies, causing blood vessels to constrict and blood pressure to rise. This supplies the surge of strength that helps a soldier brace for battle and empowers someone to leap clear of an oncoming car or escape a burning building. But our biological stress mechanisms are intended for short-term use—occasional spurts, not 24/7 endurance.

Ideally, the chemical flood subsides when the pressure or threat dies down, and the body can return to a normal level of stress hormones and other chemical messengers, but what happens if the cause for alarm never goes away? When the threat is not a temporary emergency but ongoing fear or suffering? Or when the threat *does* disappear but our bodies continue in a state of vigilance?

With extended or chronic pressure on our bodies and minds, the beneficial aspects of stress become toxic. Constant tension exhausts the muscles, leading to pain, headaches, and migraines. Ongoing constriction of the airways can cause shortness of breath, aggravating conditions like asthma, emphysema, and bronchitis. Constricted blood vessels and an elevated heart rate can raise the risk for hypertension, cardiovascular disease, or stroke. And the overload of stress hormones can exhaust the brain, causing neurons to atrophy and memory to falter. It can also damage the immune system, resulting in chronic fatigue and inflammation, depression, and metabolic disorders such as diabetes.

Since stress is one of Elissa Epel's areas of expertise, I asked her to walk me through this aspect of aging. Elissa is a professor of psychiatry at the University of California in San Francisco. I had a chance to meet her when I took a workshop she was leading on how stress can be both harmful and beneficial.

Harmful stress is the sort of grinding, relentless hardship that comes, for instance, with poverty, lack of safety, and even caregiving. "Our brain is attuned to being vigilant for danger in the environment," she said. But if we can't feel safe and turn off that danger vigilance every day, "negative stress overwhelms the body's coping mechanisms and speeds up cellular aging while lowering natural defenses against disease and infection."

The net effect of toxic stress on pregnant women can actually show up in their offspring. Male babies born prematurely at very low weight seem, as adults, to age faster than those with normal birth weight. A recent study looking at aging in people born during the Great Depression of the 1930s found that prenatal exposure to adverse economic conditions was associated with accelerated aging later in life. Using markers such as the onset of early puberty, inflammation, cellular aging, and changes in brain structure, other researchers have linked adverse experiences in childhood and early adolescence with faster biological aging and poor adult health. Growing up in poverty can mean poor nutrition and chronic illness and can even affect brain development. Abuse or violence, family breakdown, and other traumas have been found to predict cardiovascular disease risk, high cholesterol, diabetes, and cancer, as well as earlier diagnoses and onset of physical problems, all of which shorten lifespan.

Keeping an Eye on the Weather

Even if we are generally healthy, with age our bodies lose some of their ability to regulate core body temperature, and as the planet warms, dehydration and heat stroke are of greater concern. Volatile weather patterns, wildfires, hurricanes, tornadoes, and flash floods can pose particular risks to older adults, who may not be able to rapidly relocate or may become injured or lose access to needed medical equipment or medicine. Older people were the most likely to die in the first year after hurricane Katrina.

About one in ten older Americans live in places where the Environmental Protection Agency has deemed the air unhealthy. And as we get older, we become less resilient and more sensitive to dust, heat, and smog. When tested, residents living in areas with unhealthy air show many signs of accelerated aging, including higher rates of disease and cognitive and physical disability.

Environmental conditions tend to be worst in low-income areas, where toxic levels of chemicals in the air, water, and even building materials contribute to high rates of asthma. The quality of our environment can also change suddenly, as residents of East Palestine, Ohio, experienced when a train derailed in early 2023, spilling toxic chemicals into the air, ground, and waterways.

Thanks to the Clean Air Act, America's air quality has improved significantly over the past fifty years, and states have taken steps to clean up their air and waterways, necessary ingredients for any of us to live a long or healthy life. Continuing to remove harmful chemicals from our air, water, and food supply will take political will and action in communities across the country, but making such investments can help improve our health for decades to come, with the most immediate impact on children and older people.

Meanwhile we are beginning to understand the potential of climate change to impact not only our planet but our health. During the wildfires of 2020, the air quality in cities in the Northwest was the worst of any in the world. Among women getting treatment for breast cancer when Katrina hit, those impacted by the hurricane were less likely to be alive a decade later than those who were not impacted.

Many cities have long been retirement destinations because of their sunny weather. But the Southwest, particularly, is heating up and experiencing pressure on water supplies due to ongoing droughts. Since 1970, the year I was born in Phoenix, temperatures in that city have risen almost four degrees Fahrenheit, putting older residents at greater risk of dehydration and heatstroke. Like many other cities, Phoenix now has a climate action plan to reduce greenhouse gas emissions and build resiliency, including ways of keeping residents cool. The most attractive retirement destinations in the future will be those that do the most to mitigate the health effects of climate change, particularly for those who are vulnerable, whether because of age, disability, or socioeconomic conditions.

Extending Our Healthspans

I want to emphasize that despite the biological aging processes our bodies undergo and the impact of our experiences and environment, we aren't just at the mercy of our circumstances. There are many steps we can take to preserve good health and *decelerate* aging, and we now have strong evidence for the effects of these habits and practices.

The five recommended healthy habits are hardly a surprise, and most of us have already heard them from a health care provider. First of all, eat a healthy diet, maintaining a daily balance and variety of fruits and vegetables, whole grains, and proteins. Second, the less alcohol we drink, the better. Until recently, the advice was that women shouldn't have more than one drink a day, and men should limit themselves to two, but the latest evidence suggests that even moderate drinking can contribute to a slightly increased risk for certain cancers and cardiovascular diseases. Third, don't smoke. Smoking is a major aging accelerator. It increases our risk for at least twelve different cancers, can quadruple our risk for coronary heart disease and stroke, and raises our risk of lung cancer by more than twenty-five times. Smoking in old age may also increase our chances of developing Alzheimer's disease and general frailty. Quitting, even later in life, reduces the risk of early death. Men who quit smoking at sixty-five gain up to two years of life expectancy, and women gain nearly four.

The fourth healthy habit is regular daily exercise, in the form of moderate to vigorous movement. Walking works, as does taking stairs instead of the elevator or escalator. What matters is building movement into our daily routine. Thirty minutes a day is ideal, but even lesser amounts can lengthen our lives. Exercise combined with a balanced diet can help with the fifth life-enhancing habit: maintaining a healthy body weight. Surplus weight puts pressure on organs, bones, and joints, which can make it difficult and painful to move; it also triggers complex hormonal and metabolic changes, which increase the risk for hypertension, type 2 diabetes, heart disease, stroke, osteoarthritis, and some cancers. The good news is that we don't have to hit our ideal weight to see our health improve. Losing just a few pounds can make a real difference in preventing diabetes and heart attacks.

The researchers behind the healthy habits study found that people who practiced at least four of the five key habits gained eight to ten years free of major medical problems such as cancer, type 2 diabetes, heart disease, and stroke. That's a pretty big plus!

These keys to increasing our healthspan sound straightforward, and 93 percent of Americans say that a long, healthy life is important to them. So why do only one in four people report getting enough exercise, and only one in ten report eating enough fruit and vegetables? It may be down to circumstances that make those things very hard—lack of affordable fresh produce in your neighborhood, for instance. It may also be because only about half of us truly believe that our behavior affects our health. And then there's human nature. I don't smoke, and I try to exercise and watch what I eat, but some evenings I want a second glass of wine or another slice of pizza. We all have pleasures that may not, strictly speaking, be the best things for us. But knowing what the risks are can help us become more conscious of the fact that our behavior really can affect how long we will enjoy good health.

Another factor in our healthspan is how we manage stress. As I learned from Elissa, stress isn't just a negative. We all need it. Without stress, our brains grow less sharp and our muscles weaken. But we also need to manage the amount of it in our lives. We need activities that lower our stress and keep us from becoming chronically stressed, but we also have to stay actively engaged and challenge ourselves.

Elissa told me there are two pathways—"like yin and yang"—for managing stress. One involves things like taking breaks, relaxing with good friends, or going on vacation. Sounds great, as long as you've got an understanding boss, a flexible schedule, enough money, a supportive family, and time to regularly regroup. But what if you don't have those advantages? What are some other ways to manage stress that can actually support health?

What makes stress healthy or toxic has a lot to do with dose. So-called hormetic stress occurs when the body or brain adapt to levels of stress that are strong enough to induce changes—increasing skills, immunity, or stamina—but not so strong that they overwhelm us. One example is interval training, which alternates short bursts of intense activity with longer intervals of less intense activity. "Acute short-term stress leads to a response of recovery and rejuvenation," Elissa explained. "So while chronic, toxic stress speeds up aging, short bursts of positive stress help to slow aging."

We can also sharpen stress resilience by retraining our thoughts. When we dread a meeting or an obligation, Elissa explained, we set up a self-fulfilling prophecy inside the body. Our blood vessels constrict, reducing blood flow to the brain. We may become lightheaded and feel our heart racing, which triggers a whole second round of distress and self-talk, telling us we're stressed out and about to do a bad job.

But if we reframe the situation as a challenge instead of a threat to be avoided, our body responds differently. A challenge gives us an opportunity to test skills we know we possess. Unlike a threat, it inspires positive emotions and better problem solving and performance. "We have what looks more like an exercise response," Elissa said. With strong cardiac output, and higher levels of blood and oxygen to the brain, performance steps up.

I asked Elissa if the next time I'm speaking to a big audience and my heart is racing, I should remind myself that my body isn't stressed or threatened but excited.

"Yes," she said, and this strategy has an extra benefit for people in their second fifty. "When people are older, they tend to feel a diminishing sense of control and can end up limiting their activities. This is natural, especially for people who have health conditions." But staying engaged is important for our health and well-being and helps us to develop and maintain healthy habits that slow aging.

The third big component of staying healthy is social connection and relationships. Maybe you've had this feeling. You've been alone all day, buried in work or driving for hours, and you feel isolated and a bit down. That night, though, you get to go out with friends, and on your way home from seeing them, after a lot of laughter and shared confidences, you notice that you feel . . . restored.

This glow is real—I've experienced it myself many times. But recently I learned that over the long haul, that lift is reflected in my actual cells. Human beings have long known instinctively that we need to be with others, and now research is catching up.

In 1938 the Harvard Study of Adult Development began with over seven hundred young men—about one-third from Harvard and two-thirds from low-income, inner-city Boston neighborhoods. This study of mental and physical well-being is now in its ninth decade. Over time it grew to include the men's wives, and hundreds of children of its original group. The big finding? That good, close relationships not only make us happier, *they also keep us physically healthier as we age.*

Boston in the 1930s was overwhelmingly white, and the Harvard Study's original subjects reflected that (though more than half the inner-city boys came from immigrant families), so the research team presents only findings that are corroborated by other more diverse studies. People need people, whoever we are.

The subjects of the study periodically fill out questionnaires, provide health information, and submit to interviews. They answer a wide range of questions, sometimes on subjects that other studies miss—

their defense mechanisms, for example, and the amount of warmth they experienced as children.

Robert Waldinger is the fourth director of the Harvard Study. He's a clinical professor of psychiatry at Harvard Medical School, a practicing psychiatrist and psychoanalyst, and a Zen priest. When I Zoomed with Robert to learn more about the study findings, he was in his office, surrounded by books and looking cheerful. He told me he was as surprised as anyone to learn that human connections had physiological effects. "How could relationships affect our bodies?" he said, looking amazed. When the original participants reached eighty, researchers went back to the data from thirty years earlier to see what the best predictors of health and well-being had been. They expected to find cholesterol level or blood pressure. Instead they found that the best predictor of good health, both mental and physical, was participants having had good relationships in their fifties. Although they had troves of data on physical and mental health, satisfaction in relationships wasn't a metric they had been tracking. "We hadn't measured that year after year," Robert said. "We didn't even know it was a thing at that time. We were discovering it."

What about people who are shy or introverted, I asked him, or may be out of practice at striking up new friendships? "There is no set number of friends," Robert said. "It's highly individual and might change over time. Shy people may need just one or two, and I've heard stories of people who break through late in life to find love or develop a special friendship." We know, he said, that we are more likely to form relationships when we see the same people casually over and over—at the water cooler or doing something we enjoy alongside others. Some of those casual conversations can deepen and lead to ongoing relationships.

So how *do* relationships affect our health? It isn't just that when we are in a close relationship, we may be encouraged to eat healthier, exercise, or stop smoking. Something more is going on. For a better understanding of what that is, I turned to the work of Julianne Holt-Lunstad, a professor of psychology and neuroscience at Brigham Young University.

Julianne has looked at 148 studies from around the world to investigate the link between social isolation, loneliness, and the risk of early death. (Social isolation means having few relationships or little social contact, while loneliness is more subjective, referring to the gap between how much connection we want and how much we have.) Studies that followed people for years or even decades found that those who were more socially connected were 50 percent more likely to be alive in any given year. When Julianne compared risk factors, she found that loneliness, isolation, and living alone were more deadly than obesity or physical inactivity.

These health effects seem to be rooted in the fact that human beings rely on being part of a group for resources and protection. Alone, we have to be much more vigilant about threats in our environment. (Think of how you feel alone at night in a house, when every creak seems to signal danger, versus how you feel when you're part of a big family gathering in that same house.) Being alone and on guard can activate our fight-or-flight response and other physiological systems, and we use more metabolic resources. When isolation and loneliness are chronic, they take a toll. They have been linked to weakened immune functioning, higher blood pressure, raised levels of stress-related hormones such as cortisol, and increased inflammation, which is implicated in many chronic illnesses.

For me, the key takeaway of this research is that it's just as important to nurture the relationships in my life as it is to eat well and get exercise.

Shouldn't Health Care Keep Us Healthy?

You might assume that the biggest factor in whether we are healthy would be the health care system. The United States certainly puts a lot of resources into it. We spend about twice as much per person on health care as other large, wealthy countries do. This is because spending on prescription drugs and medical services is much higher in the United States than in other countries; we also use expensive diagnostics more intensively, and the cost of general physician and specialist visits are significantly greater here. Most of our peer countries have a universal public health system, while ours is much more fragmented, with many different public and private payors, which brings with it costly and complex administration. Health care spending here reached $4.3 trillion in 2021, about 18 percent of our gross domestic product. While spending during the pandemic pushed that number to its highest level in decades, other comparable countries spent about half as much on average.

Despite our greater spending, we have far worse health outcomes than our peer countries. We have the highest rates of people with multiple chronic conditions, obesity, and infant mortality, and some of the highest rates of hospitalization and death from preventable illnesses and injuries.

One big reason our health care system underperforms is the large number of people who are uninsured. In 2023 about twenty-six million people, or 8 percent of Americans, lacked health insurance. This was an all-time low—the drop due to the temporary expansion of coverage during the pandemic—but it's still an embarrassingly big number compared to countries that have universal coverage. I probably don't have to tell you that going to the doctor or hospital can be very expensive, so it's not surprising that due to cost, people without health insurance are far less likely to get needed care. Even for those with insurance, though, the out-of-pocket costs for quality care can be stratospheric. And premiums and deductibles have been eating up more and more of workers' paychecks.

The high cost of health care, even for people with insurance, is the main reason so many Americans don't get the care they need. A 2020 study comparing lower-income people in eleven wealthy countries found that in nearly all countries, adults with lower income were significantly more likely than wealthier adults to have multiple chronic conditions—but in every measure the study looked at, lower-income Americans suffered more. Half of them reported that within the last year they had skipped doctor visits, prescribed medications, and recommended tests, treatments, or follow-up care because of cost—three to four times the number who skipped care in Germany, Norway, and France. American adults with lower income also have worse access to primary care, and they make significantly higher use of the emergency department (for care that could have been delivered by regular providers had they been available).

Another reason the United States likely underperforms compared to other countries is that our insurance coverage system is a crazy-quilt of programs, and it is easy to fall through the cracks. Nearly 55 percent of Americans enroll in private health insurance through their employer. About 10 percent buy insurance on their own. Others are insured through government programs like Medicare or Medicaid.

The explanation for this hodgepodge of insurance goes back to World War II, when American GIs went off to fight. Facing a labor shortage and a cap on wages, companies at home needed incentives to attract top talent. They hit on the idea of providing health insurance and pensions, which the IRS declared tax-free for employees. That set a trend. Before the war, 9 percent of Americans had health insurance through their employers. By 1950 that number had risen to more than 50 percent.

Getting insurance through employers left out millions of Americans whose jobs didn't offer coverage or who were unemployed or retired. Presidents Franklin Roosevelt and Harry Truman both tried to get Congress to create a government-sponsored program that would provide basic coverage, but neither succeeded.

Finally in 1965, President Johnson was able to sign into law two new programs: Medicare, insuring older adults and people with disabilities, and Medicaid, for people with very low incomes. Both have been expanded over time. Medicaid eligibility for children from low-income families was increased under the Children's Health Insurance Program, which President Bill Clinton signed into law in 1997. It now provides insurance to more than nine million children, giving them an important early start on good health that will likely pay off over their lifetimes. In 2003 President George W. Bush signed into law a Medicare program to pay for prescription drugs and expanded the ability of private health plans to provide Medicare coverage. Medicare still has its shortcomings—it doesn't guarantee coverage of vision, dental, or hearing, for instance, and most people in traditional Medicare still purchase supplemental private insurance because of high out-of-pocket costs. But it has provided a hugely important support for older Americans.

The next big step in expanding health insurance coverage came in 2010, when President Barack Obama signed the Affordable Care Act (ACA) into law. The ACA dramatically reduced the number of uninsured Americans, partly by extending Medicaid coverage to more people with low incomes and by providing subsidies to middle-income families to help people afford health insurance.

Even with these programs, disparities in health insurance coverage and medical care remain. Of the twenty-six million Americans who lack health insurance today, the vast majority have modest incomes, and about half are people of color. Even with insurance and good incomes, people from communities of color are less likely to get appropriate care when they need it. For example, while increased insurance coverage has lifted rates of cancer screening for Black Americans overall, Black women are far less likely than white women to receive an early diagnosis of breast cancer. They have the highest late-stage diagnosis rate and are 42 percent more likely to die of breast cancer. Studies have shown that Black patients are significantly less likely to be prescribed pain medication and generally receive lower doses when medication is given. More generally, Black people receive poorer medical care for a wide range of conditions, from heart disease to pneumonia; they receive less basic preventive care and less care for critical procedures such as heart bypass surgery and kidney transplants.

Health care for American Indians and Alaska Natives is persistently underfunded, contributing to poor health outcomes. The federal government allocates a set amount for the Indian Health Service (IHS), the federal agency that provides health services to American Indians and Alaska Natives. Government spending was just $4,078 per person through the IHS in 2019, while it spent $12,331 per person on veterans' health and $14,173 per person on Medicare. As more than one in four American Indians and Alaska Natives are uninsured and rely on the IHS, lack of funding can have tragic consequences.

Bev Warne, the nurse I spoke with about health conditions in Oglala Lakota County, told me that better funding of the IHS would help significantly, "because the money runs out. And if you have an elder person who needs a hip replacement or a knee replacement, they say, well, it's not life threatening, so you're on hold. That's a horrendous decision to have to make."

The lack of insurance coverage and the high cost of health care in this country aren't the only roadblocks to maintaining our health as we age; the way care is provided and how we pay for it also stand in the way of healthy aging. For too long, our care has been paid for in what is called fee-for-service: that is, health care providers are paid for every visit or test we get. This is why, when you get your hospital bill, you sometimes see a long list of charges, including for a simple aspirin. Similarly, we pay for every doctor separately. If we see five doctors for each of our chronic conditions, we often receive five separate bills. If we have been given five different prescriptions or tests, we pay separately for each of them.

I see two big problems with this system. The first is that the financial incentives don't encourage either the prevention of chronic disease or the maintenance of our health. Instead, they incentivize doctors to run more tests and prescribe more drugs, with the goal of treating each illness or symptom separately. The second problem is the lack of coordination between all these doctors—no single health care provider is ultimately accountable to make sure everything we are doing makes us healthier.

This places a lot of the burden on us to manage our own care. Edmundo, who I wrote about earlier in the chapter, walked me through his approach. He prepares for every doctor visit by writing out any questions or concerns. "When my doctor changes a medication," he told me, "my first question is *Why*? What are the pros and cons? I do my research. I get all my doctors—primary care, hematologist, nephrologist, cardiologists—on the same page. When I visit one, I always remind them to send the report to all the others. It took a little prodding because they're not used to being told and directed. But you have to be proactive, you have to be your own advocate." Fortunately, Edmundo is able to do this. But imagine what happens when our health or mental capacities decline and we can't be proactive and don't have a caregiver who can coordinate and manage our care, let alone our bills.

Fortunately, many groups, including hospitals, insurers, and even the Medicare program, recognize that the old system isn't working well and are experimenting with new financial incentives to enable us to get better care. In addition, there are specialists trained to coordinate our care. Geriatricians are medical doctors who care for older patients, many of whom have complex medical needs. Like neonatologists and pediatricians, they focus on a particular phase of human development rather than a certain organ or body system. Geriatrics is a relatively new discipline, created in response to the rising number of older people.

The first department of geriatrics, at Mount Sinai Medical School, was established in the early 1980s. Although we now know a lot more about aging and age-related illnesses than we did then, we are still not training enough medical professionals to meet the growing need. There are only 7,300 geriatric doctors in the entire country, meaning that for every ten thousand patients over sixty-five, there is only one geriatrician. This number has been dropping over the last few decades even as the number of older adults is rising sharply.

I asked Louise Aronson, a geriatrician and professor of medicine in geriatrics at the University of California at San Francisco, why this was the case. She explained that finding doctors willing to go into the field is difficult. One reason is that we live in an era of medical specialization, but older people are often suffering from multiple conditions at once, as well as cognitive decline, so their problems can be very complex. The largest disincentive, though, may be financial, as geriatrics is among the lowest-paid specialties.

While some specialties have been creating different standards of care for older people—for instance, in emergency departments or for surgical patients—the broader health care system isn't keeping up. Training in medical school is still minimal—instruction lasts only for days or weeks at most. "To have a health care system that doesn't specifically train people in the care of older adults," Louise said, "is like having an education system that doesn't train people to teach children."

Louise loves being a geriatrician. "People can feel more secure in their knowledge if they know a whole lot about one small thing. But I don't want to separate the liver from the person and the person from the home or the culture. Seeing the whole picture makes it so much more rich and interesting and makes every patient different and fascinating. I feel like I do something useful most days, which is incredibly satisfying." When you take care of people who are often not taken care of, she added, they appreciate being listened to, heard, and seen. "And the longer you've lived, the more stories you have, the more interesting you are."

We need to destigmatize the aging process, Louise said. "It's natural for people not to be enthusiastic about being frail. But it happens if you live long enough. It's not a personal failing. So how do we make those losses less onerous, less shameful, less embarrassing?" We could focus on preventive standards of care for people, say, in their sixties. We could make it easier for people to go wherever they wanted by enabling them to hear better or walk steadily. We could focus on better treatments for incontinence, strengthening the pelvic floor, and exercises to maintain balance.

More than 85 percent of health care resources in the United States are used by people with chronic disease. Louise told me we could be so much healthier if our system invested more in disease prevention instead of focusing just on disease management. "There is much higher priority on the new, the scientific, the technological," she told me. We also need to put resources into the relatively low-cost preventive measures, such as food and exercise. These might be considered "unsexy," she said, but we already know they work.

We Need Science and Social Connection

I first met James Kirkland, a geriatrician and researcher at the Mayo Clinic, when we both served on an advisory board to the National Institute on Aging, a division of the National Institutes of Health that funds research on aging. When I connected with him again in 2021, he told me that he had transitioned from practicing as a geriatrician full time to studying geroscience—the field that aims to extend our years spent in good health by slowing aging—because he was no longer satisfied with "prescribing better wheelchairs, walkers, and incontinence devices." He went back to school and did a PhD in basic biology to better understand how our bodies change as we age.

James explained a basic idea behind geroscience, the so-called "pillars of aging." These are processes whose interactions result in the typical signs of aging, such as frailty, age-related bone loss, cognitive impairment, and loss of resilience to disease. While there are many ways to subdivide these pillars, James groups them into four sets of processes, which interact with each other: inflammation associated with tissue thickening or stiffening; the accumulation of damage to our DNA or cellular machinery; loss of the ability of cells to reach their mature form and function; and cellular senescence, the loss of a cell's ability to divide. Senescent cells accumulate as we age, and if the body doesn't eliminate them fast enough, they can cause neighboring cells to go senescent, setting off a cascade effect that can lead to chronic inflammation and leave us more susceptible to the diseases associated with aging.

Evidence strongly suggests that we could live both long *and* healthy lives. The models that inspire geroscientists are the super-agers, who defy the norms of biological aging. People who live to 110 rarely become sick with age-related illnesses until the last few years of their lives. By comparison, those who die in their nineties typically spend eight to ten years struggling with age-related illness. Super-agers enjoy maximal lifespan and minimal time in decline. That's a pretty good definition of optimal healthspan.

Not all super-agers are human. When I served on that advisory board with James, we heard presentations from the country's top aging experts about their latest research. I still remember one talk about the hairless naked mole rat. While most mice and rats live for a maximum of four to five years, the ugly mole rats can live for over thirty years and show few signs of aging. They are also immune to certain types of pain and cancer. By studying these rodents and other long-lived species, researchers hope to find secrets of longevity that can be applied to the human body.

Geroscientists have been investigating medicines already approved for certain diseases to see if they might be effective at slowing aging. Rapamycin, used to help reduce the rejection of organ transplants, has been shown to increase the lifespan of fruit flies and mice. In humans, rapamycin may produce unwanted side effects, and its risks can include kidney damage or increased severity of bacterial infections. Metformin, a drug approved for the treatment of diabetes, appears to influence certain metabolic and cellular processes closely related to the development of age-related conditions, such as inflammation. Researchers noticed that people with type 2 diabetes who took metformin lived longer than those who didn't. The drug has yet to undergo a clinical trial to see if these initial findings hold true for the general population or if it has potential side effects.

In his lab at Mayo Clinic, James is investigating whether killing off senescent cells—so-called "zombie cells"—can reduce disease and extend lifespans. Senolytic drugs, which selectively target senescent cells, have been used to destroy these cells in mice. In one study, the upshot for older mice was a 36 percent increase in lifespan. Older mice also gain physical strength and speed after treatment, which suggests that these drugs can extend healthspan. We don't yet know whether, used in humans, senolytics will harm healthy cells or have other unwanted side effects.

"Humans are not big mice," James reminded me. "And anything and everything can go wrong with people. I lie awake every night worried about somebody getting a side effect, and that's why we constantly say, *Do not take these things outside the context of a carefully controlled, regulated, clinical trial.* We have to be very cautious about all of this."

That warning, unfortunately, is not stopping people from paying for costly, unproven, and even potentially harmful treatments. The quest for immortality is becoming big business.

We still have a way to go before a pill or other treatment can safely slow the biological processes of aging and extend our healthspans, but I believe that medical researchers will eventually discover the means. If this happens, a priority should be to ensure that these medications are safe, affordable, and available to everyone. Otherwise, existing gaps between the long-lived and healthy haves, and the far larger group of have-nots, will only widen.

In the meantime, we need to look after our own health and support policies that make it easier for all Americans to extend and enjoy their own healthspans. This means steering people toward better health early in life—through individual behavior but also, critically, through policies that deliver equitable health, safe neighborhoods, nutritious food that is available and affordable, and so on.

We need to manage stress and develop good relationships, too. As Julianne Holt-Lunstad has said, we can't legislate for those factors—we can't "put hugs in the water." But we can regard our social relationships, in the widest sense, as a shared resource—like air or water—that are key to healthy lives. Social connections should be part of the discussion about good health, and isolation should be taken seriously as a health hazard. Both can be part of health education in schools and in medical training, and they can inform how we plan our communities—whether they are urban, suburban, or rural—so that they encourage gathering rather than isolating.

Relationships aren't the only way that the fate of our health is intertwined with the lives and health of others. The COVID-19 pandemic revealed big health disparities, but it also showed our interconnectedness. When hospitals and health systems became overburdened, for instance, cancer screenings and diagnoses dropped dramatically, and even some cancer treatments decreased. Better health for the most vulnerable contributes to better health for all, and longer healthspans make personal and economic good sense.

3

Will I Lose My Memory?

This has happened to me more than once: I walk into the kitchen, thoughts ticking through the day's chores and errands, and as I open the refrigerator, I realize I've forgotten what I'm looking for. My first reaction: *Am I losing my mind?* My second: *Is this the first stage of dementia?*

If you've also had this experience, you've got plenty of company. A full third of Americans still in their forties fear their mental sharpness is declining. Nearly six in ten of those over forty think mental decline is inevitable with aging. Among people who are retired, Alzheimer's disease and other forms of dementia loom as more frightening than cancer or stroke.

But as we age, not all incidents of forgetting signal trouble. Scientists used to believe that any kind of forgetting was due to a failure in the workings of the brain, but we now know that "everyday forgetting"—that moment at the refrigerator or the name of an acquaintance slipping our minds—is an adaptive aspect of the brain's normal functioning. I have a colleague whose ninety-two-year-old mother often joked that she couldn't remember what she had for breakfast, yet she did the *New York Times* crossword and Sudoku every day and played a mean game of bridge until just months before her death. As Scott A. Small has written, "Memory and forgetting work in unison." Small is a neuroscientist who studies memory and memory disorders. In his book *Forgetting: The Benefits of Not Remembering*, he describes how forgetting can support healthy brain function. Scientists have recently found that our brain cells, or neurons, contain mechanisms to promote not only memory but also memory erasure. This balancing act, Small writes, is "vital for our cognitive functioning, creativity and mental health."

Dementia is a reality, and I'll talk about it in detail below, but it's important to remember that while cognitive change is normal, cognitive decline is far from inevitable. The other piece of good news is that there are things we can do to lower our risk of dementia. The 2020 *Lancet* Commission report on dementia prevention, intervention, and care outlined twelve modifiable risk factors that account for about 40 percent of dementias worldwide. I'll explain these, too, later in the chapter. For now, let me lay out the basics.

The word *dementia* is a blanket term for significantly impaired thought, memory, and reasoning. The different types of dementia—such as Alzheimer's disease, the most common form in people over sixty-five—reflect the specific causes of impairment. Other causes include Lewy body dementia, frontotemporal dementia, and vascular dementia. Because these illnesses are both progressive and incurable, it's understandable that they are among the most feared diagnoses associated with aging. But they are not quite as common as we think. About half of adults believe they will likely get dementia, when in fact only about 15 percent of people between seventy-five and seventy-nine have even mild cognitive impairment. It is true that as human beings live longer and the population of older people grows, the *number* of people living with dementia is rising. But it is also true that the chance of getting dementia at any age has actually *declined* in many countries—likely due to improvements in nutrition, health care, education, and lifestyle. In the United States, the percentage of people seventy and older living with dementia has decreased from 13 percent in 2011 to 10 percent in 2019.

A lot of fear and stigma surround the basic process of cognitive aging, some of it based on misunderstanding. Having a clearer picture of the cognitive changes that are natural as we get older can help us to distinguish normal changes from those that are true signs of cognitive impairment.

Our brains, like our bodies, age. I notice that my brain functions differently than my parents' do, and also differently than my children's, who are in their late teens and early twenties. When our brains are young and healthy, we can quickly and accurately process language, form opinions, remember details, learn new skills, and make decisions. As we age, biology slows this processing activity. In certain regions of the brain, our nerve cells communicate less effectively. Blood flow may decrease, and inflammation, which escalates with disease or injury, can interfere with mental functioning, as can the normal hormonal changes that come with advancing years—for women, particularly, with menopause. Older people may need a little more time and concentration to learn new skills or perform complex memory or organizational tasks, such as balancing a checkbook. This is all perfectly natural, and in most cases older people can perform these tasks just fine if they are given enough time.

Other mental abilities, meanwhile, grow *stronger* with age. Even as words stall on the tip of our tongues, our grasp of meaning and the connections between ideas grows. We can continue to build vocabulary and verbal reasoning skills—meaning our ability to understand concepts expressed through language and to think constructively and apply logic. Age also brings more subtle emotional benefits, as Laura Carstensen explained to me. Laura is a researcher, professor of psychology and public policy, and founding director of the Stanford Center on Longevity. She studies changes in our emotions and motivations as we age, and the effect of those changes on cognitive processing. On average, she told me, "people fare better emotionally as they get older." We're less troubled by anger, sadness, and fear. This finding has been repeatedly documented over two decades of research. It reflects a greater tendency in older adults to attend to and remember positive rather than negative information.

Remarkably, studies have consistently found this resiliency across most groups, regardless of race or health and at almost every income level. "You've got to get to poverty level before you start to see declines in emotional well-being," Laura said. "Humans are pretty remarkably resilient emotionally."

How Our Brains Build Reserves

Scientists used to think we had a limited number of brain cells, and that the pool decreased over time. We now understand that our brains continue to develop and change, and that neurons can regenerate through a process called neurogenesis, which occurs at all ages.

Neurogenesis holds real promise for the treatment of brain disorders and injuries. It may also be key to understanding why some cognitive super-agers remain mentally sharp into their nineties and beyond. In the brains of super-agers, regions that are critical for memory, attention, cognitive control, and motivation remain thick and healthy, instead of atrophying, which is what normally occurs as we grow old. Super-agers' brains also contain high levels of certain neurons that affect social intelligence and awareness, more even than the brains of many younger adults. On memory tests, super-agers tend to perform like people two to three decades younger.

One theory about this stellar brainpower is based on the idea of *cognitive reserve*, which is a little like the emergency toolkit you keep in your car in case of a breakdown. Cognitive reserve doesn't prevent neurological aging, but it enables some people to work around the usual cognitive challenges that come with aging.

Researchers began learning about cognitive reserve in the late 1980s, when autopsies revealed physical signs of advanced Alzheimer's disease inside the brains of certain people who had never shown any outward symptoms of dementia. These individuals apparently had enough cognitive reserve that their brains could bypass physiological damage and find alternative ways to function normally, allowing them to remain mentally sharp.

We now know that cognitive reserve helps protect against other forms of dementia, as well as against traumatic brain injury and brain diseases such as Parkinson's, multiple sclerosis, and stroke. High levels of cognitive reserve can also increase the brain's resilience to the stress of trauma, surgery, or environmental pollution.

Why some people have more cognitive reserve than others is still a mystery, but the process of building this reserve is clearly cumulative, and lifelong learning plays a key role. Education seems to help reduce both the rate of cognitive decline and the risk of dementia. This doesn't just mean formal schooling. Learning on the job, and playing cards and strategy games such as chess, can also boost reserves. Regular exercise likely plays a role in cognitive reserve by improving blood flow to the brain and helping to thicken parts of the brain associated with cognition. Social ties and interactions are important, too, with super-agers reporting more links to family and friends.

The potential of cognitive reserve and the example of super-agers is encouraging. They offer even more reason to stay curious and pursue new learning challenges throughout life—especially in the second fifty.

When Should I Be Concerned?

If certain changes in brain function are normal as we age, how do we know what's *not* normal? This question isn't always easy to answer. Cognitive decline often occurs so gradually and inconsistently that it can go undiagnosed for years. At the same time, certain other neurological and psychiatric diseases, including diabetes, depression, and stroke, can impact brain function.

Looking at the difference between mild cognitive impairment and Alzheimer's and other dementias can help us to understand how concerned we should be about changes we notice in ourselves or others.

Mild cognitive impairment reflects memory and thinking difficulties that have a minor impact on daily life. You might be more likely to lose your keys or forget a scheduled appointment. You might need to concentrate harder to perform familiar tasks or movements. In many cases, simple tools like daily planners or to-do lists can help compensate for these lapses, and symptoms sometimes stay the same or even improve over time.

Not everyone with mild cognitive impairment will progress to Alzheimer's. (About one-third will within five years.) But it's important to check with a doctor every six to twelve months, in case the changes are signs of more serious cognitive decline. And any form of dementia can lead to severe physical and mental disability, as my dear friend and college roommate Kezia discovered when her dad, Courtney, began to decline.

Courtney had grown up in Wyoming and spent most of his life there working alongside his brothers teaching wilderness survival to kids at their summer camp. He was part of a U.S. Geological Survey Team to the Antarctic for six seasons, where he taught survival skills to scientists. An accomplished mountain climber, he even made an attempt to scale Mount Everest. Strong and fearless, Courtney had a full head of dark hair into his eighth decade. "He could still out-ski me at eighty-five," Kezia told me. "The last time we skied together, I was just in awe. And then to have it so quickly change."

The first warning signs emerged in 2020, within months of that last ski trip, when Courtney started having paranoid thoughts about someone selling his possessions and spying on him. He'd call Kezia and say, "I can't talk because they're tracking my phone." Kezia is a nurse, but she couldn't figure out what was happening. That Christmas, Courtney traveled from Wyoming to Florida, where the paranoia got worse. He began to hallucinate and became disoriented. Kezia remembered one phone call when her father said, "I'm not going to be able to talk to you for a while because they're coming to arrest me, and I've been shanghaied to Atlantic City." But Courtney wasn't in Atlantic City. He was in Florida.

A trip to the emergency room led to a visit with a neurologist. Brain scans revealed plaque buildups in Courtney's cortex. These abnormal clumps of protein, called Lewy bodies, combined with a history of hallucinations and paranoia, confirmed the diagnosis of Lewy body dementia. Around that time, Kezia said, her father started to become aggressive. "He was so afraid of people coming to get him or that we were going to leave him. He kept apologizing, saying, 'I'm so sorry.'"

Survival rates for Lewy body dementia vary. People tend to live for two to four years after being diagnosed, though some have lived as long as twenty years. Courtney lived only six months.

Alzheimer's Disease

On November 26, 1901, in a hospital in Frankfurt, Germany, a pathologist named Alois Alzheimer examined fifty-one-year-old psychiatric patient Auguste Deter. This woman knew her first name but not her last, was often disoriented, and burst into fits of jealousy and paranoia. Alzheimer made the following notes after first meeting her:

> When objects are shown to her, she does not remember after a short time which objects have been shown. . . . When she is asked to write, she holds the book in such a way that one has the impression that she has a loss in the right visual field. Asked to write *Auguste D*, she tries to write *Mrs* and forgets the rest. It is necessary to repeat every word.

Alzheimer was confounded, in part because Deter's symptoms resembled those he usually saw in much older patients. He followed her case for the next five years, until her death, at which point he performed an autopsy, using a newly developed stain to examine the cells of her brain. In otherwise seemingly normal cells, he noticed tangles of unusually thick and tough threadlike structures, called fibrils. In the cortex, he discovered clumps of "peculiar material," clusters of proteins we know today as beta-amyloid plaques. These findings would dramatically change medical understanding of a condition that until then had been generalized as "senile dementia." The disease process that Alzheimer had identified meant that dementia could be a progressive disease that started much earlier than old age. In 1910 this disease was named after him.

Today Alzheimer's disease is understood to account for 60 to 80 percent of all cases of dementia. Long before we notice any changes in behavior or memory, the beta-amyloid plaques have begun to form on the outside of neurons, while the tangled strands of another protein, called tau, are building up inside the neurons. Much about this process is still unclear, but researchers believe these formations interfere with neural communication, which can in turn lead to the damage and ultimate death of neurons. The proteins may also contribute to the inflammation and atrophy of brain tissue that is common with Alzheimer's disease.

An important caveat about the correlation between these two proteins and Alzheimer's disease is that it doesn't always hold up. A person who has plaques and tangles may not have dementia. The study of super-agers has contributed to our awareness of this fact, and research published in the Netherlands in 2021 backs it up. The Dutch study involved 340 cognitively healthy people age one hundred or more who were living independently. About a third of them agreed to donate their brains after death. Almost half of the autopsies showed brains with significant pathologies of the kind common to people with Alzheimer's and other dementias—*although these people had remained cognitively healthy even four years after reaching the age of one hundred.* Either they were resistant to the disease—possibly through genes or lifestyle—or their capacity to maintain normal cognitive abilities despite damage to their brains was linked to the cognitive reserve I talked about earlier.

So what *are* the symptoms of Alzheimer's to look out for? The disease tends to develop gradually, worsening over several years through these stages:

- Mild cognitive impairment: Changes in memory and thinking ability that aren't significant enough to affect work or relationships.
- Mild dementia: Problems with memory and thinking that impact daily functioning. Difficulty organizing thoughts. People may become withdrawn or angry, get lost in familiar places, and lose valuable items.
- Moderate dementia: Confusion and memory loss increase. People sometimes grow suspicious, aggressive, or agitated, and they often begin to wander, making it unsafe for them to be left alone.
- Severe dementia: People are unable to communicate coherently and need help with daily self-care such as eating and dressing. Eventually, they lose the capacity to sit up without assistance, swallow, or control their bladder and bowel functions.

Other forms of dementia progress differently. With Lewy body, for instance, the memory is largely intact early in the disease. But like Kezia's father, the person may experience confusion, hallucinations, or delusions. As the disease progresses, problems with movement and speech develop that resemble the symptoms of Parkinson's.

Neither Alzheimer's nor other forms of dementia follow a single trajectory, and more than half of patients have "mixed dementia," with the likelihood of developing multiple types increasing over time. On average, someone with Alzheimer's will live between three and eleven years after diagnosis, though people can live twenty years or more.

Some patients progress rapidly, while others remain vibrant, active, and socially engaged for years. Some even become activists in the campaign for more research and less stigma around dementia.

Terrie Montgomery was fifty-eight in 2015, when she was diagnosed with early-onset Alzheimer's. She first became concerned when she noticed she was forgetting passwords at work. Then one day while driving, she found herself at a railroad crossing. She panicked. For a moment she just didn't know what to do.

A visit to a neurologist, who did brain scans and other tests, resulted in the diagnosis. Terrie was shocked. She had known there was something wrong, but she wasn't expecting *that*. Terrie and her husband live in Georgia. I met with her over Zoom in the summer of 2022. The first thing that struck me was her dyed-purple hair—Terrie is vibrant, unconventional, and upbeat. "The doctor told me it was terminal, there was no cure," she said. "There was nothing like, 'You can live with this disease.' But just because you get this diagnosis doesn't mean you're going to die tomorrow. You have to *live*. And I wanted to live."

Terrie quickly became an advocate. Along with two other African Americans living with dementia, she co-founded Black Dementia Minds, under the umbrella of the nonprofit advocacy group the National Council of Dementia Minds. "In the Black community, we get hit with this disease," she said. "You've got to tell your doctor if something is wrong." Terrie's point is critical. Black Americans have higher rates of Alzheimer's than whites do, yet researchers conducting Alzheimer's studies have found that Black participants are 35 percent less likely to be diagnosed with dementia than white participants. This finding is consistent with other studies showing that Black Americans frequently have to present with more severe symptoms in a more advanced stage of the disease before a physician will give them a dementia diagnosis.

When I asked Terrie about stigma, she recalled a couple of times when people backed away when she told them her diagnosis—as she put it, it was as if she were covered in bees, and they didn't want to get stung. But mostly it was lack of understanding, among friends and even in the medical community. The first time she met her new doctor in Georgia, he told her, "You don't look like you have dementia." So she gave him links to YouTube videos of people with dementia talking about their lives.

When I asked Terrie what it was like living with dementia, she offered a poignant description of a big luxurious house. When you first get there, she said, you've got it all. You can land helicopters on the roof and go down to the pool, and you've got access to every room in between. But over time doors begin to close, sometimes slowly, other times suddenly. The door to the office where you worked. The room where you played bridge. Then the kitchen, because you can't cook anymore. The bathroom. And so on. "But along the way," she added, "there are many things you can keep doing until you get to that last room."

Getting a Diagnosis

Many of us have had a cognitive evaluation or accompanied our loved ones for a test. I decided to test my cognitive function through an online assessment. The tool was evidence-based and used a well-established database that allows people to compare themselves with others of similar age, gender, and education level. It took me through an array of mental tasks for about twenty minutes—for instance, remembering a list of words. I'm competitive, so when I misclicked a few times, I worried I wouldn't get straight As.

I did fairly well, but didn't get perfect marks. A few measures were above average, including my processing speed, which involves how well I take in information, make sense of it, and respond. It helps with things like driving safely in traffic—a great skill to have in D.C. But my working memory, which is involved in, say, remembering phone numbers or calculating a tip, was below average. As I've always been bad with phone numbers and names, I wasn't sure how to evaluate these results. But now that I have my own baseline, I can come back to the test and track any changes over time. These tests offer the benefit of showing us which parts of our thinking skills may not be as strong as we would like and how we compare with others similar to us.

You can also do an initial cognitive assessment in a doctor's office, using questions like the ones I answered online. If your doctor has known you for some time, a screening could be more informal. They could simply observe you or speak with your loved ones about changes in daily functions. There is no consensus on the best in-office screening tool for clinicians to use. The Mini-Mental State Examination is one of the most commonly used to evaluate a patient for cognitive impairment. It assesses several areas of cognitive function, including verbal recall, attention, calculation, language, and visual construction. Many clinicians feel the Montreal Cognitive Assessment—often called the "clock test," though clock-drawing is only one element of it—is more sensitive in detecting cases of early dementia. I was happy to hear from my dad that at his annual check-up, he was asked to recall a list of words and to draw a clock—far too many doctors are not using these basic tools.

Doctors who have concerns should check for other conditions that could be causing cognitive symptoms. Thyroid disease, vitamin B12 deficiency, depression, and untreated sleep apnea are a few of the things that can mimic early dementia; if they are treated, cognitive symptoms should improve. Your doctor or pharmacist should review your prescriptions, as some commonly used prescription drugs, as well as over-the-counter sleep aids, may have side effects that cause confusion, impact memory, or worsen the symptoms of existing cognitive problems. Your doctor should also schedule a more thorough assessment with a specialist, who may use a PET scan (which can detect plaques in the brain even decades before Alzheimer's symptoms appear) or an MRI (which can show change in brain volume common in Alzheimer's). The tests can also reveal tumors, strokes, or other problems that can cause dementia.

Alternative means of diagnosing Alzheimer's are in development, some involving technology—such as detecting cognitive and motor decline in the way we type—and others that focus on biomarkers and blood tests, which could simplify and standardize diagnosis. Since imaging and spinal taps (the two established methods of detection) are expensive, invasive, and not always readily available, a reliable blood test could increase access to early diagnosis.

To understand more about why early diagnosis is so important, I talked to Jason Karlawish, co-director of the Penn Memory Center and author of *The Problem of Alzheimer's* (2021). I first met Jason in 2008, when I was the staff director of the Senate Aging Committee, and he testified about ensuring that residents could exercise their right to vote while living in nursing homes. I've admired his work and his passionate commitment to geriatric medicine ever since. Jason knows this disease as well as anyone, and he's seen it up close. His father has Alzheimer's.

Jason told me he's "bullish" about early diagnosis. "If you don't get people thinking about the cognitively transforming event that is Alzheimer's, you're doing everyone a disservice." Early diagnosis gives people the ability to understand the changes they're experiencing, make informed decisions about the future, potentially begin treatments that might help, or even participate in clinical trials of new therapies. Unfortunately, we don't yet have drugs that can cure the disease, and some that may help slow its progression have potentially serious side effects.

Early diagnosis also enables people to put a plan in place. "I'm not talking about advance directives and all that," Jason said. "The more important thing is what to do *now*. Who will help me in the coming months and years, to make sure I remain safe, social, engaged? Many people live alone and don't have natural support or caregiver networks set up." Those who have family nearby can't necessarily assume that their relatives are willing and able to provide the caregiving they would like or will need. It's therefore critical to have these discussions, and a diagnosis is a catalyst for that.

Even if you're not concerned about your brain health, it's a good idea to ask the doctor for a cognitive screening so as to have a base-line against which to measure changes. Cognitive assessments are part of the annual wellness visits paid for by Medicare, but unfortunately fewer than half of doctors report performing them routinely, and only 16 percent of people over sixty-five receive them during routine check-ups—a strikingly low figure compared to the preventive care and assess-ments older people get for conditions such as cancer, diabetes, and high cholesterol.

There are multiple reasons for the low uptake. Patients may not know they are entitled to the free tests, or they could believe there is no benefit to taking them because a cure doesn't exist. Many clinicians may not understand how to use basic dementia screening tools or may feel they don't have time in an office visit to administer one. They could also be unsure how to communicate results of a test; nearly one-third of doctors report being never or only sometimes comfortable answering patient questions about dementia—despite a large majority feeling they are on the front lines of dementia care. Much of the discomfort may be due to lack of training since most primary care physicians have little or no training in dementia diagnosis and care.

Finally, there is stigma within the medical profession. Seven in ten health care providers think their patients would be ashamed or embar-rassed if diagnosed with dementia, though only one in five of their patients agree. The sad irony of this mismatch is that people can lose out on information about lifestyle changes that may impact the tra-jectory of their disease. At least three-quarters of health care providers agree that adopting brain-healthy behaviors could help slow the prog-ress of dementia, but because they wish to protect patients from dis-tress, or underestimate their willingness to adopt healthier lifestyles, they may hesitate to provide an early diagnosis. For all these reasons, dementia typically goes undiagnosed for *at least five to ten years* after neu-rodegenerative changes and decline in functioning have taken place.

The longer active symptoms are denied, the more likely they are to be a source of ongoing stress and uncertainty, disrupting social and family relationships, employment, and possibly insurance coverage. Brenda Roberts and her husband Mark are a case in point. Brenda is now the executive director of the National Council of Dementia Minds. But back in the early 2010s, when Mark started acting agitated—even threatening to get a gun and "put an end to all this" after he grew frustrated about a door installation—she never suspected dementia. She believed he had simply grown angry. She left home to stay with her daughter but made sure that Mark saw a doctor. At age sixty-two, Mark was diagnosed by a geriatric psychiatrist with vascular dementia. He became an active member of Dementia Minds and said that obtaining a diagnosis saved his marriage.

Nevertheless, people continue to have mixed feelings about being screened. A study published in 2019 looked at four thousand diverse primary care patients over sixty-five to assess whether dementia screening was harmful. Previous studies had shown that patients were concerned that screening would cause them depression or anxiety, but this study found no such harm. What the researchers found, however, was that 70 percent of participants who screened positive for cognitive impairment declined a follow-up assessment.

Ultimately, being screened for any medical condition is a choice. But as Jason Karlawish reminded me, all choices are made from within systems, shaped by the world around us. "If all you're thinking is that there is no biomedical treatment that will attack the disease," he said, "then you might say, 'Why would I want to know?' But it's so much more than that."

Terrie Montgomery talked to me about this very issue. She said that if she were a doctor delivering a dementia diagnosis, she would say, "I've got bad news and good news. You've got Alzheimer's. But we have resources. We've come so far. Walk out of here thinking about the things you *can* do. Get in touch with a support team. Start doing things you've put off. Start living."

The hesitancy around screening and the lack of clear information are things our health care system needs to address through better education and awareness among both providers and patients. People should be encouraged to follow up on cognitive screening results as they would for other conditions. The truth is that individuals are not helpless when it comes to cognitive health, and many will continue to live meaningful lives for years after being diagnosed. We can empower people to understand what they can do to reduce their risk, and we can get health care providers and their patients talking to each other— early and often.

TLC for Our Brains

First let me emphasize that *no one should be blamed for getting dementia or any illness*. People who never smoke and regularly exercise get cancer, while many lifelong smokers never develop it. There are no guarantees either way. But we know that certain health risks are either increased or lowered based on lifestyle. There is actually a lot we can do to lower our risk of dementia and support our brain health.

A growing body of evidence suggests that we could cut as much as 40 percent of dementia worldwide if we eliminated twelve* specific risk factors. Some of these—such as inadequate education and air pollution—involve the same social drivers that affect healthspan and lifespan, and addressing them requires action from government, public health initiatives, or the private sector. Other risk factors are related to personal habits and practices, such as smoking, alcohol consumption, and lack of exercise. Adopting healthy habits could help you lower your risk for dementia by anywhere from 15 to 33 percent. While

---

* The twelve risk factors are: less education, hypertension, hearing impairment, smoking, obesity, depression, physical inactivity, diabetes, low social contact, excessive alcohol consumption, traumatic brain injury, and air pollution. Gill Livingston et al., "Dementia Prevention, Intervention, and Care: 2020 Report of the Lancet Commission," *Lancet* 396, no. 10248 (August 8, 2020): 413–46.

it's best to adopt healthy habits earlier in life, doing so even late in life can make a difference.

One of the most important things we can do is look after our heart health, because what's good for the heart is good for the brain. Strokes and heart disease are critical risk factors for dementia; because blood carries oxygen from the lungs to the heart and the heart to the brain, any weakness or blockage in the vascular system can cause problems for both physical and cognitive health. Symptoms such as lightheadedness, slurred speech, sudden weakness, and fainting can all be signs that the brain isn't receiving enough oxygen-rich blood. The cause could be narrowing of blood vessels due to hardening of the arteries or other conditions, or it could involve a problem such as faulty valves within the heart chamber. If the vascular system weakens over time, the damage to the brain could be too gradual to notice at first, but it may nevertheless become permanent. The condition called "vascular dementia" reflects this connection, though some scientists believe it is not actually a distinct disease but rather damage to blood vessels in the brain depriving the brain of oxygen and leading to cognitive impairment and dementia.

Maintaining a healthy heart lowers your risk for strokes and so reduces your risk for dementia. Avoiding or minimizing behaviors and conditions that contribute to heart disease—smoking, obesity, high cholesterol, and diabetes—are critical for cognitive health. Making sure blood pressure and weight are within normal limits tends to benefit cognitive reserve and strong neural pathway connections.

Evidence supporting the heart-brain connection comes from decades-long research conducted in Framingham, Massachusetts. In the 1940s residents were enrolled in a heart health study that later resulted in the identification of key risk factors for stroke and heart attack. In the mid-1970s, the study was expanded to include surveillance for dementia. The researchers found that the more people accessed treatments and practiced behaviors to prevent heart disease—for instance, taking blood pressure medications or stopping smoking—the lower their risk of developing dementia. The only people who didn't see a cross-over benefit were those who hadn't attained at least a high school diploma. The policy implications are clear: if we want healthy hearts and brains, we need access to affordable health care and quality education.

Another risk factor for dementia, and one we can take steps to alleviate, is stress. Just as chronic negative stress contributes to health problems and shorter life expectancy, so it appears to raise the risk for cognitive decline. Ongoing stress and related mental health concerns such as depression and anxiety also seem to worsen symptoms after Alzheimer's disease is diagnosed. Research on these connections is relatively new, but one possible explanation is that high levels of certain stress hormones can damage the brain's hippocampus, where memories are made, organized, and stored. This same stress process contributes to depression and anxiety. Early-life depression has been shown to be an important risk factor for dementia, but researchers don't yet know whether it contributes to the development of dementia or whether a third factor is causing both conditions. Knowing that dementia and depression are linked, however, underscores the importance of supporting mental health as part of a holistic approach to reducing our risk of dementia.

The connections between stress, depression, anxiety, and dementia may help to explain why certain groups are more likely to develop dementia than others. Here's a sobering statistic: about two-thirds of all older adults with dementia are women. It was once believed that women's longer lifespans accounted for this gender gap. But recent studies have focused on additional factors, including hormones, genes, and differences in how tau (the tangles of protein that build up inside neurons) spreads in women's brains. Estrogen, a hormone important for brain health, decreases after menopause; the drop can lead to brain changes that may cause memory and cognitive decline, as well as lowering women's ability to resist brain diseases. At the same time, women may be more likely than men to go undiagnosed in the early stages of the illness because they tend to perform better on tests involving verbal skills and verbal memory, an advantage that can mask early signs of Alzheimer's. Women are also more likely to become caregivers for an adult with dementia, a demanding role that raises the risk of dementia for the caregiver. The depression-dementia link may be a contributing factor here, as nearly 70 percent of dementia caregivers struggle with depression.

The stress connection also shows up in disproportionately high rates of dementia among people who face racial discrimination and economic inequity. Compared to older white adults, Black adults over sixty-five are about twice as likely to develop dementia, and Hispanic/Latino adults are one and a half times as likely. The reason for these disparities, and for the course of the disease, may be a complex interaction of biology and culture, linked to the same social drivers that shorten healthspan and life expectancy for certain racial and ethnic groups. A range of research suggests that people who encounter racism in their lives, particularly Black adults, are more prone to memory problems in middle age. One 2020 study found that Black women who had experienced the highest levels of personal racism were almost three times as likely to report memory loss or frequent confusion as Black women who had suffered the lowest levels. Biological risk factors that increase the chance of developing dementia—including diabetes, high blood pressure, obesity, and heart disease—are also disproportionately high in Black adults.

Knowing that stress is a big factor in cognitive health, we can follow some clear recommendations for reducing it. Anyone who has lost a night's sleep, or suffers from insomnia, knows how terrible it feels to be sleep-deprived. Our brains need recharging on a daily basis, which happens while we sleep and dream: our neural cells build the pathways that help us process memories and clean up the day's accumulation of toxins in the brain. Adults generally need seven to nine hours sleep per night, though when we get into our sixties, we often find ourselves becoming lighter sleepers and waking several times during the night. Older people are also more likely to take medications that may contribute to sleep disruption. So while sleep may not come as easily, we shouldn't underestimate its importance.

I mentioned earlier that exercise is good for brain health because it increases blood flow, which brings more oxygen to the brain. Exercise also thickens key parts of the brain, increasing brain volume in areas associated with cognitive activities. People with a physically active lifestyle have lower rates of cognitive decline; even six to twelve months of a regular exercise program can have positive effects on the brain. Most of the science to date has focused on aerobic exercise, including everyday activities such as gardening, walking, and climbing stairs, as well as jogging, swimming, and similar kinds of athletic exercise. Most activities that support cardiovascular health appear to benefit cognitive function.

Experts generally recommend a two-pronged approach to brain-healthy exercise. First, we can weave intermittent movement into daily life—taking the stairs instead of escalators or elevators, walking or cycling short distances instead of driving, and getting up and moving around to break up long stretches of sitting. The second goal is an intentional program of moderate aerobic activity and muscle strengthening: taking at least twenty minutes a day for a brisk walk or jog; performing athletic activities such as playing tennis, dancing, cycling, or swimming; and doing muscle-strengthening activities like lifting weights at least two days a week.

As well as exercising more, we Americans could improve our diets. We tend to consume high quantities of salt, sugar, processed foods, and saturated fats. These unhealthy diets contribute to elevated blood pressure, high cholesterol, and diabetes, all harmful to both cardiovascular and cognitive health.

No single food can guarantee cognitive health, but certain food groups do a good job of providing the vitamins and minerals the brain needs—for example, a variety of fresh fruits and vegetables, especially green leafy vegetables, and seafood, which is rich in omega-3 oils. Evidence is mounting that the Mediterranean diet—built on produce, whole grains, nuts, beans, and healthy fats from foods such as fatty fish and olive oil—promotes brain health. When people consume these nutritious foods regularly as part of a balanced diet, they report better cognitive health, and the higher their consumption, the higher they rate their brain functioning. Lifelong healthy eating yields the best results, but it's never too late to begin limiting our intake of salt, red meat, fried and processed foods, and saturated fats such as butter. At the same time, we can emphasize healthy fats, including olive oil, as well as low-fat dairy foods like yogurt. Finally, drinking alcohol excessively can lead to learning and memory problems. As we age, our bodies process alcohol differently, so even moderate quantities may become too much.

A word about vitamins and dietary supplements. Adults in their second fifty spend more than $93 million a month on six supplements alone, but they're probably wasting their money. There is little or no scientific evidence that supplements touted as "brain boosters" actually improve brain health. Unless we are lacking certain nutrients, for most of us the best source of vitamins and minerals is a healthy, balanced diet.

While eating right is a big plus, breaking bread with others has added benefits. Older adults with active social lives and good relationships with family and friends tend to have sharper memories and a lower risk of dementia. This is hardly a surprise. When we're feeling lonely or disconnected, especially over long periods, we can become anxious and distressed, which can diminish our cognitive functioning. Socializing results in the secretion of chemicals in our brain such as oxytocin, one of the so-called feel-good hormones; low levels of oxytocin have been associated with depression. Close friendships are demonstrably good for our brains, providing a sense of belonging and mutual support and giving our brains positive emotional and intellectual exercise. But less intimate friendships also help to keep us mentally fit. Conversations with co-workers, neighbors, or the clerk at the checkout counter can be meaningful and beneficial.

Something that can leave us isolated even when in company with others is problems with hearing. There is a direct link between hearing and cognitive function. When we are missing much of what is going on around us, we lose touch with our environment, which abets cognitive loss. This is why, as we age, regular hearing screenings and using hearing aids are important both for staying connected and for maintaining brain health.

Throughout our lives, our brains are generating new neurons and neuronal pathways, and education and intellectual engagement at every age are important for building cognitive reserve and protecting against cognitive decline. By stimulating new thoughts and mental connections, we both maintain and strengthen the "muscle" of our brain. Keeping our brains stimulated does *not* require expensive programs or games. In fact, there is little evidence to support the claims that any commercial product can improve our memory. The real brain boosters are more mundane activities that involve memory, thinking, attention, and reasoning: learning a skill such as a language or musical instrument, or solving problems at work or while volunteering. The best activities seem to be those that challenge us cognitively in ways that are new, complex, difficult, and fun, which is why it helps to take on intellectual and creative challenges with friends. When we're both socially and intellectually engaged, we tend to have more fun, and fun keeps us coming back to learn more.

Finally, while it has been known for some time that ageism negatively affects the well-being of older adults, more recently we've learned that negative stereotypes can actually affect brain structure and pathology—changes associated with Alzheimer's disease. A study conducted by Becca Levy and colleagues compared age stereotypes measured decades ago with brain scans and autopsies performed on those same individuals years later. What they found was fascinating: the people who held more negative stereotypes earlier in life had accumulated significantly more tangles and plaques and had three times as much loss in brain volume as those with positive views of aging.

The good news is that having a generally positive view of aging appears to reduce the risk of developing dementia. People who accept and even welcome later life have been found to have lower levels of stress, and low stress can act as a protective factor—even for those otherwise at high risk. Moreover, it appears that this relationship between outlook and cognitive health is fluid and can improve over time. Everything we're learning only emphasizes the importance of interventions that combat institutional ageism and everyday ageist attitudes.

Giving and Needing Care

Even as we look after our own cognitive health, many of us will be called to care for family members or friends with dementia. One study from 2019 found that 64 percent of people with dementia live at home. (This number falls with age: among people eighty or older with dementia—those likely to need the most care—75 percent are living in a nursing home.) In 2022 more than eleven million Americans were caregivers to people with dementia, providing more than eighteen billion hours of unpaid care.

Caregiving may be emotionally and financially challenging, but it can also be a richly rewarding experience that deepens relationships and provides a sense of purpose. I have heard caregivers emphasize that the care is taking place within a relationship that has a history of mutual support and affection, elements that aren't entirely lost when one person is diagnosed with dementia. When I asked Jason Karlawish what advice he has for caregivers, he said first we should try to educate ourselves. Learn what to look out for, to remove the mysteries about what's down the line. But knowledge will only get us so far. Caring for our loved ones, he said, "is morally intense work. You're going to have to make some very difficult and even tragic choices. You'll have to think *with* them and, as they get sicker, *for* them."

These burdens can fall hardest on those with few resources, but even someone like Sandra Day O'Connor, the first woman justice on the Supreme Court, felt the weight of hard decisions and losing a loved one to dementia. In 2008, when I worked in the Senate, Justice O'Connor testified at one of our hearings. She had begun caring for her husband John in 1990 after his Alzheimer's diagnosis. She shared how in the early days of his illness, she would often bring him to court because he couldn't be left alone. She retired in 2006 to find care for John, and the two of them moved full time to Phoenix to be near their children. John died the year after her testimony, and in 2018, Justice O'Connor announced that she herself had been diagnosed with dementia. She died in 2023.

Some of the things Justice O'Connor called for in her testimony, such as increased funding for Alzheimer's research, have come about. But there is still a tremendous amount of work to do if we are to fully support people with dementia and their caregivers. (In Chapter 8, I'll dig into how the health care system and our policy choices can do this.) In the meantime, we can make our cities and communities more dementia-friendly and more supportive of caregivers. One example is the network of memory cafés that welcome people with Alzheimer's, other dementias, and mild cognitive impairment. They take place in coffee shops, restaurants, community centers, assisted living facilities, museums, libraries, and elsewhere. There are hundreds of them throughout the United States and in certain other countries. They are usually facilitated by social service or health care workers, and they offer activities such as education, games, music, dancing, and crafts; they also guide informal conversations and exercises, often aimed at fostering reminiscing and connecting with the past. Memory cafés are not a form of caregiver respite but rather a way for people to break from the daily routine, share experiences, and enjoy an outing together. They can also be a hub for learning about caregiver support resources and organizations.

Current Treatments and Future Possibilities

Given the toll of dementia—from pain and suffering to economic costs in lost wages and caregiving expenses—we desperately need effective treatments. Government funding for research on Alzheimer's and other dementias has increased more than sevenfold since 2011, with nearly $4 billion spent in 2022. A cure remains elusive, but a number of available drugs may temporarily ease certain symptoms, improve quality of life, and help people remain independent for longer. As I write this, more than one hundred other drugs are in clinical trials to treat the underlying causes of Alzheimer's. These drugs take various approaches—targeting amyloid plaques, using vaccines and chemical inhibitors to prevent the microscopic tau fibers from forming, and preventing or reducing the chronic inflammation that affects brain cells in Alzheimer's disease.

But drugs aren't the only avenue being explored. Neurology professor Alvaro Pascual-Leone directs the Berenson-Allen Center for Noninvasive Brain Stimulation at Beth Israel Deaconess Medical Center and Harvard Medical School. He is testing deep brain stimulation—an established treatment for several conditions, including Parkinson's and epilepsy, that uses implanted electrodes to interrupt abnormal electrical signaling in the brain and produce impulses that regulate it.

Unlike traditional approaches to treating Alzheimer's, brain stimulation aims to reduce the associated disabilities without curing the underlying disease. It appears that repeated stimulation sessions on people with Alzheimer's can sustain benefits for months. If proven to work consistently, such a treatment would be challenging to scale to large populations, especially given that people with Alzheimer's tend to have multiple disabilities.

As a treatment for Alzheimer's, the procedure is in its early days, but Pascual-Leone is passionate about its potential. "We have to be clear about what success looks like," he told me. "It doesn't mean your MRI looks nicer but you're equally impaired. It means that you are functioning better in the activities of daily living." After all, he added, "we're trying to help people, not just brains."

Alzheimer's is unlikely to be a disease we can solve by drugs alone. The tools for primary prevention of dementia will probably be similar to those used to manage cardiovascular disease: medications combined with lifestyle factors. Right now, however, there is a chasm between what is known about the disease and the extent to which this knowledge is being applied. This gap presents an opportunity, but closing it will require the combined efforts of individuals and communities and the support of public policies that facilitate healthy lifestyles.

While we await the development of more effective medical treatments, let's take action on the things we have some control over: engaging in behaviors that can improve our brain health, earlier diagnosis, reducing stigma, and improving support for caregivers. Investing in prevention and systems of care should be prioritized alongside the development of better drugs. It's also crucial for us to make solid investments in public education as well as in libraries, museums, and other cognitively stimulating settings that we can engage with throughout our lives. Only then can we say that we are doing everything we can for our loved ones and ourselves, adding more healthy years to our lives, and reducing the suffering and the huge social and economic costs of dementia.

4

How Long Will I Work?

I love my work. When I think about how long I want to continue, I hope it will be for at least another couple of decades. My husband feels the same about being a teacher, corralling high schoolers into learning history. We may get our wish. Our jobs are not too physically taxing, and we're both in relatively good health. Compared to our grandparents' generation, we have longer life expectancies. But those extra years will increase our financial needs. We have to assume that at some point we'll have unforeseen expenses, maybe big ones, such as staying at a nursing home. So working longer may not be just a matter of preference. Like many people, our longer lives will mean longer working lives.

The typical age of retirement in the United States has been creeping upward, a reversal of a decades-long trend. For much of the last century, even as lifespans increased dramatically, people were retiring earlier. Americans worked four or five fewer years in the 1980s than they did in the late 1950s. But since the 1980s things have shifted: the age at which people stop working has risen, driven largely by those with higher education, a group that has also seen the greatest increases in life expectancy. Meanwhile Social Security's "full retirement age"—when retirees can claim benefits without being penalized—has risen from sixty-five to sixty-seven.

This trend of working longer will likely continue, and we Americans have adjusted our expectations accordingly. Retirement simply doesn't mean what it used to—the period of life in which we no longer work. Today many people in their fifties expect to work in their retirement years.

Some policymakers have embraced the idea of people working longer as the main solution to the challenges facing our aging society. Increasing the retirement age in Social Security, for example, improves the finances of the program by reducing the total benefits people receive over their lifetime, either by providing a lower monthly benefit or fewer years of benefits or a combination of the two. People working for more years also helps grow the economy. If Americans worked, on average, until sixty-five—three years beyond the earliest age that Social Security can be claimed and on par with people in New Zealand and Iceland—our GDP would increase by double digits.

But meeting our country's economic challenges isn't going to be as simple as making us all work more years. Although many people both want and need to keep working, they aren't always able to, whether because they are in poor health, need to care for someone else, or can't find a job. If policymakers and employers are going to encourage Americans to work longer, they need to better understand the barriers that prevent people from doing so. And they must do a much better job of supporting both those who wish to work and those who are unable to keep working.

A Tale of Two Futures

Working as we get older is good for us in several ways. We know that work has cognitive benefits, and different cognitive abilities peak at different times of our lives, even into our late sixties, meaning older workers have much to contribute. I'll talk about these upsides later in this chapter. It's also the case that many people genuinely enjoy their jobs, feel a sense of purpose doing them, and want to stay employed. Given my own work on aging, I've gotten to know a lot of vibrant seventy- and even eighty-year-olds who still love their jobs and never want to stop.

Bessie is someone I met only recently, when she spoke to me from her office in Fort Washington, Maryland. She is one of those people who manages to be energetic yet exude a sense of calm. At sixty-six, she is the chief operating officer at her church. She began her career in computer programs and information systems. It was a huge learning experience, she told me, but she hated the private sector market. "I got into it back in the 1970s, when African Americans weren't looked at as people with skills, and I had to work three times as hard to get promotions," she said. "But it wasn't just that. The only way you could really get ahead seemed to be dog-eat-dog, pushing someone else down so you could get higher. And that wasn't me."

One day she was sitting in church and thought, "I want to foster community, serve people, help them have what they need." Around that time, her company downsized and laid off midlevel managers. When a full-time position in operations at a church opened up, Bessie took it.

She's been at her current job since 2002, working on day-to-day operations, handling finances, and dealing with contractors on various projects. The day Bessie and I spoke, she was working on developing a project for housing people with HIV and AIDS. When she left the private sector, she took a 50 percent salary cut, but now she loves going to the office in the morning: "When you work in a nonprofit, you get more nontangible benefits, which far outweigh some of the tangible things we think we need."

For now, Bessie says she needs a job. She and her husband aim to retire at seventy-two. They have some investments, and they both have pensions, so she feels they'll be okay. But as she gets closer to seventy, she's less sure about retiring. As long as she's healthy, she thinks she'd like to keep working.

Bessie knows she is fortunate to have options, since not everyone does.

Cindy is also sixty-six years old, but her situation is very different. Cindy spoke to me from the motel in northern Michigan where she lives. She trained as an X-ray technician and then worked as a medical assistant, but she is now a part-time greeter at a grocery store and collects Social Security. Cindy told me she can't find an affordable one-bedroom apartment. She had put aside money for retirement, but in recent years she had to buy a car and get dental work, wiping out her savings.

Cindy retired at sixty-five from her medical assistant career in the Detroit area after forty-seven years. The arthritis in her hands had made it harder to give injections and lift patients. But the deciding factor was the ageism she experienced at her last position. Co-workers criticized her for doing things *the old way*, even though she got the same results, and she would overhear them say things like *Don't hire an old person—they're too hard to train*.

"I sure would've stayed longer," Cindy told me, but their comments "had a horrible effect on me. So I packed up everything and moved north."

Cindy loves her new job. "We're like a big happy family. There is no judgment about my age. It's done great things for my self-confidence."

It's easy to see why Cindy would thrive as a greeter. She is warm, funny, and engaged. But the work isn't easy, physically. She has to stand for more than seven hours a day, and she comes home with swollen feet and legs.

Assuming she'll still be up to the physical demands of the job, Cindy plans to take on more hours in the future. She hopes the cost of rentals will come down so she can afford to move out of the motel and into her own apartment. Reflecting on her financial troubles, she said, "I never thought this would happen in retirement. This is supposed to be a great time in life."

To Retire or Not to Retire?

The kind of precariousness Cindy faces is increasingly a problem for middle-income earners too. Unless you are in the rarified group that can comfortably self-fund decades of expenses, you face significant uncertainties about whether you can afford to stop working. The average amount that people have saved for retirement simply isn't enough. For most of us, the motivation to keep working is therefore financial. In a recent survey of older adults, nearly every respondent who was still working was doing so because they needed money. The earliest we can start receiving Social Security retirement benefits is age sixty-two, but that's considered early retirement, and our benefits will be significantly reduced if we do begin claiming then. Continuing to work makes it easier to hold off claiming benefits. And the longer we put off our retirement—up to seventy—the bigger our Social Security benefits will be. Delaying retirement can also enable more years of saving, as well as extend benefits such as health insurance, pensions, and retirement savings plans.

For all these reasons, retiring early can be very costly.

But beyond the obvious financial benefits, work is often a way to stay active, socially engaged, and physically and mentally healthy. An *inactive* retirement may actually be bad for our health, especially if we're single and sedentary. Without regular exercise and social interactions, just six years of retirement can raise our risk for illness and disability and affect our cognitive functioning. Even a part-time job can mitigate these risks and result in better long-term physical and cognitive health. A recent study of more than twenty thousand Americans between the ages of fifty-five and seventy-five found that working until age sixty-seven slowed the pace of cognitive decline by more than 30 percent. Mentally stimulating work such as analyzing data, developing strategies, and creative problem solving seems to be most beneficial, with effects that last well beyond retirement age.

Working longer can also lend a sense of purpose to our lives. A giant in the field of aging, Marc Freedman, founded Encore.org (now CoGenerate), which aims to change cultural expectations for people in the second half of life. It has launched a movement to tap our talent and life experience in "encore careers." Older workers embark on such careers not only to continue receiving income but also to have meaning in their lives and a chance to make a difference through the work they do.

Something Marc said recently when we were talking stuck with me: "The most important thing is mattering. You want to feel like if you weren't there, it would be noticed."

Of course, work isn't the only source of purpose in life. Relationships can bring enormous purpose, something we tend to recognize and value more in the second fifty. Likewise, taking care of a pet, caring for a loved one who needs help, tending a garden, or engaging in creative projects can bring a sense of meaning and satisfaction. But for a lot of us, work makes us feel we matter, especially if we no longer have family responsibilities such as raising kids or caring for elderly parents. It can stimulate and challenge us and remind us that we can still make valuable contributions.

The sense of purpose derived from work doesn't have to involve a paycheck. Retirees often volunteer—putting in unpaid hours in a house of worship, organization, or club. My parents spend much of their time in retirement cleaning and doing upkeep for their church, helping out at a food pantry, and volunteering at a local public golf course. My dad doesn't even play, but he enjoys working there with his friends and chatting with the golfers. My parents also offer the kind of informal support many older people do, such as driving friends and neighbors to doctors' appointments.

A growing body of evidence shows that the physical, social, and mental activity involved in volunteering, along with the sense of purpose it provides, helps older adults to maintain their health longer—among volunteers we see, for instance, decreased symptoms of depression, less social isolation, and lower mortality. One program that has been studied to assess the benefits of volunteering is Experience Corps. Now run by AARP Foundation, this community-based volunteer program was founded in 1996 to improve child literacy. The founders, who included Marc Freedman and Linda Fried, wanted to promote the health of lower-income older adults while also addressing the social and academic needs of kids in public elementary schools.

Researchers at Washington University in St. Louis looking at twenty-three elementary schools found that during a one-year period, students working with Experience Corps tutors made over 60 percent more progress in critical reading skills than similar students not paired with tutors. The tutors also benefited: the first study to evaluate the impact on brain health of tutors in Experience Corps over a two-year period found that brain volume had increased compared to the age-related declines in nontutors, an increase correlated with improvements in memory. The program is a great example of how giving our time and energy to others supports our own well-being.

For some Americans, retirement may mark the end of a long-term, full-time job, but many of us no longer define *retirement* by whether we're still working. It may mean instead the year we begin claiming Social Security benefits or become eligible for Medicare, or perhaps the day we stop working full time at our main careers. Tracey Gendron, author of *Ageism Unmasked*, has argued that our society's use of the term *retired* is itself problematic because it takes our relationship to a particular activity—work—and applies it to an entire life stage. We are defined by a deficit: our withdrawal from something we once did but no longer do. In truth, as Gendron said, whatever our age, whatever our income or physical or cognitive functioning, we are all still engaging in life.

In the past, the question of whether to retire was less complicated. Up to the beginning of the 1900s, people worked until they were physically unable to continue, or until they died. But that changed by the mid-twentieth century. With the rise of pensions and the advent of Social Security, a new stage of life—retirement—came into being.

Alongside that, a new American dream developed, based on the premise of a three-stage life that began with school, progressed to several decades of employment—often with just one company—and culminated in years of leisure in retirement. In this model, there was a single breadwinner, the father, and a mother devoted to raising the children. Retirement was a time for relaxation, family, and perhaps volunteer work or creative activities. While this ideal certainly wasn't attainable for everyone, millions of Americans were able to achieve it. Standards of living rose, and the average retirement age dropped. Longer lives meant more time in retirement, not more time working.

My parents may belong to the last generation that could take this model for granted. After decades working for the government as a computer systems analyst, my dad retired in 1994, when he was just fifty-seven. My mom closed her real estate business a few years later. They're both now eighty-five, and with pensions, Social Security, and some savings, they are enjoying their retirement. Not many fifty-somethings today can expect a similar future. I know I won't be able to retire at fifty-seven!

Over the last several decades, these demographic and economic changes—declining pensions, a rising retirement age, and individuals shouldering more financial risk in retirement—have dramatically altered the labor landscape. As job-related pensions have declined, and a lot of us have had to take on more of the risk of financing our retirements, the age at which we stop working has been increasing. The Covid-19 pandemic complicated the retirement picture, prompting over three million older Americans to drop out of the labor force earlier than planned. Since then the share of people between fifty-five to sixty-four who work has mostly returned to its pre-pandemic level, although it remains lower for those sixty-five and older. When people lose their jobs at older ages, it takes them longer, on average, to find another one than it takes younger job-seekers—sometimes, when unemployment is high, up to twice as long. They also suffer a much larger wage loss when they do become re-employed. Only one in ten older workers ever earns as much in their new job as they did in their old one. These gaps widen when race is factored into the equation. Among older workers, it takes

African American and Hispanic men longer to become re-employed, and they suffer even sharper wage losses than their white male counterparts do. Some older workers never re-enter the workforce, and Black and Hispanic people are much more likely to retire early than their white peers, citing health problems, the need to care for family members, and a lack of available jobs.

Given the difficulties that come with involuntary retirement, I was disheartened to learn just how frequently older workers become unemployed. When Richard Johnson, who directs the Program on Retirement Policy at the Urban Institute, looked at twenty thousand workers over more than two decades, he discovered that *more than half* had been laid off or pushed out of jobs at least once after turning fifty. Rich found that by the time the workers had reached sixty-five, only 16 percent were still employed. Sometimes it was an outright termination, but other times it was subtler—job conditions became unbearable, or wages or salaries went down. Other research has shown that many older workers will take a cash payout—the buyout or "voluntary separation agreement" employers offer workers if they retire early—even if it is a fraction of what their future wages would be, fearing that they might be laid off or fired soon anyway.

The measure of our capacity to keep working as we age is related both to our lifespans and to our healthspans. It's called our "working life expectancy," and it refers specifically to the number of years we can expect to be physically or cognitively able to work after age fifty. While about a third of people who are working estimate that they will work to age seventy, far fewer manage it. For women, working life expectancy after fifty is eleven years, and for men it's thirteen years. Because our capacity to keep working is affected by a number of factors, including race and levels of education, policies that encourage longer working lives can actually deepen socioeconomic divides and worsen inequality. As more education correlates with less physically arduous jobs and better health, highly educated people are able to keep earning longer, widening disparities.

———

For older Americans who are not in great health, working longer may not be an option. More than a fifth of retirees quit work because of health problems or injuries, including many people whose jobs were not physically taxing. People with lifelong disabilities have always struggled to find and hold jobs, especially those with decent pay. The unemployment rate among workers with a disability is twice as high as it is among those without one, and people over sixty-five with a disability have the lowest labor force participation rates. Workers with a disability are more likely to have only part-time work, meaning lower income and less chance they will have access to health insurance and retirement plans. Moreover, federal law allows employers with special certificates from the Department of Labor to pay workers with a disability far below the minimum wage. In 2023 half of the 120,000 workers employed under this program were earning less than $3.50 an hour. The combination of these factors makes it more challenging for those with disabilities to work, earn, and save, leaving many financially insecure in their second fifty.

The U.S. economy has been creating more and more jobs that are "age friendly"—work that is less likely to require physical exertion or involve harsh conditions or job hazards, and more likely to involve uniquely human skills such as communication, problem solving, and relationship building. The trend toward online and remote work could help older workers and those in poorer health. But the majority of these jobs go to higher-educated workers, leaving those with less education, still—literally—doing the heavy lifting. A 2022 report found that more than 25 percent of white workers aged fifty-five to sixty-four and over 40 percent of Black and Hispanic workers in this age range toiled in physically demanding jobs. For men, such jobs include delivery work, truck driving, janitorial and cleaning services, and farming and ranching, while for older women, common jobs are personal care aides, nursing, and childcare. More than ten million older workers perform these types of jobs, and the number is growing.

People in these demanding jobs have shorter working life expectancies. Many of them have done physical labor their whole lives, and the stress on their bodies makes it more likely they will be in poor health as they age. Some of the jobs are low-income, but certainly not all. Nurses and electricians may earn a good salary, but the years of bending, lifting, twisting, and so on can make it hard for them to continue working into their sixties or seventies.

Many low-wage jobs have no retirement savings plans, and the wages aren't enough to allow workers to save on their own. Their jobs are far less likely than higher-paid jobs to come with health insurance or sick leave. Taking a day off to see a doctor or to recover from an illness may not be an option. Often these jobs pay hourly, and the hours can be long or unreliable. In the service industry, for example, a slow night can mean you immediately lose wages or tips when you are sent home from a shift.

If you earned a minimum wage your entire career, the income you will get from Social Security will be well below the poverty level. By one estimate, to make up for the shortfall between Social Security income and the cost of food, housing, and medical care, minimum-wage earners would need to work thirty-three hours every week for the rest of their lives. In other words, they will *never* be able to retire.

Mary Gatta, a sociologist who focuses on jobs and economic security for marginalized and low-wage workers, likes to stress that many people she has spoken to for her research love what they're doing. The problem is how the labor market rewards them. "We need to improve job structures," she told me, "so that people can work *and* be economically secure."

She said jobs that emphasize "aesthetic labor"—how employees look, their body and image—create additional struggles for older workers. This is another form of age discrimination (something I'll talk about more later in this chapter), and it is seen most obviously in the retail and hospitality industries. As Gatta has pointed out, you could be in perfect health, but if you're doing aesthetic labor, you may lose your livelihood as you age. "Even if you're not fired," she said, "you might be taken off more lucrative shifts or moved from the front of the house."

Sometimes the challenges of poor health, low wages, and physically arduous work overlap. Richard Johnson explained it to me this way: "People with the least amount of savings who could benefit most from working longer also tend to have the most health problems and the least marketable skills. Lower-income people often can't extend their working lives."

Many lower-income earners end up just powering through. Gatta and researcher Jessica Horning have reported on how people keep working despite pain and health problems. They call it "dying with your boots on."

Retooling for the Second Half

As we age, we continue to learn and grow, but sometimes that doesn't translate into skills the labor market needs. If I'm aiming to work into my mid-seventies, I know I'll need to keep learning to make sure I'm employable and my skills remain relevant. Jobs that a lot of us trained for thirty years ago have changed dramatically or disappeared altogether, and artificial intelligence, robotics, and automation keep transforming the workplace. (How many self-checkout kiosks have replaced human employees at your local grocery store?) But while certain jobs may vanish, new professions keep emerging. A significant number of the jobs of the future, certainly the better ones, will probably require know-how that can't be easily replicated by computers. I'm talking about uniquely human abilities such as critical thinking, social and emotional intelligence, collaboration, and communication. And a lot of these opportunities will likely be closed to workers without specialized training.

Given our longer working lives, I believe that instead of our current three-stage life, where we go to school only in our early years, periods of work will ideally need to be interspersed with episodes of learning, paving the way for new vocations and choices. For this model to become a reality, policymakers and businesses need to better support older learners. Going back to school full or even part time can be expensive, especially if you have a family and a mortgage, and you'll have fewer years of work to pay off the costs.

Opportunities do exist for older learners. Many lower-cost community colleges offer technical and vocational certificates or degrees. Employers often provide on-the-job training to build skills throughout workers' careers (though older workers may need to be proactive about seeking these opportunities, as they are often targeted at younger workers). Some organizations provide digital skills training programs, which can be invaluable for keeping on top of new technologies even after retirement. The increased availability of remote or hybrid learning in higher education can enable older workers to more easily fit a course into their busy working lives. And the rise of massive open online courses, or MOOCs, has expanded the possibilities for learners everywhere to gain skills and degrees.

More traditional education beyond high school is also an option, though less than one percent of people aged fifty to sixty-four were enrolled in post–high school education in 2021. College enrollment actually declined for people thirty to sixty-four years old between 2005 and 2020, and it continued to shrink even after the pandemic. We have to get creative about ways to help expand late-life learning. As part of a competition led by the National Academy of Social Insurance that aimed to find innovative ways to improve Social Security, I teamed up with Marc Freedman on a proposal that would allow people to get Social Security payments when they took time off to go back to school later in life. Our idea was that someone in midcareer could apply for benefits for up to two years. According to the Social Security actuaries who examined the proposal, there would be little or no cost to the system, as workers generally earn higher salaries after additional training and pay more in taxes. Although the proposal hasn't gained much traction with policymakers (no new Social Security proposals have been adopted since the 1980s), if we expect people to have careers lasting forty to sixty years, we will need to develop approaches like this to help keep workers' skills current.

While visiting Singapore in 2019, I saw an innovative approach to supporting worker education and training and to encouraging lifelong learning. Under the SkillsFuture Credit program introduced in 2015, citizens twenty-five and over are given 500 Singapore dollars (US$375), which is placed in an account to pay for education and a few years later topped up by the same amount. People in the middle of their career, aged forty to sixty, receive a second top-up. One focus of the program is keeping workers' skills current—consulting with employers themselves every year about what skills they need, then tailoring training to those areas. An upskilled workforce helps drive economic growth, but the program has benefits for all ages. The plan also established the National Silver Academy, a network of education institutions and community organizations that offer a range of classes tailored to people aged fifty and older, including gardening, cooking, financial planning, maintaining physical and mental health, and using technology. As the then-minister for health Gan Kim Yong said, Singaporeans "live to learn and learn to live."

The $600 Billion Army

I call family caregivers the invisible army, because their work is so often unseen and underappreciated, and they sometimes need to fight hard to get loved ones the care they need. All told, almost fifty million Americans care for an adult relative or friend, helping those who have physical disabilities, dementia, or mental health issues, and assuming responsibility for personal care, doctor visits and medications, transportation, and chores that keep the home running. This unpaid work was valued at $600 billion in 2021. Caregiving can play a big part in whether we're able to continue in paid work or have to take time off or even retire early. Many family caregivers find themselves sandwiched between rearing their children or putting them through college while also tending to an aging parent, and more than six in ten hold paying jobs at some point while providing care. These stressful balancing acts can affect the caregiver's own health and exact a steep emotional and financial toll. Caregivers spend more than $7,200 a year, or roughly one-quarter of their income on average, to help those they care for with meeting expenses such as rent, mortgage payments, home modifications, and out-of-pocket medical costs. The greatest financial strain falls on those who can least afford it, including women and people of color. African American family caregivers spend more than a third of their income supporting their loved ones, and Hispanic/Latino caregivers spend nearly half.

Women make up 61 percent of family caregivers in the United States, and on average they spend 37 percent more time than men do on unpaid work and care in the home. They are often forced to stop working much sooner than they want to, or are periodically absent from the workforce, which can limit their career opportunities and reduce their chances of finding employment in later life. Even years after the caregiving has concluded, women are less likely to be employed and more likely to work fewer hours and earn less money.

As age demographics shift, baby boomers' need for care will grow just as family size is shrinking. In 2010 there were seven potential family caregivers for each person over eighty. By 2050, there may be just three such caregivers, meaning workers will face more requests to support friends and ailing relatives—translating to more time, expense, physical and emotional strain, and conflicts with paid work. Or it may mean trying to find professional caregivers who are available and affordable. Our policies will need to offer much stronger support to this invisible army, something I'll come back to in my final chapter.

Gigging Our Way Through Retirement

Many people in the second half of life often downshift to part-time or gig work—anything from consulting to pet sitting to being a rideshare driver. Or they may turn to self-employment as freelancers or independent contractors, either long term or as a brief bridge to retirement. Gig work often provides a level of freedom and autonomy that full-time jobs don't. The jobs don't usually offer benefits or long-term security, so they aren't a cure-all, but they can be a partial or temporary solution to a job loss or a cash shortfall; they can provide flexibility and may help you put off filing early for Social Security benefits. One 2020 report showed that 20 percent of gig workers are fifty-five or older, and a survey of Uber and Lyft drivers found that nearly half were over sixty. A 2019 study found that more than a third of independent contractors—usually highly educated people in managerial or consulting roles—were older workers. This share had risen significantly over the last number of years, indicating just how much people rely on nontraditional working arrangements for income in the second half of life.

Some people embark on "encore careers," which I mentioned earlier, a second vocation that begins in the latter half of life. Encore careers have grown more common as lifespans have become longer, early retirement more expensive, and the nature of work for some Americans less physically strenuous. The education, health care, and nonprofit sectors are among the top areas people gravitate toward in encore careers, though some also become entrepreneurs. The transition can be challenging, particularly for people starting out, as it often involves a period of little or no income while someone is building their second career. It takes money to set yourself up in business, and if the business fails, you could jeopardize what security you have, which is harder to recover later in life. Still, many people are making it work. In fact, research shows that middle-aged entrepreneurs are actually more likely than their younger counterparts to start a successful business.

I was introduced to Sarah, who lives in Oregon, through a colleague. Sarah is now sixty-four, and when she was young, she imagined that she and her husband would retire around sixty-five, with plenty of money in their 401(k) and time to travel and do things they enjoyed. But in their fifties, they found themselves with a fair bit of debt after putting three daughters through college. They also realized that Social Security might not cover as much of their expenses as they had expected.

By the time Sarah turned sixty, she felt burned out and ready to leave her full-time job as a marketer for an architectural and engineering firm. "I was always working more than a forty-hour week," she said, "up against deadlines constantly, and two hours commuting every day." Her father was in his early nineties and on his own. He lived nearby, but she knew that if anything happened while she was at the office, it would be hard to get to him quickly. She also had grandchildren whose parents worked full time, and she wanted to be able to help more with childcare.

And then the pandemic hit. Sarah began working from home. She used the two hours she'd spent commuting to do more sewing, something she had always loved. A few years before, she had sewn her oldest daughter's wedding dress, and through word of mouth, she had begun to earn money doing wedding dress alterations. Soon she was working forty-plus hours a week for the architectural firm and another twenty doing alterations.

Sarah wanted to have her own sewing business, but whenever she did the math, she saw no way that she could afford to leave her job. Her husband, who has his own small fence and decking company, was on her health insurance. And COBRA, which allows people who leave their jobs under certain circumstances to retain their group health plan for a limited period, was so expensive it wasn't even an option.

Then in the fall of 2021, it all came together. The pandemic was easing, and weddings were picking up. Her husband turned sixty-five and was able to go on Medicare. His own business was doing well, so they had one solid income they could count on. Sarah researched her state's health insurance marketplace and found she qualified for subsidies. When her bosses announced that it was time to come back to the office, she decided to give her notice. Going part time wasn't an option, but Sarah suggested she could be on call if her company needed extra help. Her bosses agreed to try it, and she was able to set her hourly rate and take work only when she was free.

She's now booked solid for dress alterations, but the trick is figuring out how to make it all work financially—whether to keep it a one-person business run out of her home, or expand with a partner or assistant. "The finances aren't there yet," she said. "But I'm confident that will come. And I still have my on-call work to fall back on and can postpone dipping into my Social Security or my 401(k)."

Her family remarks on how much happier she is. Her blood pressure is down, and her quality of life is up: "I still have deadlines, but I control my schedule and I'm at home. I don't have it all figured out. But I'm excited about where this business is going to go."

As Sarah's story shows, the changing employment landscape has potential advantages for older workers. Gig work, telework, and self-employment can provide flexibility, and encore careers can be good for society as well as for the worker, helping to maintain an economically healthy balance between workers paying into the system and those receiving benefits. But even with these options, we can't just fall back on the idea that simply working longer, or part time, or becoming entrepreneurs, will create financial security for older people.

Instead we need policies that ensure that those who are in nontraditional working arrangements have the social and financial protections they need. This means expanding affordable health care to people who are not covered by employer plans and providing more state-sponsored retirement savings plans for those who don't have plans linked to employers. Many older people want and need to work, and they deserve these benefits, whatever the nature of their work arrangements. Sarah is an example of someone who wanted to keep working and was able to shoulder some risk. But what enabled her to transition to self-employment were certain social supports—Medicare and health insurance subsidies—as well as her employer's willingness to work with her on a step-down solution that suited everyone.

The High Cost of Age Discrimination

Discrimination against people because of age costs all of us, whether personally, socially, or economically. It leads to disproportionate numbers of older workers being laid off, not hired, or not promoted, and has spin-off effects far beyond the individuals it harms. My team at AARP released a study, undertaken with the *Economist* Intelligence Unit, showing that in 2018 the age discrimination that pushes older Americans out of the workforce cost our economy $850 billion in lost wages, salaries, taxes, and consumer spending. With a growing aging population, the study projected that this figure could rise to trillions of dollars within the next few decades. Embracing a multigenerational workforce will benefit the larger economy by extending the productive lives of *all* workers.

Ageism can run in both directions. Younger people may not be taken seriously, while older workers can be seen as less flexible or slower to pick up new concepts or technologies. Ageism against older people is a strange discrimination. As psychologist Todd Nelson has pointed out, ageism is a "prejudice against our feared future self." I wonder how many of us think of it that way as we go about our days, slipping—inadvertently, in many cases—into ageist assumptions or, on the flip side, being sidelined or demoralized by those same assumptions. Older workers can end up internalizing ageist assumptions, to their detriment. A study on the impact of stereotypes on cognitive performance found that when older people were told that aging equates with poorer memory, then were given memory tests, they fared worse than their peers who had been told that older people perform just as well as younger people.

For those already facing barriers due to gender, sexual orientation, disability, or race, getting older often amplifies those challenges. Women encounter age discrimination at earlier ages and with greater intensity than men do, and it takes women in their fifties and early sixties an average of three weeks longer to find a job than it does a man of the same age. Older people with disabilities may find that their difficulties are viewed as simply a part of aging, and they therefore don't receive the needed support in navigating barriers to access and care. Black Americans are more likely than workers of other races to report feeling unable to re-enter the workforce because of age or feeling pressured into early retirement.

Federal law prohibits age discrimination in the workplace against people who are forty and older. Yet recent court cases involving, for example, documented management discussions to reduce the number of older workers make clear that ageism is prevalent, if vastly underreported. It can also be difficult to prove in court. Victoria Lipnic, who served as commissioner of the Equal Employment Opportunity Commission, called it "an open secret." It tends to be concentrated in three main areas: recruitment and hiring, on-the-job bias (fewer training opportunities or promotions), and termination—for instance, when companies "freshen" their workforce by targeting older staff for layoffs or encouraging them to retire.

A recent survey found that over six in ten people aged forty and older believe they have seen or experienced age discrimination in the workplace, and over a third worry that their age will make it harder to find a new job. They aren't imagining it. If you apply for a job online, ageism may be embedded in the screening algorithm and automatically disqualify you. A 2017 study by the National Bureau of Economic Research involving forty thousand résumés showcasing equivalent skills found that callback rates were lower by about 18 percent for workers in their late forties and early fifties, and by about 35 percent for older workers. The authors found added discrimination against older women and suggested this was likely due to employers placing greater importance on women's appearance. This is the "aesthetic discrimination," or "lookism," that I referred to earlier. To get around these barriers, many older applicants have tried to age-proof their résumés by removing the dates of their degrees or certificates and even the dates of past positions they've held, and focusing on their most recent experience.

What Ageism Gets Wrong About Older Workers

In the previous chapter, I talked about how a certain amount of cognitive decline is normal. Am I saying now that this is irrelevant when older people seek work or want to stay in their jobs? No. I'm saying that aging is a process of both loss and accrual, and older workers bring qualities to the workplace that are acquired only through years of experience—depth of knowledge, social maturity, and sense of perspective. As writer Andrew Solomon has noted, "While all old people have been young, no young people have been old."

I'm not talking about some fuzzy notion of "wisdom." I'm referring to brain changes that we know about from rigorous research. Neuroscientists at MIT and Massachusetts General Hospital published a study showing that different cognitive skills peak at different ages. Looking at data from about fifty thousand people, researchers found that raw speed in processing information appears to peak at the end of our teens, and short-term memory is strongest between ages twenty-five and thirty-five. But emotional understanding (the ability to evaluate others' emotional states) doesn't peak until our forties and fifties, and our vocabularies continue to increase throughout our sixties. Vocabulary serves as a measure of "crystallized intelligence," which is the accumulation of facts and knowledge, and the ability to use the knowledge one has acquired. It was previously thought that crystallized intelligence peaks in our late forties, but this study showed it peaking in the late sixties or early seventies. This change may arise from the fact that people now have more education than previous generations, as well as increased access to information and to more mentally demanding work.

Even older workers doing physically arduous jobs have been shown to be as productive as younger workers. A study of a truck assembly line at a Mercedes-Benz plant found that average individual productivity actually rose between twenty-five and sixty-five years of age. Any declines in physical strength as workers aged seemed to be compensated for by abilities that tend to increase with age, such as operating well in a team in tense situations. When things went wrong on the line and required rapid fixes, older, more experienced workers knew better which errors to avoid at all costs. This focus left them slightly more inclined to make minor errors but less likely to commit the major errors that younger workers were prone to.

These and other studies support arguments in favor of multigenerational workplaces. Older workers often possess valuable contacts, institutional knowledge, and know-how that can help younger hires to integrate into organizations, providing continuity and stability. But what we're learning about the brain gives us greater insight into what people of all ages are bringing to the workplace. It's also worth noting that most people *like* working with others from different generations. One survey showed that seven out of ten people felt that having mixed-generation colleagues created new opportunities for learning and made the work environment more productive. With age diversity, we see more innovation and higher productivity in *both* younger and older workers. Turnover goes down, and workplace stability goes up.

One myth I need to debunk is the belief that retaining older workers keeps younger workers out of jobs. This is what economists call the "lump-of-labor fallacy," the mistaken idea that there is a set number of jobs to go around. This might apply within a small business or to a particular position, but it is not true for the economy as a whole. In fact, keeping more older workers helps to grow the economy, leading to more jobs overall. Younger and older workers' skills and experience most often make them complements rather than substitutes for each other.

I wanted to learn more about how employers view older workers, so I called Jacqueline Welch, the executive vice-president and chief human resources officer for *The New York Times*. Jacqueline told me that too often we're applying rules from an outdated work model, one she knows from her parents' generation. Her father was a manual laborer in a manufacturing plant where, when you reached sixty-five, you got a big retirement party and a nice going-away gift. This scenario is now the exception rather than the rule. The challenge for organizations, she said, is to reconfigure their working arrangements and reward structures to better reflect the needs and experiences of older workers.

According to Jacqueline, over a quarter of employees at *The New York Times* are over fifty. When it comes to ageism, she said, context matters. You are less likely to see older workers in tech or digital jobs. (In this, the *Times* wouldn't be unusual: the median age of tech employees at Apple, Amazon, Google, LinkedIn, and Facebook is between twenty-eight and thirty-one, more than ten years younger than the workforce in general.) But it's different in the newsroom, where you have older people who've covered big stories in the past. "It's an interesting phenomenon," Jacqueline said, "to see age in one instance be a real impediment and in another see older people regarded with reverence."

Most of us, however, aren't venerated reporters for *The New York Times*, so I asked Jacqueline how people over fifty can navigate the job market. She mentioned the gaps many older people have on their résumés and said we should think of how our experience both in and out of the workplace has equipped us to contribute to an organization. In other words, what transferable skills are we bringing with us?

For many people, that experience includes caregiving. Jacqueline has firsthand knowledge of the benefits and challenges of being a caregiver. She left a multimedia company to care for her father; he'd had two strokes and was also battling prostate cancer when he moved in with her. Balancing work, her father's care, and raising young kids proved overwhelming, so Jacqueline focused on her family. Four years later, when her father's cancer went into remission and he recovered much of the mobility lost to the strokes, Jacqueline went back to work in HR, now with a deeper understanding of the conflicting demands many workers have to juggle—but also with a new skill set.

Taking care of her father, she said, did wonders for her own organizational skills. "What the speech pathologist is telling you versus what the radiation specialist is saying are two different languages, and

I was able to knit together disparate pieces of information. Where else would I have gotten all the consulting skills that I'm now able to apply to other challenges?" She recommends that you plan how you will talk about that time you were off work and what you gained from it. Be aware, too, of how your life experience allows you to be a good coach and mentor—your age as a value-add rather than a liability.

Jacqueline also had suggestions about how to talk to employers when we need flexibility. She thinks we might be surprised by the ideas bosses will consider, especially if we clearly want to stay engaged and we offer possible solutions—not just presenting them with a problem scenario that they need to solve. The options might be time off, or a reduced schedule and adjusted pay and benefits. When it comes to retirement, Jacqueline believes employers need to create more "graceful" exit ramps for people, as many of us can't afford or just don't want that hard stop to our working lives that was common in our parents' generation. Phased retirement, part-time advisory or mentorship roles, and job shares are ways for us to stay engaged. They can also benefit our employers by facilitating deeper, more gradual transfers of knowledge, a process essential to an organization's success.

Making It Easier to Work Longer

In 2010, Julianne Taaffe and Kathryn Moon, teachers in their sixties in the English as a Second Language (ESL) program at The Ohio State University, were forwarded a troubling email written by their boss to another university. The women had worked in the program since the 1980s, helping to build it from its foundations, and both had consistently received first-rate performance reviews. But in the email, Robert Eckhart described ESL teachers as "an extraordinarily change-averse population of people almost all of whom are over 50, contemplating retirement (or not), and it's like herding hippos."

By then, older, experienced teachers in the program had noticed that their more junior colleagues were getting promotions while they lost their offices and were shifted to a cramped shared space. According to reporting in *The New York Times*, Eckhart referred to one older employee as "the Grim Reaper" and to others as "dead wood" and "millstones around my neck."

When Taaffe lodged a formal complaint, a university inquiry cleared the managers involved. After being demoted, with less pay and no sick leave, Taaffe and Moon retired, short of their full benefits. Eventually, more than twenty ESL staff left, as their positions were threatened with elimination or their salaries cut.

Taaffe and Moon filed a federal lawsuit against the university. Finally, in 2018, they were vindicated. The Equal Employment Opportunity Commission (EEOC) found reasonable cause to believe that the women and their older colleagues had been victims of age discrimination in violation of federal law. Although Ohio State denied it had acted unlawfully, it rehired both women and agreed to back pay and retroactive benefits totaling about $440,000.

The case highlighted how age discrimination is still viewed differently from other forms of bias. As Catherine Ventrell-Monsees, an EEOC attorney, said, "If the same supervisors made those comments about race or sex, they'd know trouble was coming."

If the government and businesses are truly going to support older workers—helping them stay in the workforce by reducing involuntary retirement, underemployment, and unemployment—they have to look at improving the whole life cycle of work, from recruitment practices to training to options for phased retirement. Quality jobs should have consistent scheduling, flexibility, and benefits such as sick leave and time off for caregiving. Programs must be created to help people grow on the job by continuing their educations and updating their skills. Finally, companies can't thwart the goal of working longer by creating discriminatory or hostile environments that push older people out, as happened at Ohio State.

There has been progress in certain areas, like improving health and retirement benefits for people in nontraditional jobs and supporting caregivers. The Affordable Care Act provided access to insurance and many protections for people not tied to employer health care plans. And while the federal minimum wage hasn't been raised since 2009, many states and localities have raised their own minimum wage to exceed the federal level, which may help workers to put a little aside for the future. Several states have also begun to offer paid leave so that working caregivers can take family members to the doctor or assist them in emergencies. These laws may help to keep caregivers employed while also reducing the need to put family members in nursing homes, resulting in significant saving for both the state and families.

Our increased longevity offers opportunities for us to reimagine how we work, earn, and continue to learn over the course of our lives. More must be done, though, to support and incentivize us to work longer, instead of penalizing those of us who can't keep working. However creative or industrious we may be, we can't always navigate this changing landscape on our own.

5

Will I Have Enough Money?

My grandfather did not have an easy retirement. Life expectancy, when he was born in 1897, was around forty-seven. For most of his life, he worked as a logger in Washington state—an incredibly dangerous job, especially in those days. He had a small farm with chickens, cows, and a garden that helped to keep his five kids fed. He had no pension, little savings, and only a modest check from Social Security, so he kept working almost until he died at seventy-four. My grandmother was left with little to live on, but at least she had the family farm.

My father's expectations of aging were substantially different. By the 1950s, people assumed they could live into their seventies, and they looked forward to "retirement"—then a new concept—with a base income to rely on. As my father had served in the military and then spent most of his career working for the federal government, he had a lifelong pension, a retiree health care plan, and a 401(k). When he retired in 1994, his mortgage was paid off, and he had no other debt. My parents, now in their eighties, are very fortunate; their pensions, Social Security, and retirement nest egg cover their modest expenses and allow them to travel. Like everyone, they worry about their health and independence, but they don't have to worry when it comes to money.

My husband and I are also fortunate. Our jobs will provide us with pensions, and we have been saving in retirement plans since we started working. But as I enter my own second fifty, I feel far less sanguine about my family's future than my parents did about theirs. For one thing, the Social Security system is expected to start running short of funding in 2034, the year I turn sixty-four. Based on my years of experience on Capitol Hill, I am confident that policymakers will make the changes necessary to avert a crisis before that deadline—the political consequences of doing nothing are just too severe. But not knowing what steps they will take to keep Social Security solvent—or how those will impact our benefits—makes it hard to know if my husband and I are saving enough, and if we will have enough income in retirement.

I also worry for my kids' generation. My daughter and son are now in their late teens and early twenties. Given the current trends in lifespan and employment patterns, it's likely one or both of them will live beyond their hundredth birthday, and they may never have a job that offers retirement benefits. They could be contract workers, self-employed, or members of the gig economy. Even if they do work for a large organization, they likely won't be able to count on the kinds of pensions or retiree health care plans their parents and grandparents enjoyed.

Ideally, my kids won't have to care for my husband and me. Ideally, they won't get sick themselves. Ideally, they'll figure out how to take care of themselves financially. But we live in a world where things very often aren't ideal.

What we need to support our longer lives, in my view, is a change to our systems, because much of what enables financial security in retirement—or our ability to one day retire at all—is beyond our individual control, determined by the decisions and policies of our employers and political representatives. It hinges on whether the companies we work for offer health insurance or retirement benefits, contribute to our retirement savings, and pay a living wage that allows us to save. It also depends on the solvency and adequacy of our main retirement program, Social Security, which hasn't been substantially updated since the 1980s. America's retirement-support system needs dramatic improvements to keep pace with our longer lives.

Many of us avoid thinking about retirement planning altogether. Nearly half of workers say they haven't tried to calculate how much money they'll need during retirement. But we should all think about it. The picture I'm going to paint in the next several pages isn't all wine and roses, but understanding our options and planning for the future is always better than putting our heads in the sand, and it can bring us some peace of mind.

The Price of Living Longer

Longer life is full of economic trade-offs. It means we will have more years of life to finance, with or without paychecks. We might have fewer expenses such as school tuitions or work clothes, but we'll still have plenty of household bills, and we are likely to face a host of additional health and long-term care expenses, which makes extending our healthspans that much more important.

Younger people often assume that Medicare will pay for all their health costs once they hit sixty-five. But we still have to pay insurance premiums, co-pays for doctor or hospital visits, and prescriptions. We may need many things, such as a visit to the dentist or new glasses, that Medicare won't pay for at all. By one estimate, a married couple will need to have saved at least $212,000 by age sixty-five to have an even chance of being able to pay for health care alone for the rest of their lives. To have a 90 percent chance of covering their costs, they would need to have put aside nearly $320,000. These huge figures don't even take into account the costs of long-term care (which I will talk about in Chapter 6) and other living expenses.

For a minority of people in the United States, the cost of increasing longevity is of no concern. They have plenty to cover their needs as they age, mostly because they own their own home, have a generous pension or a high-balance investment portfolio, and may still be working. In 2019 the richest 10 percent of families had an average of nearly $700,000 saved in retirement accounts. I don't want to suggest that those with sufficient assets and income live without worries—extremely high medical or care costs can eat away at even the healthiest portfolios, and I know relatively wealthy families who have struggled to cover the long-term care costs for a loved one with dementia. But having a much larger cushion means being plagued by fewer financial worries. Unfortunately, a large cushion is the exception rather than the norm. Overall, one in two families in the United States has *nothing* saved for retirement. Among those who do, families in the bottom half of the income distribution have saved less than $60,000 on average, which isn't a lot when spread over what could be decades of retirement.

Even those who have tried to save can find themselves struggling if they are hit with emergencies. A few years ago, a friend asked if I would talk with his father, Lawrence, about a reverse mortgage he was considering. I didn't know how much I could help but said I was happy to try.

I gave Lawrence a call, and he began by telling me about his life. Lawrence and his wife raised eight children in rural Utah and have forty-two grandchildren whom they adore. Now seventy-six, Lawrence was a master craftsman; he supported his family making high-quality custom cabinets in a workshop in his home. He had saved money and invested as wisely as he could. But medical bills had taken a big chunk of the family's savings when one child was born prematurely and his wife was diagnosed with cancer. Without savings to fall back on, Lawrence needed to keep working even when the arthritis in his hands made it painful. He and his wife depended on their Social Security payments and on help from family to make ends meet. Still, their debt kept climbing. They tapped the equity built up in the house to pay some bills and even considered selling their home. But the converted schoolhouse was the same building where they had met in seventh grade and later raised a family. How could they possibly let it go? But how could they make it through their second fifty if they didn't?

I shared the pros—and many cons—of reverse mortgages. Lawrence did end up getting one. He was able to keep the family home and access additional equity to draw on for emergencies. He loves that his big family can come together and that there is space for all the grandkids to sleep over. "I've always wanted a place the kids felt they could come home to," he told me.

Lawrence had worked just as hard as my father, maybe harder, given the physical nature of his job, yet in retirement he found himself in a very different financial position. It wasn't because he'd made bad choices; it was largely because he had been self-employed for most of his life and didn't have the same protections and generous health and retirement benefits my father has enjoyed.

Lawrence isn't alone in his struggle to get by. Many Americans are only a health crisis away from losing their homes or sinking into poverty. In 2021 the official poverty line for a single person in the United States was $12,880 in annual income, and more than twelve million Americans aged fifty and older lived below this line. Older Black and Latino/Hispanic people are roughly twice as likely as white adults to be poor during their second fifty, and the risk of poverty rises with age.

While twelve million is a staggering number, the reality is far worse. The poverty line is set at three times the cost of a minimum food diet in 1963 and is updated only in line with inflation; it doesn't take account of rising standards of living or factor in differences between more and less expensive parts of the country. Nor does it fully reflect the amount older adults pay in rising health care costs. When we factor in all these extra expenses, most older people today would need an income of at least twice the official poverty line just to keep a roof over their head.

By that more realistic measure, more than 60 percent of single adults over sixty-five are poor.

Balancing on a Pogo Stick

We wonks often use the analogy of a three-legged stool to describe America's retirement system. The three legs are Social Security, pensions, and savings, and if all of them are equally sturdy, the stool can support most of us throughout our retirement years.

Unfortunately, in America today, all three legs are either wobbly or collapsing completely. Traditional pensions—fixed benefits that employees receive in a monthly paycheck for life following retirement—are becoming exceedingly rare: more than two in three workers born in the 1920s through the '40s had pensions, but fewer than one in ten workers born in the mid-1960s have one, and that number keeps falling. As traditional pensions have declined, 401(k) and other employer-sponsored retirement savings accounts have grown. These accounts are different in that employees (and sometimes employers) pay into them over time, the accounts fluctuate with their investments, and an employee can draw down the funds in retirement. However, these plans are far from universal. Roughly half of American workers don't have an easy way to save for retirement through their paycheck. Even many who have saved find their balances too low to provide them with meaningful resources to cover the decades after they stop working. In all, about one in five Americans over sixty-five are completely without two of the three legs, living solely on Social Security. For them, it is like trying to get through the second fifty on a pogo stick.

Fortunately, Social Security protects almost all of us. Over 97 percent of people aged sixty and over are either getting benefits or will be at a later date. Without this monthly income, millions of older Americans would be living in poverty. But life is hardly cushy if you are living on Social Security income alone: the average monthly retirement check in 2022 was $1,670, barely enough to pay the average rent on an unfurnished apartment. That leaves little for food, clothing, medicine, and other necessities.

This financial shortfall is one reason employment is rising for people in their sixties, seventies, and even beyond. Ironically, work has become an important fourth leg of the retirement stool. Earning even a little income can make all the difference in ensuring the bills don't pile up.

Terry, who works as a cashier in the cafeteria at Howard University in Washington, D.C., is an example of someone in this situation. Terry's husband died in 2022. Continuing to work has been good for her mental health. She told me the students treat her like family, and she took great pleasure in describing Taco Tuesday and Soul Food Day, when the lines snake out the cafeteria door. But money is another factor. She gets her husband's pension—he was an electrician for thirty-five years—as well as the Social Security widow's benefit. She even has a side gig selling fresh homemade juice. She has saved a little money toward her retirement, first through a 401(k), then through an Individual Retirement Account (IRA). But working allows her to pay her bills *and* do things she enjoys, like traveling to see her children and grandchildren.

"I repeat this to all the kids," she told me. "Please do not depend on Social Security, because it's definitely not enough. Everybody thinks, 'As soon as I retire, I can fall back on it.' But it won't even get you started unless you have a 401(k) or something."

Terry is planning to retire next year. She's in good health, but she's feeling the wear and tear of years of work. "I've been in the kitchen, lifting, bending, cleaning, standing, sometimes for eight or nine hours or doing overtime." A lot of older members of her family, including her mother, have had dementia, and most of her husband's friends did not live to enjoy their retirement. Terry wants to enjoy hers while she is still healthy.

Like many Americans, Terry is perched on a four-legged stool that includes work. To understand how some people find themselves needing to work in later life, we have to take a closer look at the other three legs of the stool.

The End of the Poorhouse

Social Security is one of our country's greatest legislative achievements. Until the mid-1930s, the United States had no retirement system at all. Laborers were simply expected to work until they dropped. For those who couldn't work and didn't have wealth or family to support them, the closest thing to a safety net was the poorhouse. Paid for by local municipalities, this Dickensian institution condemned people to filth, disease, and misery.

By the time of the Great Depression, rapid industrialization had eroded the traditional protections of family and close-knit communities as desperate workers moved from rural areas to the city. With few jobs available and families in crisis, half of America's older adults were living in poverty.

In 1934, President Franklin D. Roosevelt created a cabinet-level committee to address the nation's economic insecurity. One of its assignments was to propose a plan based on European systems already in place. These programs were not means-tested or directed only at people in poverty; they were social insurance programs, built on pooled contributions from workers, that would protect them from the consequences of disability or loss of work in later life.

The committee recognized that illness and injury can derail workers at any stage of a career, while a job loss or the death of a breadwinner can devastate entire families. They recommended programs for public works, unemployment, disability, and pension and survivors' benefits. Not all of these survived the legislative process, but the national pension proposal did set the model for the Social Security Act, which Roosevelt signed into law in 1935.

The original Social Security system was designed to pay benefits only to workers who retired after turning sixty-five, but it has been updated over the years. Benefits have been added for people unable to work because of disability; for survivors and dependents; for agricultural and domestic workers; and most recently, for same-sex spouses and survivors. The early retirement eligibility age of sixty-two was established first for women in 1956 and then for men five years later. In 1975 regular cost-of-living adjustments were added to protect against inflation. And to avoid a solvency crisis in the 1980s, the "full retirement age"—when we can claim full benefits without being penalized—was gradually raised from sixty-five to sixty-seven, along with an increase in the taxes that fund Social Security.

Today sixty-six million people, roughly one in five Americans, receive some kind of Social Security benefit, including the fifty-two million who receive retirement benefits and almost six million people of all ages who get monthly survivor payments. Despite this widespread dependence on the program, there is a disconnect between how younger people view it and the reality facing older people today. In the SHOL survey, more than one-third of those under forty said they do not expect to rely on Social Security when they retire (planning to live largely off retirement plan savings), while over nine in ten older people over seventy surveyed *do* rely on it. This underestimation is worrying. It means that many young people either don't understand the realities of retirement finances or don't have faith that Social Security is going to be there for them when they need it. A lack of understanding about the program also undermines public support for Social Security, leaving it more vulnerable to cuts.

How the program works is generally misunderstood. A few years ago, when the Massachusetts Mutual Life Insurance Company gave a basic quiz about Social Security to people over fifty, more than half failed or passed with a D. In all fairness, the rules *are* confusing. But we can't plan for the future on the basis of a system we don't understand, so it's worth getting a grasp of the program's main features.

Social Security is one of the few federal programs required by law to pay for itself. This means that working Americans pay a percentage of each paycheck into the system. Our contributions flow into two U.S. Treasury accounts from which benefits are paid: the Old-Age and Survivors Insurance Trust Fund, and the Disability Insurance Trust Fund.

During times when more money was coming into the system than was being paid out in benefits, excess funds were deposited into the Social Security trust funds and invested in safe, interest-bearing government bonds. But since 2021, Social Security has been drawing down these reserves to pay out benefits.

Sometimes benefits overlap, though we can claim only one type at a time. For instance, if you qualify for a retirement benefit based on your own employment as well as a survivor benefit from your deceased spouse, you'll receive only the larger of the two benefits.

Every dollar you pay into or receive from the system is tracked, but contrary to one popular misconception, your Social Security tax contributions do *not* go into a personal account with your name on it. Instead, those taxes are used to pay for current beneficiaries, and the next generation's taxes will pay for you. My payroll taxes help cover my parents' retirement benefits, and theirs contributed to my grandmother's disability benefits. One day my children's payroll taxes will help pay for the benefits my husband and I receive.

Eligibility and the amount of Social Security benefits you receive will depend on several factors. For retirees, benefits are calculated according to a formula that considers your thirty-five highest years of earnings. The program's framers wanted to maintain some relationship between the taxes you pay and the benefits you receive. Unlike personal savings accounts, however, Social Security's retirement formula was designed to give extra help to low earners, so they receive a larger percentage of their past earnings (not a larger benefit) than people who earned more. This is what politicians mean when they say Social Security has a "progressive" benefit formula.

Several features of the program adjust for longevity. First, adjustments for inflation mean you'll be protected against rising prices. Your check will be higher when you celebrate your hundredth birthday than it was when you reached your eightieth. Second, you may claim early retirement benefits when you're as young as sixty-two, but if you wait until seventy to claim your retirement benefits, your income will be

77 percent higher every month for the rest of your life. You don't have to wait until you're seventy—each year until then that you delay will mean your benefits get larger. But if you claim benefits early, you forfeit that bump.

For people who have an illness or injury that prevents them from working, there is a whole different set of rules. While it typically takes ten years to earn credits to qualify for retirement benefits, you may gain eligibility for disability benefits with less time on the job. But Social Security Disability Insurance (SSDI) is not awarded lightly. To qualify, you must have a medical issue that is expected to last for a year or to be terminal. The condition must be so severe that you're unable to perform not only the job you used to do but any available job. The many rules make it very hard to prove your case, and long backlogs in processing applications mean you may not get a decision for years. Ultimately, two out of three people who apply for SSDI are rejected. One reason for the frequent rejections is that people's ability to work is compared to a list of jobs that has not been updated since 1991, many of which—microfilming, nut sorting, telephone quotation clerk—no longer exist. Over the past ten years, about half of appeals have been sent back to Social Security judges for new hearings, where they are often rejected all over again.

Like many people with severe disabilities, Linda had to battle to get the SSDI benefits she needed. She spoke to me from her home in Albuquerque, New Mexico. Now sixty-eight, she had been employed all her adult life in banks, but eventually her health problems—asthma, fibromyalgia, and osteoarthritis, combined with shoulder and back injuries—prevented her from working. Between her SSDI application, the original denial and her appeal, and a move from Denver to Albuquerque to get help from her sister, two and a half years passed before Linda received benefits. "I'm a very determined person," she told me. "But it was exhausting. We paid into these programs. They're supposed to be there to support us."

Fortunately, there is a growing list of over two hundred conditions that Social Security will approve within weeks, including early-onset Alzheimer's, some terminal cancers, and severe genetic disorders. But a particularly unjust rule of the program is that even after you are approved, you may have to wait up to five months to get a disability benefit check and up to two years to get health care coverage through Medicare. Patient advocacy groups have successfully fought to eliminate the Medicare waiting period for those diagnosed with ALS, but many people with other debilitating illnesses still wait far too long for the health care they need.

Disability benefits are hardly lavish—the average monthly payment in 2022 was $1,364—but they are a critical source of income for many people, especially in later life. Of the eight million former workers who receive SSDI, 75 percent are over fifty.

Our growing older population means that the Social Security leg of the retirement stool needs to be updated or it will fail to provide what people expect, and need, in retirement. Founded in 1935, the program has undergone many changes throughout its history, and its longevity is a testament to the care with which Roosevelt's panel addressed the basic financial needs of aging Americans and the best ways to provide for them. The other legs of the stool—pension benefits and savings—developed purely by accident, which helps to explain why they're wobbling.

Whatever Happened to Pensions?

In 1875, American Express became the first U.S. company to start a corporate pension plan. The catch: it helped only older workers who were disabled. Comprehensive pension plans emerged later, after President Roosevelt inadvertently created an incentive for employers to provide them. During World War II, companies were facing a severe labor shortage because so many soldiers were leaving to fight in Europe and the Pacific. Forced to compete for the best of the home-front workers, employers started to raise salaries. Fearing this would spike inflation,

Roosevelt signed an executive order in 1942 imposing a wartime wage freeze. The only incentives left to companies to attract skilled workers were add-on benefits such as health insurance and pensions.

In 1954, when the IRS confirmed that employees wouldn't be taxed on these perks, employer-based benefits became even more valuable. After the war was over, generous benefits remained a standard component of the compensation packages that many American companies used to woo top talent. The packages became so popular that unions often agreed to lower pay in exchange for higher retirement benefits.

These traditional pensions are known as "defined benefits." Employers contribute to a fund from which their long-time employees—and sometimes the employees' spouses—receive a specified monthly payment after retiring, the amount of which is based on the employee's salary and years with the company. The plan, which usually requires that employees stay with their employer full time for several decades, fit the mid-twentieth-century model of people working their way up the ladder within a single company until they retired. If the job is part time or a worker doesn't stay with the employer long enough, they won't qualify to receive retirement checks. But careers are often unpredictable. The average baby boomer held twelve jobs by the time they reached their mid-fifties.

Defined benefit pensions also depend on corporate stability. Management changes, mergers, and bankruptcy can all put pension funds in jeopardy. And not every employer pays into or protects the funds adequately. In the mid-1970s, after a series of mismanagement scandals stripped workers' pensions of their value, Congress enacted stricter funding requirements and safeguards. It also created the Pension Benefit Guarantee Corporation to protect retirees when firms went bankrupt. But no law requires companies to provide retirement benefits, and traditional pension plans in the twenty-first century have been losing favor with corporate America, especially after companies were required to show the plans as liabilities on their balance sheets. As recently as 1991, more than 100,000 companies offered these private employer plans, but by 2018 that number had plunged by half. Many of the plans surviving today are closed to new employees. Today, the small number of workers who receive traditional pensions are likely union members or federal and state employees such as teachers, police, and firefighters.

The decline in traditional pensions is one element of what has been called the "great risk shift." The last forty years have seen a transfer of financial risk—including the risk of poverty for older people—from government and business to individuals. As traditional pension plans disappear, it becomes all the more important that we strengthen the other two legs of the stool: Social Security and savings.

Is There a Secret to Saving?

The people who save the most acorns aren't necessarily more disciplined or skillful at saving. Sometimes they just have access to more bountiful trees. Our ability to save generally depends on where we work, at what level, and whether we have any money left to put aside at the end of the month, once we've paid our bills. While most big employers offer retirement savings plans, often with generous matching contributions, most small businesses do not, mainly because the plans are complex and expensive. Highly compensated workers are twice as likely to have a retirement plan as lower-wage workers, and they also benefit more from the deferred taxation of retirement savings—something that has no value for families who earn so little that they pay minimal income taxes anyway. These differences are reflected in the racial and ethnic disparities I've been tracking throughout this book. While 60 percent of white workers in the private sector are covered by some kind of employer retirement plan, just over half of Black and Asian American workers are, and only a third of Hispanic workers.

The most common employee retirement scheme today is the "defined contribution" plan, technically a retirement savings plan. It allows both employers and workers to contribute to an individual retirement account. Unlike traditional defined benefit pensions, in a defined contribution scheme, decisions about whether to contribute and how to invest are made largely by the employee. Workers are on the hook for figuring out when and how to withdraw the money when they need it, including taking loans and paying them back without facing huge tax penalties.

That these plans exist at all is another fluke of policy history. Back in 1978, Congress passed a bill to cut taxes, which also included a minor provision that delayed taxing income until employees used the money. This provision, numbered 401(k) in the tax code, went largely unnoticed until 1980, when a corporate consultant named Ted Benna scanned the tax codes in search of ideas for a client's retirement program. Benna, now known as the father of modern retirement, seized on the 401(k) as a form of retirement fund to which both employer and employee could contribute monthly. A decade later nearly forty million workers were saving in a 401(k) plan.

The plans allow employees to build nest eggs by making it simple, painless, and routine to save. Most larger companies have also adopted features such as auto-enrollment, where workers are automatically included in the plan unless they decide not to participate, and auto-escalation, which gradually increases the amount they save over time. These steps have helped to dramatically increase the likelihood that workers will save, as well as the amount they put away.

One big drawback with both defined benefit and defined contribution plans is that they're tied to all the current and former employers you have worked for. If you change jobs, it's up to you to keep track of your pensions or 401(k) accounts that stay at your former company. As the decades pass, these retirement benefits can add up, but it's easy to forget about them, and it can be even harder to find them. Transferring money in your 401(k) plan between employers can be extremely time-consuming and complicated, so most people never do it. From 2004 through 2013, more than sixteen million 401(k) accounts of $5,000 or less went unclaimed. That equals $8.5 billion in workers' savings that were never collected. Small accounts and IRAs are often sent to state treasurers, who try to locate the savers, while 401(k)s are usually retained in the former employer's retirement plan.

The bigger problem, though, is that many employers offer *no* retirement benefit. In fact, companies are not required by law to offer pensions or retirement benefits of any kind. And few companies provide benefits for most part-time or gig workers. As a result, only about half of America's workers in any given year are even offered an employment-based retirement plan.

In theory, of course, it is possible to save what you need for retirement on your own, either by investing in real estate or other assets, or by putting funds into an IRA. An IRA offers similar tax benefits to a 401(k), but it has lower contribution limits and can be set up at a bank or investment company. Unfortunately, very few of us save this way consistently.

The good news is that more than a dozen states are beginning to create state-facilitated retirement programs to allow all workers to save more easily through their paychecks. The largest in the country, California's new CalSavers retirement savings program, provides an IRA specifically for workers whose employers don't offer a retirement plan, as well as for self-employed people and others who want a way to save more. State-facilitated retirement funds are also operating in Colorado, Connecticut, Illinois, Maryland, and Oregon, with more states to come. While the programs vary, most make it easy to save by requiring that employers collect and submit worker contributions to be invested. The programs are voluntary, and workers can opt out at any time. Along with many other advocates, I have long championed these state plans. The money people put away over time may fend off a family crisis or help fund their retirement.

Given how hard many of us find saving, I asked retirement expert Anne Lester, the former head of retirement solutions for J.P. Morgan Asset Management, for her thoughts. She said many of us approach the task of saving with feelings of shame and self-blame, convinced that we should know how to do it or that we're doing it all wrong. Anne told me she used to be a terrible saver herself, and that part of figuring out how to save is understanding that "it isn't just about willpower. If you're struggling, it isn't your fault. You can take the judgment out of the picture and say, 'Okay. How do I hack my brain? How do I set up environmental cues?'"

The most important thing we can do, Anne advised, is to have money automatically deducted before it hits our checking account, so we don't even see it. She also recommended using different buckets for specific priorities, like having a separate emergency savings account in a separate bank, so that it takes that little bit of extra work to access the funds. Finally, she said we should think about our needs in terms of a hierarchy, and make sure we have made distinctions between real emergencies, things we need, things we only think we need, and things we simply want.

For a lot of us, DIY retirement planning is hard because it requires us to understand financial systems, invest on a regular basis, and have money to put aside that we can afford not to touch for decades. The last of these is particularly difficult. We have pressing obligations—mortgages, day care, school tuitions, car or student loan payments, utilities, and caregiving costs for aging parents. Or we have emergencies like car accidents, health crises, and home repairs, or sudden life changes such as job loss or divorce. If we have trouble just meeting our expenses, we're likely to let retirement saving slide or even withdraw funds from our nest egg prematurely.

Dipping into retirement savings like this is what economists call "leakage," and the amount of it is sobering. On average, for every one hundred dollars a person saves in a retirement account, twenty-two dollars is taken back out before retirement age, withdrawals that can incur steep tax penalties. Often it's young people who are taking money out, mainly to pay off credit card debt and student loans. This doesn't bode well for their future, as it denies them the benefits of long-term capital growth and undermines their chances for a financially secure retirement. And it can leave the savings leg of the retirement stool pretty wobbly.

Despite the challenge of financing our retirement, it's good to bear in mind that for many older adults, the picture is not all doom and gloom. In our SHOL survey, more than half of people aged seventy and over rated their financial situation as excellent or very good—a finding that would seem to contradict the data about how limited average retirement savings are. A few things may be at play in this anomaly. One is that money itself becomes less important as we age, while relationships take on greater significance. Another is that we become more resilient as we grow older and adapt to living within our means. Or it may be that our spending declines and we simply need less income to get by. Finally, and tragically, longevity disparities between lower- and higher-income Americans may figure in, as the lives of lower-income people are often cut short compared to people with more resources.

One of the women who participated in the SHOL survey was in her mid-fifties, still working but already anticipating a change in her spending habits. Jackie had a good salary and savings, and though she worried about inflation and how much medical care might cost in the future, she felt she'd be okay if she lived on a budget. "I don't think I'll ever be destitute or homeless," she said. "I have a big family that would always take care of me. But I couldn't just go out on a whim and spend five hundred dollars, like I can now. I can manage by being stricter and not being so loose with my wallet."

Many people simply aren't able to save for retirement because they are in debt. It is estimated that almost three-quarters of Americans aged thirty-five to fifty-four have less than one month's income saved for emergencies. With little to no cushion, when crisis strikes, it's easy to wind up borrowing. That unexpected debt can wreak havoc with retirement savings. But even without a crisis, debt can sneak up on us because of those pressing obligations I mentioned above—mortgages, student and car loans, and credit card debt, all of which have risen sharply over the past few decades. In 2019 American families headed by someone aged fifty or over owed an average of more than $93,000. And demands for payment don't let up just because we've retired. That same year more than seven in ten people over fifty had at least some debt, especially in home mortgages. Student loan debt is also following Americans into retirement. People over fifty represent the fastest-growing group owing student loans—not only their own but also loans they've taken on for their children's education. In addition, 40 percent of empty nesters report they're still paying kids' expenses, including cell phones, rent, and health care. As an empty nester with two kids in college, I can attest to how shockingly high these monthly bills can be.

Sometimes debt becomes unsustainable. In 2022 more than 92,000 people aged sixty or over filed for bankruptcy. While bankruptcy can be devastating at any age, it's particularly hard to recover financially in later life, when we have fewer options to increase our cash flow. High levels of unaffordable mortgage payments can cost older Americans their homes. I was stunned to learn that during the great recession, foreclosure rates were rising fastest among people over seventy-five. I kept thinking: What do you do when you are seventy-five and faced with losing your family home? Jessica Bruder's masterful *Nomadland: Surviving America in the Twenty-First Century* went some way toward answering that question. She tells the stories of many older people who, particularly in the wake of the 2008 recession and widespread foreclosures, took to the road as migrant laborers. While it's hard to get a precise figure for how many Americans are in this situation, Bruder estimated that as of 2021, there were at least 100,000.

Social Security was never intended to be our only source of income in retirement, so many of us try to supplement it with savings. The challenge, though, is that we must make these savings last right through to our dying day. The fear of running out can cause its own problems. Sometimes retirees live well below their means because they're afraid of tapping into their savings—preserving them for an emergency that may never happen. It isn't just rewarding experiences and pleasures they might miss out on; some skimp on essentials such as medical care.

So how do we decide what a reasonable amount of caution is? This was the conversation I had with my husband's uncle Barry. Barry was in his sixties then, living in New Jersey and still working hard as a salesman but getting tired of the long days of travel. He had set money aside for retirement but wasn't sure if it was enough. One day he said to me, "How much money can I take out of my retirement account each month and not run out?"

Because of my job, people often ask me for advice, but I had to admit I had no clue.

I said that if he wanted an accurate answer, he'd have to tell me, for starters, what the stock market was going to do, whether he would ever need to move into assisted living or a nursing home, and how much he thought his own home would be worth in the future.

Most important, I'd need to know how long he and Aunt Sheila were going to live. I spared Uncle Barry the fact that he would also have to predict how much health care and other costs would increase, what the changes in interest rates would be, and what the future of his Social Security benefits looked like. But he couldn't answer the questions I *did* pose, because they are questions none of us can answer.

It turns out I was overthinking it.

Retirement adviser Anne Lester explained to me the simple calculation she uses to estimate how much someone can afford to withdraw once they have retired. Her rule of thumb is much easier math than the sophisticated methods of calculation she helped develop in her career. She told me to imagine that I would retire at sixty-five and would live to be 105, leaving me forty years to cover. Then she said I should take my current savings and divide by forty. That's roughly how much I could spend out of my account that year. In each subsequent year, I should redo the math by dividing my savings by thirty-nine at age sixty-six, thirty-eight at age sixty-seven, and so on.

"There is no right answer," Anne said, "because you don't know what the markets are going to do, you don't know when you're going to die. So forget perfect. This is good enough. And it's giving you some wiggle room. Because you probably won't live until you're 105, and you probably will get some returns on your money—and those returns that you're not calculating into your spending pool will then be there when you break your hip and you need more money."

Is Our Retirement System Fair?

While Social Security has saved untold numbers of people from lives of complete financial insecurity, it does have its flaws. Certain inequities are baked into its design, and into our pension and retirement savings programs, that reflect larger inequalities in our society—particularly those affecting women and Black and Hispanic communities.

The American workplace stacks the deck against women throughout their working lives, leaving them less to draw on once they retire. One reason women are handicapped financially is that they bear the brunt of family caregiving, so they are more likely than men to work part time or to leave the labor force periodically to raise children or take care of family members. This can mean years without access to employer retirement plans and without contributing to Social Security. By one estimate, these gaps translate into a lifetime loss in wages and Social Security benefits of $324,000. That doesn't include the losses to retirement accounts and pensions, which can add up to tens or even hundreds of thousands in savings depending on when women leave their jobs and how much they were contributing.

Even when women are working full time, they are paid less than men. American women in 2022 averaged just eighty-two cents for every dollar earned by men. While the progressive structure of Social Security helps to even the score somewhat, older women in 2021 received an average of $4,000 less in Social Security benefits than men.

At the same time, because women tend to live longer than men, they're likely to outlive their savings and rely on Social Security for many more years. More than half of Social Security recipients over sixty-two are female, and women make up two-thirds of all beneficiaries aged eighty-five and over. About one-third of unmarried older women get virtually all their income from Social Security.

In general, people of color often end up receiving lower Social Security benefits due to being paid lower wages throughout their working lives and experiencing longer bouts of unemployment. Black American men aged sixty and over average about $4,000 less in annual Social Security benefits than older men overall. That still leaves Black men better off than Black women, who face pay discrimination to boot and have lower average yearly incomes than Black men.

The economic challenge is even harder for Hispanic women who, in 2021, were paid only fifty-eight cents for every dollar of full-time wages paid to white men. By the end of their working lives, the net effect of gender, ethnic, and racial discrimination amounts to a staggering loss of $1.1 million in earnings for Hispanic women—more than double the cost of gender inequity for white women.

Given these various disparities, it shouldn't surprise us that many older women in the United States live in poverty, or that women of color fare worst. Altogether, four million women sixty-five and older are living in poverty. In 2021 roughly one in five older Black, Native American, or Hispanic women; more than one in seven older Asian American women; and nearly one in eleven white women sixty-five and older were living in poverty.

Regarding immigrants and Social Security, I want to dispel a myth. People sometimes think that immigration weakens Social Security, but the opposite is true. On average, immigrant workers pay far more into the system through payroll taxes than they collect. Newly arrived immigrants tend to be younger than the domestic U.S. population; they are therefore more likely to be employed and less likely to be collecting retirement benefits. In addition, immigrants often have larger families, so their contribution to the program continues when their children enter the workforce and pay taxes. Even those immigrants who are undocumented are a net plus for the system's financing: Social Security taxes are often taken out of their wages, but they are not legally allowed to collect benefits. One analysis found that in 2016, undocumented immigrants contributed $13 billion to Social Security and $3 billion to Medicare.

In addition to these racial, ethnic, and gender disparities in Social Security benefits, a feature of Social Security known as the "earnings cap" affects the fairness and financing of the program, especially as income inequality increases. The cap sets a maximum amount of earnings that can be subjected to Social Security taxes, and it rises each year with overall wage growth. In 2023 Americans paid Social Security taxes only on the first $160,200 they earned. Because wages for America's top earners have been rising rapidly—while pay for lower-income workers has stayed relatively flat—the earnings cap leaves out a growing share of income subject to Social Security's payroll tax and contributes to the program's looming shortfall. The original thinking behind the earnings cap was that by limiting how much the rich pay in, you also cap how much is paid out to them, since benefits are based on what is paid in. If billionaires paid into the system at the same rates as everyone else, their Social Security checks could be enormous. But the growing gap in earnings inequality and coming deficits in the program financing has many people calling for an increase in the cap.

A second factor playing a critical role in the program's unfairness is rising inequality in life expectancy. Since the wealthiest 1 percent of men live fifteen years longer than men earning low incomes, they may get fifteen more years of Social Security payments. One panel of experts found that the top 20 percent of earners will get $100,000 more in Social Security benefits over their lifetime than the bottom 20 percent.

Touching the Third Rail

The question on most of our minds is: *Will Social Security still be there when I need it?* Our growing concerns are partly a result of Social Security's pay-as-you-go design, which presumes that each generation will pay at least as much into the system as is being paid out. That worked well during the early years of the program, when there were fewer beneficiaries and lots of workers paying taxes. During the peak working years of the baby boom generation, huge surpluses were built up in Social Security's trust funds, but as that generation retires, those surpluses are being depleted. And with increased longevity, many retirees are collecting more years of benefits than their parents did.

Factor in declining birth rates, which means fewer younger people entering the workforce, and you get a balance of payments tilted increasingly in the wrong direction.

All this explains why some people inaccurately claim that Social Security is "going bankrupt." Convincing Americans that Social Security is doomed—as some who want to make major cuts to it try to do—is one way of eroding public support for this essential program. Social Security can't go bankrupt, since contributions are constantly flowing into the coffers from America's workers. But because the system is required to pay for itself, if the reserves in the trust funds run out and nothing is done to reverse the imbalance, our benefits will—by law— have to be cut or delayed. These cuts would impact not just new or future retirees but *everyone* receiving retirement or disability payments, no matter how desperately they need the benefits.

Yet for all the challenges it faces, and all our uncertainty about exactly what it will look like in the future, Social Security will be there for you! I say that with confidence for two reasons. The first is that even if we do nothing, enough money is still going into the system to pay about 75 percent of promised benefits for the rest of the century. The second reason comes down to politics. Over the past century, popular support for Social Security has grown so strong that the program is commonly referred to in Washington as "the third rail"—a reference to the metal track supplying electric current to trains that can be deadly if touched. In other words, cutting Social Security would be political suicide. Social Security will endure because it's just too important to too many people. As things stand now, unless we update the program, benefits will be cut by 20 percent in 2034. If that were to happen, I'm pretty sure protests would break out across America. Fortunately, every politician in Washington knows this.

But political action is needed, and unfortunately, Washington works best when an issue reaches a crisis point and can no longer be ignored. It was a crisis that prompted Social Security's last set of upgrades in the early 1980s, when the program was within months of a funding shortfall that could have led to cutting benefit checks. A bipartisan commission led by Alan Greenspan created the rescue package that added decades of life to Social Security's trust funds: it cut benefits by raising the retirement age, increased revenue by bringing more people into the system (including federal workers), and added money to the trust funds by raising taxes on both workers and retirees. The state of emergency compelled both parties in Congress to work together to pass the commission's package. The commission wisely chose to phase the changes in over decades, to avoid a sudden financial shock and to give Americans time to adjust to the less palatable revisions, such as the raised retirement age and higher tax rates for workers.

Action in the absence of a looming crisis has proven more difficult. Presidents from Ronald Reagan to George Bush to Barack Obama have proposed changes to the program—creating individual retirement savings accounts, partially privatizing the system, or adopting different measures of inflation—but none of these attempts has gained traction.

To get a better understanding of the challenges the program faces today and the options we have for addressing them, I called Steve Goss, who has been the Social Security Administration's (SSA) chief actuary for more than twenty years. I've known Steve since the late 1990s when I worked for the SSA doing research, and I've always admired his passion for the program. Not many people get excited when talking about Social Security, but Steve's eyes light up when he talks about the nitty-gritty details of how to improve the program's solvency.

My favorite Steve story illustrates his commitment. At a conference in D.C. celebrating the anniversary of Social Security, a group of us were posing for a photo when a thief grabbed my iPod and a colleague's purse. While we waited for the police to arrive, Steve started dumpster diving nearby in case the thief had tossed our colleague's bag after removing her wallet. He hoped he might at least find her keys. The image of Steve half-submerged in the dumpster, going the extra mile to preserve what he could of our valuables—not unlike what he does for all Americans every day at the office—still makes me laugh.

Steve's job at the SSA requires him to project the program's sustainability for the next seventy-five years, a role he likens to being an umpire in baseball. But beyond calling the balls and strikes in the various proposals to reform Social Security, he also offers technical assistance—projecting the results of a given plan or policy and suggesting efficient, effective strategies to achieve policymakers' desired results.

Steve has worked in the Office of the Chief Actuary since 1973, and he and his team have analyzed and provided advice on countless proposals to fix the system. Current proposals to improve solvency range from large benefit cuts with no tax increases, to significant tax increases with some rise in benefits. Steve and his actuaries estimate that either extreme—raising payroll taxes from 6.2 percent to 8.24 percent on both workers and employers, or cutting all benefits by 25 percent—would do the trick and keep the program on track for the next seventy-five years. But these extremes aren't palatable to either party, and any changes to the program would require a sixty-vote majority in the Senate to pass, so would likely take compromise from both sides.

The actuaries have analyzed different ways to increase funding to Social Security or cut spending. For example, raising or eliminating the earnings cap—changing the amount of earnings that can be taxed—could solve between 22 and 73 percent of the long-term deficit in Social Security, depending on how high and how quickly the cap was raised and whether these increased payments would entitle people to higher benefits. Further raising the age for retirement benefits is another idea often proposed as a way to improve solvency. Already, Social Security's full retirement age has been gradually rising, and it is now sixty-seven for those of us born in or after 1960. Some policymakers want to push it even higher or adjust it to average life expectancy. But life expectancy in the United States varies widely, as do our health and ability to work longer. Even those of us able to work longer and delay claiming Social Security would receive lower *lifetime* benefits because we would get fewer years of payments. According to one estimate, raising the full retirement age to seventy would cost an average-earning woman born in 1990 nearly $150,000 over the course of her lifetime.

Other possibilities for strengthening the finances of Social Security have been proposed, including changing the historical practice of maintaining a self-financed system and instead allowing general revenue to supplement payroll tax revenue to make up the shortfall. Because we don't yet know which changes Congress will ultimately adopt, it's hard to plan financially for our futures. If taxes are increased, we may have less in our pockets to save. If benefits are cut, we would all need to save more to make up the difference. Punting until the crisis hits in 2034 only makes the choices harder. When I helped draft a report for the Senate Aging Committee in 2010, I was able to say that "minor tweaks" would do the job. If we keep putting off the inevitable, the next fix will be painful.

Over the past quarter-century, I've worked with many people to help Americans become more financially secure in retirement, but I haven't seen the dramatic changes this country needs. During my stints as a congressional staffer and now at AARP, I've tried to plug the holes in the leaky dike of retirement savings, help make Social Security more solvent, ensure that benefits are adequate, and highlight who will fall through the cracks with the options commonly on the table. I've managed congressional hearings to raise awareness, drafted legislation, and conducted research. I've worked with both sides of the aisle to try to create consensus and sought to bring together the financial services industry and consumers.

We have had some big wins. As I write this, more than a dozen states have enacted programs that will help people save for retirement. With national legislation stuck for decades, these states have been stepping up to expand coverage. Meanwhile the private sector is figuring out ways to make retirement accounts easier to transfer between employers, so that millions of dollars of savings don't get lost each year. One innovation would automatically transfer small retirement accounts from one employer to the next. It would be a good step, but many other countries make it very easy by having a single retirement account for each worker, to which any employer can contribute.

Some hard-fought battles have been won, only to be lost again. For a brief period, investment companies were required to act as fiduciaries, ensuring that they made decisions and recommended products that served their investors' interests rather than their own bottom line. This regulation was estimated to save investors $40 billion over ten years, but the rule was overturned by a court decision in 2018.

In many ways, we still have a broken system. In just over a decade, if no changes are made, Social Security won't be able to pay full benefits. And far too many people are reaching retirement with nothing saved and no pension. This frustrates me immensely, because a better system would help millions of people have a happier and more secure second fifty, with fewer financial worries and more personal choices.

At the height of the Great Depression, our leaders came together to create Social Security, which has helped generations of people retire with dignity. The sooner our policymakers put Social Security on more solid financial ground, the better for us all. But long-term solvency shouldn't be the only goal. People today are working in a very different world than the creators of Social Security saw in the 1930s. We have to update the program, along with our pensions and savings programs, to meet the demands of the twenty-first century—for all Americans, but especially for those who need them the most.

6

Where Will I Live?

Until her mid-seventies, Grandma Bailey, my father's mother, lived on a farm in rural Washington state. The three-bedroom house that she and my grandfather had built, and where they had raised their five kids, was isolated, down a long gravel road miles from the nearest small town. She stayed there for more than a decade after my grandfather passed away. She didn't drive, so she relied on friends and family to take her to the grocery store and Sunday mass. The house had few amenities: I remember a hand-cranked washing machine. Although it was finally upgraded, she had to hang her clothes to dry on the line outside or on a small foldable rack in the kitchen. One day she placed the rack by the stove, and it fell over and caught fire. Fortunately, she got to it in time and doused the flames with water from a mop pail.

Our family was eventually able to convince Grandma Bailey to move to a new senior apartment building in the nearby town. She missed her garden and chicken coop, but not the work it took to maintain them. She was now across the street from her regular grocery store and just a short walk from her church. She had a small one-bedroom—and the building had a full laundry room. More important, she had a group of women her own age with whom she got together for meals and card games and the walk to mass every morning.

Now in their eighties, my mom and dad live on the other side of the mountains in a small rural town in Washington. They built their two-story house in the 1970s and raised my brother and me there. They've told me in no uncertain terms that they do not want to move from the town and the home they cherish. They love spending their time admiring the beautiful view of the lake from the picture window in their living room or, on warm days, from the back deck. My parents are still healthy. But I'm worried. Bad knees and hips have thrown off my dad's balance, so stairs are tricky for him, even with the handrail I convinced them to install. Their vision isn't great and seems to be getting worse, especially at night, so they drive mostly during the day. If they eventually find themselves unable to drive at all, staying in that small town—which has no public transportation, cabs, or car-sharing services—could be difficult. No grocery stores are within walking distance, and many doctors are over eighty miles away in the nearest major city of Spokane. I live thousands of miles from them on the opposite coast. My brother is a two-hour drive away, too far to be there on a daily basis or to reach them quickly in an emergency.

As for me, I know that my current house, where Glenn and I raised our own kids, isn't our forever home. I realized that the day I watched Flo—my father-in-law's ninety-year-old girlfriend—struggle to climb the seven steps up to the main floor of our split-level. The layout of our house is going to be a problem if Glenn and I develop mobility issues. Even getting him up those steps after a recent knee surgery was tricky.

Like the three generations of my family, where you live as you age will depend on several things. Among the most important are what you can afford, of course, as well as what kind of medical care and daily support you'll need, and the types of housing available. Unfortunately, most homes in the United States are designed for young families, not for aging bodies, and our care system was set up to support older people in nursing homes rather than to help them stay in their own homes. Meanwhile, the cost of care and help with basic life functions is shockingly high, and most of it is not covered by health insurance or Medicare, leaving family members struggling to pay for care or trying to provide it themselves. On top of that, the rising number of older people—meaning more people needing assistance—isn't being matched by the number of available caregivers, either family members or paid workers. We are therefore in the midst of an escalating care crisis to go along with our housing crisis.

We can do better, and I'll talk later about how some states have already begun piloting innovative programs, moving forward with plans to help families who are struggling financially. Several are shifting away from paying for care in institutions to paying for it in the home: 2020 marked the first year that more state and federal Medicaid spending went to home and community-based services than to nursing homes. Communities are also taking matters into their own hands, with neighborhood programs sprouting up across the country to support people who want to age in place—which usually means living in their home or community for as long as possible. We are seeing more efforts to create age-friendly towns and cities and new forms of shared housing. Meanwhile, multigenerational households—a staple of the past—are once again becoming more common among certain groups, helping families to save on costs and allowing them to support each other in raising children or helping with grandparents.

The decision about where to live needs to take into account what is important *to* the person, as well as what might be good *for* them. Too often the focus is almost exclusively on what older people need to do—protect their health and safety, minimize risk—while neglecting the equally important question of what brings joy and meaning to life. A successful living or care situation will answer both of those needs.

Where We Want to Live

Like Grandma Bailey and my parents, three-quarters of people fifty and older would like to stay in their current homes or communities. Our neighborhoods and communities are where we have established ties, and our houses hold many memories. They may be near our friends, grown children, and grandchildren; our favorite grocery stores, parks, and shops; and the cultural outlets and activities we love.

All these factors contribute to a desire to "age in place," a term, as Jennifer Molinsky explained to me, that can mean many things. Jennifer is the project director of the Housing and Aging Society Program and a lecturer at Harvard's Graduate School of Design. "For some people," she said, "it means having control over where they live, and that can be anywhere in the community, not in a particular house. Some don't want to leave the home they're in. For others, it means anything but the nursing home." The common denominator is having a choice. People with physical or cognitive disabilities tend to be more interested in living in residential care communities such as assisted living or nursing homes. And perhaps not surprisingly, the desire to live in our own homes decreases as we age and begin to need help from family and friends or paid caregivers. Among people in their forties and fifties who answered our SHOL survey, 66 percent wanted to live independently in their own home, but among those in their eighties, only 43 percent did. This makes sense. If we find ourselves injured, disabled, or ill, many aspects of our homes that we may never have thought about—a staircase or the height of countertops and sinks—suddenly become barriers to daily living. Chances are our homes aren't designed or equipped for someone with mobility or health issues. Less than 1 percent of single-family detached homes in this country are fully wheelchair-accessible, and less than 4 percent are considered easily modifiable for people with moderate mobility challenges. Those who are renting apartments or houses may be allowed to make modifications, but owners could hold tenants responsible for the cost of removing them when they move out.

For the vast majority of us with inaccessible homes, if our needs change, we will either have to modify our homes or relocate. Both options can bring financial, emotional, and logistical hardships. I've spoken to many friends and colleagues who were agonizing over where they could move themselves or a family member when they were no longer able to remain at home, especially right after a fall or medical emergency.

Being able to navigate comfortably and confidently around our living spaces is key if we are going to remain safe, active, and engaged. Ideally, we should think about home modifications *before* our circumstances change, preparing our living spaces with features that will allow us to remain as independent as possible and to minimize chances of falls or other injuries. Modifications can include making simple changes such as removing throw rugs that are easy to trip over, adding a raised toilet seat with safety handles, and installing grab bars. Or they can be more substantial changes that can benefit everyone: installing an accessible bathroom on the ground floor; replacing knobs with lever-style handles that are easier to use, especially for a person with moderate arthritis; and installing a walk-in shower in place of a tub, making life easier and safer not just for an elderly person but for someone who is pregnant or has a sports injury. Accessibility is also important for visitors, as I realized when I saw Flo struggling with the stairs in my house.

Most of these changes come under the umbrella of "universal design," a set of principles based on the idea that products and our built environment should be usable, as much as possible, by everyone, regardless of our age, physical strength, mobility, or life circumstances. The approach aims to integrate accessibility features without leaving a home feeling institutional. Universal design features for the home include a no-step entry, single-floor living, doorways and halls wide enough for walkers and wheelchairs, electrical controls and toggle light switches, and lever-style handles on faucets and doors. Retrofitting an existing home can be expensive, so incorporating universal design features during initial construction or major remodels can help to minimize the cost.

In 2013 my colleague Rodney Harrell helped his parents update their home: his mother and father were fifty-nine and sixty-two years old, respectively. Rodney happens to be AARP's top housing expert, so he was putting into action what he'd been advising on the policy front for years. As even one or two steps can be a hazard, the first thing Rodney had his contractors do was cover the stairs to the front door and install paving stones at a very gradual rise across the stairs and walkway.

But modifying a living space isn't just about ensuring safety; it's also about making sure that everyone can be a part of gatherings and conversations, participate in shared spaces, help with cooking, and more. So Rodney's parents had the wall separating the dining room and kitchen taken away to allow for easier movement between them. They also installed a walk-in shower in the ground-floor bathroom, which is wheelchair accessible, and they added attractive handrails and a handheld shower. The bathroom is where a lot of falls happen, because floors and surfaces are often wet. Donna, Rodney's mother, said her favorite change was moving the washer and dryer from the basement to the first floor, so she can now do all her living on one level.

For the last several years, two housing trends have been growing rapidly in popularity: multigenerational and single-person households. The rise in the first is being driven partly by demographics—Asian American and Hispanic American families, like other immigrant families of the past, are more likely to have multiple generations under one roof—and partly by increasing housing costs and care needs. The pandemic accelerated this trend as young adults found themselves working remotely and able to avoid high rents in big cities, and grandparents came to live with their grown children to help with childcare after day care centers and schools closed. Now, one in five Americans lives in a multigenerational household, quadruple the number that did so in the 1970s. There are signs the trend will persist, as the portion of house buyers seeking homes that can accommodate multiple generations rose between 2021 and 2022.

Multigenerational living has both pros and cons. Families living in these arrangements generally say they enjoy being together and sharing the burdens of childcare and home costs. Many families also find that pooling resources from more than one generation allows them to purchase homes that would otherwise have been unaffordable. But most houses in the United States were designed for a nuclear family, not for multiple generations.

Cathy, a retired woman I spoke to, now lives with her son and daughter-in-law. Following a health scare, she moved from the Detroit area to northern Michigan to be closer to them, and at sixty-five bought her first home, a condo. Her son and daughter-in-law had their own home but rented it out and moved in with Cathy. They have the lower level with a full kitchen and living area, and she has the ground level with her own bedroom and kitchen and no stairs. "This works out real well," said Cathy, who had lived on her own for over twenty years. "It benefits all three of us. Sometimes they'll cook dinner or I will. It's nice having somebody else around in case I need it or they need me." Cathy's solution is one way of addressing the financial and social difficulties of living alone.

The rise in multigenerational living is all the more reason we need to think about the kind of housing we're creating and whether it's serving our needs. We need homes that support the privacy and independence of different generations. This may mean designing separate living spaces within a house, or separate entrances, or building "accessory dwelling units," self-contained dwellings that are either attached to the house—like a converted garage—or detached from the house but on the same property. One of the great things about accessory dwelling units, Jennifer Molinsky told me, is that they're flexible. "It could be an in-law apartment, a place for an older adult to live with their extended family, or a unit for a caregiver or an adult child back from college. It can also be a source of rental income."

The flip side of the multigenerational trend is that more and more older people are living alone, a number set to increase dramatically in the coming years. So-called solo agers make up the largest share of U.S. households; around 10 percent of people fifty and older live alone. In particular, low-income Black neighborhoods tend to have high percentages of people living alone in large houses, many of them older single women. As they age, people who live on their own typically have fewer financial resources, often relying on Social Security or retirement savings, and they receive less support with daily tasks of living. They are also at increased risk of social isolation, which is associated with mental health challenges such as anxiety and depression, and physical health concerns, including falls.

Like our housing stock, our communities haven't been designed for an aging population, particularly in the suburbs and rural areas. Most single-family homes outside cities, such as where my parents live, are not located near services or public transportation, which can be especially challenging for older people. Thirty-five percent of those eighty-five and over don't drive, but even among those over fifty, a majority say they limit their driving to certain hours and often miss activities because of driving limitations.

If our neighborhoods, communities, and cities are to support us as we get older, they need to contain a range of living options. This includes a solid stock of affordable housing for both buyers and renters, as well as access to health services, convenient transportation, grocery stores with healthy food, and opportunities for meeting others socially, whether in parks or other community spaces. Many neighborhoods and communities tick these boxes, but certainly not all. Making these services and amenities available and affordable for everyone is going to take intentional policymaking at the local, state, and federal levels.

Grassroots Innovation

Despite the fact that the number of single-person households is growing, fewer smaller homes are being built. The number has dropped dramatically in recent decades, which pushes prices up, making them difficult to afford. For low-income renters, the situation is particularly bad, with an estimated nationwide shortage of seven million rental units.

In the immediate term, some of us can take steps on our own to find housing solutions. There are now fifty-four million unoccupied spare bedrooms in the United States, mostly in the homes of older adults. By 2034, an estimated one-third of homes will be owned by people over sixty-five, and more than half of those will have just one occupant. Many older people would like to downsize to a smaller home but can't afford to. This is a key reason that shared housing—meaning unrelated people sharing a house or apartment—is on the rise among older adults, particularly for those in expensive markets who might be house-rich but cash-poor. In the last decade, the number of people over sixty-five living with nonrelatives has doubled.

A lot of us will remember seeing the show *The Golden Girls* on TV. Those four older women lived together, not necessarily to save money but for fun and companionship. Today older adults are increasingly interested in sharing living arrangements for financial reasons. Two of the main forms of sharing are a homeowner renting out a room, or a group of people renting a home or apartment together, with common living areas in both cases. A number of for-profit and nonprofit organizations are sprouting up to act as intermediaries, matching people interested in home-sharing, whether for short- or long-term arrangements.

Some older homeowners who need physical or social support take in tenants in exchange for help around the house. Many younger people who are priced out of traditional renting and homeowning are availing themselves of these formal or informal arrangements. In 2010, for instance, Judson Manor in Cleveland, a set of residential and home care retirement communities, partnered with the Cleveland Institute of Music to offer free furnished apartments to a small number of graduate students. In exchange, the students—all of whom qualify for financial assistance—perform recitals and concerts. They also just spend time with the residents, talking about art, careers, cooking, and relationships. The idea came about because the institute was short of housing, and a board member contacted Judson Manor. This is the sort of thinking outside the box that I love to hear about—ideas that are practical, cost-effective, and help people of multiple generations.

Another trend that provides some hope for those of us who want to age in place is the growing number of neighborhood groups that have been banding together to create community support and shared services. One example of this is the "Village" model, a grassroots movement that supports older adults living in their own homes who want to age in place. (It shouldn't be confused with The Villages, an age-restricted private development in Florida.) A Village is a membership organization based on geographical area—a zip code, county, or neighborhood. Members, who normally pay yearly dues, develop and manage the Village, though Villages often partner with local government aging agencies and other groups, and some have paid staff. Village members support each other through organizing social events, volunteering to help with things like transportation or household chores, and providing referrals to services in the broader community. The first Village was in the Beacon Hill area of Boston in 2002, and there are now more than 280 Villages in the United States, each tailored to the needs of its particular community.

One of the most diverse Villages in the country is the Golden Age Village in Baltimore, which serves people from more than twenty-five countries. It was founded by volunteers of the Islamic Society in Windsor Mill, Maryland. Back in the early 2000s, members of the society were already informally helping older members of the mosque with home visits, transportation, and other services. But when one member tried attending activities not related to the mosque for older people in the area, he felt out of place. His daughter, who happened to be an aging specialist, had heard of the Village model, and a series of informational meetings led to the founding of Golden Age. Now the Village, which networks with the Baltimore County Department of Aging, has services that include brunches, lectures, and knitting and chess sessions, as well as hospital and hospice visits.

Villages and similar neighborhood groups have great potential. If the model is going to be scalable, though, it will need to attract more diverse populations. So far, with a few exceptions, membership has tended to be largely white, highly educated, financially well-resourced, and fairly healthy. To expand the appeal, existing groups and people interested in starting Villages will need to think about how to recruit more broadly and consider how services can cater to people who need a lot of assistance.

The Rise of Age-Friendly Cities and Communities

Many states, cities, and communities are realizing that they weren't built for a growing aging population and are developing plans to become more age friendly. Using a framework created by the World Health Organization, local government leaders commit to creating a plan based on eight factors that shape quality of life for people of *all* ages—because what's good for older people is good for everyone. A bus designed for easy access for an older person will also be more accessible to a child, a pregnant woman, a teenager on crutches, or someone carrying luggage. In 2023 there were 754 communities in the United States, along with nine states and territories, that had made this commitment, and the numbers are rising all the time.

The process of developing age-friendly programs and policies involves local citizens and is tailored to the community's needs. What works for Washington, D.C., may not work for Macon, Georgia. In 2014, Washington, D.C., engaged over 500 volunteers in a multigenerational block-by-block walk program to identify pedestrian challenges such as broken sidewalks, missing curb ramps, and traffic signals that didn't allow for safe crossing. It also introduced a free mobile app so that people can report problems directly to transportation officials.

Communities of all sizes can benefit from age-friendly planning. Bibb County, in central Georgia, includes the urban city of Macon and many largely rural neighborhoods. More than 15 percent of its 153,000 residents are sixty-five or older. Since releasing its age-friendly plan in 2013, the city has opened a new senior center, improved walkability and bikeability, supported revitalization of a sixteen-acre park, and built or renovated different kinds of housing—from apartment buildings for older residents to "tiny homes" for people who have disabilities or were experiencing homelessness.

One of the most important steps that has been taken in the United States to create more age-friendly cities and communities was the passage of the Americans with Disabilities Act (ADA) in 1990. President George H. W. Bush worked closely with members of Congress from both sides of the aisle to pass the legislation, which required all public buildings to be accessible to people with disabilities. As a result of the ADA, most buildings are now equipped with elevators, and public transportation is accessible to people in wheelchairs. The ADA is a great example of bipartisan policymaking that has made it easier to age in America.

Getting Care and Support

The question of where to live as we get older is inextricably linked with what kind of care and support we will need and how we can get that. Do we have family we can rely on to help? Do we know what we will be able to afford? If we need housing with supportive services or even a nursing home, do options exist where we now live? If we have medical conditions or mobility limitations, does our current housing have accessibility features that support our functioning? One of the biggest barriers stopping people from being discharged from nursing facilities is that the home they would return to no longer meets their needs because of changes in their ability to function independently.

A lot of us don't want to consider these questions, but it's helpful if we can think ahead, even if we are still healthy. Recently, a colleague told me a story about a family friend who was widowed and living alone in a condominium in Florida. She was in her early eighties and in pretty good health. Her intention was to eventually move to Wisconsin where her daughter lived, though she was planning to wait until she couldn't be independent anymore. When she told her daughter of this plan, her daughter gently suggested that she move to Wisconsin sooner, so that they could enjoy time together before caregiving was needed. It was an aha! moment. Her daughter's suggestion was very fair. The woman put her condo on the market the next day and moved to Wisconsin soon afterward.

Care needs vary greatly from one person to another and at different stages of our lives as we age, but the odds are that a time will come when we need help. At some point after age sixty-five, more than 70 percent of us will need assistance, from friends and family or paid caregivers, with basic tasks such as bathing, eating, and dressing, or with things like housework, shopping, and preparing meals. That doesn't mean we'll rely on them permanently. Most of us will need only brief spells of care—for example, while recovering from a health setback such as a stroke, heart attack, or injury—after which we can function independently again. On average, only one in four of us will need paid care for more than two years. The older we get, the more likely we are to need long-term support, and some groups tend to need more than others. Those with less education, older Black and Hispanic Americans, and those living alone are apt to develop more serious care needs. We tend to underestimate not only the likelihood that we will need care but also the cost, and there is a lot of misunderstanding about what private insurance and Medicare will cover. For the one in four of us who will need care for longer than two years, the costs can be jaw-dropping. The average yearly charge for a skilled nursing home is $116,000. The average lifetime cost of paid long-term care is more than $180,000, which usually comes from a combination of private insurance, personal savings, family help, and Medicaid.

When my husband Glenn and I began to worry that his widowed father, Garrett, could no longer safely stay in his own home—even with Glenn's brother Scott living there and helping out—we used the services of a local geriatric care manager, a specialist in the needs of older adults. Alyson came to the house to help us determine what kind of living arrangement Garrett needed. She performed a cognitive test on him and surveyed the entire house, immediately recommending that we remove bathroom floor rugs that were a fall hazard. She found that Garret was struggling to get up the stairs to his bedroom, that he didn't want to cook for himself and so wasn't eating well, and that he felt lonely during the day when Scott was working. Her visits were not covered by insurance, but the few hundred dollars we spent on her fee were well worth it. We were able to quickly follow her advice and helped Garrett move into a nearby assisted living community that she recommended, one that provided meals and a more social environment.

The choices Garrett faced were similar to those many of us will face for our family members: have them remain at home and pay for professional caregivers, or help them move into an assisted living community, group home, or nursing home.

Because so many of us want to continue living at home, our first choice may be to rely on family or friends. They are the backbone of long-term care, as thirty-eight million of them provide an estimated $600 billion annually in unpaid care. But we can't, as a nation, rely only on unpaid caregivers. For one thing, their numbers relative to those who need care are dropping. In 2010 there were seven caregivers for every person over eighty—the group most likely to need care. By 2030, it's estimated there will be only four per person. The trend makes it all the more important that we invest in sustainable and affordable care options.

Meanwhile, as individuals, we need to begin creating trusted networks of potential caregivers—particularly those of us whose family members live far away or who have no immediate family. About one million Americans do not have partners, spouses, siblings, or children, and the size of this "kinless" population is expected to increase. Older LGBTQ+ adults face acute caregiver challenges: they are less likely to be married or to have children, and more likely to live alone, making social isolation and its effects on health a big issue later in life. Some are estranged from their families and thus are more dependent on networks of peers, who may themselves be experiencing difficulties of aging around the same time.

Even if you have family nearby to care for you, it is important to put a plan in place—if possible, before a crisis hits or needs escalate. You'll want to clarify what is important to you and the resources you have, in the form of both finances (including insurance) and people. You can identify potential caregivers and talk with them about your wishes. You can consider where you might move, including assisted living and nursing communities, if you can no longer remain at home. Knowing what you want can help to relieve some of the strain on loved ones, especially in the event that you are not able to communicate.

Your care network may include unpaid help from family, friends, and neighbors—as well as paid care workers such as nursing assistants, home health aides, and personal care aides. There is a lot of misunderstanding about what a paid care worker does and how difficult their job can be. Much of it involves helping people with a broad range of day-to-day activities—and that can include things like getting someone out of bed, turning them in bed in a way that avoids injury, or helping them to manage medications. These tasks require certain skills to perform safely and to allow the person receiving help to retain their dignity. A good care worker will support someone to live as active and engaged a life as they possibly can. Care workers can also provide companionship, which is especially important for older adults living on their own.

There are a variety of ways to find paid care workers, and whenever possible we should include the person who'll be receiving care in the decisions and choices made. Suppose your loved one is being released from a hospital or other medical setting and will need more help when they return home. A hospital staff member—often called a Care Manager or Hospital Discharge Planner—can suggest agencies where you can find and hire a care worker. If the older person is already at home, you can find a care manager online or through word of mouth. A place to start is your local Area Agency on Aging. This organization can provide information on agencies and point you toward additional resources, tools, and supports. Family, friends, and community organizations such as senior centers and faith-based groups can also offer good recommendations. Finally, some care workers who are employed in health care settings take on independent work as well.

When you are looking for paid care, you will want to know whether the agency is licensed, exactly what services it provides, and whether those services are available around the clock. What kind of staff does the agency have, how are they trained, and are they subject to background checks and proper supervision? You should ask about any fees and extra costs, how you'll be billed, and whether the agency is certified to be paid by Medicare and Medicaid. As there is frequent turnover in this industry, it's helpful to know what will happen if the assigned caregiver leaves the agency and whether back-up staff is guaranteed. You will want to review any contract thoroughly before signing it and question anything you don't understand.

If you need to move out of your home because of your medical care needs, disability, or mobility issues, you will probably go to an assisted living facility, a continuing care community, a group home, or a nursing home. Assisted living offers a community-like setting for people with moderate care needs. Residents typically have their own room or suite, three meals each day in a dining room, and access to medication management and clinical care around the clock. In some states, Medicaid will pay for support services for those with low incomes but not for room and board; otherwise assisted living is usually paid for out of pocket, and it can be expensive. It is also regulated differently from state to state, so quality and safety can be inconsistent. Bear in mind, if you are choosing assisted living, what the long-term costs may be. Rates are likely to rise over time, and you or your loved one may incur extra costs if care needs increase. You may not be able to stay in your assisted living apartment if your needs become more complex than the facility can manage. Pay close attention to the contracts, what services are or are not provided, and under what circumstances you would have to move from the facility.

Group homes are a form of assisted living facility that provides a similar range of services and care but are smaller—usually five to twenty people—and are often less expensive than larger assisted living facilities. Depending on where you live, they may go by another name, such as residential care homes or board and care homes, but they are regulated by each state, just as assisted living facilities are.

Continuing care retirement communities offer a range of support from independent living to assisted living to skilled nursing, all on one campus. These communities allow people to stay in one place even as their care needs increase, and they can enable couples who have different abilities to remain in the same community. They tend to be one of the most expensive options; their six-figure average entrance fees and high monthly costs make them unaffordable to most families. Contracts can be confusing, so it is important to understand what will be included, what happens if the care someone needs cannot be provided on site, and whether entrance fees will be refundable if a person moves or dies, or if the facility closes or goes bankrupt.

Nursing homes provide a greater degree of care for people with more serious health needs. Increasingly, they are also providing short-term skilled nursing care, medical care, and therapies following a hospitalization. A certain stigma has been attached to nursing homes because of a history of poor monitoring of conditions, problems with regulatory enforcement, and inadequate communication to the public of even serious infractions. Finding out if a facility is safe and high-quality used to require sorting through pages of documents on a hard-to-find website, but consumers have had better access to information since a five-star rating system was launched for nursing homes. This system was developed following a Senate hearing that I helped organize, during which one senator helpfully remarked that it was simpler to get reliable reviews of a washing machine than a nursing home.

The rating system makes it easier to vet nursing homes, weeding out those that have been cited for repeated violations. But many criticisms of this system persist, including claims that the data submitted by nursing homes is often inaccurate. There are repeated calls for more transparency and greater consumer input into these ratings so that families can weed out the bad and find the best homes in their area. Americans' confidence in nursing homes remains low. Nearly seven in ten people say they are not comfortable with the idea of living in a nursing home, chiefly because of concerns around quality of care and safety.

Despite the stigma, some facilities offer wonderful care. In 2018 I visited Pueblo of Isleta in New Mexico, one of the first pueblo-owned and -licensed assisted living and memory care facilities on tribal land. (*Pueblo* refers both to certain Native American Indian peoples and to a settlement itself.) This beautiful center was designed to provide quality care while maintaining cultural and traditional practices. The building looks like a gorgeous hotel, built in pueblo style, with adobe walls. A big kiva fireplace warms the bright main room, where visitors and residents gather. Several residents invited me to their private rooms, which they had decorated with blankets, photos, and other personal memorabilia to give them a homey feel. A memory care unit in the same building provides safe care for tribal members with dementia, and an elder center next door offers group or home-delivered meals, adult day services, and activities such as line dancing and jewelry making. What impressed me even more than the beautiful buildings and wonderful services was the way staff clearly appreciated each elder as an important member of the community, someone to learn from and value, whatever their age or health.

Pueblo of Isleta has twenty beds, so it is on the smaller side of assisted living residences. Other small facilities include those based on the Green House model, an alternative to traditional nursing homes. Green House homes have only about ten to twelve residents and are run on a very different staffing model from larger facilities. Certified nursing assistants undergo additional training that enables them to provide a much wider range of support, from meal preparation to dementia care. In a typical nursing home, staff perform only one or two specialized functions for many more residents, meaning people are often left waiting for a certain staff member who can see to their needs. The Green House model results in better quality of life for patients and better quality of work life for staff, with lower turnover rates. The model began in the early 2000s, and there are currently about three hundred licensed Green House homes in thirty-two states.

Finally, some of us will eventually need memory care if we are suffering from dementia or other cognitive impairments. Memory care is almost always a specialized service integrated into an assisted living facility or nursing home. Regulation varies from state to state, with some states having more stringent requirements regarding staffing, services, and so on.

Before you choose a nursing home or a memory care facility, you'll want to ask a lot of questions. You will need to know about their safety and licensing. Make sure they are certified and have never had their license revoked and that they conduct background checks on all their staff. Request the most recent official inspection report—nursing homes are required by law to make them available to view—and ask how any violations listed have been addressed. Find out if the facility is run by a not-for-profit or a for-profit company. Nonprofit nursing homes have been found to have higher staff-to-patient ratios and to offer better quality care. Some recent research has found that nursing homes owned by private equity are linked with increased resident hospitalizations and ER visits. Regardless of the facility's ownership, you can ask how many nurses and aides are available and how many hours of care each resident receives. Find out what the facility's visiting policies are. Does it provide transportation to medical appointments? Are its staff members trained to provide dementia care? Does it accept Medicaid? If your assets run out and your loved one qualifies for Medicaid, will the facility allow you to switch payments?

Visit the facility, and notice the atmosphere. Is it clean, and do residents look well cared for? Are staff friendly, helpful, and respectful of residents' privacy? When you are shown a room, it may be the nicest private room; make sure you also see the bedrooms with three to four residents, where Medicaid enrollees usually stay. Find out which services are considered "extras"—Medicaid enrollees may be charged for things like television or social activities. Are there easily accessible outdoor areas for fresh air and a change of scene? Does the food look appetizing, and do residents have access to snacks throughout the day? All these things are critical for the comfort and well-being of your loved one or yourself.

Barriers to Care

There are two main reasons why older Americans aren't getting the care they need and deserve. The first is cost. In 2021 the national average monthly price for a home health aide was over $5,000. A private one-bedroom in an assisted living facility cost $4,500 per month; memory care ran to nearly $7,000 per month; and a private room in a nursing home was over $9,000. Prices vary across the country, but these examples show why care is out of reach for many people, given that the average monthly Social Security retirement check in 2021 was just over $1,600. Most people mistakenly assume that Medicare will pay these expenses, but it won't generally cover most long-term care services, such as home care, assisted living, or long nursing home stays. Medicaid, the health insurance program for those with low incomes, will cover care in nursing homes, and a growing number of states are allowing home care to be covered as well. But that program has strict income and asset limits, often requiring that people spend down nearly all their savings and use some of their income to cover specific medical expenses before they

qualify for benefits. Because the rules vary by state and can be complicated, it is important to contact your state Medicaid or local legal aid
office or hire an eldercare lawyer. Rules govern how much income and
assets the spouse of the person needing care can keep for themselves.
Most states require one member of the couple to spend at least half of
their savings, up to a limit, in order to support the other. Even if you
can navigate getting someone on the program, there can be longer-term
costs. Most people are surprised to learn that after a person dies, states
are required to recover from their estate the amount that Medicaid has
spent on long-term care.

All these rules for getting help with high care costs leave middle-
income older people struggling. About half of them are likely to have
difficulty paying for care because they have too much in the way
of income or assets to qualify for Medicaid but not enough to cover
care expenses.

To help people meet these costs, Washington state is launching an
innovative program called WA Cares. Starting in 2026, it will provide
people with up to $36,500 in benefits (adjusted annually for inflation)
over the course of their lifetime. Funded by a state payroll tax, the
money can be used to pay for care in a home or facility, for transportation and meals, and even for family caregivers. Although the $36,500
benefit is modest, covering roughly one year of care at home, the program will help many families in my home state who struggle with costs.
Several other states have expressed interest in developing ways to help
their residents pay for long-term care.

This is promising, as very few of us have long-term care insurance
to help cover these expenses. The price of this insurance rises with age,
making it unaffordable for many people. In addition, some policies
won't accept applicants who have preexisting health issues. While long-
term care insurance can help offset some of the high costs of care, we
need to carefully review policies and weigh the pros and cons before
deciding whether it is right for us.

Figuring out how to pay for care can challenge even those of us who work on these issues. My colleague Amy Goyer, who wrote two books on family caregiving, cared for her mom, who'd had a stroke, and her dad, who had Alzheimer's, for more than a decade. She ended up over $100,000 in debt and had to file for bankruptcy. Her situation is not unique. One study found that only about a quarter of people in their late sixties could afford to pay for long-term care for more than five years.

The second major reason Americans are not receiving needed care is that the United States has a serious crisis in its paid care workforce. For a better understanding of how staff shortages are affecting older Americans, I talked to Ai-jen Poo, one of the most committed advocates I know, for both older people and those who care for them. Ai-jen is an expert on caregivers, and the president of the National Domestic Workers Alliance, which has secured Domestic Worker Bills of Rights in ten states and brought over two million home care workers under minimum-wage protections.

Ai-jen came to this field in part because of her grandfather. She was born the year after her mother immigrated to the United States from Taiwan. As her parents were working and studying, her grandparents played a huge part in raising her. Her grandfather was a tai chi instructor who stayed very healthy and sharp until his early nineties. Then his vision began to deteriorate, and he lost mobility and needed more assistance. His one wish was to stay at home, but Ai-jen's father couldn't figure out the right supports for him, which led to the heartbreaking decision to place him in a nursing home.

"I remember visiting my grandfather there," Ai-jen told me. "It was like, *What is this place? And why is it like this?* One worker was responsible for an entire floor of people, and everybody seemed incredibly unhappy and disconnected. Even the fluorescent lights didn't work. My grandfather really wasn't communicating with anyone there, and he had stopped eating."

Ai-jen still remembers feeling personally responsible for not having been able to help her grandfather stay home. "How could it be," she wondered, "that the people who raised us, who made everything possible for us, end up with so few dignified options at end of life?"

Around that same time, she was working with women in New York who were domestic workers. Hearing the women's stories, then seeing the staff in her grandfather's nursing home, she started to connect the dots: "I realized that we had this whole system that is really inhumane for everybody involved—but also that we could actually fix it. We can make sure that people like my grandfather have real supports to stay at home, and that those whose job it is to care for them also have supports and dignity."

A key to better care is growing the workforce dramatically. The problem, as Ai-jen and others point out, is a shortage not of potential workers but of good jobs. In every state and the District of Columbia, the median wage for a care worker is one to four dollars lower than that of other occupations with similar entry-level requirements such as janitors, fast-food workers, and retail clerks. And care jobs often have no benefits.

"There are so many passionate people who see care work as a calling and want to do it," Ai-jen said, "but we are losing them because they just can't make ends meet doing this work." She pointed out that heading into the pandemic, eight in ten home care workers didn't have a single paid sick day, so many of them lost their jobs and incomes overnight. Some, wishing to protect their clients and their own families from health risks, were using their poverty-level wages to pay for Ubers and Lyfts instead of public transportation. Others moved in with their clients, because if they didn't care for them, nobody else would.

These are the people we are relying on to care for our loved ones in the most important and personal ways. We need to recognize their value and support them by providing good jobs, living wages, and real benefits.

What Better Care Looks Like

We know there are better ways of supporting people as they age: providing care that is person-centered and helps them live in their homes and stay healthier and more independent for longer. The Program of All-Inclusive Care for the Elderly (PACE) is doing exactly this. PACE delivers comprehensive care in homes and neighborhoods, including medical services, daily care, meals, transportation, and adult day centers. The first PACE program in the United States was On Lok (the name means "peaceful, happy" abode in Cantonese), which was developed as an alternative to nursing homes for residents in the Chinatown and North Beach neighborhoods of San Francisco. Older people wanted to age at home but needed long-term care services to maintain their independence. PACE developed over the years, and in 1997 it became a permanent provider under Medicare and a state option for Medicaid. There are now 273 PACE programs in thirty-two states serving 62,000 people. The model focuses on preventive services—healthy diets, exercise to increase strength and balance, and frequent check-ups—just the sort of things that can help to keep us healthier longer.

Numerous studies have shown that Medicaid enrollees in PACE are healthier and more independent than people enrolled in comparable Medicare Advantage plans. They are far less likely to be hospitalized, use the emergency department, or go to nursing homes or other facilities. PACE benefits caregivers too. A study of thirty PACE centers found that after a family member enrolled in PACE, more than half of family caregivers reported feeling significantly less burdened in all areas—including finances, social life, and physical and emotional health. For Medicaid, the cost savings are significant—about 12 percent lower per person on the program.

In the spring of 2023, I traveled to San Francisco to see the On Lok PACE health center up close. The On Lok Senior Center, just south of the Mission District, is nestled between colorful Victorian houses. It includes a beautiful garden, tended by those who come to the center, which serves over six thousand people every year. The extensive programs it offers—including diabetes education, tai chi for arthritis, line dancing, tech support, and fall prevention—are also available to members of On Lok's PACE program. This is a place not just to receive medical care but also to gather and socialize, and it very much has that feel. No matter what our health needs, we are all more likely to thrive when we receive care that attends to our many dimensions.

What immediately struck me was the fact that the PACE health center is a one-stop shop. The team includes physicians trained in geriatrics, nurses, social workers, mental health therapists, physical and occupational therapists, and dietitians. Transportation services and home care are provided, as is podiatry, optometry, and dental care, all critical to maintaining overall health as we age. Grace Li, On Lok's CEO, talked to me about the importance of offering wrap-around services using in-house specialists. "If you don't have good hearing, good vision, good diet, good feet, good circulation, proper mobility," she said, "it's going to impair a lot of other things."

On Lok's embrace of diversity also stood out to me. Its programs and classes are tailored to different cultures, and some are offered in multiple languages. It recently partnered with Openhouse to provide the nation's first community-based adult day program designed for and with the LGBTQ+ community. The staff members were also diverse, both culturally and in terms of age. And On Lok is looking ahead. Staff train medical students from nearby colleges and universities to help foster the next generation of geriatric health care providers and are expanding the program. Recently, they brought PACE to two convents in Fremont, California, to care for elderly nuns.

PACE is proof that a system that combines both health and social care can help people thrive in their homes and communities and stay out of hospitals and nursing homes.

If we are truly going to support the growing population of older Americans, we will need deep and sustained coordination between our housing and health policies. Right now those sectors are rarely integrated, and neither of them is ready to meet growing demand. We need more investment and action—and quickly—if we are to keep millions of older people from falling through the cracks. For those who need more care, we have to ensure that assisted living and nursing facilities are of good quality and affordable, and that no one has to bankrupt themselves in order to enter them. We also have to vastly increase our stock of accessible and affordable housing to include everything from apartments to smaller single-family homes to larger homes that can accommodate multiple generations. And we must better support people who wish to age in place, which is the more economical option and what so many people want. We all want to see our loved ones living in situations that promote mental and physical health, along with happiness and dignity. And when the time comes, we will surely want that for ourselves.

How Will I Die?

The death of my husband's uncle Wayne was swift; he had a heart attack while driving, hit a tree, and died instantly. My husband's mother, Sybil, died at home with her family after a long battle with cancer, and my husband's father, Garrett, died in his mid-eighties after a single day in hospice. Garrett had had ongoing heart problems, but was still living an active life. Then one afternoon, coming home from a (not-so-healthy) fast-food lunch with a friend, he felt unwell. His son took him to the hospital to get checked out, and the doctors said his heart was failing and there was nothing more they could do. Garrett died the following day, with his three sons by his side.

The existence of so much uncertainty around the one certain thing in life makes it difficult to plan, and the very strong emotions surrounding death can make it seem too overwhelming even to contemplate. But the end of life is something we can prepare for, even amid the unknowns. I don't mean just putting our finances in order and making sure our will is notarized. Those things are very important, but it is also important to think about what will really matter to us when we are near the end of life, who we want to be with, and how we want to spend our time as life winds down. To consider such things, we need to understand what choices we'll have and what will influence our options.

When I began to write this chapter, I discovered that many of my long-held assumptions about dying were wrong. I thought older people feared it and that nobody wanted to talk about it. I thought an advance directive was the essential way to make sure our end-of-life wishes would be carried out—and that we would know, even years before we became seriously ill, what those wishes would be. And I thought people should die at home, because a hospital environment was inevitably dehumanizing.

I had a lot to learn. Much of what I've discovered has come from talking to people who have spent their working lives trying to build a more compassionate system of end-of-life care. Although the timing of death isn't predictable, and we aren't entirely in control when we are facing the end of life, we aren't entirely helpless either. We have decisions to make, and these choices help our families to know our wishes and put our affairs in order. Even more important, making these choices helps ensure that we spend the time we have left in ways more likely to be meaningful to us.

Dying Is a Natural Part of Life

For most of modern history, death was woven into the fabric of everyday life. Most people died at home, and even young children witnessed death up close, as their families cared for dying friends and relatives. For a range of reasons, including the absence of medical cures, death usually occurred at earlier ages. But changes over the last hundred years, especially in industrialized nations, have had the effect of distancing us from death. An understanding of germs and infectious diseases, the advent of antibiotics and vaccines, and improved sanitation and nutrition all contributed to a dramatic drop in infant and child mortality rates. The average American lifespan jumped from forty-seven in 1900 to seventy-seven in 2000.

Other less obvious shifts also conspired to distance us from death. In the years following World War II, the nuclear family—a couple and their dependent children—largely replaced the multigenerational family household as the norm, and young children often lived apart from older relatives. The changing employment landscape lured workers away from their hometowns and extended families. As we scattered geographically, death often became sad news conveyed over the telephone rather than a process we witnessed firsthand.

The biggest shift in our cultural attitudes about life's end, however, came with changes in the medical profession's approach to dying. In the United States, by the 1990s, 74 percent of deaths occurred in hospitals or other institutional settings, and home deaths had dropped to about 20 percent. The catalyst for this shift was the development of lifesaving drugs and medical procedures that are administered in hospitals. Since the introduction of the national emergency call system in 1968, multiple generations have grown up learning the standard drill for just about any serious health alarm: phone 911, wait for the ambulance, go to the hospital. While that system has been lifesaving for people who are injured or suddenly ill, hospitals began to treat every imminent death, even when expected, as a crisis from which people needed rescuing. Patients often got surgeries and other aggressive (and incredibly expensive) treatments that extended life only slightly while also causing considerable suffering. The result has been "medicalized dying," a dying process facilitated or prolonged by medical intervention. Of course, these interventions include many lifesaving treatments—chemotherapy, for example—so criticisms of medicalized dying focus on aggressive life supports for patients who have no chance of recovery.

The disappearance of actual death (as opposed to death in movies and TV series) from everyday life has changed the way we think, talk, and feel about it. Kathryn Mannix, a retired doctor and pioneer of palliative medicine in the U.K., believes we have lost "the rich wisdom of normal human dying." We've stopped talking about dying, Mannix says, because we consider it "impolite." We need to reclaim the process of dying, as well as the wisdom and shared consolation that go with it.

It seems that people *do* want to talk about death. I've been surprised by the results of surveys AARP has conducted about attitudes to dying and death. Eight in ten people said they were either very or somewhat comfortable talking about these issues; that figure was even higher for those over sixty-five. (In other studies, people say they want to talk about death but assume others don't, so they avoid the topic, perpetuating a taboo about this most universal of experiences.) The fear of death trends downward as we age, reaching its lowest point in those over eighty, who also report feeling most prepared for death. As those who work with the dying reminded me, perceptions and fears about death and dying, along with the willingness to talk about and prepare for them, are influenced by culture. Attitudes and preferences can look very different depending on such things as religion, race or ethnicity, socioeconomic status, and familial traditions.

How and Where We Die

Many of us would like to die quickly, avoiding difficult medical decisions and leaving no time for fear or sadness, but only about 15 percent of us will actually die suddenly and unexpectedly. The common causes of death change as we get older. For people under fifty, deaths are often due to "external" causes such as motor vehicle crashes, drug overdoses, alcohol abuse, homicide, and suicide. Adults over fifty are most likely to die of heart disease and cancer. As we get into our mid-seventies, we begin to see more strokes, respiratory diseases, and dementias causing death. In the past twenty years, deaths from drug and alcohol abuse and overdoses have more than tripled among people over sixty-five. Older people today are more likely to use drugs and alcohol than previous generations were, and these substances can be even more dangerous when they interact with multiple prescription medications or social factors such as isolation.

At the same time, modern medicine has transformed the most common and long-standing causes of sudden death in the second fifty into conditions we can survive for years or even decades. My husband is an example; it's been several years since his heart attack, and he's still thriving, thanks to rapid medical intervention, effective medications, and a healthier diet.

Eventually, though, our bodies will begin their irreversible decline, and the question arises of where we will spend our final months, weeks, or days.

Most of us want to die at home, and I had long assumed that that was always better than dying in a medicalized setting. But I've learned it's not that simple. Illness and death make great demands on family caregivers, and our system doesn't support them in caring for a dying loved one in their own home. There are also cultural differences to consider. People in some cultures, such as Taiwanese, may fear that when someone dies in the hospital, their soul might not be able to return home. In Hmong culture, death at home is believed to be very important to the spiritual well-being of both the dying person and the family. In Hindu tradition the person dying may spend their final moments lying on the ground rather than in a bed, to allow for deeper connection with the earth. However, some patients may not want to die at home because they fear being a burden to family. Moreover, being in a health care setting where their medical needs are looked after can free them to focus on being with friends and family.

As the geriatrician and palliative care specialist Diane Meier told me, "Death at home is really, really hard, because we expect families to do 95 percent of the care. Even if you're on hospice, you're lucky if a nurse comes once a week and a home health aide comes three mornings a week to help your loved one bathe. The rest of the time you're on your own."

My brother-in-law, Scott, knows all about this. He stepped in to care for his mother, Sybil, when she had ovarian cancer. After her diagnosis, Sybil had surgery, then six months of remission. But after a second surgery, she couldn't take food by mouth and was fed through a tube into her stomach that was attached to a bag. The bag had to be changed every twenty-four hours.

On weekdays, Sybil had a visiting nurse, but every weekend for five months Scott went to his parents' home, changed the bag, and administered a daily injection to his mother, making sure to avoid any infections. Scott lived closer to Sybil than his brothers did, so it was easier for him to get there, but the tasks he performed were difficult. "I was her lifeline, right?" Scott told me. "I had to help her stay around as long as she wanted to. And without the nutrients, and the medication in the shot, she wasn't going to last long."

This is a huge responsibility for someone not formally trained in health care, yet it's the reality for many families and friends. As Diane said, "We expect family caregivers to be doctor, nurse, and social worker, in addition to spouse or daughter or son." The tough reality is that not every dying person has loved ones who are willing and able to devote themselves to this level of care, and not every caregiver is cut out for the physical, emotional, and spiritual demands of tending to a dying person.

None of this is to say that hospitals are always the answer. Even with the best staff, they can feel too clinical or impersonal a setting for something as deeply personal as death. Intensive care units (ICUs), where one in three Medicare beneficiaries die, present their own problems. The heightened risk of infection in an ICU makes it the most hazardous area of a hospital, especially for people who are particularly frail. Moreover, many ICUs limit visitors, which can be hard on patients at a time when they most need the company of friends and family. In addition, health care spending for people dying in a hospital is seven times higher than for those dying at home. This means we are often spending more, both out of pocket and through insurance and

Medicare, for treatments that may not prolong our lives or add to our quality of life. I'm not suggesting that, as someone nears the end of life, they should forgo treatment they want and need; rather, we should make sure that the patient really *does* want those interventions and that they fully understand the potential benefits, risks, and implications of any treatment.

In recent decades, where Americans die has been shifting. Between 2003 and 2017, home deaths jumped by 29 percent, surpassing hospitals as the most common place of death for the first time since the early twentieth century. A likely reason that dying at home has become so much more common is the growth of hospice programs. Some experts argue that further expanding access to hospice would lead to an increase in quality home care for people with serious illnesses.

The takeaway here is that where we die should be the place that's best for us. "This notion that the home death is the good death, and the hospital death is the bad death is wrong," Diane said. "The right place is the place that meets the needs of the patient and the family."

The Comfort of Hospice Care

No matter where we die, none of us wants to suffer, and the hospice movement has done much to alleviate suffering as people approach death. The modern hospice concept originated in postwar England with Cicely Saunders, a nurse and social worker who tended to the dying. Convinced that more compassionate treatment was needed and that too many patients felt deserted at the end of life, Saunders became a doctor and began studying pain management for those with incurable illnesses. Her approach bucked prevailing norms, which had patients waiting until their medications wore off before they were given relief. She advocated for constant control of constant pain. When patients no longer feared the return of their pain, their anxiety was greatly reduced, which in turn actually reduced their pain.

In 1967 Saunders founded the first modern hospice facility, in South

West London. By then, her ideas about caring for the dying had spread to the United States, where she was a visiting faculty member at Yale in the mid-1960s. In 1969 Elisabeth Kübler-Ross changed the public conversation about the end of life when she published her hugely influential *On Death and Dying*. It took another few years, but in 1974, Florence Wald, a former dean of the School of Nursing at Yale, along with two pediatricians and a chaplain, founded the first hospice facility in the United States, in Branford, Connecticut.

You may be familiar with hospice if someone you were close to died while they were in hospice care, but there is still a lot of misunderstanding about what it is, who qualifies, and what Medicare does and doesn't pay for.

Hospice is team-based care for a person with a terminal illness that focuses on comfort and quality of life rather than on extending life. Hospice covers many services not traditionally paid for by insurance, including regular home visits by doctors, nurses, and aides, and access to psychosocial support from social workers, spiritual professionals, and grief specialists. Volunteers may sit with a patient or offer services such as walking the dog. Hospice will pay for, deliver, and set up expensive medical equipment—such as a hospital bed or a walker that can make someone more comfortable or allow them independence. It will bring prescription drugs, including those for pain management, directly to the patient. The patient and their family can receive emotional and psychological support to help with depression, anxiety, and fear, and after the death family members can receive grief counseling.

Most hospice services are provided wherever the person calls home—whether that is their own house, a nursing home, or an assisted living facility. But hospice services can also be provided at a hospital or nursing home or an in-patient hospice facility. Stays in these "hospice houses" are usually short-term, for crisis management or to give a caregiver some respite—a short period of rest or relief. In some communities, a dying person may be able to stay at a hospice house for a longer duration, but this isn't the norm.

Under Medicare, in order to receive hospice services, you must meet three conditions: your regular doctor (if you have one) and a hospice doctor must certify that you have a terminal illness and a life expectancy of six months or less (you can be "recertified" after six months if doctors confirm that you are still terminally ill); you must forgo any treatments that attempt to cure the illness, including participation in medical trials; and you must sign a statement choosing hospice care instead of other Medicare-covered treatments for the illness. If you don't have Medicare, most state Medicaid programs and the Veterans Health Administration offer similar hospice benefits. Many private insurance plans also cover hospice services, though eligibility criteria and benefits can vary.

Hospice does have its limitations. It does not provide around-the-clock care. Although someone from the hospice team is available by phone, and members of the team will visit, the actual hands-on care is intermittent. So unless the dying person is in a hospital or a nursing facility, most of the day-to-day caregiving will be provided by friends and family or by paid caregivers. In addition, hospice does *not* pay for room and board beyond brief stays at a hospice inpatient unit, hospital, or nursing facility, when pain or symptoms become too difficult to manage at home.

Despite these limits, hospice performs an invaluable service. I know from speaking to social workers, nurses, and other clinicians who work in hospice care that many feel it is a privilege to sit with people at one of the most vulnerable times of their lives. An important part of their work is helping those in their care come to terms with the life they've lived, see the legacy they are leaving behind, and make peace with the areas of their life they feel are unsettled.

The number of hospice providers and people receiving such care continues to grow. About half of people who die while on Medicare are enrolled in hospice. Their time under hospice care tends to be short—about half of enrollees receive it for less than eighteen days, a figure that hasn't changed significantly since the early 2000s. Receiving hospice care so late in the course of an illness—whether because of lack of awareness, bureaucratic hurdles, the requirement to give up any potentially curative treatment, or cultural or personal inclinations—means missing out on extra support and the chance to focus on what matters most at the end of life.

To better understand hospice and how it can be improved, I talked to Sarah Creed. Sarah was a nurse for many years and is now vice-president of nursing operations at Good Shepherd Community Care, a not-for-profit organization just outside Boston that specializes in hospice and palliative care. She is involved in clinical operations but is also deeply informed about health care policy related to hospice. Her passion for what she does is extraordinary, which is why she is frustrated by the fact that people often receive hospice services very late, when it's hard, or even impossible, for caregivers to build a trusting relationship with them or get them all the services they're entitled to.

When Sarah meets new patients, she begins by finding out what their biggest worry is. It might be fear of pain, concern about what will happen to their families when they're gone, or whether they can still do any of the things they enjoy. She asks what they want to do with the time that's left. What would quality of life look like? Are they willing to tolerate some pain in order to do something they love, or is their priority to be pain free, even if that means being groggy? This type of in-depth conversation can also allow a clinician to better understand any cultural traditions important to the patient that need to be respected.

"I will do my best to keep them as comfortable as I can," Sarah said, "and we have a lot of tools in our toolbox. But I also think it's really important to be honest. I try to shift the hope of a cure to the hope of being able to live each day to the fullest extent they can. That's where more time is better. As a hospice nurse, I have a better chance of improving your quality of life four months before you're going to die than I do four days before you're going to die."

Sarah tries to strike a balance between easing a person's symptoms and enabling them to do what matters to them. One patient loved going out to eat and wanted to have a nice dinner with her family, but she was tethered to an oxygen tank. Sarah's team found a portable tank that her family could carry, helped her get dressed up, and gave her medication that was strong enough to stabilize her respiratory rate without making her sleepy. The woman was delighted to have her dinner out. Another patient used to be a swimmer and really wanted to go swimming. One of the social workers was a lifeguard and was able to take the man into a pool.

"These are our favorite hospice moments," Sarah told me, "where someone is really getting what they want. This is why we do the work."

Where Palliative Care Comes In

Hospice is available only to people who are dying and choose to no longer receive treatment. But palliative care, a key component of hospice, can help many people who are living with chronic conditions such as multiple sclerosis, cardiac disease, Parkinson's, or ALS—and could benefit from the symptom management and support it provides. Palliative care goes beyond simply treating a disease and focuses on quality of life for both the patient and the family, through a whole range of medical, practical, social, spiritual, and emotional supports. It can begin on the day of diagnosis and does not depend on whether that diagnosis is terminal or how long a patient is expected to live.

Beyond specialist doctors and nurses, the palliative care team is likely to include social workers, nutritionists, and spiritual counselors, all of whom work to reduce or eliminate suffering, whether from pain, depression, fatigue, or worry. They help patients understand their choices for medical treatment, clarify their goals for care, and avoid unnecessary treatments. In other words, they help them get what they want from the medical system.

A lot of what I know about palliative care I've learned from Diane Meier, who has transformed the way we treat people suffering from serious illnesses. When my mother-in-law Sybil was suffering due to the spread of ovarian cancer, we were at a complete loss as to how to help her. I put her in touch with Diane. I don't know everything she discussed with Sybil, but I noticed that afterward my mother-in-law was more peaceful.

I first met Diane in 2010 after she received a MacArthur Foundation "genius" award and was taking a year off from practicing medicine. She had come to work as a fellow (an overqualified intern) in the U.S. Senate. By that time, she was the director of the Center to Advance Palliative Care, a national organization working to increase the number and quality of palliative care programs around the country, and she wanted to better understand how to influence policymakers to expand palliative care.

As a young doctor in the 1980s, Diane saw many patients who were very ill—suffering from pain, shortness of breath, fatigue, sleeplessness, depression, and anxiety. But because they weren't dying, they were not eligible for hospice. They were in medical limbo, in desperate need of a different kind of help: relief from psychological distress, better communication with their doctors, and better pain management.

When Diane and I spoke in the summer of 2021, she remembered those patients. "We had nothing for them," she told me. "You couldn't work in an acute care hospital and not see that all we were doing was providing disease-specific treatment and ignoring all the other aspects of the human experience." The failure to address mental and emotional health was actually undermining the benefits of all that medical care. Untreated depression, pain, or shortness of breath, for instance, increases the risk of dying from the underlying disease.

For generations, Diane said, doctors had been taught to "mechanistically treat the illness and not think about the fact that the brain and the body are one organism that you can't separate." When we're in so much pain that we can't move comfortably, eat well, go outside, or socialize with friends—the things that make life worth living—our emotional health suffers right along with our physical health.

In 1983, Diane established a palliative care institute at Mount Sinai Hospital in New York. Since then, largely due to the work of Diane and her colleagues, the field has expanded, with palliative care programs in U.S. hospitals more than tripling in the last few decades.

There is growing evidence that palliative care helps people not only have a better quality of life but live longer. A study of terminal lung cancer patients who received either traditional cancer treatment or the same treatment plus palliative care found that those who received palliative care ended up feeling less depressed, stopped chemotherapy sooner, chose hospice earlier—and lived two months longer than patients who received traditional treatment alone. What's more, the palliative care group spent fewer days in the hospital and were less likely to die there.

Providing palliative care services isn't just good for patients—it reduces spending on other types of health care. One recent study showed that home-based palliative care patients used significantly fewer services, particularly in the last three months of life, leading to far lower costs than those incurred by patients not enrolled in palliative care. Other studies of patients receiving palliative care have consistently shown fewer ER visits, lower ICU admission rates, reduced stays in ICUs and hospitals, and markedly lower hospital costs.

Better Access to Hospice and Palliative Care

Despite all the benefits of hospice and palliative care, too many people are still missing out on these services. When it comes to hospice, not all patients and families are willing to accept that the end is near. Giving up on treatment and the hope for a cure is hard for everyone, including doctors. The criteria for entering hospice can also impede access, as predicting someone's remaining lifespan is quite difficult, even for medical specialists. Some doctors overestimate life expectancies of their terminal patients, which can have implications for hospice refer-

ral because of the six-month life expectancy requirement. Poor communication is another challenge. A 2022 study showed that patients
seventy years or older who were being treated for incurable cancer estimated that they had a higher chance of curability than their doctors
did. Such disconnects may lead doctors to delay important discussions
and refer their patients very late to hospice services.

Residents report receiving very limited training in end-of-life conversations during medical school and residency, so their reluctance to
discuss prognosis, treatments, and options is unsurprising. The fact
that these discussions became politically contentious doesn't help. I
was working in the Senate in 2009 during the debate over the Affordable Care Act, when a provision that would reimburse doctors for the
time they spent talking with patients about their advance care wishes
was twisted into a false claim that the bill would create "death panels."
Medicare eventually began paying for these important conversations,
though they remain politically divisive.

As in every other aspect of the U.S. health care system, significant
disparities along racial and economic lines persist in our access to and
use of hospice. A 2020 study of Medicare patients found that 35 percent
of Black participants who died over the study period used hospice services in the last six months of life, compared to 46 percent of white participants. Black patients were more likely in their final months to have
multiple visits to the emergency room, hospitalizations, and intensive
treatments (such as mechanical ventilation and feeding tubes), while
white patients more often opted for hospice. The disparity could be due
to several factors. Given well-documented differences in care, Black
patients may have less trust in the medical system and wonder if they
are being offered every option available; that could make them less
willing to forgo treatments that could conceivably prolong life. Poor
communication between health care providers and their Black patients
may also contribute to lower use of services, as well as cultural views
or spiritual beliefs about forgoing life-sustaining procedures. Finally,
Black patients may have less convenient access to higher-quality end-

of-life care, as hospitals located in poor, rural, or racially and ethnically diverse communities tend to be least likely to offer hospice care teams.

With regard to palliative care, there seems to be a general lack of awareness about it. One recent study looking at unpaid family caregivers, some of whom were making health care decisions for a person with a serious chronic illness, found that over half of them had never heard of palliative care. Those from racially and ethnically diverse communities and caregivers without a college degree were the least likely to be aware of it. Among caregivers who had heard of palliative care, a significant portion believed it was the same as hospice.

If you are seeking palliative care, you can start by asking your primary care doctor about it, or the specialist overseeing your treatment. Unfortunately, doctors are often reluctant to refer patients for palliative care. A survey of oncologists across the country found that sometimes even physicians aren't aware that palliative care is different from end-of-life care. Just 17 percent of the oncologists referred patients to palliative care at the time of a metastatic cancer diagnosis, despite clinical guidelines recommending that it begin early in the disease. One in five offered it only at the end of life. Doctors cited a lack of time and tools to educate patients, as well as perceived patient resistance—the concern that patients view palliative care as their doctor giving up on them.

You may therefore need to do your own research. The Center to Advance Palliative Care offers a comprehensive online directory of providers. It is searchable by zip code and by where you would like to receive palliative services—in a hospital or clinic, at home, or in a nursing home. At your first consultation with a palliative care doctor, you will want to discuss your symptoms, the services you are interested in, activities you feel are essential to maintain in order to live meaningfully, and your fears and concerns about your medical care.

We need to educate both patients and health care providers about this invaluable service, and also increase the ranks of palliative care physicians. Even when patients and doctors agree on the need for palliative care, a study found, there has been a shortage of trained personnel. As with geriatric medicine, there are simply not enough doctors trained in palliative care. When I checked the provider directory of the Center to Advance Palliative Care, I found very few specialists in my own area and none even close to where my parents live.

Finally, the barrier that affects our attitudes toward both palliative care and hospice, one that cuts across all racial, ethnic, and socioeconomic groups, is fear. As Sarah Creed told me, people too often try to put death out of their minds. "I'm not saying I'm not afraid of death," she said, "but I don't think we are accepting of the whole life cycle in our culture. When you're pregnant, you plan for the birth, for what that is going to entail. But when we're dying, we 'fight.' And that word really gets me. We *fight* to stay alive, and it's the *fight* against cancer. And through that fighting, there's not a lot of acceptance or thinking about what's going to happen if I can't beat this."

We can do both: support people medically and psychologically who are struggling with long-term illnesses, *and* ensure that those who are reaching the end of life have the care they want and need.

Preparing for the End

One of the best things about my job at AARP is that I get to study programs for aging populations in other countries so that we can import their innovations to the United States. In 2022 I took a trip to New Zealand and stopped in the town of Rotorua to meet with some older people who have been building their own coffins—and having a lot of fun doing it.

It all started in 2010 at a meeting of the Rotorua University of the Third Age, which supports learning after retirement. Attendees were asked which classes they wanted to see offered. Katie Williams, a former midwife and hospice nurse, raised her hand and said she wanted to learn how to make her own coffin. There was an uncomfortable silence, but after the meeting a group of people approached her and said they liked the idea.

The Coffin Club Rotorua now has about sixty volunteers making what they call "underground furniture," coffins they decorate with images or motifs important to those who will one day use them—scenes of mountains for an avid hiker or images of Elvis for a devoted fan. It was incredibly moving to get a sense of someone's life and personality this way. The members used to build the coffins themselves, but now they buy them at low cost and personalize them. The day I visited, one woman told me about a coffin she was designing for her best friend who had dementia. The group also makes coffins to donate to Rotorua hospitals for stillbirths and to help low-income families. "People can't afford to live," Katie said, "and they can't afford to die."

The club is part art studio, part social club, and part charity. I saw coffins lined up in the garage, with stencils and paints available for any-one to use. Tea was brewing in the common area, and couches and board games invited people to hang out inside. Through this program, club members have found a way to demystify death and build community. Their work frees families to have conversations about end-of-life wishes that might otherwise have been taboo. Speaking with club members, it was clear to me that people do want to talk about these things, and that they want death to be personalized. In Katie's words, "How splendid we can have control of our last journey."

As we said goodbye, Katie gave me one of her famous "cuddles," a big hug from a small woman, and I drove away thinking about the beauty and power of accepting that the end will come—and about what design I would want on my own coffin.

The visit also made me think about what choice means to us as we near the end, about which things we have a say in and how we can get closer to realizing our wishes or those of someone we care about. I'm a little wary of the idea of the "good death." Broadly defined, a good death is one that aligns with the wishes of the patient and family, does not involve avoidable suffering and distress, and abides by ethical, clinical, and cultural standards. Such a death would take into account things like pain management, informed decision-making, and the protection of someone's dignity. I'm certainly not against any of these things, and some circumstances are unquestionably better than others. But setting up a good death as a goal can create false expectations. Death can't always be neatly managed, and the patient and family who've planned for a good death may feel cheated or guilty if the final days or hours involve more suffering than anticipated. Also, religious practices and cultural beliefs differ in their definitions of the ideal death. Finally, what matters to someone near the end isn't always clear and can change as death approaches.

I was struck by a story Deborah Kado, a Stanford geriatrician and chief of geriatrics research, told me. In the early 1990s Deborah was treating a patient who was dying of prostate cancer. He desperately wanted to go home, but he had an infection. "I felt obliged to lay it out," Deborah recalled. " 'Your infection isn't completely treated, that means that it will likely kill you.' He never acknowledged any of that. Ever. He just said every day, 'I want to go home.'" Finally, she gave in and sent him home. At two a.m. the morning after discharge, she got a call. Her patient had died. His partner said, "Thank you so much, Dr. Kado, for allowing him to come home."

Deborah hadn't known her patient was gay, so she didn't realize that the restrictive visitation rules then in place concerning same-sex partners had left him cut off from his loved one. What the man most wanted was to be with his partner and his dog. That was the best death he could have had. Deborah had almost, inadvertently, stood in the way. She told me she's never forgotten that man. "He taught me something. I was listening to him, but I wasn't communicating."

We can't assume that our doctor or even those closest to us will know what we want in our final days, so we should take important practical steps to document our end-of-life health care and financial wishes. We should, for example, create an advance directive and will. Some of these documents involve multiple forms and incur legal costs, and they require us to make difficult choices that can change over time. It isn't surprising, then, that many of us have not completed them or kept them up to date.

While I was doing research for this chapter, I realized that I needed to update my own plans and wishes. I hadn't looked at my will since my kids, who are now adults, were little, back when my biggest worry was making sure I had guardians in place for them, in case something happened to me. I wasn't sure where I'd put my document specifying my health wishes, so it would hardly be useful in an emergency. And while I talk openly with my family about where I'd like to have my ashes scattered, I don't think I've ever spoken, even with my husband, about the care I would or would not want if I were incapacitated. Honestly, I'm not sure I even know that myself. So if you're in a similar position, know that you're not alone.

Let's start with the basics of how to designate our medical wishes. *Advance directive* is a broad term that refers to any legal document related to our future medical care. It includes a living will and medical power of attorney. State laws vary about the specifics of these documents, the terms they use, and whether you need a standardized legal form or can draft your own.

A living will specifies what medical treatment we would or would not want if we were terminally ill or injured or in a "persistent vegetative state." For instance, we can specify whether we would want food and water provided intravenously ("tube feeding"), and whether certain kinds of medical machinery should be used, such as heart-lung machines or ventilators that may sustain or extend our life without curing our condition.

A medical power of attorney means we designate a trusted person to be our health care "proxy" or "surrogate," giving that person the authority to make medical decisions on our behalf if we are unable to do so ourselves. We can draft it so that it is implemented immediately or only if we become incapacitated. Our proxy has broader power to carry out our wishes than is provided in a living will; besides consenting to or refusing treatments, this person can access our medical records, select and discharge health care providers, and approve or instruct the withholding of such care as heart resuscitation. We should choose someone who knows and respects our wishes, whom we trust to make difficult decisions for us, and who understands and accepts this responsibility. It can be a challenging role, especially if the proxy is carrying out decisions other loved ones oppose. That is why, ideally, we should have the conversation about our end-of-life wishes with all our family and close friends present, including the person who will act as our health care proxy.

If we become incapacitated and haven't completed an advance directive, doctors will ask certain family members for guidance, according to the law in our state. In complicated cases, a court may appoint a relative, friend, or independent guardian (which may be someone we have never met) who they believe will act in our best interests.

Since the passage of the 1990 Patient Self-Determination Act—intended to protect patient rights and ensure their treatment wishes are followed—there has been a push for patients to file end-of-life care plans while they are healthy. As of 2020, 72 percent of American adults sixty-five and older had a living will. During the first months of the pandemic, the creation of advance directives increased.

Yet although the law requires that our wishes be followed, advance directives may not have the impact we expect. According to numerous studies, advance care plans don't influence medical decisions at the end of life; nor, in the opinion of patients and families, do they improve quality of care. Carrying out a patient's written wishes can be complicated. Family members may object to stipulations in the directive and pressure the proxy not to follow them. Some requests may not be feasible to honor—for instance, the dying person wants to be cared for at home but no team of caregivers is available. Doctors may lack access to the directive or may interpret it differently, depending on the treatment options available. The documents also tend to be tied to the patient's state of residence and are not always recognized in another state.

One of the most complicating factors is not bureaucratic but human: as our health changes, we often change our minds about what care we want. This is something I learned from talking to Diane Meier and others who work with terminally ill patients. For most of us, the desire for human connection and the ability to engage with those closest to us holds true to the end. But other priorities can shift in ways we wouldn't have foreseen.

"While you are independent," Diane explained, "you prioritize remaining independent. But when you become dependent, people adjust. And life is still worth living." She finds it cruel that we ask people to "make hypothetical decisions about circumstances they are not in and can't really comprehend until they are in them." For example, if you came to the hospital with a severe case of COVID-19, going onto a ventilator could well save your life, but if your living will said "no ventilator," and your doctor was following it to the letter, you wouldn't get that ventilator, and you could die. Treatment directives written outside the reality of a medical situation and its specific circumstances, and far in advance, can result in devastating, unintended consequences.

None of this is to argue that we shouldn't make *any* advance plans; it's only to say that there are ways of arriving at better results. First, choosing a health care proxy, discussing our wishes with that person, and putting those in writing are essential. When we lose decisional capacity, we need to have someone who can make real-time decisions for us. In conversations with her patients, Diane encourages them to identify who they would trust in that situation. "I don't ask them if they do or don't want a ventilator or feeding tube," she said, "because that's contingent on the specifics of the situation."

It's also a good idea for us to talk with our loved ones about sickness and death when we're in good health in order to understand what decisions and feelings might be involved when life-or-death situations do arise. In the end it may matter less where I put my own living will than how I've communicated my end-of-life wishes to my doctor, my husband, and my children—so I need to start doing that now. Because I know my wishes may change over time, I'll also need to have those conversations throughout my life.

When my mother-in-law, Sybil, became sick, I gave her and my father-in-law a copy of the Five Wishes document to discuss and fill out. I'm a fan of this resource because it goes beyond providing instructions for medical care to specifying how we want to be treated by others as we die, how comfortable we want to be, and so on. (Do we want prayers or music? Do we want someone holding our hand? Do we want pain-relieving medication even if it means we will sleep?) It also covers how we want to be remembered, where we want to be buried, and many other preferences. Five Wishes is available in thirty languages and meets legal requirements for advance directives in all but four states.

Discussing end-of-life wishes can lead to unexpected and even lighthearted moments. When my friend Kelly asked her mother, Molly, about her wishes, some were more specific than others. Molly said that at her funeral she would like Kelly and her daughter to sing "Ave Maria" and read aloud her favorite prayer from Saint Francis. As for her medical wishes, Molly, who was a lifelong equestrian, told Kelly to treat her like a horse: "If a horse colics once, you fix him. Same with twice. At three times, you let him go." Kelly wasn't sure the response fit on the Five Wishes form, but she understood that her mom wanted care, up to a point.

Having a document like Five Wishes can help us to think about what is important at the end—spiritually, emotionally, and psychologically. Not surprisingly, studies that have looked at what matters to people as they near death have found that close personal relationships are a major component of well-being, including relationships with God or a higher power. Communicating the importance of these relationships through love and gratitude was very important to them. People invari-

ably said that personal relationships were strengthened as they neared
the end of life. I find this helpful to think about. What matters at the
end might just be, well, what matters.

Aside from making our end-of-life wishes clear, we all face the very
practical matter of estate planning. These documents help ensure that
we have a say in who will care for our dependents after we die and how
our belongings will be distributed. Typically, we'll need to visit an estate
planning attorney, who will help us determine whether a will or trust
is more appropriate. A living trust is a trust fund that holds our assets
until a predetermined time, which could be a time *before* our death.
A will provides instructions for allocating real estate, bank accounts,
jewelry, stocks, cars, retirement accounts, and even pets, and it can
minimize the cost of transferring assets and associated taxes. It also
includes plans for the surviving spouse or partner. The rise in blended
families and households can make financial arrangements complex,
leading to potential conflict following a death. We should review our
documents regularly, especially in the event of a divorce or disability or
the death of a loved one—milestones that may change our mind about
how to distribute our assets.

Most Americans say they believe that having a will is important, and
the share of people who have wills has risen since the pandemic, significantly among those under thirty-five. Nevertheless, as of 2023, only one
in three American adults has a will. The main reason people give for
not having done their estate planning is procrastination. Estate planning requires thinking about mortality. It takes a little work, and it
costs some money, although low-cost and even free legal aid services
are available.

It is important to get estate planning right. If you use online software to create a will or trust, you should be sure that the guidance it
offers applies in the state where you live. A colleague who specializes

in elder law shared with me the story of a woman who used software based on California estate law to make her trust. The woman realized only later that because she didn't live in California, her documents had a host of problems. A friend told me about the case of her mother and stepfather, who believed they had a common-law marriage. Only when her stepfather died did her mother discover that their state did not recognize common-law marriages, which created headaches when settling his estate. It pays to get advice that's specific to your state and circumstances.

Many people assume a will is only for the well-off and isn't worth the cost if their assets aren't large. But even a small cash inheritance can affect a family's long-term wealth, as it may help pay for education or boost homeownership for the next generation. Not having a will can end up costing more money than estate planning would have. It effectively delegates important decisions about your assets, and even your dependents, to the courts, and it leaves loved ones struggling with difficult decisions or arguments in the midst of their grief.

The likelihood of having a will depends a lot on age, income, education, and race. People with more education and higher incomes are more likely to have an estate plan, while racial disparities in estate planning mean that white families are far more likely to inherit than Black or Hispanic families. This disparity has big social impacts, since homeownership figures prominently into a family's wealth.

The decisions and costs of planning a funeral, burial, or cremation for someone else can feel overwhelming, and planning our own can feel a little strange. But if we can think beforehand about what is important to us, we can be clear about our wishes, gain some peace of mind, and save others added difficulty when they are grieving. And as the Coffin Club in Rotorua taught me, even our caskets can be approached in a spirit of celebration.

Funerals and burials are getting steadily more expensive. A 2021

study showed that the median cost of an adult funeral with viewing and burial was $7,848, while that of a funeral with viewing and
cremation was nearly $7,000. Burial plots for caskets will add some-
where between $500 to $5,000, though they can go as high as $25,000,
depending on the type and location of the cemetery. Interest in "green
burials" is rising; they aim to have a minimal impact on the environment by avoiding, among other things, the use of concrete vaults and
embalming fluids, instead burying bodies in biodegradable contain-
ers. A space to bury an urn containing cremated remains will cost anywhere from $350 to $2,500. That is all before you figure in the cost of a
headstone. Not surprisingly, more than half of American families now
opt for cremation. A "direct" or "simple" cremation omits the embalming, viewing, funeral, and burial, cremates the remains very soon after
death, and places the ashes in a simple container.

People are amazingly creative when it comes to scattering—or not—
their loved ones' ashes. It's possible to strap them to a firework and
arrange a special send-off display. Or you can place them in a biodegradable urn and hire a helium balloon, which will burst at 100,000
feet, sending the ashes far and wide. You can even arrange ahead of time
to have your ashes compressed into a vinyl record, which will actually
play a prerecorded personal message, your chosen play mix, or whatever
takes your fancy. The sculptor Ruth Asawa arranged for her son to mix
clay with her ashes to create a beautiful vessel. Most of us will probably
go a more mundane route. Though regulations vary by state, it is legal
to scatter ashes at sea or in areas of natural beauty, provided we follow
certain health and safety guidelines from the Environmental Protection Agency, the Bureau of Land Management, and the state where we
will leave the ashes.. My husband has requested that we carry his ashes
up a high mountain in Colorado and then release them at the top. I
hope that when that time comes, I am still able to climb, or I may have
to meet my kids at the top of the gondola.

Whatever we choose, there are several ways of paying ahead of time
for our funerals—through setting aside money in a trust or designated

savings account or buying special life insurance policies. Some people prepay for their funerals, to lock in a price and hopefully ease the burden on their families. But we need to be careful about this arrangement. The regulation of prepaid funerals varies by state, and we may not get our money back if, for example, we move to another state and need to cancel the contract or if the funeral home goes out of business.

Choosing to Die

While many people who are seriously ill want to pursue every available treatment option, others who are suffering at the end of life want to have a choice about when they will die. Medical aid in dying is the practice by which a terminally ill, mentally competent adult requests a lethal dose of medication for the purpose of ending their own life, and a doctor prescribes it. Public support for this is growing. A 2020 Gallup survey showed that 74 percent of adults say doctors should be allowed to end the life of patients "by some painless means" if they have an incurable disease and if they and their family request it.

As of 2023, ten U.S. states and the District of Columbia have laws that allow medical aid in dying. While the rules vary by state, the patient must generally meet several conditions related to residency, diagnosis, prognosis, and the ability to self-administer the medication. There are also set waiting periods. Doctors can choose not to participate, and most states require more than one doctor to certify that the conditions are met.

Data from several states shows that the majority of patients who die with medical aid are white, over sixty-five, and have at least some college education. The most common diagnosis is cancer. In states that have medical aid in dying laws, only a small fraction of the population uses them. In 2017 in California, just 577 patients received prescriptions out of a total of over 269,000 deaths. This gap between the percentage of Americans who say they approve of access to aid in dying and those who use it suggests that while most people would not choose it for themselves, they support giving others the option. It may also point to the challenge, for someone with a very serious health condition, of meeting all the criteria to qualify. Self-administration, for instance, could be difficult for a person suffering from advanced ALS.

While public support for medical aid in dying has increased, there is also strong opposition. The American Medical Association, the largest organization representing doctors across the country, argues that it is incompatible with the physician's role as healer. Several religious groups oppose it, though some make a distinction between taking active steps to end a life and forgoing treatments to prolong that life. Many disability rights groups worry that people who are marginalized, vulnerable, or living with a disability may be encouraged, or even coerced, to end their lives when what they actually need are the resources and supports to enable them to live well and with dignity.

My aim here is not to come down on one side or the other of the debate over medical aid in dying. It is clear no one should ever be coerced or forced to end their life, and I feel strongly that our society needs to provide much more health care, services, counseling, housing, and financial support, so that people with any level of disability or illness won't feel that death is their only option. With or without these laws, however, far too many older adults are making the excruciating decision to end their own lives, and not always due to advanced illness. Suicide is often regarded as a tragedy of the young, so I was shocked to learn that the highest rates of death by suicide are among those over eighty-five, while the rate of death by suicide for men seventy-five and older is twice that for men in their teens. The high rates among older people are linked to major depression and other mental illnesses, poor physical health or function, cognitive impairment, the feeling of being a burden to caregivers, and stressful life events. Isolation is also a factor, and social connectedness with family, friends, and community has been shown to act as a buffer against risk of death by suicide.

It is important to watch for warning signs.* If you or someone you know is struggling and needs emotional support, reach out for help or call the crisis hotline (988) or the Friendship Line (1-800-971-0016), a twenty-four-hour crisis intervention and nonurgent support service for people over sixty, disabled adults of all ages, and caregivers. Elder death by suicide is a crisis that gets far too little attention. We can all be on the lookout for signs, in our friends or family members, that may point to a danger of self-harm or suicide.

One famous case of elder death by suicide is that of Chester Nimitz, Jr., and his wife, Joan, in 2002. Chester, son of the commander of the Pacific Fleet during World War II, was himself a highly decorated admiral. Joan was a trained dentist who became a full-time mother to their three daughters. I got to know the family through my sister-in-law, Beth, who is the granddaughter of Chester and Joan. In the summer of 2022, I talked with their eldest daughter, Betsy, about her parents.

Betsy said that for more than a decade, Chester and Joan were very clear about their wishes. It wasn't that they were opposed to medical interventions; Chester had already undergone major heart surgery. But in their eighties, their health began to deteriorate. Joan had terrible back pain due to severe osteoporosis and had gone blind from macu-

---

* According to the American Association of Marriage and Family Therapy, specific warning signs include: loss of interest in things or activities usually found enjoyable; decreased social interaction, self-care, and grooming; breaking medical regimens (such as going off prescriptions); experiencing or expecting a significant personal loss (such as a spouse); feeling hopeless and/or worthless; putting affairs in order, giving things away, or making changes in wills; stockpiling medications or obtaining other lethal means; and having a preoccupation with death or lacking concern about personal safety. Remarks such as "This is the last time you'll see me" or "I won't be needing any more appointments" should raise concern. The most significant indicator is an expression of suicidal intent. See American Association of Marriage and Family Therapy, "Suicide in the Elderly," AAMFT.org.

lar degeneration. Chester had awful gastrointestinal problems, chronic back pain, and impaired vision. As Betsy told me, "The best medicines and the best doctors didn't help. They said over and over again, 'We've had fantastic lives. Life doesn't owe us a whole lot now.'"

The Nimitzes had a loving family and resources to get all the care and support they needed, yet they decided they didn't want to suffer any longer. They would have availed themselves of medical aid in dying had it been obtainable, but they did not have terminal diagnoses and lived in Massachusetts, which at the time didn't have a medical aid in dying statute. So they couldn't ask for assistance from their doctors. Instead, they spent years planning for what they would need.

They put their affairs in order and said their final goodbyes. On January 1, 2002, when they were eighty-six and eighty-nine, they took their own lives.

This experience has certainly had an impact on the family. Betsy went on to become an advocate for Compassion & Choices, a nonprofit group that supports medical aid in dying, and my sister-in-law, Beth, volunteered with hospice for many years.

Being with Someone Who Is Dying

Many of us will be close to someone in their final months and days. We may even be the one to make decisions for them if they're unable. In fact, a third of older Americans say they have had to decide about ending life support for a loved one. Talking with people like Sarah Creed and Diane Meier, and seeing my husband's brother caring for their dying mother, has made me think about how I can best support someone who is nearing the end of life and help them have the death they wish for.

Being with someone in their last days can be hard, both physically exhausting and emotionally challenging. We may not always be sure how to help ease suffering—sometimes the most important thing may simply be staying present, listening, and conveying how much we love them. But as many of us know who have accompanied a loved one facing death, it can also be a privilege and a profoundly meaningful, even sacred, experience.

People who are dying need care related to their physical comfort; their mental, emotional, and spiritual needs; and the practical concerns of their lives. I've already talked about some of these needs in the context of thinking about our own deaths: understanding what might be most important at the end of life, clarifying what kinds of medical care we believe we will or won't want, getting a sense of what our concerns or fears might be. When we are close to someone who is dying, these conversations are essential if we are going to act as the health care proxy, but even if we aren't in that official role, knowing these things can help us to provide the best support.

Likely, but not always, a team of family, friends, and medical experts will be involved in a person's end-of-life care, hopefully a hospice or palliative care team, and we can discuss particulars of medical care with them. We can help a person who is ill to understand whether a proposed treatment would benefit them, if its burdens would outweigh those benefits, and whether the quality of life after a treatment would align with their values and goals of care.

There are also things only a family member or close friend would know. My brother-in-law Scott figured out that Sybil, in order to die in peace, needed to know that her husband of sixty-one years would be okay. Scott decided that after Sybil died, he would move in with his father. He laughs now when he remembers Sybil's initial reaction to the idea: "Are you kidding me? You guys will kill each other!" Scott reassured her that it would work. (He made good on his promise, and though he and his dad would definitely have their moments, they lived together for five years.) Knowing that her husband wouldn't be alone was a big factor in Sybil saying she was ready to die. She passed with her husband and sons by her side.

We can also try to understand what to expect if we are present at the actual time of death. I asked Sarah Creed, who has been at so many bedsides, to describe it for me. She said the first sign that someone is approaching death is that they "start to go inward." Someone who was always chatty isn't talking so much. Maybe they loved watching the news but now just want music on in the house. The person becomes less mobile, getting out of bed less often, until eventually they aren't getting up at all. Their body isn't hungry anymore, so eating declines or stops. Sarah said that when this happens, it's very important not to force feed. "Food is love," she said, "and we always want to feed people." She and her team do a lot of work with families on this issue, letting them know that forcing someone to eat can actually cause problems and pain.

The person begins sleeping more and more, Sarah said, until they may be sleeping all day. Then we might hear a gurgling in the throat. Although Sarah has seen the "death rattle" go on for a full week, it tends to mean that the end is very near. The breaths get further apart, the spaces between them longer. It's hard for families to hear this sound, Sarah said, "but it's so much worse for us to hear than it is for the person who's experiencing it."

This stage can vary in length and intensity. There may be a big pain crisis, or death may come suddenly if, for instance, a few hours before dying, the person experiences a pulmonary embolism—a blocked blood vessel in the lungs—and gets very short of breath. In such cases, pain medication would likely be increased to make the person more comfortable. Whatever the progression to the end, it will arrive.

Living with Loss—but Living

Having nearly become a widow in my forties, I'm particularly sensitive to those who have lost a spouse, close family member, or good friend. I've talked a lot about the dangers of isolation throughout this book, and losing key people in our life, whoever they may be, can hit us hard, both emotionally and financially.

When I was on a retreat in early 2023, I struck up a conversation with a woman named Lark from Iowa. Lark was seventy-seven. Four months earlier she had lost her husband of forty-six years to cancer. She had cared for Lew until near the end. They put a hospital bed next to their own bed at home so they could hold hands at night. When Lark could no longer manage his care, Lew went to a hospice facility. The nurses there told Lark, "You can be his wife now instead of his nurse."

When Lark could see that the end was near, she held Lew's hand and said, "It's okay if you go. But I will miss you." And then Lew died.

Since Lew's passing, one of the things Lark was finding hardest was visiting the grocery store. She had loved to cook for Lew and had always shopped with him in mind, but now she had no idea what to buy. One day she left the store with just bananas. On Lew's birthday, she baked him a chocolate cake, just as she always had, even though he was no longer there to enjoy it. She took it to her sister's, and they ate the whole thing. For two days, Lark couldn't stop crying.

Lark is one of more than eleven million widows in the United States. About 3.5 million men are widowers. Of adults seventy-five or older who have been married at least once, 58 percent of women and 28 percent of men have lost a spouse, so as we grow older, widowhood is a very common experience.

Lark had never traveled alone before, but her daughter helped her arrange a trip to the retreat. She was feeling courageous, she told me, but she was also lonely without Lew. I was glad to see her getting out. Many older people who live on their own end up spending a huge amount of their time alone. We know that social isolation isn't good for us, and losing a spouse can actually shorten our lives. Older adults face a 66 percent increase in risk of death during the first few months of grieving the loss of a spouse. While the causes of this "widowhood effect" are unclear, we know that caring for someone at the end of their life can have a big impact on a person's health. Grief has psychological effects, and social connections may be lost. If a loved one's death is sudden and traumatic, the survivor's heart muscle can actually weaken. It's as though one literally dies of a broken heart. Speaking to a therapist, staying busy and connected with others, getting a pet, and practicing good self-care (eating well, exercising, and getting enough rest) have all been shown to help in the aftermath of loss.

In addition to its emotional and psychological challenges, widowhood brings practical concerns too. In the first two years of being widowed, women overall experience a 22 percent drop in income and a 10 percent loss of wealth, even as many household expenses stay the same. (Widowers tend to remain financially stable, but their mental and emotional health deteriorates more sharply, and they experience greater loneliness and depression.) Becoming the sole financial decision-maker can be challenging for widows, especially those who shared management of finances with their spouse or whose spouses managed the finances alone. They may lack access to bank accounts, credit cards, and other important bills and records if their spouse didn't leave instructions and passwords. Given that half of widows over sixty-five will survive their spouse by fifteen years, they can face big responsibilities alone over long periods of time. Experts advise new widows to get an objective review of their financial situation, and not to rush into making decisions about finances or where they will live while still in the midst of grief.

The good news is that grief eases over time. In a survey of seventy thousand widows, women in their first year after loss reported higher rates of depressed mood, poorer social and physical functioning, and lower mental health. But when interviewed three years later, their mental health, moods, and social functioning had all improved.

We need to mourn at our own pace and acknowledge that grieving doesn't always start with the passing of our loved one. It can begin at diagnosis, then ease when we know that our loved one is no longer suffering. Grief occurs in stages, and it comes and goes, so it's important to understand that our grief doesn't need to look a certain way. Lark told me that even as she still grieved, "It's more about how do I live. How do I make a life? I want to live out these years in a good way, a full way."

Lark's comment strikes me as a nice summary of what all of us tend to want as we grow older: a good, full life, however we define it. And near the end, we want compassionate and sensible care that we can afford. The people I spoke to while writing this chapter have worked incredibly hard to alleviate suffering and to make the treatment of chronic illness and dying more humane. They have laid a solid foundation, and our policymakers and health care system need to build on it. We need a system guided by the goal of treating the whole person—right up to our last breath.

8

A Better Second Fifty

Americans are caught in some grim contradictions. We live in the richest country in the world, which spends more per person on health care than any other nation, but our lives are shorter than those of citizens of certain poorer countries. We boast of having some of the most sophisticated medical technology and know-how, and yet in 2019 the health outcomes of Americans aged fifty-five to sixty-nine were so much worse than those of citizens of our peer nations; if our health was on par with theirs, 200,000 fewer of us would have died. And while we have a history of tackling big challenges successfully, many of our institutions and policies that support older citizens—the infrastructure that makes it easier to age well—have become sadly outdated.

Unless we make big changes, this picture is only going to worsen as our older population gets bigger. By 2030, one in five Americans will be over sixty-five. More people than ever are living into their eighties, nineties, and even past one hundred. Many of these older adults and their families are struggling with the high costs of medical care while trying to meet their monthly housing bills. They continue to work despite physical pain and chronic illness. They wonder if they will outlive their savings, and if Social Security can keep them afloat.

I had always expected that the aging and retirement of the baby boom generation would awaken policymakers to the needs of older people. And there has been progress. When Medicare was first established, for example, it did not cover the cost of most prescription drugs; this changed in 2003, when President George W. Bush signed the Medicare Prescription Drug, Improvement, and Modernization Act. And even as the number of people on Medicare and Medicaid has risen, the per-person growth in costs has dropped dramatically. The reasons are many: shifts in care from hospitals to cheaper settings; changes in legislation; increased use of technology and generic drugs; and a shift from Medicaid payments for nursing homes to payments for less expensive home care. This reduction in spending can free up billions of dollars in federal and state budgets for nonhealth social care and preventive care, which could reduce health spending even more.

But the progress we've made has been mostly at the margins of issues rather than at the big-picture level, which would take into account the interconnectedness of problems and solutions. In the meantime, other countries have been forging ahead. Currently more than one hundred countries have taken steps toward creating and implementing plans for their aging populations, either at the local level or nationwide. Some U.S. states have them in place. Often referred to as action plans or master plans for aging, their goal is to serve as a strategic and comprehensive framework for providing the services and supports needed by an aging population. When designed well, these plans touch on every part of society, recommending or mandating actions to be taken by the nonprofit, private, and public sectors, and by individuals. They provide a blueprint for policymakers to efficiently allocate resources and ensure funding, and they can be updated as new issues emerge. Importantly, action plans reject the traditional single-issue approach and instead address health, finances, housing, and social support needs together.

An action plan needs long-term political and financial commitment, so that it isn't just shelved when those who championed it are no longer in office. It's not a minor undertaking. But the playbook for implementing big solutions to the big problems facing an aging society has worked in the past: President Roosevelt's Committee on Economic Security created Social Security, and President Johnson's Great Society created Medicare and Medicaid. Without such plans, many of us would be far worse off today in our second fifty. What we need now is a plan on the scale of the Great Society, one containing an entire series of reforms and new programs to meet our current challenges. We need a plan for a Great Aging Society.

Two Models of a Plan for Aging

In 2021, the state of California released its Master Plan for Aging, envisioning "a California for all ages by 2030." I had heard a lot of buzz about this plan and wondered how it might differ from previous initiatives there that had been full of good ideas but had mostly gathered dust on the shelf. To find out, I called Fernando Torres-Gill, who is a giant in the fields of aging and disability. He served as the first ever assistant secretary on aging under President Bill Clinton and is now a professor at UCLA and the University of Southern California. The son of migrant farm workers, Fernando developed polio as a child and underwent numerous surgeries. His mother, who was raising nine children in public housing, got him into Shriners Hospital, which offered free care to children with disabilities. While there, he got a very good education and excellent services. This experience has influenced how he approaches his work. "Facing disability at an early age gave me skills, resilience and a sense of humor," he said, then added, with a laugh, "Always finding a silver lining even if it's not there."

In California, aging advocates worked together to ensure that Governor Gavin Newsom was personally committed to developing and implementing a master plan. Then they essentially locked everyone into a room—academics, health care providers, disability rights groups, older adults, and government stakeholders—and said, "If you're going to grow old in California, what are the four or five things that are most important to allow you to have a quality of life?"

Ultimately, Fernando said, they realized they couldn't do all things for all people. But common ground, five things everyone wanted, did emerge: housing, health care, inclusion and equity, caregiving, and economic security. Based on those overarching goals, the Master Plan for Aging contains twenty-three strategies and more than one hundred initiatives for action, and it encourages collaboration across government, the private sector, and community-based organizations. Fortunately, the process unfolded at a time of fiscal surplus, so the governor directed resources to making sure the plan was implemented.

The plan wasn't just about addressing the problems facing older people—it had to be about helping *everyone* age better. "If we don't invest in younger people," Fernando said, "their health, their education, their income security, they're going to grow old as poor and very sick people." There was also a critical equity component. California is a majority-minority state, and as Fernando pointed out, young children, particularly in communities of color, have high rates of obesity and diabetes that have to be addressed in order to reduce long-term medical and health costs. Lastly, the plan brought aging and disability together, including people of all ages who have disabilities.

Three years into implementation, California's Master Plan has taken important steps toward creating a more age- and disability-friendly state. It is reducing co-payments for low-income people on Medicaid, increasing the number of people who can access services—including assisted living—and exploring options for offering its own statewide long-term care insurance. It hasn't solved every problem, but it is an important step in the right direction.

California is not the only state to have a multisector plan; a handful of others have developed plans or have state mandates to do so. There is only so much, though, that individual states can do—they can't improve Social Security or Medicare, for instance. We also need big policy solutions at the national level.

A number of countries have developed multisector plans for aging. One I've seen up close is in Singapore. Roughly the size of Rhode Island, this city-state boasts an average life expectancy of almost eighty-five years, one of the world's longest. In 2015 the government unveiled its multipronged action plan to support people of all ages in living active, engaged, and healthy lives. It contains policies and programs in education, employment, volunteering, housing, wellness, retirement security, and social inclusion. The plan is well funded and monitored and pays special attention to vulnerable older adults. The "Skills Future Credit" support that I mentioned in Chapter 4, which gives citizens money to set up education accounts and helps workers keep their skills current, is part of this plan.

Here in the United States, at the federal level, we need to learn from what's happening around the world and within our own states and build on the best ideas. I'm going to outline my own action plan and describe strategies that the private sector can adopt. I could write an entire book on each one of these policy solutions, and a slew of reports have been written calling for action in many of these areas—the National Academy of Medicine's recently released Global Roadmap on Healthy Longevity is a good one. But I'll stick to a few broad ideas and some specific proposals for meeting the challenges raised in the previous seven chapters.

Three Guiding Priorities

A few issues cut across virtually everything we need to do to enable a healthier, happier, and more financially secure second fifty. Working on them will have positive ripple effects. Failing to address them will make it hard, if not impossible, to bring about real change.

Eliminate Ageism and Age Discrimination

Ageism is the belief that older people are less capable or of less worth as human beings. It involves stereotypes and prejudices we hold and forms of discrimination we enact based on age. When we turn ageism on ourselves, it worsens our health and shortens our longevity.

In the policy arena, ageism means discounting the needs of older adults, especially when they require care or have disabilities or cognitive issues. The fact that we still don't properly fund quality, affordable, long-term care is an example of our failure to prioritize older people's needs.

As a result of age discrimination in employment, older workers are less likely to be hired and are more likely to be passed over for promotions or laid off. This discrimination doesn't just marginalize, or even impoverish, people; it's bad for the economy. In 2018 the economy could have been 4 percent larger if older workers had not faced discriminatory barriers to working longer; this staggering figure will grow dramatically by the middle of this century if we don't make changes. Employers need to understand the costs of age discrimination in terms of lost talent and their own bottom line. Businesses hurt their own growth by not having a workforce that represents their customer base—and in an aging society, this base will include more and more older people.

In addition to having an unbiased workplace culture, older workers should have an easier time proving age discrimination in court. A federal law makes discriminating against people over forty illegal, yet a Supreme Court ruling has made it extremely challenging for any private sector workers to bring cases against their employers, even when there is a clear track record of ageism in the workplace. The Court ruled that it is not enough to show that age was a factor in the discrimination; a worker must now prove age was the *decisive* factor. This is a much higher bar than the legal standards required in complaints of discrimination based on race, gender, or religion. For more than a decade, a bill to restore the previous legal standard has languished in Congress.

Ageism is particularly harmful within the health care system. Older people's health concerns may be dismissed, and care and treatment withheld, because of biases about what aging should look and feel like. One in five people over fifty report having experienced this kind of discrimination; of that group, three in ten said it led to their health declining. Training health care workers to become aware of their own ageist prejudices can lead to more compassionate, effective care.

Reducing ageism will require a shift in mindset. Younger people need more intergenerational contact so that they encounter positive role models of aging. We must all catch ourselves and check others when ageist stereotypes are used, so that they become taboo. And we have to shed the myths and negative stereotypes that say aging is solely a time of decline and understand that the second half of life is also a period of growth, optimism, and meaningful participation. What we do during these years can be just as valuable as what we do in the first half of our lives.

Eliminate Disparities

It is easier to take a step up from the bottom stair than to raise the ceiling. The most effective way to increase our collective healthspans, lifespans, and even economic security is to level the playing field so that everyone has a fair chance at a long and healthy life.

The cost of inaction is high. Individuals experience personal loss, and our society misses out on their potential talents and productivity. One study found that over a four-year period, Americans lived an aggregate of 3.5 million years less due to premature death and spent $230 billion on medical care due to racial and ethnic health disparities. By 2030, if these inequities in life expectancy are not addressed, the U.S. gross domestic product will be more than 5 percent lower, and the United States will have around ten million fewer jobs. As our peer countries reap the benefits of healthier populations and more productive workforces, our own economy will continue to fall behind.

Racial and ethnic disparities often widen over whole lifetimes, so narrowing them requires taking a whole-life approach. This means improving maternal health, expanding pre-K education, and reducing high school dropout rates for communities of color. It means addressing residential segregation and poverty and improving both community safety and infrastructure. Eliminating disparities in access to care is critical, but ensuring equal treatment by the health care system has to follow.

Men and women must have an equal chance to live a good second half of life. Evidence from around the world shows that when gender equity improves, the life expectancy of both women and men rises. Workforce inequities must be eliminated, the responsibilities of child care and caregiving more equally shared, and access to capital expanded for women who want to start businesses and purchase homes. These changes can help remove the economic obstacles that rob women of long-term financial security.

While we can't change biology, we can take steps to address the social and cultural causes of men's shorter lives. One immediate reason for men's earlier deaths is that they often put off visits to doctors even when they suspect something might be wrong. Programs such as the Cleveland Clinic's MENtion It! encourage men to confide in their doctors when they notice symptoms, thereby helping to remove the stigma around seeking medical care. A comprehensive approach to reducing the rising death toll among men in mid- to late life from suicide and alcohol and drug poisoning—deaths of despair—is critical.

Increase Educational Attainment

If education were a pill, every doctor would prescribe it. It increases life expectancy, heads off deaths of despair, and even lengthens our healthspan. Low-quality education for children has been correlated with higher rates of dementia later in life. Expanding educational opportunities must start at the preschool level and continue throughout life. While the share of adults with a bachelor's degree has risen, more than one in three people over twenty-five have only a high school diploma or less. One study showed that closing the health gap between those who do and don't have a college degree would save more lives than all our investments in medical advances. If everyone in the United States had the same longevity as those with a college degree, this country would be among the longest lived of its peer countries rather than at the bottom of that list.

According to research by Jennifer Karas Montez at Syracuse University, education functions as a kind of "personal firewall," blunting the differences in longevity between states. "If you have a college degree or more," she told me, "it pretty much doesn't matter where you live. But as you have less and less education, where you live matters so much." This is because the more education we have, the more resources we are likely to have, and the less we are at the mercy of safety net programs such as unemployment insurance and affordable health insurance.

Expanding affordable higher education helps to reduce income inequality by giving more people access to better and higher-paying jobs that provide them with the kind of health and retirement benefits that make a real difference as they get older.

We are being hindered as a nation by rising tuition costs that make college unaffordable for many. Skyrocketing student debt is being carried by multiple generations, often into retirement. A majority of Americans now feel that a four-year college degree isn't worth the cost. In fact, 2023 marked the sixth straight year of declining enrollment for both two- and four-year colleges. These trends may have a long-term impact not only on our economy but on the health, wealth, and longevity of future generations as they age.

In Wisconsin, an innovative program was proposed to establish 401(K)ids accounts. These savings accounts would be given to every child, seeded with contributions from the government, philanthropies, and families, then invested to build wealth over their lifetime. The money could be used for education, medical emergencies, first-time home purchases, and even retirement. Studies of similar education-focused accounts that have been set up for kids show they increase financial resources and change parents' expectations, as being college bound improves children's social and emotional development.

In addition to making college more affordable for anyone who wants to attend, we need a range of better and more secure jobs for people with all levels of education. Investing in community colleges, apprenticeships, vocational programs, and specialized training for skilled labor will help those who don't need a full college education to do high-paying work. The Tennessee Promise program, for example, offers a scholarship for two years of tuition-free community college or technical school to all recent high school graduates or adults without an associate's degree. At the same time, private companies and many states have begun to recognize that people can develop skills and valuable experience outside a four-year college, and they are removing requirements for job applicants to have a bachelor's degree—including for state jobs, senior-level posts, and positions in finance, health care, and other areas.

Finally, we need continuous education and training throughout our lives, not just in our younger years. Investment in innovative models that target middle-age and older students to support lifelong learning—such as allowing those who took time off work to return to school to collect their Social Security payments, and offering reduced tuition or even free programs at public universities or community colleges—will enable more of us to keep our skills fresh and challenge our brains as we age.

Chapter-by-Chapter Solutions

1. We Could Be Living Longer

One reason for Americans' lower life expectancy is that far too many of us are dying before our fiftieth birthday. Our infant mortality rate is one of the highest among wealthy countries, despite having proven interventions such as quality prenatal and infant care and safe sleep environments for infants. But midlife mortality is also rising, and addressing that will take a multipronged approach. Implementing the recommendations in the 2021 National Academies consensus report on reducing deaths of despair would be a good place to start: its long list of policy solutions ranges from addressing the opioid crisis to improving cardiometabolic health.

TARGET DISPARITIES

One of the most effective ways to increase life expectancy is to direct more help toward those most in need. American longevity differs by more than a decade between people at the top of the economic ladder and those at the bottom, but in our peer countries, poverty doesn't result in such a big gap. Compared with other developed nations, our social protection benefits are stingy. Social Security replaces less of a worker's earnings than do public pensions in most developed countries. Our rules for qualifying for unemployment payments are stricter, and the benefits are smaller and of shorter duration. As the pandemic revealed, many workers have no sick leave at all. According to one study, U.S. life expectancy would gain five and a half years if our antipoverty spending matched that of Denmark, Finland, Norway, or Sweden.

Policies at the state and local level have a big impact on life expectancy. There is a nearly nine-year gap in average lifespan between the longest lived state (Hawaii) and the shortest (Mississippi). Jennifer Karas Montez and her colleagues found that states with longer life expectancies have strong policies on, for example, raising taxes on tobacco and curbing its use, supporting workers through increased minimum wage, and paid family leave.

Local policies, as well as investments by nonprofits and the private sector, also matter. Beaufort County, in the Lowcountry region of South Carolina, went from having one of the lowest life expectancies in the state to having one of the highest over the last two decades. In large part this was due to a community health center that, among other things, located its health clinic, pharmacy, and senior center in adjoining buildings on the same campus. That proximity enables older people coming to the center to maintain social connections while having their health concerns addressed. The community health center also forged partnerships with local farms to provide farmworker health programs, and it stays open in the evenings so that more people can access its services.

ADDRESS THE SOCIAL DRIVERS OF HEALTH

Social drivers of health—including economic and social mobility, education, neighborhood environment, housing, transportation, and nutrition—are the most important factors in determining our health and longevity. If we want to remedy persistent health disparities across populations, we will need systemic solutions to these interconnected problems. Improving the health of those with chronic conditions requires providing them not only with better access to health care but also affordable supportive housing. Making it easier for people to engage in healthy behaviors (eating a nutritious diet, exercising, and quitting smoking) requires bringing resources to low-income communities and situating affordable housing in areas where opportunities for quality education, recreation, and access to jobs already exist. We need to make sure people have easy access to affordable healthy food and to expand nutrition programs such as Meals on Wheels, which delivers meals to more than 2.2 million of the ten million people over sixty who struggle with food insecurity.

Poverty and racism intersect with these social drivers, so reducing disparities in our longevity and health will require tackling both. Data from nearly four hundred Black adults collected over three decades found that by the time they reached fifty those who had been targeted by racism multiple times and in multiple contexts had aged biologically about *six years more* than white people of the same chronological age. In practical terms, this means that many older black Americans face more disability and experience more pain and suffering, and so they have greater need for physical assistance.

There is no silver bullet or single solution to these issues. Addressing the social drivers of health will require the public and private sectors to partner on a range of solutions that invest in health, housing, and other supportive services and to improve access and service delivery for those most in need. Expanding evidence-based programs that utilize a "Health in All Policies" approach—which incorporates health and equity into all levels of policymaking—is an important start.

Finally, we need to take action on the "social" part of the social drivers of health. Feeling connected to others is key to our mental and physical health and our longevity. The U.K. and Japan have actually established Ministers for Loneliness, who work to reduce the stigma around loneliness, ensure that it is taken into account when policy is made, and support citizens to have meaningful social relationships. In 2023 the U.S. surgeon general, Vivek Murthy, issued a report on the "epidemic" of loneliness and isolation. It affirmed the healing effects of social connection and community and proposed a range of actions that government bodies, organizations, media, and individuals can take. Some of the recommendations for individuals are straightforward and have the added benefit of being enjoyable, which isn't to say they are always easy: nurturing relationships, practicing gratitude, joining community groups, and seeking opportunities to support others. We also need to be open with our health care providers if we're struggling.

2. Extending Our Healthspans

Most of the recent gains in life expectancy have led to additional years of poor rather than good health. Americans' lives are not just shorter than those of people in many other countries, they are also less healthy. In 2019 the average sixty-year-old American could expect to enjoy good health until age sixty-six—four years fewer than a sixty-year-old in Japan and three fewer than someone of that age in France. If our physical condition varies so much across borders, it clearly isn't determined by our birthdate.

Maintaining or even improving our health as we age will require healthy behaviors, better access to quality health care, the prevention or delay of chronic illnesses, and a better-trained workforce to care for us. Continued investment in the science of extending our healthspans is critical, as is ensuring that any future geroprotective treatments that slow the aging process are safe, affordable, and accessible to everyone.

EVERYONE NEEDS HEALTH INSURANCE

The passage of the Affordable Care Act, along with new rules put in place during the pandemic to ensure consistent coverage and extra financial help for buying insurance, led to a historic high in the number of insured Americans in 2022. However, 5.6 million people between fifty and sixty-four were still uninsured, leaving them less likely to get the medical care they need. A wide range of policy solutions could improve affordability and access to insurance. Some states have not expanded health coverage through Medicaid for low-income residents—despite the fact that federal taxes from those states are subsidizing expanded coverage in other states. Researchers from the National Bureau of Economic Research estimated that the lack of coverage in these holdout states led to more than fifteen thousand preventable deaths. Expanding access to affordable health insurance by increasing subsidies and tax credits that lower costs, along with strong outreach and enrollment efforts so that people know which programs they are eligible for, would help ensure that everyone can access the health care they need.

Evidence is building that oral, hearing, and vision care are all important components of maintaining good overall health. Despite the fact that our teeth, ears, and eyes are all affected by aging, most insurance programs, including Medicare, provide minimal coverage for their care. One in five adults over sixty-five has untreated tooth decay, over two-thirds have gum disease, and nearly one in five has lost all their teeth. Research has linked poor oral health to chronic conditions such as heart disease, diabetes, depression, and dementia. Similarly, older adults with untreated hearing loss end up in the hospital more often and are more likely to develop dementia. Vision loss impacts not only the quality of our lives, but also our ability to function and live independently. If oral, vision, and hearing care could be fully integrated with medical care, the savings from improved health could help offset some of the costs of the new benefits.

SUPPORT PRIMARY CARE AND PREVENTIVE SERVICES

The best way to keep ourselves healthy is to avoid becoming sick in the first place. Yet only 5 percent of U.S. health spending is on prevention and public health activities, and we continue to undervalue primary care. Numerous studies have shown that greater use of primary care is associated with fewer hospitalizations and emergency department visits, and with lower mortality. In contrast to specialty care, primary care is linked to a more equitable distribution of health across populations; it can also offset the negative impact on health of poor economic circumstances. Primary care doctors can help patients manage chronic diseases earlier, enabling better outcomes over the long term and reducing costs. In Oregon, an assessment of the Patient Centered Primary Care Home Program found that for every dollar the state invested in primary care, it saved thirteen dollars in other areas, such as specialty care, emergency department use, and inpatient expenses. Unfortunately, adults in the United States are less likely to have a regular doctor or a long-standing relationship with a primary care provider than people in other wealthy countries.

Increasing investments in preventive care can help Americans reach midlife and the years beyond in better health. Every year more than 1.5 million of us have a heart attack or stroke, making cardiovascular disease the leading cause of death in the United States and a key reason life expectancy here is falling behind that of other countries. We can reduce our risk for heart disease by stopping smoking, managing our weight, and exercising regularly. But heart disease is not the only cause of mortality that can be prevented or delayed. Only 25 percent of adults aged fifty to sixty-four are up to date on core CDC-recommended preventive services such as screenings for chronic conditions, immunizations for diseases like influenza and pneumonia, and counseling about personal health behaviors. Meanwhile, the United States ranks first in obesity among the world's largest and wealthiest nations. Obesity rates in children are skyrocketing, potentially shortening future generations' lifespans and healthspans. One in five deaths in people between forty and eighty-five can now be traced to obesity. Life expectancy in the United States would rise by three to four months if everyone were able to maintain their recommended weight. Finally, making it harder and more expensive to smoke can improve our healthspan and extend our lives. Doctors should encourage their patients who use tobacco to enroll in tobacco-use cessation counseling sessions. It is never too late to get the health benefits of stopping smoking, and Medicare covers up to eight smoking and tobacco-use cessation counseling sessions per year.

INCREASE THE NUMBER OF GERIATRICIANS

The United States has a severe shortage of health care providers, including doctors, nurses, and direct care staff, all needed in an aging society. Especially troubling is the fact that the number of geriatricians has been falling since 2000, even as the population of older Americans grows. Geriatrics is one of the lowest-paid medical specialties, despite the fact these specialists see patients with some of the most complex health concerns, including multiple chronic health conditions. Programs that promote aging sensitivity training to medical students can help bring more professionals into the field, as can greater incentives for students and young doctors such as scholarships, grants, and assistance repaying loans. Changing aspects of Medicare could incentivize young doctors to provide better care—geriatric as well as primary—through insurance reimbursement that takes account of the often complex needs of older patients.

Beyond training more geriatric specialists, it's critical that we "geriatricize" the medical profession, meaning every health care provider should be trained in the needs of older adults, including dementia care. Rather than limit this important knowledge to a relatively small subset of practitioners, we should emphasize geriatrics and the unique

needs of older patients in training, education, and continuing education standards for all health care providers. The federally funded Geriatrics Workforce Enhancement Program provides grants to schools of
medicine and nursing, primary care practices, long-term care settings,
and other institutions to improve the health of older people, in part
by integrating geriatrics into primary care. Increasing funding for this
program and prioritizing geriatrics training for all medical professionals could help us achieve a health care workforce that is better prepared
for an aging society.

INVEST IN THE SCIENCE OF HEALTHY LONGEVITY

Investments in geroscience research are currently only a tiny fraction
of our total spending on medical research. Putting money into geroscience will lead to better understanding of the biology of aging, and
potentially find ways to prevent, delay, alleviate, or treat age-related diseases and conditions. Ideally that research will help to uncover effective
and, hopefully, affordable geroprotectors—medications and strategies
that can slow the processes of aging—which have the potential to give
us more years in good health. The financial benefits to society of delaying disease are huge: one study conducted by researchers at London
Business School, University of Oxford, and Harvard Medical School
found that a slowdown in aging that increases life expectancy by one
year could be worth up to $38 trillion. Delaying the onset of age-related
diseases such as cancer, cardiovascular disease, or dementia increases
the likelihood that we'll live longer lives, spending more time in good
health and, potentially, more time working. All this results in economic
benefit for individuals and societies.

3. Support Better Brain Health

While dementia is not an inevitable element of aging, the number of
people with dementia and cognitive decline is expected to rise dramatically as the world's population ages. In the absence of new treatments,
the number of older Americans diagnosed with Alzheimer's disease is

projected to reach 8.5 million by 2030 and fourteen million by 2060. Those numbers don't include the millions of people with other forms of dementia and cognitive decline. Some groups will be affected more than others. Among Black Americans aged sixty-five or older, 14 percent have Alzheimer's disease or a related dementia, compared to 12 percent of Hispanic older adults, and 10 percent of white adults. As we work to reduce the number of people with Alzheimer's, it will be essential to create tailored solutions to simultaneously reduce risks for all communities.

Investments in slowing down the incidence and progression of these diseases can pay big dividends. Alzheimer's is already the most expensive disease in the United States. In 2019 the cost per person, including health care and the value of unpaid care, was about $81,000 a year—four times that of care for people of similar age without the disease. That year the total cost related to people with dementia was $290 billion, between Medicare, Medicaid, private insurance, and out-of-pocket payments. If the onset of dementia could be delayed by even five years, it would save $145 billion in direct health care costs.

REDUCE RISK AND SLOW PROGRESSION

Solutions are needed urgently to slow the progression of the disease and to target its underlying causes. In the meantime, we all must become aware of what we can do to support our own brain health and lower our risk of cognitive decline and dementia. In 2022 an Alzheimer's disease risk study conducted predominantly on lower-income Black adults followed more than seventeen thousand people sixty-five and older. The researchers found that healthy lifestyles (including exercising, limiting alcohol consumption to low or moderate levels, not smoking, and following a nutritious diet) were associated with an 11 to 25 percent reduction in risk of Alzheimer's and other dementias. The more healthy habits people had, the greater their risk reduction: those in the top quarter saw a *36 percent reduced risk of dementia*. But effective strategies for brain health must go beyond individual behavior. Making healthier lifestyles more accessible and affordable to diverse populations, and addressing the social drivers of health and the inequities that result in food deserts, unsafe neighborhoods, limited or low-quality education, and poor health care, are essential for eliminating disparities in dementia risk.

The National Plan to Address Alzheimer's Disease, released in 2012, includes ambitious goals, such as the effective treatment and eventual prevention of Alzheimer's disease and other dementias and expanded support for the millions of families coping with dementia. By coordinating related activities across the federal government, it has broken down long-standing silos and forged partnerships between public and private stakeholders. A new goal adopted in 2021 expands research on risk factors and advances actions to promote healthy aging, especially among those at greatest risk, such as Black, Hispanic, and American Indian populations, and lower-income adults. Thankfully, federal funding of the National Institutes of Health for research into Alzheimer's disease and related dementias has increased nearly eightfold in the last decade.

PROVIDE BETTER CARE AND TREATMENT

The American health care system needs to be reformed so that people receive quality care at all stages of an illness—beginning with screening and diagnosis. Screening can help with early detection and create a baseline against which to compare change. But today the majority of people with dementia either aren't being diagnosed or are unaware that they have the condition even when they have been diagnosed. Medicare began paying for cognitive assessments and dementia care planning in 2017, but only 1.5 percent of those on Medicare who were eligible for screening received it in 2020. Clinicians need training in how to detect warning signs of cognitive decline, the effective use of screening tools, and perhaps most important, how to communicate their findings to patients. Providing patients with an accurate diagnosis that explains changes they are experiencing is critical so that they can start thinking about putting a care plan and caregiver network in place. Doctors need to tell families how symptoms may change over time and how they can support their loved ones and care for themselves.

Quality care for people with dementia is complex because it involves addressing the medical, mental, emotional, legal, and social problems of both patients *and* their caregivers. Medicare was generally designed to pay only for acute medical services delivered to a patient by doctors or hospitals one visit at a time. It is not set up to pay for the type and level of services needed to address the complex problems that come with dementia or nonmedical care for the patient or direct support for caregivers. Medicare could be expanded to pay for things like in-home services to help with bathing, dressing, cooking, and medication management; caregiver support such as respite and training in managing behavioral and psychological symptoms; social services, including adult day care to provide cognitive engagement and prevent social isolation; and disease management support to help avoid legal and financial crises. Such payment reform would enable patients to maintain independence and a better quality of life and could help sustain caregivers and support them in keeping their loved one at home as long as possible. It would also help to prevent crises that too often land people with dementia in hospitals and nursing homes, an outcome that increases suffering and unnecessarily drives up costs for both Medicare and the family.

It is very welcome news that a new program is being tested within Medicare to provide these types of supports for people with dementia and their caregivers. The GUIDE Model provides access to a dementia-trained "care navigator," who serves as a point of contact and helps to facilitate communication between a family and their loved one's clinical team; schedules appointments and other care activities; and provides support to caregivers. The program also provides much-needed respite for caregivers and a 24/7 support line. The GUIDE Model will run as an experiment with a limited number of families for eight years and, if shown to be successful at keeping people out of nursing homes, could be integrated into Medicare for those living with dementia and their caregivers going forward.

4. Helping Those Who Want or Need to Work Longer

Older Americans are working longer and in larger numbers than ever before. Today twice as many people fifty-five and older either have a job or are looking for one as were working or seeking work in the 1990s. Yet far too many older workers are pushed out of the workforce due to age discrimination, a lack of competitive skills, declines in health, or the need to care for a loved one. Federal and state governments, employers, and people of all ages need to reimagine what it means to earn over a lifetime.

END AGE DISCRIMINATION IN EMPLOYMENT

Recognizing the value of older, experienced workers and eliminating age bias is a win-win for workers and employers alike. Older workers get access to the jobs they need, while employers benefit from older employees' high level of engagement and lower rates of turnover. Firms with more age diversity, especially those with higher numbers of older workers, have been found to be more productive and make better decisions. Age-inclusive recruitment, advancement, and retention practices can allow companies to attract and keep multigenerational talent. Ending the use of age or graduation dates in résumés or the requirement of certain qualifications—"digital natives," "recent college grads," or maximum years of experience—can encourage an age-diverse talent pool for new hires. Small innovations in company practices, such as opening internships to people of all ages—and offering "returnships" for workers who have had to step away from their jobs for their own health or to be a caregiver—can also ensure that a workplace is age-diverse.

PROVIDE BETTER JOBS WITH GOOD BENEFITS

The quality of our jobs early in life can have a big impact on our later health and financial security. Jobs that offer reasonable compensation, retirement, health, wellness and caregiving benefits, and options for phased retirement can provide a solid foundation for retirement security. Workplace benefits need to evolve, especially to accommodate the growing number of workers who are trying to balance their jobs with responsibilities as family caregivers. The system we have, in which employers can choose whether to offer health and retirement benefits, leaves far too many Americans without the basic protections that citizens in most other developed countries enjoy. This is where federal, state, and even local policies can have the biggest impact, covering those who do not have paid leave, health insurance, or retirement savings through their employer.

Over the course of our lifetime, we spend on average ninety thousand hours working, so the physical environment of our workplace is an important social driver of health, whether it is a factory, an office, or our home. Our health and well-being obviously suffer from exposure to hazards and pollutants, physical strain, and stressors such as long working hours and shift work. Advance scheduling, so that workers know their shifts days or weeks in advance, can reduce stress and improve productivity. Investment in a healthy work environment and workplace health programs can benefit both companies and the larger economy by extending the productive lives of all workers.

PROVIDE OPPORTUNITIES TO KEEP JOB SKILLS UP TO DATE

The skills we gain when young, whether at school or at work, may, decades later, no longer be relevant to the job market, as technologies and entire industries evolve or disappear completely. By providing workers with continued education and training, especially enhanced opportunities to remain and grow on the job, our society can help them stay employable as they age. Federal and state job-training programs must focus on older job seekers, informing them about the skills that are most in demand. Reliable information on the quality of training programs can be hard to find amid the blizzard of degrees and certificate programs, and oversight of institutions is needed to safeguard against fraud. Financial aid could be reformed to make grants available for short-term training to help people who need to update their skills. Tax credits could be expanded and deductions offered for education-related expenses such as transportation and caregiving. Lifelong learning accounts, like those set up for workers in Singapore, could be established for training and educating older job seekers. Finally, educational programs themselves could be more flexible, allowing people to juggle their work and personal commitments by incorporating supports such as childcare and accelerated class schedules.

SUPPORT CAREGIVERS

One reason people of all ages quit their jobs, turn down promotions, or cut back to part-time hours, is the need to care for a family member or friend with a serious illness or disability. Workplaces that support us in caring for both children and adults can help us manage our responsibilities without sacrificing our careers or immediate or long-term financial security. Flexible scheduling along with paid sick, family, and caregiving leave can allow someone who needs to take time off for child or adult care to remain in the workforce longer. Lower-cost programs, such as training for middle managers and employee resource groups, can help support working caregivers. Access to high-quality and affordable adult and child day care and backup care helps workers balance home and work responsibilities. Expanding the federal Family Medical Leave Act or state family leave laws would help more caregivers take the unpaid time off they need and ensure that they will have a job to return to.

5. We Could Be More Financially Secure in Retirement

The living standards of older Americans have improved over the past sixty years, with poverty rates falling and average income rising. The trends are due largely to expansions in retirement and health benefits via Social Security and Medicare, as well as Medicaid and other programs for people with low incomes. But inequality has also increased and the number of people over sixty-five who are living in poverty has begun rising, reaching eight million in 2022. The retirement security picture is bleak for many Americans because of the numerous cracks in our system. Social Security hasn't been significantly amended since the 1980s, and half of us don't have an easy way to save for retirement. Rising health care costs eat away at what little savings people do have. We can make our retirements more secure by updating important financial systems to align with twenty-first-century realities.

SHORE UP SOCIAL SECURITY

Social Security is one of the few self-financed programs in the federal government. But beginning in 2034, the reserve funds will run out, and the payroll and other taxes that fund the program will be insufficient to pay all benefits. Within the next decade, policymakers will need to develop a comprehensive plan to shore up finances for current and future generations and to ensure that benefits are adequate to provide a stable foundation of income in retirement. While 2034 can seem far away compared to more immediately pressing issues or crises, the sooner Congress acts, the less difficult the fix will be.

Among the options frequently discussed to address the financial shortfall are reducing benefits for current or future retirees, raising payroll taxes on all workers (or just those with high incomes), and adding additional funding from other sources, such as the general tax revenues that fund most other federal programs. Proposals have been offered that only raise taxes or only cut benefits, but most bipartisan initiatives have included a mix of both options. Because making changes to the program requires a supermajority in Congress, any final legislation will likely involve compromises and a mix of solutions.

In addition to making the Social Security program solvent for current and future generations, we must also ensure that it works better, especially for those who need it the most. Older workers with physically demanding jobs often find it hard to wait until their late sixties to collect their full benefit checks. People with disabilities sometimes must wait years for their claims for SSDI benefits to be approved, due to the complexity of the process and long delays. And far too many people fall into poverty as they age, especially widows. Even though a significant portion of older adults rely heavily on Social Security, the benefits are not generous, and many receive checks that are below the poverty level. In fact, the United States ranks in the bottom third of wealthy countries on this metric. Benefits should provide enough income that recipients can afford food, medicines, and a safe place to live in retirement.

RETIREMENT SAVINGS

Most of our peer countries include all workers in their retirement savings systems, but in the United States only about half of workers can automatically save for retirement through their employer. This lack of coverage is one reason half of Americans have nothing saved as they approach retirement. This is a problem not just for retirees. The lack of sufficient retirement savings will cost state and federal governments trillions of dollars over the next two decades in increased public assistance and reduced tax revenue.

Saving though paychecks should be made easy for everyone. In hopes of getting more employers to offer retirement plans, lawmakers at the federal level have recently made it easier for businesses to band together. Many states are creating retirement savings programs of their own through public-private partnerships, where workers whose employers don't offer a retirement plan can easily invest for their future. This idea of state-sponsored "work and save" programs has swept across the country, and I see it as a big step toward solving the gaps in coverage, especially for employees of small businesses. While I am a big believer in the states serving as laboratories of democracy to develop solutions, I would like to see all Americans have the option to save, no matter where they live. The idea of a more universal system of retirement savings, where every worker would be automatically enrolled in a savings plan at work but could opt out if they wanted, has been supported by conservative and liberal policymakers alike, and both President Obama and Senator John McCain backed it as presidential candidates. But federal legislation to create it has been stuck in Congress for decades.

A related issue is the lack of emergency savings. In any given year, 60 percent of U.S. households experience at least one financial shock that can put them into debt or force them to use retirement savings prematurely. Being able to automatically put money aside out of each paycheck into an emergency savings account would be a big step forward.

6. Housing and Care for All

Where we live as we get older is inextricably linked to the kind of housing available to us and the amount of care we need. Ideally, our care needs and our living situation will align—and we will be able to afford appropriate housing, whether in our own homes, an assisted living community, or a nursing home.

CREATE MORE ACCESSIBLE AND AFFORDABLE HOUSING OPTIONS

We have a severe shortage of homes that are accessible to people of all needs and capacities. As constructing homes that are accessible is much less expensive than retrofitting inaccessible ones later, incorporating universal design features in new construction makes sense. Accessibility allows people to more easily age in place and enables friends and family of all abilities to visit. For homes that are already built, low-cost loans, tax credits, state Medicaid waiver funding, and grants for builders or homeowners to pay for modifications can help to offset accessibility investments. Community Aging in Place—Advancing Better Living for Elders (CAPABLE) is a program that provides home repair and modifications; it has helped reduce spending on health care and allowed people with disabilities to live safely in their home and better care for themselves.

We also need communities to offer a wider range of housing types—not just single-family homes but also smaller options for individuals and those downsizing, "middle" housing such as townhomes and duplexes, and larger homes for multigenerational families or people who are house sharing. In many places, this will require new zoning and land-use regulations, and the removal of regulatory barriers to construction of both housing and accessory dwelling units (ADUs). These separate living spaces, either attached to or detached from a single-family home, can help people age in their communities by providing lower-cost housing options or even rental income. Some innovative models that address both accessibility and availability of housing exist around the world. A program in Ireland helps older homeowners modify their homes while creating separate rental units that can provide additional income to the owner and affordable living for renters. The program partners with nearby hospitals, placing health care workers in the homes of older people—a true win-win.

Expanding our use of other tools to increase the availability of affordable and appropriate housing can allow people who have deep ties to their communities to stay there, regardless of their circumstances. These tools include housing vouchers for renters, subsidies for developers to build more affordable housing, and low-income-housing tax credits. Prohibiting discrimination against tenants who use housing subsidies or receive public assistance can also help people find more affordable housing options.

High housing costs, including property taxes, are a burden, especially for older adults living on fixed incomes. Roughly one in three people aged sixty-five and above spend more than a third of their incomes on housing, forcing them to make tough choices about paying for food, utilities, and other bills. Having more affordable options and providing property tax relief and deferral programs, some of which allow homeowners to delay paying their taxes until their properties are sold, can help people who are struggling to stay in their homes.

A more troubling trend is the steep rise of adults over fifty who are experiencing homelessness or living in homeless shelters. Many of these people have suffered job loss, eviction, or foreclosure. Because disabilities increase with age, older people experiencing homelessness are likely to be living with chronic illnesses that are made worse by exposure to the elements and lack of access to medical care.

Several government programs support expansion of housing for low-income older people, including one specifically aimed at housing assistance in rural areas. These programs work by funding the construction, acquisition, or rehabilitation of properties; supporting provision of services; and providing rental assistance. They also offer loans and grants for older adults to modify their homes to help them age in place. But waiting lists for the programs can be long, in some cases up to two years. Funding must be expanded to accommodate increasing demand.

MAKE OUR COMMUNITIES BOTH AGE- AND DEMENTIA-FRIENDLY

A movement to make cities, states, and communities more age-friendly has been sweeping the nation. Over 750 communities, as well as nine states and territories, are developing plans and advancing policies that make them more accessible to people of all ages. Efforts to promote these policies must continue so that broader swaths of the country are prepared to accommodate the needs of their aging populations.

It is estimated that 70 percent of people with dementia live at home and a quarter live alone. Neighbors and community members therefore play a big role in supporting these individuals and their families, especially given what we know about the importance of social engagement to brain health. We need more "dementia-friendly" communities, including education campaigns that reduce stigma, and increased services for people with dementia and their caregivers. Public spaces such as memory cafés can support people with dementia both socially and cognitively. Cultural venues can become dementia-friendly, and museums from Seattle, Washington, to Fishers, Indiana, to New York City are creating programs that encourage and support people with dementia to engage with art. These sorts of programs can help us to become a society that truly includes rather than excludes those with dementia.

HELP FAMILIES PAY FOR LONG-TERM CARE

The cost of providing aid for bathing, dressing, or other daily needs is shockingly high and mostly falls on individual families, as it is not covered by private health insurance or Medicare. Very few people have purchased long-term care insurance because of its cost and complexity, so some states are creating new ways to help people pay for long-term care. The WA Cares program in Washington state—which provides funding to people for services related to long-term care—is a great example. Several other states have expressed interest in developing ways to help their residents pay for long-term care costs.

Those who can afford to pay for care themselves have a range of options as to where they receive care—the home, assisted living communities, or nursing homes. Those who cannot afford to pay rely primarily on Medicaid, the main government payer for care. Medicaid is available only to qualifying individuals with low incomes (or to people who have become impoverished from paying for care). Moreover, Medicaid is required to pay only for nursing home care.

In a promising trend, states have begun shifting their Medicaid payments to provide services in people's homes rather than just in nursing homes. In 2020 half of U.S. states were spending most of their Medicaid and state funding for long-term services and supports on services to keep older people and adults with physical disabilities in their homes. Getting help in their own home is what most people want, and it is more cost effective: Medicaid pays more than twice as much for someone to live in a nursing home as it does for in-home and community-based services. Still, access to home and community-based care options vary widely depending on where you live.

SUPPORT FOR THE "CARE FORCE"

An invisible army takes care of Americans as we age—if we're lucky. Friends, family, and professional caregivers—including home care workers, hospice caregivers, and nursing assistants—together form what long-time advocate Ai-jen Poo calls the "care force." We rely on this force, numbering one hundred million people, to support us, or our loved ones, in having a dignified quality of life. But professional caregivers tend to experience low pay, long hours, strenuous work, and poor benefits, all of which make it unlikely that our aging society will have enough of them to meet the growing demand. Qualified, caring aides often receive lower pay than workers in less demanding roles. We must provide the "care force" with better pay, benefits, and increased training and certifications in order to keep carers from leaving the profession, allow them to advance in their careers, and provide the sense of empowerment they need to thrive in their jobs.

The costs of caregiving incurred by families and friends can be high— including costs to their own health and well-being as well as the financial burdens. Policies such as caregiver tax credits, paid family and sick leave, paying family caregivers, and respite (giving caregivers a break from duties) can all make a difference. After years of bipartisan efforts, in 2022 the Department of Health and Human Services released the National Strategy to Support Family Caregivers. This strategy calls on federal agencies, state and local governments, and the private sector to take action on over five hundred recommendations, including support for caregivers in coordinating care and help with understanding what resources and tools are available.

7. Better Care at the End of Life

We are all mortal, so we all have a stake in making it easier to live with life-limiting illnesses and getting better care at the end of life. One key step that will improve every aspect of end-of-life care is better training for health providers on how to have conversations with patients about their wishes for end-of-life care and treatment. This training should include an awareness of how different cultural backgrounds can influence attitudes toward these conversations and the actual decisions that follow.

EXPAND AND IMPROVE PALLIATIVE CARE AND HOSPICE SERVICES

Better care at the end of life starts with improved and expanded palliative care, especially better treatment for emotional distress and the elimination of barriers for pain management. We need increased access to palliative care services not only in hospitals but also in nursing homes and in our own homes. Palliative care improves people's lives, and it more than pays for itself. Since roughly one in five Medicare dollars is spent in the last year of life, the use of hospice and palliative care can often generate savings by avoiding expensive and futile treatments. A study analyzing the potential of a well-designed hospice benefit in California's Medicaid program found that spending on palliative care could generate significant cost savings to the program.

Many people never receive hospice benefits because of the requirement that they have a prognosis of six months or less to live and the rule prohibiting potentially curative care. The Affordable Care Act allows children enrolled in Medicaid or the Children's Health Insurance Program to receive hospice services while also receiving curative or life-extending care. Although commercial insurers are not required to cover such "concurrent care" for children, many now do. People of any age with a life-limiting illness, regardless of insurance, shouldn't have to make the difficult choice between hospice and curative care.

Improving access to hospice and palliative care starts with raising awareness. State laws requiring clinicians to offer information and counseling about care options to terminally ill patients make it more likely that patients will die in their homes or in a hospice rather than in a hospital. Improving palliative care is not only good for patients, it can also save the health care system a lot of money. Palliative care expert

Diane Meier calculated in a 2011 paper that palliative care, at its then level of penetration in U.S. hospitals, would save $1.2 billion annually over standard care—a figure she estimated could rise to $4 billion per year if implemented at nearly all hospitals. More thoroughly coordinated care and clear discussion of care goals would help patients avoid unwanted imaging, consultations, and procedures. By carefully managing pain and other symptoms, palliative care allows more patients to remain at home rather than make expensive visits to the emergency department or stay in the hospital.

Insurance plans, including Medicare and Medicaid, typically provide only limited coverage of palliative care services, such as home visits, advance care planning, and family support. There is movement toward expanding coverage, and we are seeing innovations, particularly in state Medicaid programs. Several states have started to cover community-based palliative care. California, Hawaii, and Maine have begun reimbursing for palliative care education and services, setting up a system for referrals, monitoring quality, and working with community organizations to deliver care at home. This kind of coverage, which provides better quality care at lower cost, should be expanded across the country.

IMPROVE MENTAL HEALTH CARE

Far too many older Americans are not getting the mental health diagnosis or treatment they need. Those over eighty-five have the highest rates of death by suicide of any age group. In 2019 one in five people on Medicare—twelve million older people—reported symptoms of depression. Yet even though the biggest risk factor for death by suicide among older adults is depression, it is often underdiagnosed in this group, partly because it is mistakenly assumed that depression is a normal part of aging. Although Medicare covers depression screening as part of the Annual Wellness Visit, only 6 percent of people with traditional Medicare were screened for depression in 2018. Almost half of Medicare recipients said they were never asked about depression by a medical provider. We need our health care system to do a much better of job addressing mental health problems and the suffering that comes with them.

Given my experience with my grandmother's severe mental illness, one of the pieces of legislation I worked on in the Senate that I am most proud of is the Mental Health Parity and Addiction Equity Act, which was signed into law in 2008. It requires health insurers to pay for mental health and substance use disorder therapies the same way they pay for medical and surgical treatments. Unfortunately, the legislation's requirements did not apply to Medicare, which continues to limit the number of days of inpatient mental health treatment a person can get over their lifetime. Expanding coverage of needed treatments, training health providers in the unique needs of older adults, increasing the number and diversity of mental health providers, and combating mental health stigma can all help to address the crises of high rates of depression and suicide in older adults.

PLANNING FOR THE END

Many of us avoid end-of-life planning, partly because it can be complicated. The estate planning process needs to be simplified and made more widely accessible. Technology can be used to expand the availability and convenience of estate planning services, including electronic wills and trusts to govern the distribution of property at death and remote notarization of documents so that people in nursing homes or hospitals can more easily complete them. Policymakers need to encourage advance care planning, especially to ensure that we have legally specified our medical power of attorney, the person who can help advocate for our wishes in the event that we can no longer make decisions for ourselves. It is important that we have these difficult conversations with our family and friends about what we would want, if that time came.

A Final Word

Having worked on these issues for decades, I can imagine pushback to the recommendations I have presented. One objection may arise out of the "scarcity mindset," the belief that supporting longer healthier lives for older Americans will take from our support for the educational, health, and other needs of young people—or, conversely, that supporting young people is not connected to their health in later life. But we are all on the same trajectory from young to old, and a lack of investment in our youngest citizens can have detrimental consequences throughout their lives. Children who grow up poor tend to struggle at every stage of life, and they are more likely to experience poverty as adults and early death. Children who grow up with certain advantages, such as quality education, tend to build on those and benefit over the course of their lives from higher incomes, better access to health care, and greater financial security in retirement. My recommendations for addressing the challenges facing an aging society therefore aim to help *all* generations. The generations to come will face many of the same issues that older people face today, as well as a few we probably can't anticipate. By creating a better society for older people now, we are laying the foundation for a better future for younger people. In other words, what is good for the second fifty is also good for the first, and vice versa.

The second argument, I imagine, will concern costs. Yes, some of my proposals may sound like big, expensive agenda items, but if there is one thing I've learned in my line of work, it's that doing nothing costs more in the long run. The less we spend now to improve health care, income, employment, and long-term services and supports, the more we will spend down the line to care for people as they age. The absence of a plan doesn't make costs disappear; it just shifts them to individuals or families, often when they are in crisis, or to state or federal social safety net programs.

The costs and benefits of improving the way we age aren't solely financial. Providing the foundation for a longer healthspan and a more financially secure second fifty would mean that Americans experience less physical suffering, less psychological stress, and more chance to enjoy our final years. Society benefits, too, through an increased economic output that improves the standard of living for the country overall. These investments may require us to make difficult choices regarding the structure and funding of health and financial programs. Policymakers at the federal, state, and local levels will therefore need to present their arguments transparently so that constituents understand the long-term impact of these important investments.

Finally, Americans will always disagree about the extent of the role of government. The government can't solve every problem. We all have a part to play in helping make our own second half better. The private sector has a role too. But many things that are key to living healthier and more financially secure lives are beyond our individual control; they are linked to factors such as affordable education, safe neighborhoods, and good jobs, and policymakers must take them on.

At the same time, we can engage with policymakers. When I was talking to Brian Smedley from the Urban Institute, I asked him what we could do as individuals, beyond striving for healthier habits and putting more money in our retirement accounts. Brian talked about having seen communities come together, organize politically, and campaign for policy changes. It isn't always easy or possible to get involved when you're busy working, raising a family, or caring for a loved one, but over my many years working on these issues, I've seen a lot of grassroots activists instigate real change. When West Virginia senator Joe Manchin was given petitions with more than thirty thousand signatures of his constituents, detailing their struggles with high drug costs, he committed to taking action on the spot, helping to pave the way for federal legislation negotiating prescription drug prices in Medicare. The ALS community lobbied hard, educating policymakers and the public, until the ALS Disability Insurance Access Act was passed in 2020. As a result, people with an ALS diagnosis are the only group that does not have to wait for five months before they can start receiving Social Security Disability Insurance benefits. Hopefully, the same criteria will be set for other disabling conditions. And I've long admired the tenacity of disability rights advocates, especially the late Judy Heumann, whose push for civil rights and the Americans with Disabilities Act will help nearly all of us as we age.

Getting involved has its own benefits. "Political activism is one of the most health-enhancing behaviors people can engage in," Brian said. "Not only are you creating political will for the changes you need, but you're also building social solidarity and social cohesion, which are critically important for health. Collectively, we can shape a better future."

ACKNOWLEDGMENTS

The Second Fifty would not have come to fruition without an army of help and support.

Nearly every week for the last three years, my core book team has joined a Friday afternoon call and freely engaged in debates about what to include, what to leave out, and how to distill sometimes complicated research into a clear point. Each member of the team is lovely, which made those weekly calls actually fun (most of the time!), and I am deeply indebted to their hard work and dedication to this project.

Meredith Rucker, my communications director, was one of the first people I told that I was considering writing a book, and since that day so long ago, she has carefully and consistently shepherded the many parts of this project. The encouragement Meredith gave me over these last three years allowed me to envision a complete book, even when it was just a jumble of ideas in my head.

A million thanks go to William Lewis, who managed all the details of the project—arranging meetings with experts, corralling comments, and keeping the moving parts on track. Will joined me to explore why the On Lok Senior Services Center is so successful, and he contributed unique ideas and perspectives to many parts of the book. Will's magical ability to know what I needed and when I'd need it allowed me to focus on the writing instead of on all the logistical details.

I can't thank Molly McCloskey enough for her incredible collaboration in writing the book. Molly is a beautiful storyteller, a dedicated researcher, and a great wit. I absolutely loved working with her and was consistently impressed by how she could turn my wonky sentences into an easy-to-read and engaging prose. An award-winning author in her own right, she was able to capture my voice and tell this story in the way I had always dreamed.

This book has over one thousand endnotes, and many of them are due to the detailed research of Mary-Genevieve Moisan. Serving first as my intern and then as my research assistant, she brought her incredibly quick and accurate fact-finding skills to the project, all while being the ray of sunshine she just is.

I was lucky to have a lot of support to ensure that I was able to keep doing my day job at AARP while writing this book. Britta Berge, my trusted chief of staff, has been with me on this journey from the beginning, providing valued feedback and strategic guidance to the team. Her steady support and leadership also helped me keep the trains running. Sherita Alexander, my steadfast assistant of twelve years, was the only reason I could come close to balancing my work and writing schedule, and all the while she kept me laughing. David Green, importantly, made sure we stayed within budget and all the bills were paid on time.

When I started out, I knew nothing about the world of publishing, but I was able to rely on the wisdom and experience of Jodi Lipson, who directs AARP's books division. Jodi held my hand through the many steps of the process and provided vital feedback along the way. I would have been lost without her. I also want to thank my wonderful agent, Tom Miller, from Liza Dawson Associates, for pushing me to broaden my audience and for navigating the ins and outs of the publishing world. My thanks to Leslie Nettleford Freeman for her wise legal counsel and close review of the final chapters.

This book has benefited enormously from the guidance and feedback from my incredible editor Alane Mason at Norton. She championed the book from the beginning and helped shape it at every stage. Everyone at Norton who worked on *The Second Fifty*—copyediting, designing, marketing, and promoting it—certainly deserve thanks too, especially Mo Crist, Julia Druskin, Don Rifkin, Jason Heuer, Erin Lovett, and Meredith McGinnis.

I was fortunate to work with the late John Butman on the proposal for this book. He pulled the many ideas I had together and suggested I use questions to frame the chapters. He and his beautiful writing are greatly missed. The talented writer Aimee Liu got me started turning that proposal into a book and worked with me through the worst of the pandemic. I appreciated her encouraging me to take a more in-depth look at those who were struggling through their second fifty.

I am grateful for the support of a few early contributors to this project. Julia Elrod served as my project manager before I had even written a proposal. My incredibly bright research interns Grace Cerand and Hannah Diamond helped me immeasurably by delving deeply into the wide-ranging topics I wanted to cover.

I am indebted to the many experts from my team at AARP who generously shared their knowledge, reviewed drafts, and provided valuable feedback. They continue to inspire me daily with their dedication to making the world a better place for us as we age. My gratitude goes to: Jean Accius, Carrie Amero, S. Kathi Brown, Selena Caldera, Beth Carter, Lona Choi-Allum, Rita Choula, Lindsay Chura, Olivia Dean, Joel Eskovitz, Stephanie Firestone, Brendan Flinn, Amanda Fredriksen, Jeff Gullo, Jilenne Gunther, Shannon Guzman, Edem Hado, Rodney Harrell, Ian Hartman-O'Connell, Vijeth Iyengar, David John, Gary Koenig, Justin Ladner, Sarah Lock, Susanna Montezemolo, Tobey Oliver, Jim Palmieri, David Parkes, Rebecca Perron, Leigh Purvis, Susan Reinhard, Jennifer Schramm, Jane Sung, Erwin Tan, Colette Thayer, Lori Trawinski, and Lina Walker. I appreciated the reviews and recommendations from my AARP colleagues David Certner, Nancy McPherson, and Bill Sweeney. Mollie Gurian from LeadingAge deepened my understanding of hospice and palliative care, connected me with key people, and helped ensure that I got the language right on these important issues. Rita Jojola, director of the Pueblo Isleta Elder Center, kindly arranged my visit to the center. I appreciate the time she and her team took to share the great work the Pueblo does to care for their elders. I want to thank Grace Li, Katherine Kelly, and the entire On Lok staff for giving me a tour of the PACE facilities and answering my many questions about how their program works and how others might replicate their success.

I want to especially recognize several members of my team for their specific contributions. Vicki Levy and Patty David developed and analyzed the Second Half of Life Survey. Kadeem Thorpe found people for me to speak with whose personal experiences helped make the sometimes abstract issues I wrote about come to life. Scott Tanaka and Angela Houghton helped ensure that diverse populations were sensitively referenced. My incredible library team, including Holly Havlicek, Alison Seese, and Veralrose Hylton, pulled together sources and primary research. Dorothy Siemon reviewed every chapter (sometimes several times) and offered insight and feedback throughout.

Stephanie Abramson and Dee Khun performed thorough fact-checking; both Dee and Sarah Sampson worked diligently formatting the thousand endnotes. Jonathan Peterson provided valuable written contributions. I am thankful for the AARP communications team, who ensured that the ideas in the book would reach beyond the page. My appreciation goes to Diane Renzulli, Kathryn Schnoor, and Emily Pickren. In addition to her expert communications guidance, Laura Segal read a complete draft and offered suggestions throughout the writing process.

My AARP colleagues have been a source of inspiration and support. I want to thank our CEO Jo Ann Jenkins for her years of encouragement and for allowing me to balance my day job with the weekend and evening job of writing a book. My appreciation also goes to Kevin Donnellan and Myrna Blyth for their early and continued advice and backing and to David Morales for his counsel. I hope I have done justice in these pages to the incredible work of my colleagues Edna Kane Williams, Nancy LeaMond, and Martha Boudreau.

I am so very grateful to the many people who shared their personal stories or took the time to talk with me about their research. Only a fraction of them are included in these pages, but they all enlarged my understanding of the issues we face in the second half of our lives.

I also want to thank my former colleagues who served with me in the U.S. Senate, the Library of Congress, and the Social Security Administration. I learned so much from these talented public servants, and I hope I have adequately represented the many battles we fought together.

The Second Fifty would not have come together without the contributions of all these people, and my sincere apologies if I have left anyone off this list. Any errors in the text are entirely my own.

More gratitude than I can express goes to my family, who have been my biggest champions and muses. Thank you to my parents for letting me share your stories and for all the love and sacrifices you have made for your family. I have learned a lot about aging well and giving back to the community from watching you both. My brother-in-law Scott Whitman and I were in tears as he told me about the joys and the difficulties of caring for his parents. My sister-in-law Beth Whitman shared both her family history and her beautiful pond house. Uncle Barry and Aunt Sheila always set me straight. My brother Scott Bailey and sister-in-law Junko have given me a lifetime of support and art that enabled me to consider the possibility that I, too, could do something creative.

This book is dedicated to my kind, bright, and wonderful kids, Grace and Owen, who inspire me every day. I wrote it in the hope that it might make the second half of life a little easier for them and their generation. Their love and encouragement were unwavering throughout the long writing process, and I am so proud to be their mom.

Finally, to my husband, Glenn, the best partner a person could ask for. Thank you for trying to tiptoe through the kitchen all those weekends when I was glued to my laptop for many long hours. Your constant cheerleading and belief that I actually could write a book (how did you write two?) got me through some of the hardest points. Thank you for sharing your life with me and for letting me share your story. I will love you until 103 and then carry you up Aspen Mountain.

NOTES

Introduction

ix **In 1900 the average:** Brigham Bastian et al., "Mortality Trends in the United States, 1900–2018," National Center for Health Statistics, August 25, 2020.

ix **high-water mark:** Kenneth D. Kochanek, Sherry L. Murphy, Jiaquan Xu, and Elizabeth Arias, "Mortality in the United States, 2016," NCHS Data Brief no. 293, December 2017.

ix **50 percent chance:** Marie-Pier Bergeron-Boucher, Francisco Villavicencio, Erwin J. Tan, and James W. Vaupel, "Longevity and Equity," *AARP International: The Journal* 13 (2020): 26–29.

ix **expected to quadruple:** Katherine Schaeffer, "U.S. Centenarian Population Is Projected to Quadruple over the Next 30 Years," Pew Research Center, January 9, 2024.

x **Liana Munro:** Jeryl Brunner, "It's Never Too Late to Reunite with Your Dream—Just Ask This 77-Year-Old Ballroom Dance Champion," *Forbes*, June 26, 2021.

x **Fauja Singh:** Ronald Chettiar, "Fauja Singh: Oldest Marathon Runner an Inspiration for Youngsters," International Olympic Committee, March 31, 2023.

x **Iris Apfel:** Chloe Foussianes, "Iris Apfel, 97-Year-Old Style Icon, Has Just Signed with a Modeling Agency," *Town and Country*, January 31, 2019.

x **Apo Whang-Od:** Audrey Carpio, "Meet the 106-Year-Old Woman Keeping an Ancient Filipino Tattooing Tradition Alive," *Vogue*, April 7, 2023.

x **Barbara Hillary:** Katherine Q. Seelye, "Barbara Hillary, 88, Trailblazer on Top (and Bottom) of the World, Dies," *New York Times*, November 26, 2019.

xiii **Second Half of Life Study (SHOL):** Vicki Levy and Patty David, *Second Half of Life Study*, AARP Research, June 2022.

xiv　**How much money and care:** Pieter Coenen, "Do Highly Physically Active Workers Die Early? A Systematic Review with Meta-Analysis of Data from 193,696 Participants," *British Journal of Sports Medicine* 52 (2018): 1320–26.

xiv　**deadlier than obesity:** Julianne Holt-Lunstad, Timothy B. Smith, and J. Bradley Layton, "Social Relationships and Mortality Risk: A Meta-Analytic Review," *PLoS Medicine* 7, no. 7 (2010): e1000316.

xiv　**other health problems:** National Institute on Aging, "Social Isolation, Loneliness in Older People Pose Health Risks," NIA.NIH.gov, April 23, 2019; Malissa Underwood, "Social Isolation and Loneliness in Older Adults: the Unseen Determinant of Health," *Public Health Insight*, August 18, 2022; Cleveland Clinic, "What Happens in Your Body When You're Lonely?" *HealthEssentials Newsletter*, February 23, 2018.

xv　*nearly fifteen years longer:* Raj Chetty et al., "The Association Between Income and Life Expectancy in the United States, 2001–2014," *Journal of the American Medical Association* 315, no. 16 (2016): 1750–66.

xv　**about seventy-six years:** Elizabeth Arias, Betzaida Tejada-Vera, Kenneth D. Kochanek, and Farida B. Ahmad, "Provisional Life Expectancy Estimates for 2021," *NVSS Vital Statistics Rapid Release*, Report no. 23, August 2022.

xv　**average healthspan:** World Health Organization, "Healthy Life Expectancy (HALE) at Age 60 (Years)," WHO.int, 2020.

xv　**40 percent of dementias:** Gill Livingston et al., "Dementia Prevention, Intervention, and Care: 2020 Report of the Lancet Commission," *Lancet* 396, no. 10248 (August 8, 2020): 413–46; Mark Mather and Paola Scommegna, "Up to Half of U.S. Premature Deaths Are Preventable; Behavioral Factors Key," Population Reference Bureau, September 14, 2015.

xv　**sheer number:** Population Reference Bureau, "U.S. Dementia Trends" (fact sheet), PRB.org, October 21, 2021; V. A. Freedman, J. C. Cornman, and J. D. Kasper, *National Health and Aging Trends Chart Book: Key Trends, Measures and Detailed Tables,* National Health and Aging Trends Study, 2021.

xv　**view aging positively:** Becca R. Levy et al., "Longevity Increased by Positive Self-Perceptions of Aging," *Journal of Personality and Social Psychology* 83, no. 2 (2002): 261–70.

xvi　**more strokes and heart attacks:** Becca R. Levy et al., "Age Stereotypes Held Earlier in Life Predict Cardiovascular Events in Later Life," *Psychological Science* 20, no. 3 (2009): 296–98; Becca R. Levy et al., "A Culture-Brain Link: Negative Age Stereotypes Predict Alzheimer's Disease Biomarkers," *Psychology and Aging* 31, no. 1 (2016): 82–88; Becca R. Levy et al., "Association Between Positive Age Stereotypes and Recovery from Disability in Older Persons," *Journal of the American Medical Association* 308, no. 19 (2012): 1972–73.

xvi　**need some kind:** Richard Johnson, *What Is the Lifetime Risk of Needing and Receiving Long-Term Services and Supports?*, Research Brief, Assistant Secretary for Planning and Evaluation, U.S. Department of Health and Human Services, April 2019.

Chapter 1: How Long Will I Live?

1　**Boulder Mountain Rescue:** Alpine Rescue Team, "About Alpine," Alpinerescueteam. org.

2　**survival rate:** UMPC Health Beat, "What Is a Widowmaker Heart Attack?," Share. UPMC.com, September 2, 2022.

2   **fared little better**: Thomas F. Lüscher and Slayman Obeid, "From Eisenhower's Heart
     Attack to Modern Management: A True Success Story!," *European Heart Journal* 38, no.
     41 (2017): 3066-69.

2   **coronary stents:** Javaid Iqbal, Julian Gunn, and Patrick W. Serruys, "Coronary Stents:
     Historical Development, Current Status and Future Directions," *British Medical Bulle-
     tin* 106, no. 1 (June 2013): 193-211.

3   **eighteen years longer:** Arias, Tejada-Vera, Kochanek, and Ahmad, "Provisional Esti-
     mates for 2021."

4   **forty-eight years:** Brigham Bastian et al., "Mortality Trends in the United States,
     1900-2018," National Center for Health Statistics, August 25, 2020.

4   **77.3 years:** Elizabeth Arias, Betzaida Tejada-Vera, Farida Ahmad, and Kenneth D.
     Kochanek, "Provisional Life Expectancy Estimates for 2020," *NVSS Vital Statistics Rapid
     Release,* Report no. 15, July 2021.

4   **die during childbirth:** Centers for Disease Control and Prevention, "Achievements
     in Public Health, 1900-1999: Healthier Mothers and Babies," *Morbidity and Mortality
     Weekly Report,* October 1, 1999.

4   **dramatic gains:** Theodore A. Kotchen, "Historical Trends and Milestones in Hyper-
     tension Research," *Hypertension* 58, no. 4 (2011): 522-38.

4   **lung transplants:** Associated Press, "Organ Transplant Demand Increases," *New York
     Times,* February 23, 2001.

4   **motor vehicle death rate:** National Safety Council, "Car Crash Deaths and Rates,"
     Injuryfacts.NSC.org.

5   **roughly six hours:** Population Reference Bureau, "More of Us on Track to Reach
     Age 100: Genes, Habits, Baboons Examined for Longevity Clues," PRB.org, June 24,
     2011.

5   **78.8 years:** Organization for Economic Cooperation and Development, "Life Expec-
     tancy at Birth," Data.OECD.org.

5   **ranked fortieth:** World Health Organization, "Life Expectancy at Birth (Years),"
     WHO.int, 2020.

5   **fall for the first time:** Aaron O'Neill, "Life Expectancy in the United States, 1860-
     2020," Statista, June 21, 2022.

5   **it dropped from:** World Bank, "Life Expectancy at Birth, Total (Years)—United
     States," Data.WorldBank.org, 2022.

5   **dying at younger ages:** Dylan Matthews, "What a Striking New Study of Death in
     America Misses," *Vox,* October 4, 2023.

5   **spike in deaths:** O'Neill, "Life Expectancy in the United States, 1860-2020."

5   **four times more likely:** Anne Case and Angus Deaton, *Deaths of Despair and the Future
     of Capitalism* (Princeton, NJ: Princeton University Press, 2020), 40, 60.

5   **deaths of despair:** Case and Deaton, *Deaths of Despair,* 2.

5   **158,000 such deaths:** Case and Deaton, *Deaths of Despair,* 94.

5   **"long-term drip":** Roge Karma, " 'Deaths of Despair': The Deadly Epidemic that Pre-
     dated Coronavirus," *Vox,* April 15, 2020.

5   **compounded the tragedy:** National Center for Health Statistics, "Suicide in the U.S.
     Declined During the Pandemic," CDC.gov, November 5, 2021.

5   **more than 107,000 people:** F. B. Ahmad, J. A. Cisewski, L. M. Rossen, and P. Sutton,
     "Provisional Drug Overdose Death Counts," National Center for Health Statistics,
     November 15, 2023.

5   **for 76.1 years:** Arias, Tejada-Vera, Kochanek, and Ahmad, "Provisional Life Expectancy Estimates for 2021."

6   **highest household incomes:** Juan M. Sánchez and Olivia Wilkinson, "COVID-19 Death Gap by Country Income Widened after Vaccine Availability," Federal Reserve Bank of St. Louis, March 11, 2022.

6   **never graduated:** Jarvis T. Chen et al., "Intersectional Inequities in COVID-19 Mortality by Race/Ethnicity and Education in the United States," Harvard Center for Population and Development Studies, Working Paper 21, no. 3, February 23, 2021.

6   **varied significantly**: Author's calculations from Jordan Allen et al., "Coronavirus in the U.S.: Latest Map and Case Count," *New York Times,* April 16, 2021.

6   **highest rates of infection:** José Manuel Aburto et al., "Significant Impacts of the COVID-19 Pandemic on Race/Ethnic Differences in US Mortality," *Proceedings of the National Academy of Sciences* 119, no. 35 (2022): e2205813119; Office of Diversity, Inclusion and Health Equity, "Communities of Color and the Disproportionate Impact of COVID-19," HopkinsMedicine.org, February 2021; Katherine Leggat-Barr, Fumiya Uchikoshi, and Noreen Goldman, "COVID-19 Risk Factors and Mortality Among Native Americans," *Demographic Research* 45 (2021): 1185–218.

6   **death toll in nursing homes:** Rebecca J. Gorges and R. Tamara Konetzka, "Factors Associated with Racial Differences in Deaths Among Nursing Home Residents with COVID-19 Infection in the US," *Journal of the American Medical Association* 4, no. 2 (2021): e2037431.

6   **10 to 20 percent:** A. Michael McGinnis, Pamela Williams-Russo, and James R. Knickman, "The Case for More Active Policy Attention to Health Promotion," *Health Affairs* 21, no. 2 (2002); J. Graham Ruby et al., "Estimates of the Heritability of Human Longevity Are Substantially Inflated Due to Assortative Mating," *Genetics* 210, no. 3 (2018): 1109–24.

6   **health care we receive:** McGinnis, Williams-Russo, and Knickman, "Case for More Active Policy"; Lauren A. Taylor et al., *Leveraging the Social Determinants of Health: What Works,* Blue Cross Blue Shield of Massachusetts Foundation and Yale Global Health Leadership Institute, June 2015; Office of Disease Prevention and Health Promotion, *Healthy People 2030: Building a Healthier Future for All,* Health.gov.

6   **social drivers:** Rachel Nuzum, Corinne Lewis, and Debbie I. Chang, "Measuring What Matters: Social Drivers of Health," Commonwealth Fund, November 2, 2021.

7   **more accurately reflects:** National Association of Community Health Centers, "Social Drivers vs. Social Determinants: Using Clear Terms," NACHC.org, January 23, 2023.

7   **about 60 percent:** McGinnis, Williams-Russo, and Knickman, "Case for More Active Policy."

7   **Thomas Perls:** Thomas Perls, interview by the author, October, 29, 2020.

7   **two thousand centenarians:** Perls interview.

7   **Long Life Family Study:** National Institute on Aging, *Long Life Family Study*, NCBI. NLM.NIH.gov.

7   **Seventh-day Adventists:** Gary E. Fraser and David J. Shavlik, "Ten Years of Life: Is It a Matter of Choice?," *Archives of Internal Medicine* 161, no. 13 (2001): 1645–52; Gary E. Fraser et al., "Lower Rates of Cancer and All-Cause Mortality in an Adventist Cohort Compared with a US Census Population," *Cancer* 126, no. 5 (March 1, 2020).

7   **healthy lifestyle:** Aaron Gilbreath, "Why Do Seventh-Day Adventists Live Longer Than Most Americans?" *Longreads*, February 28, 2020.

7   **very low rates:** Loma Linda University Health, "Adventist Health Study–2: Early Findings," AdventistHealthStudy.org.

8   **For every one hundred:** Thomas Perls, "Male Centenarians: How and Why Are They Different from Their Female Counterparts?," *Journal of the American Geriatrics Society* 65, no. 9 (2017): 1904–6.

8   **women outlive them:** Population Reference Bureau, "Around the Globe, Women Outlive Men," PRB.org, September 1, 2001.

8   **gender paradox:** Steven Austad and Kathleen Fischer, "Sex Differences in Lifespan," *Cell Metabolism* 23, no. 6 (2016): 1022–33; Gabriel A. B. Marais et al., "Sex Gap in Aging and Longevity: Can Sex Chromosomes Play a Role?," *Biology of Sex Differences* 9, no. 33 (2018): 33.

8   **the two terms:** Carolyn M. Mazure, "What Do We Mean by Sex and Gender?," Yale School of Medicine, September 19, 2021. Gendered identity and behavior do not always fall neatly under "male" or "female" labels, of course, and this complexity poses a challenge of its own for researchers. A big part of the problem is that until recently, U.S. birth and death certificates identified people only as male or female, so vital statistics on gender-diverse populations were nonexistent. They are only now becoming available. Some initial studies are finding that older transgender people are at higher risk for poor physical health, disability, depression, and perceived stress compared to their LGB counterparts, but overall, we know very little about life expectancy for people who do not identify as cisgender male or female.

9   **Sex hormones:** Natalie Angier, "Secrets of the Y Chromosome," *New York Times*, June 11, 2018; Clare Ansberry, "Women and Men Age Differently—in More Ways Than Just Longevity," *Wall Street Journal*, July 14, 2020.

9   **vary with age:** Marais et al., "Sex Gap in Aging"; Rita Ostan et al., "Gender, Aging and Longevity in Humans: An Update of an Intriguing/Neglected Scenario Paving the Way to a Gender-Specific Medicine," *Clinical Science* 130, no. 19 (2016): 1715.

9   **ramps up immune responses:** Alfred T. Harding and Nicholas S. Heaton, "The Impact of Estrogens and Their Receptors on Immunity and Inflammation During Infection," *Cancers* 14, no. 4 (2022): 909.

9   **rates of breast cancer** Fox Chase Cancer Center, "Breast Cancer Inherited Risk," Temple Health, FoxChase.org; Marais et al., "Sex Gap in Aging"; Ostan et al., "Gender, Aging and Longevity."

9   **actively suppresses:** Harding and Heaton, "Impact of Estrogens."

9   **a decade younger:** Harvard Health Publishing, "Testosterone and the Heart," Health.Harvard.edu, March 1, 2010.

9   **nonreproductive cancer:** Franck Mauvais-Jarvis et al., "Sex and Gender: Modifiers of Health, Disease, and Medicine," *Lancet* 396, no. 10250 (August 2020): 565–82.

9   **across all societies:** World Cancer Research Fund International, "Worldwide Cancer Data," WCRF.org; Hyuna Sung et al., "Global Cancer Statistics 2020: GLOBOCAN Estimates of Incidence and Mortality Worldwide for 36 Cancers in 185 Countries," *CA: A Cancer Journal for Clinicians* 71, no. 3 (2021): 209–49.

9   **156 countries:** Ana-Catarina Pinho-Gomes, Sanne A. E. Peters, and Mark Woodward, "Gender Equality Related to Gender Differences in Life Expectancy Across the Globe Gender Equality and Life Expectancy," *PloS Global Public Health* 3, no. 3 (March 6, 2023): e0001214.

10   **surviving childbirth:** Ulf Högberg, "The Decline in Maternal Mortality in Sweden: The Role of Community Midwifery," *American Journal of Public Health* 94, no. 8 (2004): 1312–20.

10   **maternal deaths:** Donna L. Hoyert, "Maternal Mortality Rates in the United States, 2020," NCHS *Health E-Stats*, February 2022; Centers for Disease Control and Prevention, "Pregnancy Mortality Surveillance System," CDC.gov, March 23, 2023; Latoya Hill, Samantha Artiga, and Usha Ranji, "Racial Disparities in Maternal and Infant Health: Current Status and Efforts to Address Them," KFF, November 1, 2022.

10   **physical injury:** Susan B. Sorenson, "Gender Disparities in Injury Mortality: Consistent, Persistent, and Larger Than You'd Think," *American Journal of Public Health* 101, suppl. 1 (December 2011): S353–S358.

10   **at least a year:** Andrew Fenelon, Li-Hui Chen, and Susan P. Baker, "Major Causes of Injury Death and the Life Expectancy Gap Between the United States and Other High-Income Countries," *Journal of the American Medical Association* 315, no. 6 (2016): 609–11.

10   **almost three women:** Violence Policy Center, "Female Homicide Victimization by Males," VPC.org; "3 American Women Are Murdered Every Day by Their Husband or Boyfriend," *Politifact*, February 19, 2018; Kaofeng Lee, "Each Day, Three Women Die because of Domestic Violence," National Network to End Domestic Violence, n.d.

10   **nuns and monks:** Marc Luy, "Causes of Male Excess Mortality: Insights from Cloistered Populations," *Population and Development Review* 29, no. 4 (2003): 647–76.

11   **men avoid going:** Cleveland Clinic, "Men Will Do Almost Anything to Avoid Going to the Doctor" (press release), My.ClevelandClinic.org, September 4, 2019.

11   **five of the thirty years:** John P. Bunker, Howard S. Frazier, and Frederick Mosteller, "Improving Health: Measuring Effects of Medical Care," *Milbank Quarterly* 72, no. 2 (1994): 225–58.

11   **five leading causes:** Mather and Scommegna, "Up to Half of U.S. Premature Deaths Are Preventable"; Centers for Disease Control and Prevention, "Potentially Preventable Deaths from the Five Leading Causes of Death" (graphic), CDC.gov, 2014.

11   **trillions spent annually:** Organization for Economic Cooperation and Development, "Health Expenditure and Financing," Data-Explorer.OECD.org.

12   **Dawes explains:** Daniel Dawes, interview by the author, February 11, 2021.

12   **richest women:** Chetty et al., "Association Between Income and Life Expectancy."

12   **men in Sudan and Pakistan:** Chetty et al., "Association Between Income and Life Expectancy."

12   **correlated with education:** Current Population Survey data in U.S. Bureau of Labor Statistics, "Earnings and Unemployment Rates by Educational Attainment, 2022" (chart), BLS.gov, September 6, 2023.

13   **lifetime value:** Jaison R. Abel and Richard Deitz, "Do the Benefits of College Still Outweigh the Costs?," *Current Issues in Economics and Finance* 20, no. 3 (2014).

13   **enrolled in college:** Thomas D. Snyder, *120 Years of American Education: A Statistical Portrait*, National Center for Education Statistics, January 1993.

13   **completed four years:** Snyder, "120 Years of American Education."

13   **more women than men:** Snyder, "120 Years of American Education."

13   **gap is widening:** "Educated Americans Live Longer, As Others Die Younger," *Economist*, March 17, 2021.

13   *disadvantages* **also:** Stephen Crystal and Dennis Shea, "Cumulative Advantage, Cumulative Disadvantage, and Inequality Among Elderly People," *Gerontologist* 30, no.

4 (August 1, 1990): 437–43; Stephen Crystal, Dennis G. Shea, and Adriana M. Reyes, "Cumulative Advantage, Cumulative Disadvantage, and Evolving Patterns of Late-Life Inequality," *Gerontologist* 57, no. 5 (October 1, 2017): 910–20.

13 **gap that has *doubled*:** Author's calculation from U.S. Census Bureau, "Selected Measures of Equivalence-Adjusted Income Dispersion: 1967 to 2019," Table A-5, Census.gov, 2020.

13 **around three years:** Chetty et al., "Association Between Income and Life Expectancy."

14 **Brian is now:** Brian Smedley, interview by the author, December 5, 2022.

14 **Place Matters:** Joint Center for Political and Economic Studies, Place Matters: Advancing Health Equity, NationalCollaborative.org, 2016.

14 **major grocery store:** Sammy Schuck, "Detroit's Status as 'Food Desert' Challenged as More Produce Options Emerge," Capital News Service, January 21, 2022.

15 **greatest gap:** Jeremy Ney, "Life Expectancy and Inequality," Social Policy Lab, January 24, 2022.

15 **Oglala Lakota County:** U.S. Census Bureau, "Oglala Lakota County, South Dakota; Summit County, Colorado," Census.gov.

15 **Bev Warne, an Oglala elder:** Bev Warne, interview by the author, April 11, 2023.

15 **schools were set up:** Charla Bear, "American Indian Boarding Schools Haunt Many," NPR, May 12, 2008.

15 **eradicating Native culture:** Bear, "Boarding Schools"; U.S. Department of the Interior, "Federal Indian Boarding School Initiative," BIA.gov.

15 **closed in the 1960s:** American Indian Resource Center, "Native American Boarding Schools," AIRC.UCSC.edu.

15 **about 21 percent:** Office of Minority Health, "Population Profiles: American Indian/Alaska Native," MinorityHealth.HHS.gov, February 24, 2023.

15 **serve as coordinator:** Addison Dehaven, "Bev Warne: A Nurse's Life," South Dakota State University, December 8, 2022.

15 **retention rates shot up:** Dehaven, "Bev Warne."

16 **to 61 percent:** Joel Achenbach et al., "An Epidemic of Chronic Illness Is Killing Us Too Soon," *Washington Post*, October 3, 2023.

16 **five years longer:** Chetty et al., "Association Between Income and Life Expectancy."

16 **largest gains:** Chetty et al., "Association Between Income and Life Expectancy."

16 **shortest life expectancies:** Haidong Wang et al., "Left Behind: Widening Disparities for Males and Females in US County Life Expectancy, 1985–2010," *Population Health Metrics* 11, no. 8 (2013).

16 **lowest expenditures:** U.S. Census Bureau, "2017 Public Elementary-Secondary Education Finance Data," Census.gov, October 28, 2021.

16 **prioritizing key services:** Jennifer Karas Montez and Mateo P. Farina, "Do Liberal U.S. State Policies Maximize Life Expectancy?," *Public Policy and Aging Report* 31, no. 1 (2021): 7–13.

17 **most vulnerable residents:** Stephanie Weber et al., "Policy-Relevant Indicators for Mapping the Vulnerability of Urban Populations to Extreme Heat Events: A Case Study of Philadelphia," *Applied Geography* 63 (2015): 231–43.

17 **mapping heat levels:** Academy of Natural Sciences of Drexel University, "Academy of Natural Sciences Leads Effort to Map Philly's Heat and Air Quality This Summer," ANSP.org, April 26, 2022.

17 **Solutions included:** Penn Institute for Urban Research, "How Philly Can Stay Ahead

of the Curve in Addressing Climate Change," PennIUR.Upenn.edu, November 29, 2022; City of Philadelphia, *Beat the Heat: Hunting Park: A Community Heat Relief Plan*, Phila.gov, 2020.

17 **approximately forty-five lives:** Kate Weinberger et al., "Effectiveness of National Weather Service Heat Alerts in Preventing Mortality in 20 US Cities," *Environment International* 116 (2018): 30–38.

17 **Ron Howell:** Ron Howell, interview by the author, March 13, 2023.

17 **Yale College reunion:** Ronald Howell, "Before Their Time," *Yale Alumni Magazine*, May–June 2011.

18 **female undergraduates:** Women at Yale, "A Timeline of Women at Yale," Celebrate-women.Yale.edu.

18 **intensive stress:** Howell, "Before Their Time"; Reed T. DeAngelis, "Striving While Black: Race and the Psychophysiology of Goal Pursuit," *Journal of Health and Social Behavior* 6, no. 1 (2020): 24–42.

18 **fairly constant:** National Equity Atlas, "Life Expectancy," NationalEquityAtlas.org; GBD US Health Disparities Collaborators, "Life Expectancy by County, Race, and Ethnicity in the USA, 2000–19: A Systematic Analysis of Health Disparities," Lancet 400, no. 10345 (2022): 25–38; Elizabeth Arias, Betzaida Tejada-Vera, and Farida Ahmad, "Provisional Life Expectancy Estimates for January through June, 2020," NVSS Vital Statistics Rapid Release, Report no. 10, February 2021; Latoya Hill, Nambi Ndugga, and Samantha Artiga, "Key Data on Health and Health Care by Race and Ethnicity," KFF, March 15, 2023.

18 **between whites and other races:** Case and Deaton, *Deaths of Despair*, 6.

18 **drop by nearly three years:** Arias, Tejada-Vera, Kochanek, and Ahmad, "Provisional Estimates for 2021."

19 **two and a half years:** Arias, Tejada-Vera, Kochanek, and Ahmad, "Provisional Estimates for 2021."

19 **concerning disparities:** Arias, Tejada-Vera, Kochanek, and Ahmad, "Provisional Estimates for 2021."

19 **Researchers don't agree:** Alberto Palloni and Elizabeth Arias, "Paradox Lost: Explaining the Hispanic Adult Mortality Advantage," *Demography* 41, no. 3 (2004): 285–415; Carmen Alcántara, Cindy D. Estevez, and Margarita Alegría, "Latino and Asian Immigrant Adult Health: Paradoxes and Explanations," in *The Oxford Handbook of Acculturation and Health*, ed. Seth J. Schwartz and Jennifer Unger (Oxford: Oxford University Press, 2016), 197–220.

19 **lower levels of smoking:** Paola Scommegna, "Exploring the Paradox of U.S. Hispanics' Longer Life Expectancy," Population Reference Bureau, July 12, 2013; Francesco Acciai, Aggie J. Noah, and Glenn Firebaugh, "Pinpointing the Sources of the Asian Mortality Advantage in the USA," *Journal of Epidemiology and Community Health* 69, no. 10 (2015): 1006–11.

19 **immigration patterns:**, Mariele Macaluso, "The Influence of Skill-Based Policies on the Immigrant Selection Process," *Economia Politica* 39, no. 2 (2022): 595–621; Fernando Riosmena, Randall Kuhn, and Warren C. Jochem, "Explaining the Immigrant Health Advantage: Self-Selection and Protection in Health-Related Factors Among Five Major National-Origin Immigrant Groups in the United States," *Demography* 54, no. 1 (2017): 175–200.

19 **historical experiences:** Mosi Adesina Ifatunji et al., "Black Nativity and Health Dis-

parities: A Research Paradigm for Understanding the Social Determinants of Health," *International Journal of Environmental Research and Public Health* 19, no. 15 (2022).

19 **conceals wide variations:** Alcántara, Estevez, and Alegría, "Latino and Asian Immigrant Adult Health."

19 **Roseto, Pennsylvania:** Brenda Egolf et al., "The Roseto Effect: A 50-Year Comparison of Mortality Rates," *American Journal of Public Health* 82, no. 8 (August 1992): 1089–92.

20 **cardiovascular disease:** Egolf et al., "Roseto Effect."

20 **neighboring communities:** Egolf et al., "Roseto Effect."

20 **differences in biology:** Theresa M. Duello et al., "Race and Genetics Versus 'Race' in Genetics," *Evolution, Medicine, and Public Health* 9, no. 1 (2021): 232–45.

20 *thirty-year difference:* Joint Center for Political and Economic Studies, *Place Matters for Health in Baltimore: Ensuring Opportunities for Good Health for All*, JointCenter.org, November 2012.

20 **redlining was:** Candace Jackson, "What Is Redlining?," *New York Times*, August 17, 2021.

20 **stopped using:** Andre M. Perry and David Harshbarger, "America's Formerly Redlined Neighborhoods Have Changed, and So Must Solutions to Rectify Them," Brookings, October 14, 2019.

21 **"Chinatowns":** Mary Szto, "From Exclusion to Exclusivity: Chinese American Property Ownership and Discrimination in Historical Perspective," *Journal of Transnational Law and Policy* 25 (2017): 73–74.

21 **frequently bordered:** U.S Commission on Civil Rights, *Not in My Backyard: Executive Order 12,898 and Title VI as Tools for Achieving Environmental Justice*, USCCR.gov, October 2003.

21 **83 percent Black:** U.S. Census Bureau, "Jackson City, Mississippi," Census.gov.

21 **boil their water:** Char Adams, "Jackson, Mississippi's Water Crisis Persists as National Attention and Help Fade Away," NBC News, January 17, 2023.

21 **"weathering":** Allana T. Forde et al., "The Weathering Hypothesis as an Explanation for Racial Disparities in Health: A Systematic Review," *Annals of Epidemiology* 33 (2019): 1–18.e3; Kayla Yup, "Black Women Excluded from Critical Studies Due to 'Weathering,'" Yale School of Medicine, December 1, 2022.

21 **chronic exposure:** Forde et al., "Weathering Hypothesis"; Ana Sandoiu, "'Weathering': What Are the Health Effects of Stress and Discrimination?," *MedicalNewsToday*, February 26, 2021; A. T. Geronimus, "The Weathering Hypothesis and the Health of African-American Women and Infants: Evidence and Speculations," *Ethnicity and Disease* 2, no. 3 (1992): 207–21; Jenny Guidi et al., "Allostatic Load and Its Impact on Health: A Systematic Review," *Psychotherapy and Psychosomatics* 90, no. 1 (2021): 11–27.

21 **"producing ever-greater":** A. T. Geronimus et al., "'Weathering' and Age Patterns of Allostatic Load Scores Among Blacks and Whites in the United States," *American Journal of Public Health* 96, no. 5 (2006): 826–33.

21 **difference of six years:** Sarah Forrester et al., "Racial Differences in Weathering and its Associations with Psychosocial Stress: The CARDIA Study," SSM-Population Health 7 (2019).

22 **similar effects:** Gilbert C. Gee et al., "Racial Discrimination and Health Among Asian Americans: Evidence, Assessment, and Directions for Future Research," *Epidemiologic Reviews* 31, no. 1 (2009): 130–51; Kristine M. Molina, Margarita Alegría, and

Ramaswami Mahalingam, "A Multiple-Group Path Analysis of the Role of Everyday Discrimination on Self-Rated Physical Health Among Latina/os in the USA," *Annals of Behavioral Medicine* 45, no.1 (2013): 33–44; Jane A. Tiedt and Lori A. Brown, "Allostatic Load: The Relationship Between Chronic Stress and Diabetes in Native Americans," *Journal of Theory Construction and Testing* 18, no. 1 (2014): 22–27.

22 **genetic changes:** Steve W. Cole, "Social Regulation of Human Gene Expression," *Current Directions in Psychological Science* 18, no. 3 (2009): 132–37; Ana V. Diez Roux, "Complex Systems Thinking and Current Impasses in Health Disparities Research," *American Journal of Public Health* 101, no. 9 (2011): 1627–34; Chantel L. Martin et al., "Understanding Health Inequalities Through the Lens of Social Epigenetics," *Annual Review of Public Health* 43 (April 5, 2022): 235–54.

22 **over half of premature deaths:** Martin Loef and Harald Walach, "The Combined Effects of Healthy Lifestyle Behaviors on All Cause Mortality: A Systematic Review and Meta-Analysis," *Preventive Medicine* 55, no. 3 (2012): 163–70; Monique Tello, "Healthy Lifestyle: 5 Keys to a Longer Life," Harvard Health Blog, March 25, 2020.

22 **five healthy habits:** Yanping Li et al., "Impact of Healthy Lifestyle Factors on Life Expectancies in the US Population," *Circulation* 138, no. 4 (2018): 345–55.

23 **two years longer:** Tello, "Healthy Lifestyle."

23 **all five by age fifty:** Tianna Hicklin, "Healthy Habits Can Lengthen Life," National Institutes of Health, May 8, 2018; Li et al., "Impact of Healthy Factors."

23 **boost health:** Becca R. Levy et al., "Longevity Increased by Positive Self-Perceptions of Aging," *Journal of Personality and Social Psychology* 83, no. 2 (2002): 261–70.

23 **her 2022 book:** Becca R. Levy, *Breaking the Age Code: How Your Beliefs About Aging Determine How Long and Well You Live* (New York: William Morrow, 2022).

23 *7.5 years longer:* Levy et al., "Longevity Increased."

23 **ageism is associated:** Becca R. Levy et al., "Age Stereotypes Held Earlier in Life Predict Cardiovascular Events in Later Life," *Psychological Science* 20, no. 3 (2009): 296–98; Becca R. Levy et al., "A Culture-Brain Link: Negative Age Stereotypes Predict Alzheimer's Disease Biomarkers," *Psychology and Aging* 31, no. 1 (2016): 82–88; Becca R. Levy et al., "Association Between Positive Age Stereotypes and Recovery from Disability in Older Persons," *Journal of the American Medical Association* 308, no. 19 (2012): 1972–73.

24 **much bigger picture:** Louise Aronson, *Elderhood: Redefining Aging, Transforming Medicine, Reimagining Life* (London: Bloomsbury, 2019), 256.

24 **midlife is the time:** David G. Blanchflower and Andrew J. Oswald, "Is Well-Being U-Shaped Over the Life Cycle?," *Social Science and Medicine* 66, no. 8 (2008): 1733–49; Arthur A. Stone et al., "A Snapshot of the Age Distribution of Psychological Well-Being in the United States," *Proceedings of the National Academy of Sciences* 107, no. 22 (2010): 9985–90.

24 **circumstances that often:** Aronson, *Elderhood.*

24 **make us happier:** Koichiro Shiba et al., "Purpose in Life and 8-Year Mortality by Gender and Race/Ethnicity Among Older Adults in the U.S," *Preventive Medicine* 164 (2022): 107310; Health and Retirement Study, *The Health and Retirement Study,* HRS. USR.umich.edu.

24 **goals and direction:** Robby Berman, "Having a Sense of Purpose May Help You Live Longer, Research Shows," *MedicalNewsToday,* November 21, 2022.

24 **lower risk of dying:** Aliya Alimujiang et al., "Association Between Life Purpose and

Mortality Among US Adults Older Than 50 Years," *JAMA Network Open* 2, no. 5 (2019): e194270; Shiba et al., "Purpose in Life."

24 **Purpose has:** Awais Aftab et al., "Meaning in Life and its Relationship with Physical, Mental, and Cognitive Functioning: A Study of 1,042 Community-Dwelling Adults Across the Lifespan," *Journal of Clinical Psychiatry* 81, no. 1 (2019); Patrick L. Hill et al., "The Value of a Purposeful Life: Sense of Purpose Predicts Greater Income and Net Worth," *Journal of Research in Personality* 65, no. 5 (2016).

24 **help us live longer:** Berman, "Having a Sense of Purpose."

24 **Richard Leider** Richard Leider, interview by author, January 13, 2023.

24 **purpose is fundamental:** Richard J. Leider and David Shapiro, *Who Do You Want to Be When You Grow Old?: The Path of Purposeful Aging* (n.p.: Berrett-Koehler, 2021).

25 **"Those who have":** Victor Frankl, *Man's Search for Meaning* (1946), trans. Ilse Lasch (Boston: Beacon Press, 1959), 68; Friedrich Nietzsche, *Twilight of the Idols or How to Philosophize with a Hammer* (1889), 6.

25 **risk of becoming isolated:** National Academies of Science, Engineering, and Medicine, *Social Isolation and Loneliness in Older Adults: Opportunities for the Health Care System* (Washington, DC: National Academies Press, 2020).

25 **up to fifteen years:** Julianne Holt-Lunstad et al., "Loneliness and Social Isolation as Risk Factors for Mortality: A Meta-Analytic Review," *Perspectives on Psychological Science* 10, no. 2 (2015): 227-37.

25 **"bigger than we":** Adrianna Rodriguez, "US Life Expectancy Problem Is 'Bigger Than We Ever Thought,' Report Finds," *USA Today*, June 2, 2023.

26 **American disadvantage:** Steven H. Woolf, "Falling Behind: The Growing Gap in Life Expectancy Between the United States and Other Countries, 1933-2021," *American Journal of Public Health* 113, no. 9 (2023): 970-80.

26 **skewing the national average:** Rodriguez, "US Life Expectancy Problem."

26 **we all pay a price:** Smedley interview.

26 **In 2018, a bill:** National Strategy to Increase Life Expectancy Act, H.R. 7035, 115th Congress (2018).

Chapter 2: Will I Be Healthy?

27 **geroscience:** American Federation for Aging Research, "What Is Geroscience?," AFAR. org; B. Anton et al., "Can We Delay Aging? The Biology and Science of Aging," *Annals of the New York Academy of Sciences* 1057, no. 1 (2005): 525-35; *The Fountain of Youth? The Quest for Aging Therapies: Hearing Before the Subcommittee on Investigations and Oversight of the Committee House Science, Space and Technology*, 117th Cong. (2022) (statement of S. Jay Olshansky, University of Illinois at Chicago); Matt Kaeberlein, "How Healthy Is the Healthspan Concept?," *GeroScience* 40, no. 4 (2018): 361-64.

27 **modified in animals:** Ibrahim Mohammed et al., "A Critical Review of the Evidence That Metformin Is a Putative Anti-Aging Drug That Enhances Healthspan and Extends Lifespan," *Frontiers in Endocrinology* 12 (2021): 718942; Vladimir Anisimov, "Aging Delay: of Mice and Men," *Acta Biomedica* 92, no. 1 (2021): e2021073; Salk Institute for Biological Studies, "Cellular Rejuvenation Therapy Safely Reverses Signs of Aging in Mice," *Salk News*, March 7, 2022.

28 **enormous benefits:** Olshansky, testimony at *Fountain of Youth*; Andrew J. Scott, Martin Ellison, and David A. Sinclair, "The Economic Value of Targeting Aging," *Nature Aging* 1 (2021): 616-23.

28 **Jennifer Karas Montez:** Jennifer Karas Montez, interview by the author, September 7, 2022.

28 **based on studies:** Jennifer Karas Montez et al., "U.S. State Policies, Politics, and Life Expectancy," *Milbank Quarterly* 98, no. 3 (2020): 668–99.

28 **similar laws:** Montez et al., "U.S. State Policies, Politics."

28 **Connecticut and Oklahoma:** Jennifer Karas Montez and Jacob M. Grumbach, "U.S. State Policy Contexts and Population Health," *Milbank Quarterly* 101, no. S1 (April 2023): 196–223.

29 **13 percent:** Nader Mehri and Jennifer Karas Montez, "The Chances of Dying Young Differ Dramatically Across U.S. States," Lerner Center for Public Health Promotion and Center for Aging and Policy Studies, Data Slice no. 54, June 21, 2022.

29 *twenty years:* Jennifer Karas Montez, Mark D. Hayward, and Douglass A. Wolf, "Do U.S. States' Socioeconomic and Policy Contexts Shape Adult Disability?" *Social Science Medicine* 178 (2017): 115–26.

29 **nearly two years:** World Health Organization, "Life Expectancy at Birth (Years)," WHO.int, 2020; World Health Organization, "Healthy Life Expectancy (HALE)," WHO.int, 2020.

30 **sixty-six years:** Brigham Bastian et al., "Mortality Trends in the United States, 1900–2018," National Center for Health Statistics, August 25, 2020; WHO, "Life Expectancy at Birth (Years)."

30 **report poor health:** Eileen M. Crimmins, Jung K. Kim, and Teresa E. Seeman, "Poverty and Biological Risk: The Earlier 'Aging' of the Poor," *Journals of Gerontology: Series A, Biological Sciences and Medical Sciences* 64A, no. 2 (2009): 286–92.

30 **financial hardships:** Rebekah J. Walker et al., "The Longitudinal Influence of Social Determinants of Health on Glycemic Control in Elderly Adults with Diabetes," *Diabetes Care* 43, no. 4 (2020): 759–66.

30 **racial disparities:** Samantha Artiga, Latoya Hill, and Anthony Damico, "Health Coverage by Race and Ethnicity, 2010–2021," KFF, December 20, 2022.

30 **leveled off:** Dana Goldman, "The Economic Promise of Delayed Aging," *Cold Spring Harbor Perspectives in Medicine* 6, no. 2 (2015).

30 **future generations:** Péter Hudomiet, Michael D. Hurd, and Susann Rohwedder, "Trends in Health in Midlife and Late Life," *Journal of Human Capital* 16, no. 1 (2022): 133–56.

30 **very satisfied:** Vicki Levy and Patty David, *Second Half of Life Study*, AARP Research, June 2022; David J. Lowsky et al., "Heterogeneity in Healthy Aging," *Journals of Gerontology: Series A, Biological Sciences and Medical Sciences* 69, no. 6 (2014): 640–49.

30 **technical fixes:** Medical Device Network, "Ageing Population and Medical Devices: Technology Trends," MedicalDeviceNetwork.com, March 21, 2022; Gustavo J. Almeida, Samannaaz S. Khoja, and Boris A. Zelle, "Effect of Prehabilitation in Older Adults Undergoing Total Joint Replacement: An Overview of Systematic Reviews," *Current Geriatrics Reports* 9, no. 4 (2020): 280–87.

31 **Four in ten:** Danielle M. Taylor, "Americans with Disabilities: 2014," Current Population Reports no. P70-152, Census.gov, November 2018.

31 **one in ten:** Taylor, "Americans with Disabilities."

31 *successful aging:* Annele Urtamo, K. Jyväkorpi Satu, and E. Strandberg Timo, "Definitions of Successful Ageing: A Brief Review of a Multidimensional Concept," *Acta Biomedica* 90, no. 2 (2019): 359–63.

31 **prevailing assumption:** Tracey Gendron, *Ageism Unmasked: Exploring Age Bias and How to End It* (Westminster, MD: Steerforth, 2022), 80.

31 **at least one:** Jane L. Tavares, Marc A. Cohen, Susan Silberman, and Lauren Popham, *Measuring Disease Cost Burden Among Older Adults in the U.S.: A Health and Retirement Study Analysis*, LeadingAge and National Council on Aging, 2022.

32 **Edmundo:** Edmundo, interview by the author, March 8, 2023.

33 **many theories:** João Pinto da Costa et al., "A Synopsis on Aging—Theories, Mechanisms and Future Prospects," *Ageing Research Reviews* 29 (2016): 90–112.

33 **less collagen:** Suzan Obagi, "Why Does Skin Wrinkle with Age? What Is the Best Way to Slow Or Prevent This Process?" *Scientific American*, September 26, 2005.

33 **melanocytes:** Peter Urban, "Why Does Hair Turn Gray As You Age?" AARP, January 5, 2021.

33 **sleeping more fitfully:** National Institute of Neurological Disorders and Stroke, "Brain Basics: Understanding Sleep," NINDS.NIH.gov, August 13, 2019.

33 **sexual intimacy:** National Institute on Aging, "Sexuality in Later Life," NIA.NIH. gov, November 30, 2017; Brittne Kakulla and Stephanie Childs, *Ageless Desire: Relationships and Sex in Middle Age and Beyond (Ages 40-Plus)*, AARP Research, 2023.

33 **symptoms such as:** National Institute on Aging, "What Is Menopause?," NIA.NIH. gov, September 30, 2021.

33 **some symptoms often:** Elizabeth Agnvall, "Expert Advice to Help Symptoms of Menopause," AARP, December 20, 2022; Cleveland Clinic, "Menopause," My.Cleveland Clinic.org; Juli Fraga, "Menopause Transition Ushers in Memory Problems for Many Women," *Washington Post*, December 11, 2022.

33 **arteries gradually stiffen:** National Institute on Aging, "Heart Health and Aging," NIA.NIH.gov, June 1, 2018.

33 **metabolism naturally slows:** Herman Pontzer et al., "Daily Energy Expenditure Through the Human Life Course," *Science* 373, no. 6556 (2021): 808–12; Gina Kolata, "What We Think We Know About Metabolism May Be Wrong," *New York Times*, August 12, 2021; National Institute on Aging, "Maintaining a Healthy Weight," NIA.NIH.gov, April 7, 2022.

34 **cells require:** Qian-Li Xue, "The Frailty Syndrome: Definition and Natural History," *Clinics in Geriatric Medicine* 27, no. 1 (2011): 1–15.

34 **lose muscle mass:** Elena Volpi, Reza Nazemi, and Satoshi Fujita, "Muscle Tissue Changes with Aging," *Current Opinion in Clinical Nutrition and Metabolic Care* 7, no. 4 (2004): 405; Centers for Disease Control and Prevention, "The Truth About Aging and Dementia," CDC.gov, September 8, 2021; Stephanie Studenski et al., "Gait Speed and Survival in Older Adults," *Journal of the American Medical Association* 305, no. 1 (2011): 50–58.

34 **fastest marathon:** For marathoner times, see Sean McAlister, "How Fast Was Kelvin Kiptum's Men's Marathon World Record? Chicago Marathon 2023 Race Pace Breakdown and Split Times," Olympics, October 9, 2023; Cathal Dennehy, "Alcohol Nearly Killed Tommy Hughes. Now He Holds the Over-60 Half Marathon Record," *Runner's World*, September 22, 2020; Jere Longman, "85-year-old Marathoner Is So Fast that Even Scientists Marvel," *New York Times*, December 28, 2016.

34 **regarded telomeres:** Masood A. Shammas, "Telomeres, Lifestyle, Cancer, and Aging," *Current Opinion in Clinical Nutrition and Metabolic Care* 14, no. 1 (2011): 28–34; Elissa S. Epel et al., "Accelerated Telomere Shortening in Response to Life Stress," *Proceedings of the National Academy of Sciences* 101, no. 49 (2004): 17312–15.

34 **genetic mutations increase**: Valentina Salvestrini, Christian Sell, and Antonello Lorenzini, "Obesity May Accelerate the Aging Process," *Frontiers in Endocrinology* 10 (2019): 266.

34 **question the reliance**: Alexander Vaiserman and Dmytro Krasnienkov, "Telomere Length as a Marker of Biological Age: State-of-the-Art, Open Issues, and Future Perspectives," *Frontiers in Genetics* 11 (2020): 630186; Emily A. DeBoy et al., "Familial Clonal Hematopoiesis in a Long Telomere Syndrome," *New England Journal of Medicine* 388 (2023): 2422–33.

34 **"epigenetic clock"**: Steve Horvath and Kenneth Raj, "DNA Methylation-Based Biomarkers and the Epigenetic Clock Theory of Ageing," *Nature Reviews: Genetics* 19 (2018): 371–84; Elaine Schmidt, "Epigenetic Clock," Harvard Medical School, September 29, 2016.

34 **lead to inflammation:** lvi Zahava Vadasz et al., "Age-Related Autoimmunity," *BMC Medicine* 11, no. 1 (2013): 1–4.

34 **chronic inflammatory:** Claudio Franceschi et al., "Inflamm-aging: An Evolutionary Perspective on Immunosenescence," *Annals of the New York Academy of Sciences* 908, no. 1 (2000): 244–54.

34 *inflamm-aging*: Franceschi et al., "Inflamm-aging"; Juana Serrano-López and Beatriz Martín-Antonio, "Inflammaging, an Imbalanced Immune Response That Needs to Be Restored for Cancer Prevention and Treatment in the Elderly," *Cells* 10, no. 10 (2021): 2562; Luigi Ferrucci and Elisa Fabbri, "Inflammageing: Chronic Inflammation in Ageing, Cardiovascular Disease, and Frailty," *Nature Reviews: Cardiology* 15, no. 9 (2018): 505–22.

35 **bruises and paper cuts:** David Gerstein et al., "Wound Healing and Aging," *Dermatologic Clinics* 11, no. 4 (1993): 749–57.

35 **fight-or-flight:** Bruce S. McEwen, "Stressed or Stressed Out: What Is the Difference?," *Journal of Psychiatry and Neuroscience* 30, no. 5 (2005): 315–18.

35 **neurons to atrophy:** Bruce S. McEwen, "Structural Plasticity of the Adult Brain: How Animal Models Help Us Understand Brain Changes in Depression and Systemic Disorders Related to Depression," *Dialogues in Clinical Neuroscience* 6, no. 2 (2004): 119.

35 **damage the immune system:** McEwen, "Stressed or Stressed Out."

35 **Elissa Epel's:** Elissa Epel, interview by the author, July 26, 2021.

36 **Harmful stress:** Si-Sheng Huang, "Depression Among Caregivers of Patients with Dementia: Associative Factors and Management Approaches," *World Journal of Psychiatry* 12, no. 1 (2022): 59–76.

36 **born prematurely**: Ryan J. Van Lieshout et al., "Extremely Low Birth Weight and Accelerated Biological Aging," *Pediatrics* 147, no. 6 (2021).

36 **prenatal exposure**: Lauren L. Schmitz and Valentina Duque, "In Utero Exposure to the Great Depression Is Reflected in Late-Life Epigenetic Aging Signatures," *Proceedings of the National Academy of Sciences* 119, no. 46 (2022): e2208530119; La Follette School of Public Affairs, "Schmitz Publishes Study Linking Early-Life Poverty with Accelerated Aging," Lafollette.wisc.edu, December 18, 2022.

36 **adverse experiences in childhood:** Mark T. Berg et al., "Childhood Adversities as Determinants of Cardiovascular Disease Risk and Perceived Illness Burden in Adulthood," *Journal of Youth and Adolescence* 49, no. 6 (2020): 1292–308; Injury Prevention Research Center, "Adversity's Effect on Heart Health and Biological Aging," Iprc.public-health.uiowa.edu, March 8, 2022; Madelon M. E. Riem and Annemiek Karre-

man, "Childhood Adversity and Adult Health: The Role of Developmental Timing and Associations with Accelerated Aging," *Child Maltreatment* 24, no. 1 (2019): 17–25; "Experiencing Childhood Trauma Makes Body and Brain Age Faster," *ScienceDaily*, August 3, 2020.

36 **Growing up in poverty:** Office of Disease Prevention and Health Promotion, "Poverty," *Healthy People 2030*, Health.gov.

36 **as the planet warms:** Bruce A. Carnes, David Staats, and Bradley J. Willcox, "Impact of Climate Change on Elder Health," *Journals of Gerontology: Series A, Biomedical Sciences and Medical Sciences* 69, no. 9 (2014): 1087–91.

37 **after hurricane Katrina:** Vincanne Adams et al., "Aging Disaster: Mortality, Vulnerability, and Long-Term Recovery Among Katrina Survivors," *Medical Anthropology* 30, no. 3 (2011): 247–70.

37 **deemed the air unhealthy:** J. Ailshire, "The Role of Air Pollution in Healthy Aging," *Innovation in Aging* 2, no. 1 (2018): 863–64.

37 **dust, heat, and smog:** Carnes, Staats, and Willcox, "Impact of Climate Change."

37 **areas with unhealthy air:** Ailshire, "Role of Air Pollution."

37 **high rates of asthma:** Bruce S. McEwen and Pamela Tucker, "Critical Biological Pathways for Chronic Psychosocial Stress and Research Opportunities to Advance the Consideration of Stress in Chemical Risk Assessment," *American Journal of Public Health* 101, no. S1 (2011): S131–S39; Bhargavi Ganesh, Corianne Payton Scally, Laura Skopec, and Jun Zhu, *The Relationship Between Housing and Asthma Among School-Age Children*, Urban Institute, October 2017.

37 **train derailed:** Jill Neimark, "Experts Weigh in on Potential Health Hazards Posed by Chemicals in Ohio Train Derailment," *STAT*, February 21, 2023; Aria Bendix and Uwa Ede-Osifo, "As Residents Near Ohio Train Derailment Begin to File Lawsuits, Some Report Lingering Coughs or Chest Pain," NBC News, February 18, 2023.

37 **necessary ingredients:** U.S. Environmental Protection Agency, "Progress Cleaning the Air and Improving People's Health," EPA.gov, May 1, 2023; Maryland Department of Environment, *Clean Air in Maryland 2020*, MDE.Maryland.gov, 2020; Centers for Disease Control and Prevention, "Massachusetts's Success," CDC.gov, March 9, 2018; American Rivers, "National River Cleanup," Americanrivers.org; Chesapeake Bay Foundation, "The History of Chesapeake Bay Cleanup Efforts," CBF.org.

37 **cities in the Northwest:** Evan Bush, David K. Li, and Aria Bendix, "Seattle and Portland Endure the World's Worst Air Quality as Wildfires Burn," NBC News, October 20, 2022.

37 **impacted by the hurricane:** Sue Anne Bell et al., "The Effect of Exposure to Disaster on Cancer Survival," *Journal of General Internal Medicine* 35, no. 1 (2020): 380–82.

37 **pressure on water supplies:** Michael Doudna, "Will the Valley Be Habitable in 2050? An Environmental Scientist Says Yes, But with These Changes," NBC News, September 28, 2022.

37 **temperatures in that city:** David Knowles, "Can Phoenix, the Hottest City in America, Survive Climate Change?" Yahoo!News, July 2, 2022; Olivia Dow, "Here's What You Need to Know About Phoenix's Climate Action Plan," Cronkite News, January 7, 2022.

38 **climate action plan:** City of Phoenix, *Climate Action Plan: 2021 Edition*, Phoenix.gov, September 27, 2021.

38 **strong evidence:** Mini E. Jacob et al., "Can a Healthy Lifestyle Compress the Dis-

abled Period in Older Adults?" *Journal of the American Geriatrics Society* 64, no. 10 (2016): 1952–61.

38   **a healthy diet**: Harvard School of Public Health, "Healthy Eating Plate," HSPH.Harvard .edu, January 2023.

38   **more than one drink**: U.S. Department of Agriculture and U.S. Department of Health and Human Services, *Dietary Guidelines for Americans 2020–2025*, 9th ed., DietaryGuidelines.gov, December 2020; Benjamin Anderson et al. "Health and Cancer Risks Associated with Low Levels of Alcohol Consumption," *Lancet* 8, no. 1 (2023): E6–E7; Kiran J. Biddinger et al., "Association of Habitual Alcohol Intake with Risk of Cardiovascular Disease," *Journal of the American Medical Association* 5, no. 3 (2022): e223849.

38   **risk of lung cancer**: Centers for Disease Control and Prevention, "Smoking and Tobacco Use: Benefits of Quitting," CDC.gov, September 23, 2020.

38   **Smoking in old age**: Ruth Peters et al., "Smoking, Dementia and Cognitive Decline in the Elderly, A Systematic Review," *BMC Geriatrics* 8, no 1 (2008): 1–7; Gotaro Kojima et al., "Does Current Smoking Predict Future Frailty? The English Longitudinal Study of Ageing," *Age and Ageing* 47, no. 1 (2018): 126–31.

38   **Quitting, even later**: Centers for Disease Control and Prevention, "Benefits of Quitting," CDC.gov, October 25, 2023.

38   **quit smoking at sixty-five**: Donald H. Taylor, Jr., et al., "Benefits of Smoking Cessation for Longevity," *American Journal of Public Health* 92, no. 6 (2002): 990–96.

39   **Thirty minutes a day**: Monique Tello, "Activity: It All Counts," Harvard Health Blog, April 23, 2019.

39   **hormonal and metabolic**: Stanford Center of Longevity, *The Sightlines Project: Seeing Our Way to Living Long, Living Well in the 21st Century*, Longevity.Stanford.edu, February 2016; National Heart, Lung and Blood Institute, "Overweight and Obesity," NHLBI. NIH.gov, March 24, 2022; Centers for Disease Control and Prevention, "Health Effects of Overweight and Obesity," CDC.gov, September 24, 2022.

39   **make a real difference**: Donna H. Ryan and Sarah Ryan Yockey, "Weight Loss and Improvement in Comorbidity: Differences at 5%, 10%, 15%, and Over," *Current Obesity Reports* 6, no. 2 (2017): 187–94.

39   **eight to ten years free**: Monique Tello, "Five Healthy Habits Net More Healthy Years," Harvard Health Blog, February 19, 2020; Yanping Li et al., "Healthy Lifestyle and Life Expectancy Free of Cancer, Cardiovascular Disease, and Type 2 Diabetes: Prospective Cohort Study," *BMJ* 368 (January 8, 2020): 16669; Karen Feldscher, "Five Healthy Habits to Live By," *Harvard Gazette*, April 30, 2018.

39   **93 percent**: American Heart Association, "Living Longer Is Important, But Those Years Need to Be Healthy Ones" (press release), Newsroom.Heart.org, January 29, 2020.

39   **only one in four**: Nazik Elgaddal, Ellen A. Kramarow, and Cynthia Reuben, "Physical Activity Among Adults Aged 18 and Over: United States, 2020," NCHS Data Brief no. 443 (August 2022); Seung Hee Lee et al., "Adults Meeting Fruit and Vegetable Intake Recommendations—United States, 2019," *Morbidity and Mortality Weekly Report* 71, no. 1 (January 7, 2022).

39   **down to circumstances**: Brian Elbel et al., "Assessment of a Government-Subsidized Supermarket in a High-Need Area on Household Food Availability and Children's Dietary Intakes," *Public Health Nutrition* 18, no. 15 (2015): 2881–90; Yan-Bo Zhang et

al., "Associations of Healthy Lifestyle and Socioeconomic Status with Mortality and Incident Cardiovascular Disease: Two Prospective Cohort Studies," *BMJ* 373 (April 14, 2021).

39   **half of us truly believe:** AHA "Living Longer Is Important."

40   **a lot to do with dose**: Thomas Rutledge, "When Stress Is Good for You: The Hormesis Effect," *Psychology Today*, December 1, 2022.

40   **interval training:** Zsolt Radak et al., "Exercise, Oxidative Stress and Hormesis," *Ageing Research Reviews* 7, no. 1 (2008): 34–42; Elissa S. Epel, "The Geroscience Agenda: Toxic Stress, Hormetic Stress, and the Rate of Aging," *Ageing Research Reviews* 63 (2020): 101–67.

41   **Harvard Study of Adult Development:** Massachusetts General Hospital and Harvard Medical School, *Harvard Study of Adult Development*, AdultDevelopmentStudy.org.

41   **Over time it grew:** Massachusetts General Hospital and Harvard Medical School, *Harvard Second Generation Study*, AdultDevelopmentStudy.org.

41   **presents only findings:** Robert Waldinger, interview by the author, February 15, 2023.

42   **Robert Waldinger:** Waldinger interview.

42   **satisfaction in relationships:** Robert Waldinger and Marc Schulz, *The Good Life: Lessons from the World's Longest Scientific Study of Happiness* (New York: Simon & Schuster, 2023).

43   **148 studies:** Dr. Julianne Holt-Lunstad, "The Effects of Loneliness and Social Isolation," *A Second Opinion* (audio podcast), May 11, 2020; Julianne Holt-Lunstad et al., "Loneliness and Social Isolation as Risk Factors for Mortality: A Meta-Analytic Review," *Perspectives on Psychological Science* 10, no. 2 (2015): 227–37.

43   **few relationships:** Holt-Lunstad, "Effects of Loneliness"; Holt-Lunstad et al., "Loneliness and Social Isolation."

43   **more socially connected:** Holt-Lunstad et al., "Loneliness and Social Isolation."

43   **more deadly than obesity:** Julianne Holt-Lunstad, Timothy B. Smith, and J. Bradley Layton, "Social Relationships and Mortality Risk: A Meta-Analytic Review," *PloS Medicine* 7, no. 7 (2010): e1000316.

43   **alone and on guard:** Holt-Lunstad, "Effects of Loneliness."

43   **stress-related hormones:** National Institute on Aging, "Social Isolation, Loneliness in Older People Pose Health Risks," NIA.NIH.gov, April 23, 2019; Malissa Underwood, "Social Isolation and Loneliness in Older Adults: the Unseen Determinant of Health," *Public Health Insight*, August 18, 2022; Cleveland Clinic, "What Happens in Your Body When You're Lonely?" *HealthEssentials Newsletter*, February 23, 2018.

43   **twice as much:** Matthew McGough et al., "How Does Health Spending in the U.S. Compare to Other Countries?" *Health System Tracker*, February 9, 2023; Roosa Tikkanen and Melinda K. Abrams, "U.S. Health Care from a Global Perspective, 2019: Higher Spending, Worse Outcomes?" Commonwealth Fund, January 30, 2020; William H. Shrank, Teresa L. Rogstad, and Natasha Parekh, "Waste in the US Health Care System: Estimated Costs and Potential for Savings," *Journal of the American Medical Association* 322, no. 15 (2019): 1501–9.

43   **cost of general physician:** Organization for Economic Cooperation and Development, *Understanding Differences in Health Expenditure Between the United States and OECD Countries*, OECD.org, September 2022.

44   **much more fragmented:** OECD, *Understanding Differences.*

44 **$4.3 trillion in 2021:** Apoorva Rama, "National Health Expenditures, 2021: Decline in Pandemic-Related Government Spending Results in 8-Percentage Point Decrease in Total Spending Growth," American Medical Association, 2023.

44 **far worse health outcomes:** Tikkanen and Abrams, "U.S. Health Care 2019"; Munira Z. Gunja, Evan D. Gumas, and Reginald D. Williams II, "U.S. Health Care from a Global Perspective, 2022: Accelerating Spending, Worsening Outcomes," Commonwealth Fund, January 31, 2023.

44 **lacked health insurance:** Brian Tsai, "U.S. Uninsured Rate Hits Record Low in First Quarter of 2023," NCHS Blog, August 2, 2023.

44 **universal coverage:** Aiden Lee et al., "National Uninsured Rate Reaches All-Time Low in Early 2022," Data Point HP-2022-23, Assistant Secretary for Planning and Evaluation, U.S. Department of Health and Human Services, August 2022; Jason Furman and Matt Fiedler, "The Economic Record of the Obama Administration: Reforming the Health Care System," Office of the President of the United States, 2016.

44 **people without health insurance:** Jennifer Tolbert, Patrick Drake, and Anthony Damico, "Key Facts About the Uninsured Population," KFF, December 19, 2022.

44 **out-of-pocket costs:** Sara R. Collins, Lauren A. Haynes, and Relebohile Masitha, "The State of U.S. Health Insurance in 2022: Findings from the Commonwealth Fund Biennial Health Insurance Survey," Commonwealth Fund, September 29, 2022; David Squires and Chloe Anderson, "U.S. Health Care from a Global Perspective: Spending, Use of Services, Prices, and Health in 13 Countries," Commonwealth Fund, October 8, 2015.

44 **premiums and deductibles:** Preeti Vankar, "Percentage of Median Income Spent on Premium Contribution and Deductible by U.S. Employees from 2008–2020," *Statista*, March 22, 2023.

44 **high cost of health care:** Ana B. Ibarra, "Electing to 'Opt Out' of Obamacare," *KFF Health News*, November 17, 2016.

44 **in eleven wealthy countries:** Michelle M. Doty et al., "Income-Related Inequality in Affordability and Access to Primary Care in Eleven High-Income Countries," *Health Affairs* 40, no. 1 (2020); Commonwealth Fund, "New International Study: Americans with Lower Income are the Sickest, Most Likely to Struggle to Afford Care and Other Basic Needs Compared to Lower-Income People in Other Wealthy Countries" (press release), CommonwealthFund.org, December 9, 2020.

45 **through their employer:** Katherine Keisler-Starkey and Lisa N. Bunch, *Health Insurance Coverage in the United States: 2021*, Current Population Reports no. P60-278, Census .gov, September 2022.

45 **10 percent:** Keisler-Starkey and Bunch, *Health Insurance Coverage.*

45 **IRS declared tax-free:** Aaron E. Carroll, "The Real Reason the U.S. Has Employer-Sponsored Health Insurance," *New York Times*, September 5, 2017.

45 **more than 50 percent:** Carroll, "Real Reason."

45 **neither succeeded**: Kaiser Family Foundation, "Timeline: History of Health Reform in the U.S.," KFF.org, 2011.

45 **two new programs:** Centers for Medicare and Medicaid Services, "About CMS—History," CMS.gov, December 1, 2021.

45 **Children's Health Insurance Program:** Medicaid, "2020 Number of Children Ever Enrolled Report," Medicaid.gov.

45 **pay for prescription drugs:** Medicare Prescription Drug, Improvement, and Modernization Act of 2003, H.R. 1, 108th Congress (2003).

46   **supplemental private insurance:** Wyatt Koma, Juliette Cubanski, and Tricia Neu-
     man, "A Snapshot of Sources of Coverage Among Medicare Beneficiaries in 2018,"
     KFF, March 2021; Wafa Tarazi et al., *Medicare Beneficiary Enrollment Trends and Demo-
     graphic Characteristics,* Issue Brief no. HP-2002-08, Assistant Secretary for Planning and
     Evaluation, U.S. Department of Health and Human Services, March 2, 2022.

46   **extending Medicaid coverage:** Tolbert, Drake, and Damico, "Key Facts about the
     Uninsured."

46   **twenty-six million:** Tolbert, Drake, and Damico, "Key Facts about the Uninsured";
     Christen Linke Young, "There Are Clear, Race-Based Inequalities in Health Insurance
     and Health Outcomes," Brookings, February 19, 2020.

46   **half are people of color:** Brian D. Smedley, Adrienne Y. Stith, and Alan R. Nelson,
     eds., *Unequal Treatment: Confronting Racial and Ethnic Disparities in Health Care* (Washing-
     ton, DC: National Academies Press, 2003).

46   **increased insurance coverage:** Vann R. Newkirk, "America's Health Segregation
     Problem," *Atlantic,* May 18, 2016; Erica T. Warner et al., "Time to Diagnosis and Breast
     Cancer Stage by Race/Ethnicity," *Breast Cancer Research and Treatment* 136, no. 3 (2012):
     813–21; American Cancer Society Cancer Action Network, "Disparities in Breast Can-
     cer: African American Women," Fightcancer.org, January 2017.

46   **less likely to be prescribed:** Frank Batten School for Leadership and Public Pol-
     icy, "Black Americans are Systematically Under-Treated for Pain. Why?," Batten.
     Virginia.edu, June 30, 2020; Nancy Morden et al., "Racial Inequality in Prescrip-
     tion Opioid Receipt—Role of Individual Health Systems," *New England Journal of
     Medicine* 385 (2021): 342–51; Salimah H. Meghani, Eeeseung Byun, and Rollin M.
     Gallagher, "Time to Take Stock: A Meta-Analysis and Systematic Review of Anal-
     gesic Treatment Disparities for Pain in the United States," *Pain Medicine* 13, no. 2
     (2012): 150–74; Kelly M. Hoffman et al., "Racial Bias in Pain Assessment and Treat-
     ment Recommendations, and False Beliefs About Biological Differences Between
     Blacks and Whites," *Proceedings of the National Academy of Sciences* 113, no. 16 (2016):
     4296–301.

46   **poorer medical care:** Anna Flagg, "The Black Mortality Gap, and a Document Writ-
     ten in 1910," *New York Times,* August 30, 2021; Joe Feagin and Zinobia Bennefield,
     "Systemic Racism and US Health Care," *Social Science and Medicine* 103 (2014): 7–14;
     Smedley, Stith, and Nelson, *Unequal Treatment;* Urban Institute, "*Unequal Treatment* at
     20: Accelerating Progress toward Health Care Equity—Morning Session," Urban.org,
     March 21, 2023.

46   **persistently underfunded:** Cristina Boccuti, Christina Swoope, and Samantha
     Artiga, "The Role of Medicare and the Indian Health Service for American Indians
     and Alaska Natives: Health, Access and Coverage," KFF, December 18, 2014.

46   **Government spending:** U.S. Department of Veterans Affairs, *Annual Benefits Report:
     Fiscal Year 2019,* Benefits.VA.gov, 2019, 8; Indian Health Service, "I Profile," HIS.gov;
     Boards of Trustees of the Federal Hospital Insurance and Federal Supplementary
     Medical Insurance Trust Funds, *2021 Annual Report,* CMS.gov, 207.

47   **rely on the IHS:** Collette Adamsen, "Health Care Coverage by Age for American
     Indian/Alaska Native Elders," Native Fact Sheet no. 105, National Resource Center
     on Native American Aging, November 2015; Matthew Tobey, Katrina Armstrong, and
     Donald Warne, "The 2019 Partial Government Shutdown and Its Impact on Health
     Care for American Indians and Alaska Natives," *Journal of Health Care for the Poor and*

Underserved 31, no. 1 (2020): 75–80; Boccuti, Swoope, and Artiga, "Role of Medicare and Indian Health Service."

47 **don't encourage either:** Susan Levine et al., "Health Care Industry Insights: Why the Use of Preventive Services Is Still Low," *Preventing Chronic Disease* 16 (2019).

47 **Edmundo:** Edmundo interview.

48 **particular phase:** Mary Ann Forciea, "Geriatric Medicine: History of a Young Specialty," *Virtual Mentor* 16, no. 5 (2014): 385–89.

48 **first department of geriatrics:** John E. Morley, "A Brief History of Geriatrics," *Journals of Gerontology: Series A, Biomedical Sciences and Medical Sciences* 59, no. 11 (2004): 1132–52; Paula E. Lester, T. S. Dharmarajan, and Eleanor Weinstein, "The Looming Geriatrician Shortage: Ramifications and Solutions," *Journal of Aging and Health* 32, no. 9 (2020): 1052–62.

48 **7,300 geriatric doctors:** Lester, Dharmarajan, and Weinstein, "Looming Geriatrician Shortage."

48 **number has been dropping:** Lester, Dharmarajan, and Weinstein, "Looming Geriatrician Shortage."

48 **Louise Aronson:** Aronson interview.

48 **lowest-paid specialties:** Ariadne A. Meiboom et al., "Why Medical Students Do Not Choose a Career in Geriatrics: A Systematic Review," *BMC Medical Education* 15 (2015): 1–9; American Geriatrics Society, "Geriatric Medicine: A Clinical Imperative for an Aging Population, Part IA Policy Statement," HMPGlobalLearningNetwork.com, March 2005; Doximity, "2020 Physician Compensation Report," C8y.doxcdn.com, October 2020.

49 **More than 85 percent:** Halsted R. Holman, "The Relation of the Chronic Disease Epidemic to the Health Care Crisis," *ACR Open Rheumatology* 2, no. 3 (2020): 167–73.

50 **James Kirkland:** James Kirkland, interview by the author, December 16, 2021.

50 **Senescent cells accumulate:** Mayo Clinic, "James L. Kirkland, M.D., Ph.D.," Mayo.edu; Michael Tabb and Tulika Bose, "Can We Stop Aging?" *Scientific American*, February 1, 2023.

50 **super-agers, who defy:** Paola Sebastiani and Thomas T. Perls, "The Genetics of Extreme Longevity: Lessons from the New England Centenarian Study," *Frontiers in Genetics* 3 (2012): 277.

50 **live to 110:** Stacy L. Anderson et al., "Health Span Approximates Life Span Among Many Supercentenarians: Compression of Morbidity at the Approximate Limit of Life Span," *Journals of Gerontology: Series A, Biomedical Sciences and Medical Sciences* 67, no. 4 (2012): 395–405.

50 **die in their nineties:** Anderson et al., "Health Span Approximates Life Span."

51 **ugly mole rats:** Vera Gorbunova, Michael J. Bozzella, and Andrei Seluanov, "Rodents for Comparative Aging Studies: From Mice to Beavers," *Age* 30, no. 2–3 (2008): 111–19; Lindsey Valich, "Why Do Naked Male Rats Live Long, Cancer-Free Lives?" University of Rochester News Center, February 6, 2018.

51 **medicines already approved:** National Library of Medicine, "Metformin for Preventing Frailty in High-risk Older Adults," ID no. NCT02570672, ClinicalTrials.gov, January 10, 2023.

51 **Rapamycin:** Mikhail V. Blagosklonny, "Rapamycin for Longevity: Opinion Article," *Aging* 11, no. 19 (2019): 8048–67; Peter Mrak et al., "Discovery of the Actinoplanic Acid Pathway in *Streptomyces rapamycinicus* Reveals a Genetically Conserved Synergism with

Rapamycin," *Journal of Biological Chemistry* 293, no. 52 (2018): 19982-95; Damir Bara-nasic et al., "Draft Genome Sequence of *Streptomyces rapamycinicus* Strain NRRL 5491, the Producer of the Immunosuppressant Rapamycin," *Genome Announcements* 1, no. 4 (2013): e00581-13; Max Planck Institute for Biology of Ageing, "Brief Exposure to Rapamycin Has the Same Anti-Aging Effects as Lifelong Treatment, Shows Study in Fruit Flies and Mice," *ScienceDaily*, August 29, 2022; Paula Juricic et al., "Long-Lasting Geroprotection from Brief Rapamycin Treatment in Early Adulthood by Persistently Increased Intestinal Autophagy," *Nature Aging* 2 (2022): 824-36.

51 **unwanted side effects:** Blagosklonny, "Rapamycin for Longevity."

51 **Metformin:** Nir Barzilai et al., "Metformin as a Tool to Target Aging," *Cell Metabolism* 23, no. 6 (2016): 1060-65; Scott, Ellison, and Sinclair, "Economic Value."

51 **with type 2 diabetes:** C. A. Bannister et al., "Can People with Type 2 Diabetes Live Longer Than Those Without? A Comparison of Mortality in People Initiated with Metformin or Sulphonylurea Monotherapy and Matched, Non-Diabetic Controls," *Diabetes, Obesity and Metabolism* 16, no. 11 (2014): 1165-73; Chen-Pin Wang et al., "Differential Effects of Metformin on Age Related Comorbidities in Older Men with Type 2 Diabetes," *Journal of Diabetes and Its Complications* 31, no. 4 (2017): 679-86.

51 **killing off senescent cells:** Yi Zhu et al., "Past and Future Directions for Research on Cellular Senescence," *Cold Spring Harbor Perspectives in Medicine* (2023): a041205-a041205.

51 **36 percent increase:** Ming Xu et al., "Senolytics Improve Physical Function and Increase Lifespan in Old Age," *Nature Medicine* 24, no. 8 (2018): 1246-56.

51 **used in humans:** Georgina M. Ellison-Hughes, "First Evidence That Senolytics are Effective at Decreasing Senescent Cells in Humans," *EBioMedicine* 56 (June 2020).

51 **"Humans are not big":** Kirkland interview.

52 **people from paying:** U.S. Food and Drug Administration, "Statement from FDA Commissioner Scott Gottlieb, M.D., and Director of FDA's Center for Biologics Evaluation and Research Peter Marks, M.D., Ph.D., Cautioning Consumers Against Receiving Young Donor Plasma Infusions that are Promoted as Unproven Treatment for Varying Conditions" (press release), FDA.gov, February 19, 2019.

52 **deliver equitable health:** Schmitz and Duque, "In Utero Exposure to the Depression"; Lowsky et al., "Heterogeneity in Healthy Aging."

52 **"put hugs":** Holt-Lunstad, "Effects of Loneliness."

53 **health systems became:** Harvey W. Kaufman et al., "Changes in the Number of US Patients with Newly Identified Cancer Before and During the Coronavirus Disease 2019 (COVID-19) Pandemic," *Journal of the American Medical Association* 3, no. 8 (2020): e2017267; Linda Wang, "Working to Close the Cancer Screening Gap Caused by COVID," National Cancer Institute, May 17, 2022; Debra Pratt et al., "Impact of COVID-19 on Cancer Care: How the Pandemic Is Delaying Cancer Diagnosis and Treatment for American Seniors," *JCO Clinical Cancer Informatics*, no. 4 (2020): 1059-71.

Chapter 3: Will I Lose My Memory?

55 **fear their mental sharpness:** Laura Mehegan and Chuck Rainville, *2021 AARP Survey on the Perceptions Related to a Dementia Diagnosis: Adults Age 40-plus*, AARP Research, 2021.

55 **loom as more frightening:** Edwin Jones and Age Wave, *The Four Pillars of the New Retirement: What a Difference a Year Makes*, AgeWave.com, June 2021.

56   **"Memory and forgetting":** Scott Small, "We Will Forget Much of the Pandemic. That's a Good Thing," *New York Times,* March 9, 2022.

56   **"vital for our cognitive":** Scott Small, *Forgetting: The Benefits of Not Remembering* (New York: Crown, 2021).

56   **40 percent of dementias:** Gill Livingston et al., "Dementia Prevention, Intervention, and Care: 2020 Report of the Lancet Commission," *Lancet* 396, no. 10248 (August 8, 2020): 413–46.

56   *dementia*: National Institute on Aging, "What Is Dementia? Symptoms, Types, and Diagnosis," NIA.NIH.gov, December 8, 2022.

56   **most common form:** National Institute on Aging, "Memory, Forgetfulness, and Aging: What's Normal and What's Not?" NIA.NIH.gov, October 21, 2020.

56   **likely get dementia:** Mehegan and Rainville, *2021 Survey on Perceptions*; Cleveland Clinic, "Mild Cognitive Impairment," My.ClevelandClinic.org, March 2019; Ronald C. Peterson et al., "Practice Guideline Update Summary: Mild Cognitive Impairment. Report of the Guideline Development, Dissemination, and Implementation Subcommittee of the American Academy of Neurology," *Neurology* 90, no. 3 (January 2018): 126–35.

56   **actually *declined*:** Population Reference Bureau, "U.S. Dementia Trends" (fact sheet), PRB.org, October 21, 2021.

57   **living with dementia:** V. A. Freedman, J. C. Cornman, and J. D. Kasper, *National Health and Aging Trends Chart Book: Key Trends, Measures and Detailed Tables,* National Health and Aging Trends Study, 2021.

57   **brains are young:** Lynda A. Anderson et al., "The Public's Perceptions About Cognitive Health and Alzheimer's Disease Among the U.S. Population: A National Review," *Gerontologist* 49, no. S1 (June 2009): S3–S11.

57   **interfere with mental:** National Institute on Aging, "How the Aging Brain Affects Thinking," NIA.NIH.gov, June 27, 2023; National Institute on Aging, "Cognitive Super Agers Defy Typical Age-related Decline in Brainpower," NIA.NIH.gov, July 31, 2020.

57   **a little more time:** NIA, "How the Aging Brain."

57   **grasp of meaning:** NIA, "How the Aging Brain."

57   **understand concepts:** Memory and Aging Center, "Healthy Aging," Memory.UCSF. edu.

57   **Laura Carstensen:** Laura L. Carstensen, interview by the author, November 5, 2021.

58   **remember positive:** Laura L. Carstensen and Marguerite DeLiema, "The Positivity Effect: A Negativity Bias in Youth Fades with Age," *Current Opinion in Behavioral Sciences* 19 (February 2018): 7–12.

58   **neurons can regenerate:** Global Council on Brain Health, *Debunking Myths About the Aging Brain. 7 Facts About Your Brain,* AARP.org, 2017.

58   **Neurogenesis holds:** Owji Shahin and Mohammadali M. Shoja, "The History of Discovery of Adult Neurogenesis," *Clinical Anatomy* 33, no. 1 (January 2020): 41–55.

58   **remain mentally sharp:** NIA, "Cognitive Super Agers."

58   **memory tests:** NIA, "Cognitive Super Agers."

58   *cognitive reserve*: Harvard Health Publishing, "What Is Cognitive Reserve?," Health. Harvard.edu, January 6, 2023.

59   **never shown any outward:** HHP, "What Is Cognitive Reserve?"

59   **helps protect against:** Shelli R. Kesler et al., "Premorbid Intellectual Functioning,

Education, and Brain Size in Traumatic Brain Injury: An Investigation of the Cognitive Reserve Hypothesis," *Applied Neuropsychology* 10 (2003): 153–63; HHP, "What Is Cognitive Reserve?"

59 **brain's resilience:** HHP, "What Is Cognitive Reserve?"

59 **Education seems to help:** Yaakov Stern and Daniel Barulli, "Cognitive Reserve," *Handbook of Clinical Neurology* 167 (2019), chap. 11.

59 **Learning on the job:** Jean F. Dartiques et al., "Playing Board Games, Cognitive Decline and Dementia: A French Population-Based Cohort Study," *BMJ* 3, no. 8 (2013); Yaakov Stern, "Cognitive Reserve in Ageing and Alzheimer's Disease," *Lancet Neurology* 11, no. 11 (November 2012): 1006–12.

59 **exercise likely plays:** Jane E. Brody, "The Secrets of 'Cognitive Super-Agers,'" *New York Times*, June 21, 2021; Yaakov Stern et al., "Effect of Aerobic Exercise on Cognition in Younger Adults. A Randomized Clinical Trial," *Neurology* 92, no. 9 (February 26, 2019).

59 **more links:** NIA, "Cognitive Super Agers."

60 **lose your keys:** National Institute on Aging, "What Is Mild Cognitive Impairment?" NIA.NIH.gov, April 12, 2021.

60 **compensate for these lapses:** NIA, "What Is Mild Cognitive Impairment?"

60 **progress to Alzheimer's:** National Institute on Aging, "Memory, Forgetfulness, and Aging: What's Normal and What's Not?" NIA.NIH.gov, October 21, 2020; Alex Ward et al., "Rate of Conversion from Prodromal Alzheimer's Disease to Alzheimer's Dementia: A Systematic Review of the Literature," *Dementia Geriatric Cognitive Disorder Extra* 3, no. 1 (2013): 320–32.

60 **Kezia:** Kezia, interview by the author, November 16, 2021.

61 **as long as twenty years:** Annabel Price et al., "Mortality in Dementia with Lewy Bodies Compared with Alzheimer's Dementia: A Retrospective Naturalistic Cohort Study," *BMJ* 7, no. 11 (November 3, 2017): e017504; Cleveland Clinic, "Lewy Body Dementia," My.ClevelandClinic.org, August 18, 2022.

61 **Alois Alzheimer:** Alzheimer's Disease International, "Alois Alzheimer," Alzint.org.

61 **"When objects are shown":** Konrad Maurer, Stephan Volk, and Hector Gerbaldo, "Auguste D and Alzheimer's Disease," *Lancet* 349, no. 9064 (May 24, 1997): 1546–49.

62 **"peculiar material":** Maurer, Volk, and Gerbaldo, "Auguste D."

62 **60 to 80 percent:** Alzheimer's Association, "What Is Alzheimer's Disease?," Alz.org.

62 **inflammation and atrophy:** Alzheimer's Assoc., "What Is Alzheimer's?"

62 **important caveat:** NIA, "Cognitive Super Agers."

62 **may not have dementia:** Karen S. SantaCruz et al., "Alzheimer Disease Pathology in Subjects Without Dementia in 2 Studies of Aging: The Nun Study and the Adult Changes in Thought Study," *Journal of Neuropathology and Experimental Neurology* 70, no. 10 (2011): 832–40.

62 **Dutch study:** Nina Beker et al., "Association of Cognitive Function Trajectories in Centenarians with Postmortem Neuropathology, Physical Health, and Other Risk Factors for Cognitive Decline," *Journal of the American Medical Association* 4, no. 1 (2021).

63 **linked to the cognitive reserve:** Thomas T. Perls, "Cognitive Trajectories and Resilience in Centenarians—Findings from the 100-Plus Study," *Journal of the American Medical Association* 4, no. 1 (January 15, 2021): e2032538.

63 **these stages:** Mayo Clinic, "Alzheimer's Stages: How the Disease Progresses," Mayo Clinic.org, April 29, 2021.

63 **memory is largely intact:** Esther Heerema, "Stages of Lewy Body Dementia: What to Expect As Condition Progresses," *Verywell Health*, September 28, 2022.

63 **movement and speech:** Heerema, "Stages of Lewy Body Dementia."

63 **multiple types:** Sarah Lenz Lock and Jonathan Peterson, *It's Time to Act: The Challenges of Alzheimer's and Dementia for Women*, AARP, 2020; Alzheimer's Association, *2023 Alzheimer's Disease Facts and Figures*, Alz.org, 2023.

63 **between three and eleven years:** Mayo, "Alzheimer's Stages."

64 **Terrie Montgomery:** Terry Montgomery, interview by the author, August 5, 2022.

64 **railroad crossing:** Dementia Minds, "Hello My Name Is Terry," Dementiaallianceinternational.org, July 18, 2022.

64 **National Council of Dementia Minds:** National Council of Dementia Minds, Dementiaminds.org.

64 **more severe symptoms:** National Institute on Aging, "Data Shows Racial Disparities in Alzheimer's Disease Diagnosis Between Black and White Research Study Participants," NIA.NIH.gov, December 16, 2021; Alzheimer's Impact Movement and Alzheimer's Association, "Race, Ethnicity, and Alzheimer's" (fact sheet), AAIC.Alz.org, March 2020.

65 **online assessment:** AARP Staying Sharp, "Assessment," Stayingsharp.aarp.org.

66 **simply observe you:** Rachel Nania, "4 Reasons You Shouldn't Shy Away from a Cognitive Screening," AARP, June 24, 2022.

66 **Mini-Mental State Examination:** PsychDB, "Mini-Mental Status Exam (MMSE)," Psychdb.com.

66 **Montreal Cognitive Assessment:** Ziad S. Nasreddine et al., "The Montreal Cognitive Assessment, MoCA: A Brief Screening Tool for Mild Cognitive Impairment," *Journal of the American Geriatrics Society* 53 (2005): 695–99.

66 **mimic early dementia:** Nania, "Cognitive Screening."

66 **review your prescriptions:** Armon B. Neel, "Caution! These 10 Drugs Can Cause Memory Loss," AARP, February 9, 2016; Memory and Aging Center, "Medication and Dementia," Memory.ucsf.edu.

66 **assessment with a specialist:** Alzheimer's Drug Discovery Foundation, "Alzheimer's Diagnosis and Treatment," Alzdiscovery.org.

66 **tests can also reveal:** NIA, "What Is Dementia? Symptoms, Types."

67 **the way we type:** George Underwood, "Can Your Typing Patterns Reveal If You Have Alzheimer's?" Pharmaphorum, April 26, 2021; Ashley A. Holmes et al., "A Novel Framework to Estimate Cognitive Impairment via Finger Interaction with Digital Devices," *Brain Communications* 4, no. 4 (July 28, 2022).

67 **Jason Karlawish:** Jason Karlawish, interview by the author, August 10, 2022.

67 **Early diagnosis gives:** Rachel Nania, "4 Reasons You Shouldn't Avoid Talking to Your Doctor About Dementia," AARP, June 21, 2021.

67 **drugs that can cure:** Winston Chiong et al., "Decisions with Patients and Families Regarding Aducanumab in Alzheimer Disease, with Recommendations for Consent: AAN Position Statement," *Neurology* 98, no. 4 (2022): 154–59.

68 **have a baseline:** Nania, "Talk to Your Doctor."

68 **annual wellness visits:** Medicare Coverage Database, "Cognitive Assessment and Care Plan Services," CMS.gov; Alzheimer's Association, *2019 Alzheimer's Disease Facts and Figures*, Alz.org, 2019.

68 **basic dementia screening tools:** Marwan N. Sabbagh et al., "Early Detection of Mild

Cognitive Impairment (MCI) in Primary Care," *Journal of Prevention of Alzheimer's Disease* 7, no. 3 (2020): 165–70.

68 **one-third of doctors:** Alzheimer's Association, "Primary Care Physicians on the Front Lines of Diagnosing and Providing Alzheimer's and Dementia Care: Half Say Medical Profession Not Prepared to Meet Expected Increase in Demands" (media kit), Alz.org, March 11, 2020.

68 **little or no training:** Alzheimer's Assoc., "Primary Care Physicians."

68 **embarrassed if diagnosed:** AARP Press Room, "AARP Report Shows Disconnect Between Patient, Health Care Provider Views of Dementia" (press release), Press. AARP.org, June 22, 2021.

68 **health care providers agree:** Mehegan and Rainville, *2021 AARP Survey on Perceptions.*

68 **at least five to ten years:** Valgeir Thorvaldsson et al., "Onset and Rate of Cognitive Change Before Dementia Diagnosis: Findings from Two Swedish Population-Based Longitudinal Studies," *Journal of the International Neuropsychological Society* 17, no. 1 (2011): 154–62.

69 **Brenda Roberts:** Claire Ansberry, "Their Dementia Diagnosis Doesn't Mean They're Keeping Silent," *Wall Street Journal*, October 12, 2021; "Paving a New Path in Life After a Dementia Diagnosis," YouTube, September 13, 2021.

69 **published in 2019:** Nicole R. Fowler et al., "Risks and Benefits of Screening for Dementia in Primary Care: The Indiana University Cognitive Health Outcomes Investigation of the Comparative Effectiveness of Dementia Screening (IU CHOICE) Trial," *Journal of the American Geriatrics Society* 68, no. 3 (2019).

70 **empower people:** Milken Institute, "Dementia: Addressing the Stigma of America's Most Feared Diagnosis," MilkenInstitute.org, June 22, 2021.

70 **same social drivers:** Livingston et al., "Dementia Prevention."

70 **15 to 33 percent:** Livingston et al., "Dementia Prevention."

71 **even late in life:** Livingston et al., "Dementia Prevention."

71 **what's good for the heart:** Global Council on Brain Health, *The Brain-Heart Connection: GCBH Recommendations to Manage Cardiovascular Risks to Brain Health*, AARP.org, 2020.

71 **lowers your risk for strokes:** GCBH, *Brain-Heart Connection.*

71 **contribute to heart disease:** GCBH, *Brain-Heart Connection.*

71 **within normal limits:** GCBH, *Brain-Heart Connection;* AARP Staying Sharp, "Staying Sharp's Six Pillars of Brain Health," StayingSharp.aarp.org.

71 **conducted in Framingham:** Claudia L. Satizabal et al., "Incidence of Dementia over Three Decades in the Framingham Heart Study," *New England Journal of Medicine* 374 (February 11, 2016): 523–32; Jason Karlawish, *The Problem of Alzheimer's: How Science, Culture, and Politics Turned a Rare Disease into a Crisis and What We Can Do About It* (New York: St. Martin's Press, 2021), 236–37.

72 **policy implications:** Karlawish, *Problem of Alzheimer's.*

72 **chronic negative stress:** Nicholas J. Justice, "The Relationship Between Stress and Alzheimer's Disease," *Neurobiology of Stress* 8 (February 8, 2018): 127–33.

72 **depression and anxiety:** Claus M. Escher, Lena Sannemann, and Frank Jessen, "Stress and Alzheimer's Disease," *Journal of Neural Transmission* 126, no. 9 (2019): 1155–61; Martin Prince et al., *World Alzheimer Report 2014: Dementia and Risk Reduction: An Analysis of Protective and Modifiable Factors*, Alzheimer's Disease International, September 2014; Sofie Holmquist, Anna Nordström, and Peter Nordström, "The Association

of Depression with Subsequent Dementia Diagnosis: A Swedish Nationwide Cohort Study from 1964 to 2016," *PLoS Medicine* 17, no. 1 (2020): e1003016; Livingston et al., "Dementia Prevention."

72 **the brain's hippocampus:** Willa D. Brenowitz et al., "Depressive Symptoms Imputed Across the Life Course Are Associated with Cognitive Impairment and Cognitive Decline," *Journal of Alzheimer's Disease* 83, no. 3 (2022): 1379–89.

72 **same stress process:** Shuichi Chiba et al., "Chronic Restraint Stress Causes Anxiety- and Depression-Like Behaviors, Downregulates Glucocorticoid Receptor Expression, and Attenuates Glutamate Release Induced by Brain-Derived Neurotrophic Factor in the Prefrontal Cortex," *Progress in Neuro-Psychopharmacology Biological Psychiatry* 39, no. 1 (October 1, 2012): 112–19; Thomas Steckler, Florian Holsboer, and Johannes Reul, "Glucocorticoids and Depression," *Best Practice and Research Clinical Endocrinology and Metabolism* 13, no. 4 (December 1999): 597–614.

72 **researchers don't yet know:** Amy L. Byers and Kristine Yafee, "Depression and Risk of Developing Dementia," *Nature Reviews: Neurology* 7 (May 3, 2011): 323–31.

72 **connections between stress:** Javier Santabárbara et al., "Anxiety and Risk of Dementia: Systematic Review and Meta-Analysis of Prospective Cohort Studies," *Maturitas* 119 (January 2019); 14–20; Willa Brenowitz, "Happiness in Early Adulthood May Protect Against Dementia," *ScienceDaily*, September 28, 2021; Brenowitz et al., "Depressive Symptoms Imputed."

72 **sobering statistic:** Lock and Peterson, *It's Time to Act.*

72 **additional factors:** Erin E. Sunderman et al., "Sex Differences in Alzheimer's-Related Tau Biomarkers and a Mediating Effect of Testosterone," *Biology of Sex Differences* 11, no. 33 (June 19, 2020).

72 **decreases after menopause:** Lisa Mosconi, *The XX Brain: The Groundbreaking Science Empowering Women to Maximize Cognitive Health and Prevent Alzheimer's Disease* (New York: Avery, 2020), 9, 11.

73 **mask early signs:** Marilynn Marchione, "New Clues on Why Women's Alzheimer's Risk Differs from Men's," AP News, July 16, 2019.

73 **nearly 70 percent:** Anne-Marie Botek, "Alzheimer's Caregivers Six Times More Likely to Develop Dementia," Aging Care, n.d.; Victoria Omranifard, Ebrahim Haghighizadeh, and Shahla Akouchekian, "Depression in Main Caregivers of Dementia Patients: Prevalence and Predictors," *Advanced Biomedical Research* 7, no. 1 (January 22, 2018): 34.

73 **Compared to older:** Alzheimer's Association, *2023 Alzheimer's Disease Facts and Figures,* Alz.org, 2023.

73 **complex interaction:** Alexander L. Chin, Selamawit Negash, and Roy Hamilton, "Diversity and Disparity in Dementia: The Impact of Ethnoracial Differences in Alzheimer's Disease," *Alzheimer's Disease and Associated Disorders* 25, no. 3 (July–September 2011): 187–95.

73 **more prone:** Patricia Coogan et al., "Experiences of Racism and Subjective Cognitive Function in African American Women," *Alzheimer's and Dementia: Diagnosis, Assessment and Disease Monitoring* 12, no. 1 (July 21, 2020): e12067; Negar Fani et al., "Association of Racial Discrimination with Neural Response to Threat in Black Women in the US Exposed to Trauma," *JAMA Psychiatry* 78, no. 9 (July 28, 2021): 1005–12.

73 **One 2020 study:** Coogan et al., "Experiences of Racism."

73 **disproportionately high:** Lock and Peterson, *It's Time to Act.*

73   **need recharging:** Andy R. Eugene and Jolanta Masiak, "The Neuroprotective Aspects of Sleep," *MEDtube Science* 3, no. 1 (2015): 35.

74   **sleep disruption:** National Institute of Neurological Disorders and Stroke, "Brain Basics; Understanding Sleep," NINDS.NIH.gov.

74   **brain volume:** Brody, "Secrets of 'Super-Agers'"; Stern et al., "Effect of Aerobic Exercise."

74   **regular exercise program:** Global Council on Brain Health, *The Brain-Body Connection: GCBH Recommendations on Physical Activity and Brain Health,* AARP.org, 2016.

74   **brain-healthy exercise:** GCBH, *Brain-Body Connection.*

74   **intentional program:** GCBH, *Brain-Body Connection.*

74   **unhealthy diets:** Global Council on Brain Health, *Brain Food: GCBH Recommendations on Nourishing Your Brain Health,* AARP.org, 2021.

74   **food groups:** GCBH, *Brain Food.*

74   **Mediterranean diet:** GCBH, *Brain Food*; Hallie Levine, "4 Steps to Boost Brainpower. The Key Activities That May Help You Stay Sharp," *Consumer Reports,* August 9, 2021.

75   **balanced diet:** Chuck Rainville, Laura Mehegan, and Laura Skufca, *2017 Brain Health and Nutrition Survey,* AARP Research, 2018.

75   **healthy fats:** GCBH, *Brain Food.*

75   **drinking alcohol:** National Institute on Alcohol Abuse and Alcoholism, "Alcohol Alert. Alcohol's Damaging Effects on the Brain," NIAAA.NIH.gov, October 2004.

75   **$93 million a month:** GCBH, *Brain Food.*

75   **"brain boosters":** Global Council on Brain Health, *The Real Deal on Brain Health Supplements: GCBH Recommendations on Vitamins, Minerals, and Other Dietary Supplements,* AARP.org, 2019.

75   **best source:** Kathleen Fifield, "New Report Pans Supplements for Brain Health," AARP, June 11, 2019.

75   **active social lives:** Global Council on Brain Health, *Social Engagement and Brain Health,* AARP.org, 2017.

75   **feel-good hormones:** Lin W. Hung et al., "Gating of Social Reward by Oxytocin in the Ventral Tegmental Area," *Science* 357, no. 6358 (September 29, 2017): 1406–11; Harvard Health Publishing, "Oxytocin: The Love Hormone," Health.Harvard.edu, June 13, 2023.

76   **direct link:** Yasue Uchida et al., "Age-Related Hearing Loss and Cognitive Decline— The Potential Mechanisms Linking the Two," *Auris Nasus Larynx* 46, no. 1 (February 2019): 1–9.

76   **intellectual engagement:** Mateo P. Farina et al., "Racial and Educational Disparities in Dementia and Dementia-Free Life Expectancy," *Journals of Gerontology: Series B, Psychological Sciences and Social Sciences* 75, no. 7 (September 2020): e105–e112.

76   **By stimulating:** Global Council on Brain Health, *Engage Your Brain: GCBH Recommendations on Cognitively Stimulating Activities,* AARP.org, 2017.

76   **challenge us:** GCBH, *Engage Your Brain.*

76   **negatively affects:** World Health Organization, "Ageism Is a Global Challenge: UN" (press release), WHO.int, March 18, 2021.

76   **age stereotypes:** Becca R. Levy et al., "A Culture-Brain Link: Negative Age Stereotypes Predict Alzheimer's Disease Biomarkers," *Psychology and Aging* 31, no. 1 (2016): 82–88.

76   **three times as much:** Levy et al., "Culture-Brain Link."

76   **positive view of aging:** Becca R. Levy et al., "When Culture Influences Genes: Pos-

itive Age Beliefs Amplify the Cognitive-Again Benefit of APOE ε2," *Journals of Gerontology: Series B, Psychological Sciences and Social Sciences* 75, no. 8 (October 2020): e198–e203.

77 **fluid and can improve:** Global Council on Brain Health, *Brain Health and Mental Well-Being: GCBH Recommendations on Feeling Good and Functioning Well*, AARP.org, 2018.

77 **live at home:** Krista L. Harrison et al., "Care Settings and Clinical Characteristics of Older Adults with Moderately Severe Dementia," *Journal of the American Geriatrics Society* 67, no. 9 (August 7, 2019): 1907–12.

77 **falls with age:** Nora Super, Rajiv Ahula, and Kevin Proff, *Reducing the Cost and Risk of Dementia: Recommendations to Improve Brain Health and Decrease Disparities*, Milken Institute, 2019.

77 **eleven million Americans:** Alz. Assoc., *2023 Alzheimer's Facts and Figures*.

77 **Sandra Day O'Connor:** Sandra Day O'Connor, statement before the Special Committee on Aging, U.S. Senate, May 14, 2008; Matthew Haag, "Sandra Day O'Connor, First Woman on Supreme Court, Reveals Dementia Diagnosis," *New York Times*, October 23, 2018; Sandra Day O'Connor to the public, October 23, 2018, SupremeCourt.gov.

78 **memory cafés:** Memory Cafe Directory, "What Is a Memory Cafe?," Memorycafedirectory.com.

79 **$4 billion spent:** Alzheimer's Association, "Research Funding," Alz.org.

79 **other drugs:** Jeffrey Cummings et al., "Alzheimer's Disease Drug Development Pipeline: 2022," *Alzheimer's and Dementia* 4, no. 8 (2022): e12295.

79 **various approaches:** Mayo Clinic, "Alzheimer's Treatments: What's on the Horizon?," MayoClinic.org.

79 **Alvaro Pascual-Leone:** Alvaro Pascual-Leone, interview by the author, July 13, 2022.

79 **deep brain stimulation:** Cleveland Clinic, "Deep Brain Stimulation," My.ClevelandClinic.org; Pascual-Leone interview.

79 **associated disabilities:** Yinpei Luo et al., "Deep Brain Stimulation for Alzheimer's Disease: Stimulation Parameters and Potential Mechanisms of Action," *Frontiers in Aging Neuroscience* 13 (2021): 619543.

80 **primary prevention:** Roland Thorpe, Jr., Kristine Yaffe, Carlos Mendes de Leon, and Scott Hofer, "Preventing Cognitive Aging and Dementia" (video of panel discussion), Academy of Behavioral Medicine and Research, October 2021.

80 **chasm between:** Global Council on Brain Health, *How to Sustain Brain Healthy Behaviors: Applying Lessons of Public Health and Science to Drive Change*, AARP.org, 2022.

Chapter 4: How Long Will I Work?

81 **four or five fewer:** Murray Gendell and Jacob S. Siegel, "Trends in Retirement Age by Sex, 1950–2005," *Monthly Labor Review*, July 1992.

81 **driven largely:** Alicia H. Munnel, *What Is the Average Retirement Age?* Center for Retirement Research at Boston College, August 2011, 5, 2; Marc Luy et al., "The Impact of Increasing Education Levels on Rising Life Expectancy: A Decomposition Analysis for Italy, Denmark, and the USA," *Genus* 75, no. 11 (2019).

82 **"full retirement age":** Courtney Coile, *The Evolution of Retirement Incentives in the U.S.*, National Bureau of Economic Research, Working Paper 25281, November 2018.

82 **expect to work:** Organization for Economic Cooperation and Development, *Promot-*

ing an Age-Inclusive Workforce. Living, Learning and Earning Longer, OECD.org, December 16, 2020.

82   **double digits:** OECD, *Promoting Age-Inclusive Workforce.*

82   **cognitive abilities peak:** Anne Trafton, "The Rise and Fall of Cognitive Skills: Neuroscientists Find That Different Parts of the Brain Work Best at Different Ages," *MIT News,* March 6, 2015.

83   **Bessie:** Bessie, interview by the author, September 23, 2022.

84   **Cindy:** Cindy, interview by the author, November 17, 2022.

85   **average amount:** Mary Gatta, interview by the author, August 12, 2022.

85   **they needed money:** Lona Choi-Allum, *Understanding a Changing Older Workforce: An Examination of Workers Ages 40-Plus,* AARP Research, January 2023.

85   **considered early retirement:** Social Security Administration, "Early or Late Retirement," SSA.gov.

85   **way to stay active:** Health and Retirement Study Staff, *Aging in the 21st Century: Challenges and Opportunities for Americans,* HRS.ISR.umich.edu, January 2017.

85   **just six years:** Dave Dhavel, Rashad Inas, and Jasmina Spaspjevic, "The Effects of Retirement on Physical and Mental Health Outcomes," *Southern Economic Journal* 75, no. 2 (August 1, 2008): 497–523.

85   **part-time job:** Yujie Zhan et al., "Bridge Employment and Retirees' Health: A Longitudinal Investigation," *Journal of Occupational Health Psychology* 14, no. 4 (October 2009): 374–89.

85   **age sixty-seven:** Jo Mhairi Hale, Maarten J. Bijlsma, and Angelo Lorenti, "Does Postponing Retirement Affect Cognitive Function? A Counterfactual Experiment to Disentangle Life Course Risk Factors," *SSM Population Health* 15 (June 26, 2021): 100855.

85   **Mentally stimulating:** Gwenith G. Fischer et al., "Mental Work Demands, Retirement, and Longitudinal Trajectories of Cognitive Functioning," *Occupational Health Psychology* 19, no. 2 (April 2014): 231–42.

85   **Marc Freedman:** Marc Freedman, interview by the author, November 4, 2022.

85   **Encore.org:** The organization changed its name to CoGenerate to reflect its growing emphasis on solving problems by reaching across generational divides.

86   **enormous purpose:** Robert Waldinger and Marc Schulz, *The Good Life: Lessons from the World's Longest Scientific Study of Happiness* (New York: Simon & Schuster, 2023).

86   **involved in volunteering:** Corporation for National and Community Service, *Longitudinal Study of Foster Grandparent and Senior Companion Programs: Service Delivery Implications and Health Benefits to the Volunteers,* AmeriCorps.gov, April 2019, 68; Sei J. Lee, Michael A. Steinman, and Erwin J. Tan, "Volunteering, Driving Status and Mortality in U.S. Retirees," *Journal of the American Geriatrics Society* 59, no. 2 (February 11, 2011): 274–80.

87   **social and academic needs:** Jeanine M. Parisi et al., "Can the Wisdom of Aging Be Activated and Make a Difference Societally?," *Educational Gerontology* 35, no. 10 (2009): 867–79.

87   **over 60 percent more:** Yung Soo Lee et al., "The Effect of the Experience Corps® Program on Student Reading Outcomes," *Education and Urban Society* 44, no. 1 (2010).

87   **brain health of tutors:** Michelle C. Carlson, "Impact of the Baltimore Experience Corps Trial on Cortical and Hippocampal Volumes," *Alzheimer's and Dementia* 11, no. 11 (2015): 1340–48.

87   **whatever our age:** Tracey Gendron, *Ageism Unmasked. Exploring Age Bias and How to End It* (Westminster, MD: Steerforth, 2022), 49, 71.

87   **physically unable:** Munnel, *Average Retirement Age.*

88   **more time in retirement:** Dave Goodsell, *It'll Take a Miracle: The Search for Retirement Security in an Insecure World*, Natixis Investment Managers, 2021.

88   **to drop out:** Schwartz Center for Economic Policy Analysis, *The Stalled Jobs Recovery Pushed 1.1 Million Older Workers Out of the Labor Force*, EconomicPolicyResearch.org, February 10, 2021.

88   **pre-pandemic level:** Current Population Survey data in U.S. Bureau of Labor Statistics, "Employment" (chart), Data Tools, BLS.gov.

88   **up to twice as long:** Richard W. Johnson and Corina Mommaerts, *Age Differences in Job Loss, Job Search, and Reemployment*, Retirement Policy Discussion Paper no. 11-1, Urban Institute, January 2011; Richard W. Johnson and Peter Gosselin, *How Secure Is Employment at Older Ages?* Research Report, Urban Institute, December 28, 2018.

88   **earns as much:** Johnson and Gosselin, *How Secure Is Employment.*

89   **African American and Hispanic:** Johnson and Gosselin, *How Secure Is Employment.*

89   **never re-enter:** Board of Governors of the Federal Reserve System, *Report on the Economic Well-Being of U.S. Households in 2018*, FederalReserve.gov, May 2019.

89   *more than half:* Peter Gosselin, "If You're Over 50, Chances Are the Decision to Leave a Job Won't Be Yours," *ProPublica*, December 28, 2018; Johnson and Gosselin, *How Secure Is Employment.*

89   **still employed:** Johnson and Gosselin, *How Secure Is Employment.*

89   **it was subtler:** Richard Johnson, interview by the author, November 10, 2021.

89   **"voluntary separation":** AARP, "Buyout Offers Raise Important Issues for Older Workers," AARP.org, November 13, 2018; Richard Eisenberg, "Fidelity Latest to Offer Older Worker Buyouts: Double-Edge Sword?," *Forbes*, March 1, 2017.

89   **far fewer manage:** Employee Benefit Research Institute and Greenwald & Associates, "Expectations About Retirement," Fact Sheet no. 2, *2020 Retirement Confidence Survey*, EBRI.org, 2020.

89   **expectancy after fifty:** Christian Dudel and Mikko Myrskylä, "Working Life Expectancy at Age 50 in the United States and the Impact of the Great Recession," *Demography* 54, no. 6 (2017): 2101–23.

89   **number of factors:** Marty Parker et al., "Population-Based Estimates of Healthy Working Life Expectancy in England at Age 50 Years: Analysis of Data from the English Longitudinal Study of Ageing," *Lancet Public Health* 5, no. 7 (July 2020): e395–e403; Laura D. Quinby and Gal Wettstein, *Are Older Workers Capable of Working Longer?* Center for Retirement Research at Boston College, July 20, 2021.

89   **more education correlates:** Quinby and Wettstein, *Are Older Workers*; Lisa F. Berkman and Beth C. Truesdale, eds., *Overtime: America's Aging Workforce and the Future of Longer Working* (New York: Oxford University Press, 2022), 11–12.

90   **quit work:** HRS Staff, *Aging in the 21st Century.*

90   **lifelong disabilities:** Lisa Schur et al., "Disability at Work: A Look Back and Forward," *Journal of Occupational Rehabilitation* 27, no. 4 (2017): 482–97.

90   **unemployment rate:** U.S. Bureau of Labor Statistics, "Persons with a Disability: Labor Force Characteristics Summary," Economic News Release no. USDL-23-0351, BLS.gov, February 23, 2023.

90   **only part-time work:** BLS, "Persons with a Disability."

90 **far below the minimum:** Wage and Hour Division, "Subminimum Wage," DOL.gov, n.d.

90 **less than \$3.50 an hour:** U.S. Government Accountability Office, *Subminimum Wage Program: DOL Could Do More to Ensure Timely Oversight*, February 24, 2023, GAO-23-105116, GAO.gov.

90 **financially insecure:** U.S. Census Bureau, "Age by Disability Status by Poverty Status," Table no. B18130, Data.Census.gov, 2022.

90 **"age friendly":** Daron Acemoglu, Nicolaj Søndergaard Mülbach, and Andrew J. Scott, "The Rise of Age-Friendly Jobs," *Journal of the Economics of Ageing* 23 (2022): 100416.

90 **majority of these jobs:** Anna Zajacova and Jennifer Karas Montez, "Physical Functioning Trends Among US Women and Men Age 45–64 by Education Level," *Biodemography and Social Biology* 63, no. 1 (March 13, 2017): 21–30.

90 **physically demanding jobs:** Jessica Forden et al., *Physically Demanding Jobs and Involuntary Retirement Worsen Retirement Security*, Status of Older Workers Report Series, Schwartz Center for Economic Policy Analysis, New School, November 1, 2022.

90 **such jobs include:** Richard W. Johnson and Claire Xiaozhi Wang, *What Are the Top Jobs for Older Workers?*, Urban Institute, December 1, 2017; U.S. Bureau of Labor Statistics, "Occupational Requirements Survey," BLS.gov, July 10, 2015.

90 **ten million older workers:** National Academy of Social Insurance, "Older Workers in Physically Challenging Jobs Need Stronger Social Insurance Supports" (press release), September 6, 2023.

91 **shorter working life:** Jacob Pedersen et al., "High Physical Work Demands and Working Life Expectancy in Denmark," *Occupational Environmental Medicine* 77 no. 8 (2020): 576–82.

91 **no retirement savings:** Beth Brockland and Tanya Ladha, *Financial Health of Workers in Low-wage Jobs*, Financial Health Network, July 28, 2022.

91 **far less likely:** U.S. Bureau of Labor Statistics, "Lower-Wage Workers Less Likely Than Other Workers to Have Medical Care Benefits in 2019," *TED: The Economics Daily*, March 3, 2022.

91 **hours can be long:** Joel Goh, Jeffrey Pfeffer, and Stephanos Zenios, "Exposure to Harmful Workplace Practices Could Account for Inequality in Life Spans Across Different Demographic Groups," *Health Affairs* 34, no. 10 (October 2015).

91 **below the poverty level:** Social Security Works, "Enacting a \$15 Minimum Wage Is a Win for Social Security," SocialSecurityWorks.org, February 2021.

91 **thirty-three hours:** Mary Gatta and Jessica Horning, "Dying with Your Boots On: The Realities of Working Longer in Low-Wage Work," in *Overtime: America's Aging Workforce and the Future of Working Longer*, ed. Lisa F. Berkman and Beth C. Truesdale (New York: Oxford University Press, 2022), 178.

91 **"We need to improve":** Gatta interview.

92 **"People with the least":** Johnson interview.

92 **"dying with your boots":** Gatta and Horning, "Dying with Your Boots On."

92 **changed dramatically:** James Manyika et al., *Jobs Lost, Jobs Gained: What the Future of Work Will Mean for Jobs, Skills, and Wages*, McKinsey & Co., November 28, 2017.

92 **certain jobs may vanish:** Kenneth Terrell, "20 Jobs That Could Disappear Forever," AARP, August 20, 2020.

92 **require know-how:** World Economic Forum, *The Future of Jobs Report 2020*, WEForum.org, October 20, 2020, 28–31.

92   **uniquely human abilities:** Debra Whitman and Heather E. McGowan, "The Future of Work for All Generations," OECD Forum, October 7, 2019.

92   **specialized training:** Carl E. Van Horn, Kathy Krepcio, and Maria Heidkamp, *Improving Education and Training for Older Workers*, AARP Public Policy Institute, March 2015.

93   **targeted at younger workers:** Employment and Training Administration, *Report of the Taskforce on the Aging of the American Workforce*, Aging.Senate.gov, February 2008, 13–14.

93   **massive open online courses:** Fact.MR, "Massive Open Online Course (MOOC) Market to Register 35% CAGR, Surpassing US$152 Billion by 2032," *PR Newswire*, August 17, 2022.

93   **post–high school:** Melanie Hanson, "College Enrollment and Student Demographic Statistics," Education Data Initiative, July 26, 2022.

93   **enrollment actually:** Hanson, "College Enrollment"; National Student Clearinghouse Research Center, "First Look at Fall 2023 Highlights," NSCResearchCenter.org, September 28, 2023.

93   **innovative ways:** Debra Whitman, Marc Freedman, and Jim Emerman, "Social Security Lifelong Learning Benefits," *Public Policy and Aging Report* 28, supp. 1 (2018): S55–S63.

94   **SkillsFuture Credit:** SkillsFuture, "SkillsFuture Credit: For Singaporeans Aged 25 Years and Above to Offset SSG-Approved Training Course Fees," SkillsFuture.gov.sg.

94   **National Silver Academy:** C3A Ageing Well and National Silver Academy, "Frequently Asked Questions," C3a.org.sg.

94   **"live to learn":** Debra Whitman and Lina Walker, "Singapore: An Island Nation with a Big Vision for Aging," AARP International, October 1, 2020.

94   **fifty million Americans:** C. Grace Whiting and Susan Reinhard, *Caregiving in the United States 2020*, AARP Public Policy Institute and National Alliance for Caregiving, May 2020.

94   **$600 billion in 2021:** Susan C. Reinhard et al., *Valuing the Invaluable: 2023 Update, Strengthening Supports for Family Caregivers*, AARP Public Policy Institute, March 2023.

95   **while providing care:** Lynn Friss Feinberg and Laura Skufca, *Managing a Paid Job and Family Caregiving Is a Growing Reality: Nearly 30 Million Family Caregivers of Adults Are in the Labor Force*, AARP Public Policy Institute, 2020.

95   **more than $7,200:** Laura Skufca and Chuck Rainville, *Caregiving Out-of-Pocket Costs Study*, AARP Research, June 2021.

95   **roughly one-quarter:** Skufca and Rainville, *Caregiving Out-of-Pocket Costs*.

95   **unpaid work:** Cynthia Hess, Tanima Ahmed, M. Phil, and Jeff Hayes, *Providing Unpaid Household and Care Work in the United State: Uncovering Inequality*, Briefing Paper no. C487, Institute for Women's Policy Research, January 2020.

95   **after the caregiving:** Sean Fahle and Kathleen McGarry, "How Caregiving for Parents Reduces Women's Employment: Patterns Across Sociodemographic Groups," in Berkman and Truesdale, *Overtime*, 231.

95   **seven potential family:** Donald Redfoot, Lynn Feinberg, and Ari Houser, *The Aging of the Baby Boom and the Growing Care Gap: A Look at Future Declines in the Availability of Family Caregivers*, AARP Public Policy Institute, 2013.

95   **often downshift:** Eileen Applebaum, Arne Kalleberg, and Hye Jin Rho, *Nonstandard*

Work Arrangements and Older Americans, 2005–2017, Economic Policy Institute, February 28, 2019.

95 **gig work:** Cody Cook, Rebecca Diamond, and Paul Oyer, "Older Workers and the Gig Economy," *AEA Papers and Proceedings* 109 (May 2019): 372–76.

96 **Uber and Lyft drivers:** Ahu Yildirmaz, Mita Goldar, and Sara Klein, *Illuminating the Shadow Workforce: Insights into the Gig Workforce in Businesses*, ADP Research Institute, February 1, 2020; Erick Burgueno Salas, "Share of Ride-Hailing Services Drivers by Age U.S. 2019, by Age," *Statista*, May 6, 2022.

96 **managerial or consulting:** Lona Choi-Allum, "High on Priority List for Older Workers: Meaningful Employment and Flexibility," AARP, January 18, 2023; U.S. Bureau of Labor Statistics, "Contingent and Alternative Employment Arrangements—May 2017," News Release no. USDL-18-0942, BLS.gov, June 7, 2018.

96 **nontraditional working:** Applebaum, Kalleberg, and Rho, "Nonstandard Work Arrangements."

96 **"encore careers":** Julie Kagan, "Encore Career," *Investopedia*, January 16, 2022.

96 **top areas:** Kagan, "Encore Career"; MetLife Foundation and Civic Ventures, *Encore Career Choices: Purpose, Passion and a Paycheck in a Tough Economy*, Encore, 2011.

96 **start a successful:** Pierre Azoulay et al., "Age and High-Growth Entrepreneurship," *American Economic Review: Insights* 2, no. 1 (2020): 65–82.

96 **Sarah:** Sarah, interview by the author, September 21, 2022.

97 **COBRA:** U.S. Department of Labor, "Continuation of Health Coverage (COBRA)," DOL.gov.

98 **economically healthy:** Kagan, "Encore Career."

98 **This means expanding:** Applebaum, Kalleberg, and Rho, "Nonstandard Work Arrangements."

99 **$850 billion:** AARP and *Economist* Intelligence Unit, *The Economic Impact of Age Discrimination*, AARP.org, 2018.

99 **multigenerational workforce:** AARP International, "How and Why Modern Employers Should Embrace Longevity," AARPInternational.org.

99 **taken seriously:** Emma Waldman, "Am I Old Enough to Be Taken Seriously?" *Harvard Business Review*, November 25, 2020.

99 **"prejudice against":** Todd D. Nelson, "Ageism: Prejudice Against Our Feared Future Self," *Journal of Social Issues* 61, no. 2 (May 16, 2005): 207–21.

99 **impact of stereotypes:** Thomas M. Hess et al., "The Impact of Stereotype Threat on Age Differences in Memory Performance," *Journals of Gerontology: Series B, Psychological Sciences and Social Sciences* 58, no. 1 (January 1, 2003): P3–P11.

99 **Women encounter:** AARP and *Economist* Intelligence Unit, *Economic Impact of Age Discrimination*; Ian Burn et al., *Why Retirement, Social Security, and Age Discrimination Policies Need to Consider the Intersectional Experiences of Older Women*, National Bureau of Economic Research, Working Paper no. 27450, June 2020.

100 **Older people with disabilities:** Anastasia Campbell and Matthew McKenna, "Ageism and Ableism: The Intersectional Discrimination Faced by Older Adults with Disabilities," Maynooth University Assisted Living and Learning Institute, July 9, 2021.

100 **unable to re-enter:** AARP and *Economist* Intelligence Unit, *Economic Impact of Age Discrimination*.

100 **Federal law prohibits:** U.S. Equal Employment Opportunity Commission, "Age Discrimination," EEOC.gov.

100 **recent court cases:** Thomas Claburn, "IBM Settles Age Discrimination Case That Sought Top Exec's Emails," *Register*, June 27, 2022.

100 **difficult to prove:** *Gross v. FBL Financial Services*, 557 U.S. (2009).

100 **"an open secret.":** U.S. Equal Employment Opportunity Commission, "EEOC Acting Chair Lipnic Releases Report on the State of Older Workers and Age Discrimination 50 Years After the ADEA" (press release), EEOC.gov, June 26, 2018.

100 **three main areas:** Joe Kita, "Workplace Age Discrimination Still Flourishes in America," AARP, December 30, 2019.

100 **over a third worry:** Lona Choi-Allum, *Understanding a Changing Older Workforce: An Examination of Workers Ages 40-Plus*, AARP Research, 2023.

100 **forty thousand résumés:** David Neumark, Ian Burn, and Patrick Button, *Is it Harder for Older Workers to Find Jobs? New and Improved Evidence from a Field Experience*, National Bureau of Economic Research, Working Paper no. 21669, November 2017.

100 **"aesthetic discrimination":** Alyssa Dana Adomaitis, Rachel Raskin, and Diana Saiki, "Appearance Discrimination: Lookism and the Cost to the American Woman," *Seneca Falls Dialogues Journal* 2, no. 6 (2017).

101 **"While all old people":** Andrew Solomon, "The Middle of Things: Advice for Young Writers," *New Yorker*, March 11, 2015.

101 **cognitive skills peak:** Trafton, "Rise and Fall of Cognitive Skills."

101 **truck assembly line:** Axel Börsch-Supan and Matthias Weiss, "Productivity and Age: Evidence from Work Teams at the Assembly Line," *Journal of the Economics of Aging* 7, no. C (April 2016): 30–42.

102 **Older workers:** Organization for Economic Cooperation and Development, *Promoting an Age-Inclusive Workforce. Living, Learning and Earning Longer*, OECD.org, December 16, 2020.

102 **Turnover goes down:** OECD, *Promoting an Age-Inclusive Workforce.*

102 **it is not true:** Börsch-Supan and Weiss, "Productivity and Age."

102 **make them complements:** OECD, *Promoting an Age-Inclusive Workforce.*

102 **Jacqueline Welch:** Jacqueline Welch, interview by the author, December 1, 2021.

103 **median age:** Statista Research Department "Average Age of Tech Company Employees 2016" (chart), Statista.com, May 31, 2016; Tricia Lucas, "Blatant Ageism in Tech: Why You Should Hire Employees over 50," Ellevate, n.d.; U.S. Census Bureau, "U.S. Census Bureau Releases 2019 Population Estimates by Demographic Characteristics," Press Release no. CB20-99, June 25, 2020.

104 **The Ohio State University:** Narrative and quotations are from Paula Span, "He Called Older Employees 'Dead Wood.' Two Sued for Age Discrimination," *New York Times*, July 6, 2018; Elizabeth Olson, "Claims of Age Bias Rise, but Standards of Proof Are High," *New York Times*, May 18, 2016.

105 **"If the same supervisors":** Span, "He Called Older Employees."

106 **hasn't been raised:** Economic Policy Institute, "Minimum Wage Tracker," EPI.org, March 1, 2023.

106 **offer paid leave:** National Conference of State Legislators, "State Family and Medical Leave Laws," NCSL.org, September 9, 2022.

106 **significant saving:** Kanika Arora and Douglas A. Wolf, "Does Paid Family Leave Reduce Nursing Home Use? The California Experience," *Journal of Policy Analysis and Management* 37, no. 1 (November 3, 2017): 38–62.

Chapter 5: Will I Have Enough Money?

107 **worked as a logger:** U.S. Bureau of Labor Statistics, "Civilian Occupations with High Fatal Work Injury Rates" (chart), Data Tools, BLS.gov, 2021.

108 **running short:** Social Security Administration, *The 2023 OASDI Trustees Report*, SSA.gov.

109 **calculate how much:** Employee Benefit Research Institute and Greenwald & Associates, "Preparing for Retirement in America," Fact Sheet no. 3, *2020 Retirement Confidence Survey*, EBRI.org, 2020.

109 **married couple will need:** Jake Spiegel and Paul Fronstin, "Projected Savings Medicare Beneficiaries Need for Health Expenses Remained High in 2022," Employee Benefit Reseach Institute, Issue Brief, February 9, 2023.

109 *nearly $320,000:* Spiegel and Frontstin, "Projected Savings."

110 **richest 10 percent:** Neil Bhutta et al., "Changes in U.S. Family Finances from 2016 to 2019: Evidence from the Survey of Consumer Finances," *Federal Reserve Bulletin* 106, no. 5 (September 2020).

110 *nothing* **saved:** Bhutta et al., "Changes in Family Finances."

110 **Lawrence:** Lawrence Cook, interview by the author, February 23, 2023.

111 **official poverty line:** U.S. Department of Health and Human Services, "Annual Update of the HHS Poverty Guidelines," *Federal Register*, January 19, 2023; U.S. Census Bureau, "American Community Survey 1-year Public Use Microdata Samples," Data.census.gov, 2021.

111 **poor during their second:** John Creamer, "Poverty Rates for Blacks and Hispanics Reached Historic Lows in 2019," U.S. Census Bureau, 2020; John Creamer, Emily A. Shrider, Kalee Burns, and Frances Chen, *Poverty in the United States: 2021*, Current Population Reports no. P60-277, U.S. Census Bureau, September 2022, table A-1.

111 **doesn't take account:** U.S. Department of Health and Human Services, Office of the Assistant Secretary for Planning and Evaluation, "Frequently Asked Questions Related to the Poverty Guidelines and Poverty," ASPE.HHS.gov.

112 **more than 60 percent:** Congressional Budget Office, *Measuring the Adequacy of Retirement Income: A Primer*, CBO.gov, October 2017; Elder Index, "Measuring the Income Older Adults Need to Live Independently," ElderIndex.org, 2022.

112 **Traditional pensions:** U.S. Department of Labor, "Types of Retirement Plans," DOL.gov; Kimberly Blanton, "Boomers Lament Disappearance of Pensions," Center for Retirement Research at Boston College, March 29, 2022.

112 **accounts fluctuate:** DOL, "Types of Retirement Plans."

112 **don't have an easy way:** David John, Gary Koenig, and Marissa Malta, *Payroll Deduction Retirement Programs Build Economic Security*, AARP Public Policy Institute, 2022.

112 **living solely on Social Security:** National Academy of Social Insurance, "The Role of Benefits in Income and Poverty," NASI.org.

112 **getting benefits or will be:** Social Security Administration, "Population Profile: Never Beneficiaries, Aged 60 or Older, 2020," SSA.gov, August 2021.

112 **hardly cushy:** Irene Dushi, Howard M. Iams, and Brad Trenkamp, "The Importance of Social Security Benefits to the Income of the Aged Population," *Social Security Bulletin* 77, no. 2 (2017); Social Security Administration, "Fact Sheet: Social Security," SSA.gov, 2023; ApartmentAdvisor, "National Rent Report," ApartmentAdvisor.com, February 2023.

113 **employment is rising:** U.S. Bureau of Labor Statistics, "Employment Protections—2022–2032," News Release no. USDL-23-1941, BLS.gov, September 6, 2023; U.S. Bureau of Labor Statistics, "Number of People 75 and Older in the Labor Force Is Expected to Grow 96.5 Percent by 2030," *TED: The Economics Daily*, November 4, 2021.

113 **Terry:** Terry, interview by the author, September 23, 2022.

114 **the poorhouse:** Erin Blakemore, "History Stories: Poorhouses Were Designed to Punish People for Their Poverty," History Channel, August 30, 2018.

114 **Dickensian institution:** Blakemore, "Poorhouses."

114 **rapid industrialization:** Social Security Administration, "Traditional Sources of Economic Security," SSA.gov.

114 **few jobs available:** Benjamin Veghte, "Social Security's Past, Present and Future," National Academy of Social Insurance, August 13, 2015.

114 **social insurance programs:** SSA, "Traditional Sources of Economic Security,"

114 **illness and injury:** Committee on Economic Security, *Report of the Committee on Economic Security*, SSA.gov.

114 **Benefits have been added:** Edward D. Berkowitz, "Statement Before the Subcommittee on Social Security of the Committee on Ways and Means," Disability Policy and History, SSA.gov, July 13, 2000; Social Security Administration, "1986 Disability History Report," SSA.gov, January 1986; Jim Borland, "What Same-Sex Couples Need to Know," Social Security Matters Blog.SSA.org, August 19, 2021.

115 **early retirement eligibility age:** Martha A. McSteen, "Fifty Years of Social Security," SSA.gov.

115 **cost-of-living adjustments:** Social Security Administration, "Cost-of-Living Adjustments" SSA.gov.

115 **"full retirement age":** Social Security Administration, "Summary of P.L. 98–21 (H.R. 1900) Social Security Amendments of 1983—Signed on April 20, 1983," SSA.gov, November 26, 1984.

115 **roughly one in five:** Social Security Administration, "Number of People Receiving Social Security, Supplemental Security Income (SSI), or Both," Table 1, SSA.gov, February 2023; SSA, "Fact Sheet"; AARP, "How Do Survivor Benefits Work?," AARP.org, December 22, 2022.

115 **do not expect to rely:** Vicki Levy and Patty David, *Second Half of Life Study*, AARP Research, June 2022.

115 **a basic quiz:** MassMutual, "2020 MassMutual Social Security Retirement Benefits Consumer Poll Topline Report," MassMutual.com, March 17, 2020.

115 **required by law:** SSA, "Traditional Sources of Economic Security."

115 **contributions flow:** Social Security Administration, "What Are the Trust Funds?," SSA.gov.

116 **larger of the two:** AARP, "What Are My Options If I Am Eligible for Both a Social Security Retirement Benefit and a Survivor Benefit?," AARP.org, May 5, 2023.

116 **benefits are calculated:** Social Security Administration, "Social Security Benefit Amounts," SSA.gov.

116 **retirement formula:** Congressional Budget Office, *CBO's 2023 Long-Term Projections for Social Security*, CBO.gov, June 2023.

117 **77 percent higher:** Social Security Administration, "Full Retirement and Age 62 Benefit by Year of Birth," SSA.gov.

117 **gain eligibility:** Social Security Administration, "Disability Benefits: How You Qualify," SSA.gov.

117 **medical issue:** Social Security Administration, *Understanding the Benefits*, Publication no. 05-10024, SSA.gov, January 2023.

117 **hard to prove:** SSA, "Disability Benefits"; Social Security Administration, "Average Wait Time Until Hearing Held Report (For the Month of September 2023)," SSA.gov, September 2023.

117 **two out of three:** Center on Budget and Policy Priorities, "Chart Book: Social Security Disability Insurance," CBPP.org, February 12. 2021.

117 **not been updated:** Social Security Administration, "Occupational Information System (OIS) Project," SSA.gov; Lisa Rein, "Social Security Denies Disability Benefits Based on List with Jobs from 1977," *Washington Post*, December 27, 2022.

117 **half of appeals:** Lisa Rein, "Judges Rebuke Social Security for Errors as Disability Denials Stack Up," *Washington Post*, May 25, 2023.

117 **Linda:** Linda, interview by the author, March 8, 2023.

118 **approve within weeks:** Social Security Administration, "Compassionate Allowances Conditions," SSA.gov.

118 **diagnosed with ALS:** Social Security Administration, "Removing the Waiting Period for Entitlement to Social Security Disability Insurance Benefits for Individuals with Amyotrophic Lateral Sclerosis," *Federal Register* 86l no. 164 (August 27, 2021).

118 **average monthly payment:** Social Security Administration, "2023 Social Security Changes: Cost-of-Living-Adjustment (COLA)" (fact sheet), SSA.gov.

118 **who receive SSDI:** Social Security Administration, "Disabled Worker Beneficiaries in Current Payment Status at the End of December 2016, Distributed by Age And Sex" (table), SSA.gov.

118 **undergone many changes:** Geoffrey Kollmann, "Social Security: Summary of Major Changes in the Cash Benefits Program," SSA.gov, May 18, 2000.

118 **pension plans:** Patrick W. Seburn, "Evolution of Employer-Provided Defined Benefit Pensions," *Monthly Labor Review* 114, no. 12 (1991): 16–23.

119 **IRS confirmed:** Selma Mushkin, "The Internal Revenue Code of 1954 and Health Programs," *Public Health Reports* 70, no. 8 (August 1955).

119 **"defined benefits":** DOL, "Types of Retirement Plans."

119 **they won't qualify:** Jonathan Moody and Anthony Randazzo, *The National Landscape of State Retirement Benefits: How Good Are Public Retirement Systems at Putting Employees on a Path to Retirement Income Security?*, Equable Institute, 2021.

119 **held twelve jobs:** U.S. Bureau of Labor Statistics, "Number of Jobs, Labor Market Experience, Marital Status, and Health for Those Born 1957–1964," News Release no. USDL-23-1854, BLS.gov, August 22, 2023.

119 **mismanagement scandals:** James Wooten, "'The Most Glorious Story of Failure in the Business': The Studebaker-Packard Corporation and the Origins of ERISA," *Buffalo Law Review* 49 (2001); Pension Benefit Guaranty Corporation, "History of PBGC," PBGC.gov, November 16, 2023.

119 **Pension Benefit Guarantee Corporation:** Pension Benefit Guarantee Corporation "General FAQs About PBGC," PBGC.gov, August 22, 2023.

120 **plunged by half:** Employee Benefits Security Administration, *Private Pension Plan Bulletin Historical Tables and Graphs 1975–2020*, DOL.gov, October 2022.

120 **closed to new employees:** Xiaofeng Peng, "The Impact of Off-Balance-Sheet Pension

Liability under SFAS No. 87 on Earnings Quality, Cost of Capital, and Analysts' Forecasts" (PhD diss., Kent State University Graduate School of Management, May 2008).

120 **small number:** U.S. Bureau of Labor Statistics, "67 Percent of Private Industry Workers Had Access to Retirement Plans in 2020," *TED: The Economics Daily*, March 1, 2021.

120 **"great risk shift":** Jacob S. Hacker, *The Great Risk Shift: The New Economic Insecurity and the Decline of the American Dream* (New York: Oxford University Press, 2008).

120 **most small businesses:** Lona Choi-Allum, "Utah Small Business Owners Support Access to a Retirement Savings Program," AARP, May 19, 2022; Jennifer Sauer, "Pennsylvania Small Business Owners Support a State Retirement Savings Bill," AARP, June 13, 2022; Lona Choi-Allum, "AARP Kansas Work and Save Small Business Survey," AARP, December 13, 2021.

120 **Highly compensated workers:** BLS, "67 Percent of Private Industry Workers."

120 **in the private sector:** Advisory Council on Employee Welfare and Pension Benefit Plans, *Gaps in Retirement Savings Based on Race, Ethnicity and Gender*, DOL.gov, December 2021.

120 **"defined contribution":** *Investopedia* Team, "401(k) vs. Pension Plan: What's the Difference?," *Investopedia*, November 30, 2022.

121 **minor provision:** Act to Amend the Internal Revenue Code of 1954 to Reduce Income Taxes, and for Other Purposes, Public Law 96–500, 95th Congress, November 6, 1978.

121 **Ted Benna:** Alyssa Fetini, "A Brief History of the 401(k)," *Time*, October 16, 2008.

121 **401(k) as a form:** Tim Stobierski, "401(k) Basics: When It Was Invented and How It Works," Northwestern Mutual, March 2018.

121 **nearly forty million:** Leona Friedburg and Michael T. Owyang, *Not Your Father's Pension Plan: The Rise of 401(k) and Other Defined Contribution Plans*, Federal Reserve Bank of St. Louis, January–February 2002.

121 **increase the likelihood:** Jeffrey W. Clark and Jean A. Young, *Automatic Enrollment: The Power of the Default*, Vanguard Research, 2021.

121 **change jobs:** U.S. Bureau of Labor Statistics, "Number of Jobs, Labor Market Experience, Marital Status, and Health for Those Born 1957–1964," News Release no. USDL-23-1854, BLS.gov, August 22, 2023.

121 **went unclaimed:** U.S. Government Accountability Office, *Workplace Retirement Accounts. Better Guidance and Information Could Help Plan Participants at Home and Abroad Manage Their Retirement Savings*, GAO-18-19, GAO.gov, January 2018.

121 **$8.5 billion in workers':** GAO, *Workplace Retirement Accounts*.

122 **state treasurers:** Anita Mukherjee and Corina Mommaerts, *Frictions in Saving and Claiming: An Analysis of Unclaimed Retirement Accounts*, Retirement and Disability Research Center, Center for Financial Security, University of Wisconsin-Madison, 2019.

122 **only about half:** Alicia H Munnell and Anqi Chen, *401(k)/IRA Holdings in 2019: An Update from the SCF*, Center for Retirement Research at Boston College, October 2020.

122 **IRA offers similar:** Internal Revenue Service, "IRA Facts," IRS.gov.

122 **few of us save:** Sarah Holden and Daniel Schrass, "The Role of IRAs in US Households' Savings for Retirement, 2021," *ICI Research Perspective* 28, no. 1 (January 14, 2022).

122 **state-facilitated retirement:** Georgetown University Center for Retirement Initiatives, "State Programs 2023: More Programs Are Open and Enrolling Workers, Smaller States Actively Explore Partnership Opportunities, while Other States Continue to Introduce Legislative Proposals," CRI.Georgetown.edu, 2023.

122 **Anne Lester:** Anne Lester, interview by the author, October 21, 2022.
123 **"leakage":** Shai Akabas and Brian Collins, "Leakage: Taking the Money Too Early," Bipartisan Policy Center, September 19, 2014.
123 **twenty-two dollars:** Joint Committee on Taxation staff, Estimating Leakage from Retirement Savings Accounts, no. JCX-20-21, JCT.gov, April 26, 2021; Internal Revenue Service, "Early Retirement Distributions and Your Taxes," IRS.gov, March 3, 2016.
123 **mainly to pay:** "Financial Independence: The Ultimate Goal and Biggest Hurdle for Today's Early Adults, Merrill Lynch Study Finds," *Business Wire*, April 18, 2019.
124 **rated their financial:** Levy and David, *Second Half of Life Study*.
124 **need less income:** Ann C. Foster, "Consumer Expenditures Vary by Age," *BLS Beyond the Numbers* 4, no. 14 (December 2015).
124 **cut short compared:** U.S. Government Accountability Office, *Retirement Security: Income and Wealth Disparities Continue Through Old Age*, GAO-19-587, GAO.gov, August 9, 2019.
124 **Jackie:** Levy and David, *Second Half of Life Study*.
124 **they are in debt:** S. Kathi Brown, *Financial Security Trends: Wave 2 Report*, AARP Research, 2022: S. Kathi Brown, "Rising Prices Lead to Changes in Lifestyle and Shopping Habits," AARP, November 1, 2022.
124 **less than one month's:** Caroline Ratcliffe et al., *Emergency Savings and Financial Security Insights from the Making Ends Meet Survey and Consumer Credit Panel*, Data Point no. 2022-01, Office of Research, Consumer Financial Protection Bureau, March 2022.
124 **debt can sneak up:** Wenli Li, *The Graying of Household Debt in the U.S.*, Federal Reserve Bank of Philadelphia, 2021.
124 **owed an average:** Bill Fay, "Demographics of Debt," Debt.org, November 21, 2023.
125 **at least some debt:** Lori Trawinski, "Surging Debt of Families Age 50+ Threatens Long-Term Financial Security," AARP Blogs, March 16, 2022; Center for Microeconomic Data, *Quarterly Report on Household Debt and Credit, 2022:Q4*, NewYorkFed.org, February 2023.
125 **fastest-growing group:** Lori Trawinski, Susanna Montezemolo, and Alicia R. Williams, The Student Loan Debt Threat: An Intergenerational Problem, AARP Public Policy Institute, May 2019.
125 **40 percent of empty nesters:** "Survey Reveals Empty Nesters Still Supporting Children Financially," 55places.com, September 17, 2019.
125 **filed for bankruptcy:** Center for Microeconomic Data, *Quarterly Report on Household Debt and Credit*.
125 **foreclosure rates:** Lori A. Trawinski, Nightmare on Main Street: Older Americans and the Mortgage Market Crisis, AARP Public Policy Institute, August 2012.
125 *Nomadland*: Jessica Bruder, *Nomadland: Surviving America in the Twenty-First Century* (New York: W. W. Norton, 2017).
125 **below their means:** Chris Browning et al., "Spending in Retirement: Determining the Consumption Gap," Financial Planning Association, February 2016; Kimberly Blanton, "Half of Retirees Afraid to Use Savings," Center for Retirement Research at Boston College, September 26, 2019.
126 **Anne Lester:** Lester interview.
127 **handicapped financially:** Social Security Administration, "Social Security Is Important to Women" (fact sheet), SSA.gov, September 2023; U.S. Government

Accountability Office, *Retirement Security: Older Women Report Facing a Financially Uncertain Future*, GAO-20-435, GAO.gov, July 14, 2020.

127 **lifetime loss:** MetLife Mature Market Institute, *The MetLife Study of Caregiving Costs to Working Caregivers. Double Jeopardy for Baby Boomers Caring for Their Parents*, Caregiving.org, June 2011.

127 **losses to retirement accounts:** Fidelity, "The Hidden Costs of Caregiving," Fidelity.com, November 2, 2021.

127 **eighty-two cents:** Rakesh Kochhar, "The Enduring Grip of the Gender Pay Gap," Pew Research Center, March 1, 2023.

127 **average of $4,000:** SSA, "Social Security Important to Women."

127 **make up two-thirds:** SSA, "Social Security Important to Women."

128 **virtually all:** Reliance on Social Security is estimated from U.S. Census Bureau, "Current Population Survey Annual Social and Economic Supplement," Census.gov, March 2022.

128 **$4,000 less in annual:** Social Security Administration, "Projected Profile of Beneficiaries by Race and Ethnicity," SSA.gov, 2022.

128 **pay discrimination:** Robin Bleiweis, "Quick Facts About the Gender Wage Gap," Center for American Progress, March 2020; U.S. Census Bureau, "Historical Income Tables: People," Census.gov.

128 **fifty-eight cents:** U.S. Government Accountability Office, *Women in the Workforce: The Gender Pay Gap Is Greater for Certain Racial and Ethnic Groups and Varies by Education Level*, GAO-23-106041, GAO.gov, December 15, 2022.

128 **net effect of gender:** National Women's Law Center, "The Lifetime Wage Gap, State by State," NWLC.org, March 6, 2023.

128 **four million women:** Juliette Cubanski, Wyatt Koma, Anthony Damico, and Tricia Neuman, "How Many Seniors Live in Poverty?," KFF, November 19, 2018.

128 **roughly one in five:** Shengwei Sun, *National Snapshot: Poverty Among Women and Families*, National Women's Law Center, January 2023.

128 **less likely to be collecting:** Theresa Cardinal Brown, Jeffrey Mason, Kenneth Megan, and Cristobal Ramón, *Immigration's Effect on the Social Security System*, Bipartisan Policy Center, November 2018.

128 **children enter the workforce:** Brown et al., *Immigration's Effect on Social Security*.

129 **contributed $13 billion:** Nina Roberts, "Undocumented Immigrants Quietly Pay Billions Into Social Security and Receive No Benefits," Marketplace, January 28, 2019; Stephen Goss et al., "Effects of Unauthorized Immigration on the Actuarial Statis of the Social Security Trust Funds," Actuarial Note no. 151, SSA.gov, April 2013; Boards of Trustees of the Federal Hospital Insurance and Federal Supplementary Medical Insurance Trust Funds, *2017 Annual Report*, CMS.gov, July 13, 2017.

129 **first $160,200:** Social Security Administration, "Cost-of-Living Adjustments," SSA.gov.

129 **increase in the cap:** Office of the Chief Actuary, "Provisions Affecting Payroll Taxes," SSA.gov, 2023.

129 **wealthiest 1 percent:** Raj Chetty et al., "The Association Between Income and Life Expectancy in the United States, 2001–2014," *Journal of the American Medical Association* 315, no. 16 (2016): 1750–66.

129 **get $100,000 more:** National Academies of Sciences, Engineering, and Medicine,

The Growing Gap in Life Expectancy by Income: Implications for Federal Programs and Policy Responses (Washington, DC: National Academies Press, 2015).

130 **if we do nothing:** Social Security Administration, *The 2023 OASDI Trustees Report,* SSA.gov.

130 **"the third rail":** Tim W. Ferguson, "Social Security: Testing the Third Rail," *Milken Institute Review,* August 31, 2020; Michelle Clark Neely, "Shaking the Third Rail: Reforming Social Security," Federal Reserve Bank of St. Louis, October 1, 1996.

130 **cut by 20 percent:** Social Security and Medicare Boards of Trustees, "A Summary of the 2023 Annual Reports. A Message to the Public, " SSA.gov.

131 **last set of upgrades:** Matthew Dallek, "Bipartisan Reagan-O'Neill Social Security Deal in 1982 Showed It Can Be Done," *U.S. News & World Report,* April 2, 2009.

131 **added decades:** Geoffrey Kollmann, "Social Security: Summary of Major Changes in the Cash Benefits Program," SSA.gov, May 18, 2000; Social Security Administration, "Myths and Misinformation About Social Security—Part 2," SSA.gov.

131 **commission's package:** Geoffrey Kollmann and Carmen Solomon-Fears, "Major Decisions in the House and Senate on Social Security: 1935–2000," SSA.gov, March 26, 2001.

131 **less palatable revisions:** Social Security Administration, "Summary of P.L. 98–21 (H.R. 1900) Social Security Amendments of 1983—Signed on April 20, 1983," SSA.gov, November 26, 1984.

131 **Presidents from:** Social Security Administration, "Myths and Misinformation"; White House, "Seniors and Social Security," ObamaWhiteHouse.Archives.gov.

131 **Steve Goss:** Steve Goss, interview by the author, July 14, 2021; "Stephen C. Goss," Docs.House.gov.

132 **countless proposals:** Social Security Administration, "Office of the Chief Actuary's Estimates of Proposals to Change the Social Security Program or the SSI Program," SSA.gov.

132 **program on track:** Social Security Administration, *The 2022 OASDI Trustees Report,* SSA.gov.

132 **sixty-vote majority:** Kollmann and Solomon-Fears, "Major Decisions in the House and Senate."

132 **between 22 and 73 percent:** Congressional Research Service, *Social Security: Raising or Eliminating the Taxable Earnings Base,* CRSReports.Congress.gov, December 22, 2021.

132 **now sixty-seven:** Social Security Administration, *Retirement Benefits,* Publication no. 05-10035, SSA.gov, January 2023.

133 **nearly $150,000:** John B. Shoven, Sita Slavov, and John G. Watson, *How Does Social Security Reform Indecision Affect Younger Cohorts?,* National Bureau of Economic Research, Working Paper no. 28850, May 2021.

133 **"minor tweaks":** U.S. Senate, *Social Security Modernization: Options to Address Solvency and Benefit Adequacy,* Report 111-187, Govinfo.gov, May 13, 2010.

133 **help people save:** Georgetown University CRI, "State Programs 2023."

134 **easier to transfer:** Retirement Clearinghouse, "America's Leading 401(k) Providers and Retirement Clearinghouse Collaborate to Implement a Nationwide Network for Auto Portability. Fidelity, Vanguard, Alight and Retirement Clearinghouse Establish First-Ever Industry Consortium to Help Improve Retirement Outcomes of America's Under-Saved and Under-Saved Workers" (press release), RCHL.com, October 5, 2022.

134	**from one employer:** U.S. Senate, "Secure 2.0 Act of 2022," Finance.Senate.gov, 120.

134	**many other countries:** Organization for Economic Cooperation and Development, *Formal Access to Retirement Savings Plans of Workers in Non-Standard Forms of Work: Country Profiles of Design Features,* OECD.org, 2019.

134	**overturned by a court:** AARP, "Labor Department's Proposed Rules for Retirement Plan Advisers Could Hurt Investors," AARP.org, July 31, 2020; U.S. Court of Appeals for the Fifth Circuit, "Appeal no. 17–10238," CA5.uscourts.gov, March 2018.

Chapter 6: Where Will I Live?

137	**escalating care crisis:** Jennifer Molinsky, *Housing for America's Older Adults: Four Problems We Must Address,* Joint Center for Housing Studies of Harvard University, August 18, 2022.

137	**spending went to home:** Susan Reinhard et al., *Innovation and Opportunity: A State Scorecard on Long-Term Services and Supports for Older Adults, People with Physical Disabilities, and Family Caregivers,* AARP Public Policy Institute, September 2023.

137	**neighborhood programs:** Habitat for Humanity, "Aging in Place with Habitat for Humanity," Habitat.org; Melissa Stanton, "6 Creative Housing Options," AARP, n.d.; Joint Center for Housing Studies of Harvard University, *Housing America's Older Adults: Meeting the Needs of an Aging Population,* JCHS.Harvard.edu, 2014.

137	**multigenerational households:** D'Vera Cohn et al., "The Demographics of Multigenerational Households," Pew Research Center, 2022.

138	**current homes:** Joanne Binette, *2021 Home and Community Preference Survey: A National Survey of Adults Age 18-Plus,* AARP Research, September 2022.

138	**Jennifer Molinsky:** Jennifer Molinsky, interview by the author, March 8, 2023.

138	**more interested:** LeadingAge-NORC, "How Do Older Baby Boomers Envision Their Quality of Life If They Need Long-Term Care Services?" (survey findings), LeadingAge. org, March 2019.

138	**our SHOL survey:** Levy and David, *Second Half of Life Study.*

138	**single-family detached:** Molinsky interview; Office of Policy Development and Research, *Assessing the Accessibility of America's Housing Stock for Physically Disabled Persons,* HUDuser.gov; Office of Policy Development and Research, *Accessibility of America's Housing Stock: Analysis of the 2011 American Housing Survey,* HUDuser.gov, March 19, 2015.

138	**hold them responsible:** Maya Brennan, "For Owners and Renters, Home Modification Assistance Can Be a Lifeline," Urban Institute, August 17, 2017.

139	**"universal design":** Office of Disability Employment Policy, "Universal Design," DOL.gov.

139	**integrate accessibility:** JCHS, *Housing America's Older Adults.*

139	**features for the home:** JCHS, *Housing America's Older Adults.*

139	**initial construction:** Ty Pennington and Amy Goyer, "Simple Home Design Changes to Keep You Comfortable and Safe," AARP, December 12, 2022.

140	**partly by demographics:** Joanne Binette, Angela Houghton, and Stephanie Firestone, "Pandemic's Economic Pressures Pushing Generations Under One Roof," AARP, December 31, 2020.

140	**pandemic accelerated:** Erica Pandey, "Working from (Your Parents') Home," *Axios,* September 15, 2020; Erica Pandey, "Coronavirus Reshapes American Families," *Axios,* April 4, 2020.

140   **quadruple the number:** Pew Reseach Center, "U.S. Population in Multigenerational Households Quadrupled Since 1971" (table), PewResearch.org, March 22, 2022.

141   **buyers seeking homes:** Oyin Adedoyin, "More Parents Are Moving In with Adult Children—At Younger Ages," *Wall Street Journal*, February 22, 2023.

141   **enjoy being together:** D'Vera Cohn et al., "Financial Issues Top the List of Reasons U.S. Adults Live in Multigenerational Homes," Pew Research Center, March 24, 2022.

141   **Cathy:** Cathy, interview by the author, November 29, 2022.

141   **"accessory dwelling units":** Binette, Houghton, and Firestone, "Pandemic's Economic Pressures."

142   **older people are living alone:** Jennifer Molinsky, "The Number of People Living Alone in Their 80s and 90s Is Set to Soar," Joint Center for Housing Studies of Harvard University, March 10, 2020; Dana Goldstein and Robert Gebeloff, "As Gen X and Boomers Age, They Confront Living Alone," *New York Times*, December 1, 2022.

142   **solo agers:** Chrysanthe Broikos and Melissa Stanton, *Making Room: Housing for a Changing America*, AARP Livable Communities, 2019: Stephanie Childs, *Solo Agers: Attitudes and Experiences*, AARP Research, April 2023.

142   **alone in large houses:** Goldstein and Gebeloff, "As Gen X and Boomers Age."

142   **fewer financial resources:** Office of Financial Protection for Older Americans, *Financial Well-Being of Older Americans*, Files.ConsumerFinance.gov, December 2018: Childs, *Solo Agers*; Katherine G. Giefer and Michael D. King, "One in Six Older Americans Received Needs-Based Assistance Even Before Pandemic," U.S. Census Bureau, October 28, 2021; Samara Scheckler, "Older Adults Living with a Partner Were Better Able to Cope with the Pandemic," Joint Center for Housing Studies of Harvard University, April 19, 2023.

142   **mental health challenges:** Julie Zissimopoulos and Johanna Thunell, "Older Adults Living Alone Report Higher Rates of Anxiety and Depression," *USC Schaeffer Evidence Base*, April 21, 2020; Nicola Petersen, Hans-Helmut König, and André Hajek, "The Link Between Falls, Social Isolation and Loneliness: A Systematic Review," *Archives of Gerontology and Geriatrics* 88 (2020): 104020.

142   **limit their driving:** Joanne Binette and Fanni Farago, "Where We Live, Where We Age: Trends in Home and Community Preferences," AARP, November 18, 2021; JCHS, *Housing America's Older Adults*.

142   **cities are to support:** JCHS, *Housing America's Older Adults*.

142   **smaller homes:** Goldstein and Gebeloff, "As Gen X and Boomers Age."

143   **shortage of seven million:** National Low Income Housing Coalition, "The Gap: A Shortage of Affordable Rental Homes," NLIHC.org.

143   **unoccupied spare bedrooms:** Noelle Marcus, "Tackling the Housing Crisis and Bridging Generational Divides Through Home-Sharing," *Stanford Social Innovation Review*, March 21, 2021.

143   **just one occupant:** Marcus, "Tackling the Housing Crisis."

143   **like to downsize:** Freddie Mac, "Housing Supply: A Growing Deficit," FreddieMac.com, May 7, 2021; Goldstein and Gebeloff, "As Gen X and Boomers Age."

143   **shared housing:** Jennifer Molinsky, "Are More Older Adults Sharing Housing?," Joint Center for Housing Studies of Harvard University, August 20, 2018; Soo Youn, "The New Golden Girls: Baby Boomers Are Moving in Together to Save Money," *Washington Post*, February 25, 2022.

143   **living with nonrelatives:** Jon Marcus, "Have a Spare Room? Try Renting It to a Grad

Student," AARP, October 25, 2019; Office of Policy Development and Research, *Insights into Housing and Community Development Policy*, HUDuser.gov, June 2021.

143 **financial reasons:** Binette and Farago, "Where We Live"; Marcus, "Have a Spare Room?"

143 **main forms of sharing:** OPDR, *Insights into Housing and Community Development Policy.*

143 **for-profit and nonprofit:** Marcus, "Have a Spare Room?"

143 **Judson Manor:** Jon Hanc, "In Cleveland, Young and Old Keep Tempo of Life," *New York Times*, May 13, 2015; Judson Senior Living, "Student Residents," JudsonSmart Living.org; Heather Hansman, "College Students Are Living Rent-Free in a Cleveland Retirement Home," *Smithsonian*, October, 2015.

144 **"Village" model:** Villages NW, "Beacon Hill: The First Village," Villages NW.org; Carrie Graham and Shannon Guzman, *The Village Model: Current Trends, Challenges, and Opportunities*, AARP Public Policy Institute, October 2022; Jonathan M. Pitts, "'Village' Brings Light, Joy to Seniors' Golden Years," *Baltimore Sun*, n.d.; Andrew E. Scharlach et al., *Creating Age-Friendly Communities Through the Expansion of Villages: Summary of Longitudinal Member Outcomes*, School of Social Welfare, University of California, Berkeley, June 1, 2017.

144 **Golden Age Village:** Jonathan M. Pitts, "Diverse Baltimore County 'Village' Helps Seniors Stay Safer, Healthier, While Still Living at Home," *Baltimore Sun*, February 6, 2023.

145 **membership has tended:** Graham and Guzman, *Village Model.*

145 **eight factors:** AARP Livable Communities, "The 8 Domains of Livability: An Introduction," AARP.org, n.d. The eight domains are: transportation; housing; outdoor spaces and buildings; social participation; respect and social inclusions; civic partnership and employment; community and health services; communication and information.

145 **754 communities:** AARP Livable Communities, "The Member List," AARP.org, 2014.

145 **block-by-block walk program:** District of Columbia, "Age Friendly DC: 2015 Progress Report," AgeFriendly.DC.gov, 2015.

145 **free mobile app:** Coalition for Smarter Growth, "Moving an Age-Friendly D.C.: Transportation for All Ages," SmarterGrowth.net, September, 2014.

146 **More than 15 percent:** U.S. Census Bureau, "Macon-Bibb County, Georgia," Census. gov, 2022.

146 **age-friendly plan:** AARP Livable Communities, "Age-Friendly Greater Macon-Bibb, Georgia," AARP.org, 2020.

146 **Americans with Disabilities Act:** U.S. Department of Justice Civil Rights Division, "Americans with Disabilities Act of 1990, As Amended," ADA.gov.

146 **biggest barriers:** Rhonda Meador et al., "Going Home: Identifying and Overcoming Barriers to Nursing Home Discharge," *Care Management Journals*, 12, no. 1 (2011): 2–11.

147 **don't want to consider:** Deborah Schoch, "11 Housing Options for Older Adults Who Need a Little—or More—Help," AARP, November 18, 2022.

147 **70 percent of us:** Medicare, "Long-term Care," Medicare.gov; Richard Johnson, *What Is the Lifetime Risk of Needing and Receiving Long-Term Services and Supports?* Research Brief, Assistant Secretary for Planning and Evaluation, U.S. Department of health and Human Services, April 2019.

147 **only brief spells:** Anek Belbase, Anqi Chen, and Alicia H. Munnell, *What Resources*

Do Retirees Have for Long-Term Services and Supports?, Center for Retirement Research of Boston College, 2021.

147 **more than two years:** Johnson, *What Is the Lifetime Risk.*

147 **more serious care:** Belbase, Chen, and Munnell, *What Resources Do Retirees*; Richard Johnson and Judith Dey, *Long-Term Services and Supports for Older Americans: Risks and Financing, 2022*, Research Brief, Assistant Secretary for Planning and Evaluation, U.S. Department of Health and Human Services, September 27, 2022.

147 **tend to underestimate:** Melissa Favreault and Judith Dey, *Long-Term Services and Supports for Older Americans: Risks and Financing*, Research Brief, Assistant Secretary for Planning and Evaluation, U.S. Department of Health and Human Services, February 2016; J. Wiener et al., *What Americans Think About Long-Term Care*, Assistant Secretary for Planning and Evaluation, U.S. Department of Health and Human Services, 2015; Jason Kane, "Americans Seriously Unprepared for Long-Term Care, Survey Finds," *PBS NewsHour*, April 24, 2013; Trevor Tompson et al., *Long-Term Care: Perceptions, Experiences and Attitudes Among Americans 40 or Older*, Associated Press and NORC Center for Public Affairs Research, 2013.

147 **skilled nursing home:** New York Life, "What Is the Cost of Long-Term Care?," NewYork Life.com, 2023.

147 **cost of paid long-term care:** PwC and MIB, *Formal Cost of Long-Term Care Services*, PWC.com, 2021.

148 **$600 billion annually:** Susan C. Reinhard et al., *Valuing the Invaluable: 2023 Update, Strengthening Supports for Family Caregivers*, AARP Public Policy Institute, March 2023.

148 **seven caregivers:** Redfoot, Feinberg, and Houser, *Aging of Baby Boom.*

149 **"kinless" population:** Ashton M. Verdery and Rachel Margolis, "Projections of White and Black Older Adults Without Living Kin in the United States, 2015 to 2060," *Proceedings of the National Academy of Sciences* 114, no. 42 (2017): 11109-14.

149 **less likely to be married:** National Center on LGBT Aging and SAGE, *Facts on LBGT Aging*, SAGEusa.org, 2020.

149 **dependent on networks:** Robert Espinoza, *Out and Visible: The Experiences and Attitudes of Lesbian, Gay, Bisexual and Transgender Older Adults, Ages 45–75*, SAGE, 2014; Ben R. Inventor, Olimpia Paun, and Erik McIntosh, "Mental Health of LGBTQ Older Adults," *Journal of Psychosocial Nursing and Mental Health Services* 60, no. 4 (2022): 7-10.

149 **clarify what is important:** Kim Painter, "When Denial Gets in the Way of Long-Term Care Planning," AARP, October 11, 2022.

150 **Area Agency on Aging:** Association for Community Living, "Eldercare Locator," Eldercare.ACL.gov, 2023.

150 **looking for paid care:** Amy Goyer, "Choosing an Agency for In-Home Care," AARP, September 27, 2021; Lee Woodruff, "Choosing the Right Long-Term Care Facility," AARP, September 14, 2021.

150 **frequent turnover:** Joanne Spetz et al., "Home and Community-Based Workforce for Patients with Serious Illness Requires Support to Meet Growing Needs," *Health Affairs* 38, no. 6 (2019): 902-9; Stephen Campbell et al., *Caring for the Future: The Power and Potential of America's Direct Care Workforce*, PHI, 2021.

150 **you will probably go:** Schoch, "11 Housing Options."

150 **paid for out of pocket:** AARP, "Assisted Living Facilities: Weighing the Options," AARP.org, December 3, 2021.

151 **incur extra costs:** AARP, "Assisted Living Facilities."

151   **Group homes:** Sally Abrahms, "Group Homes: A Small-Scale Option for Assisted Living," AARP, October 26, 2022.

151   **most expensive options:** AARP, "How Continuing Care Retirement Communities Work," AARP.org, January 27, 2022.

151   **greater degree of care:** Ari Houser, "Nursing Homes" (fact sheet), AARP Public Policy Institute, 2007; Congressional Research Service, "Overview of Federally Certified Long-Term Care Facilities," CRSReports.Congress.gov, 11, 2020.

151   **certain stigma:** Robert Gebeloff, Katies Thomas, and Jessica Silver-Greenberg, "How Nursing Homes' Worst Offenses Are Hidden from the Public," *New York Times*, December 10, 2021.

152   **five-star rating system:** Medicare, "Find and Compare Providers Near You," Medicare.gov.

152   **washing machine:** *Nursing Home Transparency and Improvement: Hearing Before the U.S. Senate*, 110th Cong. (2007).

152   **But many criticisms:** Jessica Silver-Greenberg and Robert Gebeloff, "Maggots, Rape and Yet Five Stars: How U.S. Ratings of Nursing Homes Mislead the Public," *New York Times*, August 4, 2021.

152   **Nearly seven in ten:** Megan Brenan, "Americans Give Nursing Homes D+ Grade for Quality of Care," Gallup, September 12, 2023.

152   **Pueblo of Isleta:** Centers for Medicare and Medicaid Services, "Tribal Nursing Home and Assisted Living Facility Directory," CMS.gov, February 2021.

152   **first pueblo-owned:** Pueblo of Isleta, "Assisted Living Facility," IsletaPueblo.com.

153   **Green House homes:** Susan Reinhard and Edem Hado, "LTSS Choices: Small-House Nursing Homes," AARP, January 6, 2021.

153   **undergo additional training:** Susan C. Reinhard et al., *Empowered Direct Care Worker: Lessons from the Green House Staffing Model*, AARP Public Policy Institute, 2022; Michelle Cottle, "Nobody Wants to Live in a Nursing Home. Something's Got to Give," *New York Times*, August 1, 2021.

153   **specialized functions:** Reinhard and Hado, "Small-House Nursing Homes."

153   **better quality of life:** Reinhard et al., *Empowered Direct Care Worker*.

153   **three hundred licensed:** Reinhard and Hado, "Small-House Nursing Homes."

153   **Memory care is:** Michelle Crouch, "Memory Care: Specialized Support for People with Alzheimer's or Dementia," AARP, December 6, 2021.

153   **safety and licensing:** Woodruff, "Choosing the Right Long-Term Care Facility."

153   **owned by private equity:** Vikram R. Comondore et al., "Quality of Care in For-Profit and Not-For-Profit Nursing Homes: Systematic Review and Meta-Analysis," *BMJ* 339 (2009); Robert Tyler Braun et al., "Association of Private Equity Investment in US Nursing Homes with the Quality and Cost of Care for Long-Stay Residents," *JAMA Health Forum* 2, no. 11 (2021): e213817.

154   **considered "extras":** Medicaid, "Nursing Facilities," Medicaid.gov.

154   **home health aide:** Genworth, *Genworth Cost of Care Survey: Median Cost Data Tables*, Publication no 282102, Genworth, January 31, 2022.

154   **$4,500 per month:** Genworth, *Genworth Cost of Care Survey*.

154   **just over $1,600:** Social Security Administration, *Annual Statistical Supplement to the Social Security Bulletin, 2022,* table 5A, SSA.gov, 2022.

154   **won't generally cover:** Centers for Medicare and Medicaid Services, *Medicare Coverage of Skilled Nursing Facility Care*, Medicare.gov, December 2022.

154 **care in nursing homes:** Medicaid, "Medicaid Eligibility," Medicaid.gov.

155 **hire an eldercare lawyer:** National Council on Aging, "What Is Medicaid Estate Recovery? And How Does It Work?," NIA.NIH.gov, June 2017.

155 **spend at least half:** Medicaid, "Spousal Impoverishment," Medicaid.gov.

155 **states are required:** Medicaid, "Estate Recovery," Medicaid.gov.

155 **in the way of income:** Caroline F. Pearson, "The Forgotten Middle: Many Middle-Income Seniors Will Have Insufficient Resources for Housing and Health Care," *Health Affairs* 38, no. 5 (April 24, 2019).

155 **up to $36,500:** WA Cares Fund, "About the WA Cares Fund," WACaresFund.wa.gov.

155 **Several other states:** Mark Miller, "States Try Easing the Burden of Long-Term Care's Cost," *New York Times,* June 16, 2023.

155 **long-term care insurance:** Reinhard et al., *Innovation and Opportunity.*

155 **policies won't accept:** Kathleen Ujvari, *Disrupting the Marketplace: The State of Private Long-Term Care Insurance, 2018 Update,* AARP Public Policy Institute, 2018.

156 **Amy Goyer:** Clare Ansberry, "Caring for Older Relatives Is So Expensive That Even AARP's Expert Filed for Bankruptcy," *Wall Street Journal,* February 20, 2022.

156 **could afford to pay:** Belbase, Chen, and Munnell, *What Resources Do Retirees Have.*

156 **Ai-jen Poo:** Ai-jen Poo, interview by the author, November 30, 2022.

156 **National Domestic Workers Alliance:** National Domestic Workers Alliance, "Ai-jen Poo," Domesticworkers.org.

157 **but of good jobs:** Ann Oldenburg, "Real Problems, Real Solutions to the Long-Term Care Crisis," AARP, May 3, 2022.

157 **wage for a care worker:** PHI, "Competitive Disadvantage: Direct Care Wages Are Lagging Behind" (fact sheet), PHInational.org, 2020.

157 **have no benefits:** Poo interview; PHI, *Direct Care Workers in the United States: Key Facts,* PHInational.org, September 6, 2022.

158 **delivers comprehensive care:** Reinhard, Tilly, and Flinn, *Scaling Innovations.*

158 **first PACE program:** On Lok, "Our History," OnLok.org.

158 **273 PACE programs:** Susan Reinhard, Jane Tilly, and Brendan Flinn, *From Ideation to Standard Practice: Scaling Innovations in Long-Term Services and Supports,* AARP Public Policy Institute, 2022; Lisa Harootunian et al., *Improving Access to and Enrollment in Programs of All-Inclusive Care for the Elderly* (PACE), Bipartisan Policy Center, October 2022.

158 **focuses on preventive services:** Medicaid, "Programs of All-Inclusive Care for the Elderly Benefits," Medicaid.gov.

158 **less likely to be hospitalized:** Harootunian et al., *Improving Access and Enrollment.*

158 **significantly less burdened:** Harold Urman, "PACE Enrollment Reduces Burden on Family Caregivers," Vital Research; Edem Hado and Harriet Komisar, *How the PACE Model Integrates Medical Care with Long-Term Services and Supports,* AARP Public Policy Institute, 2023.

158 **cost savings are significant:** Hado and Komisar, *How the PACE Model;* National PACE Association, "PACE by the Numbers Infographic," NPAOnline.org, 2023.

159 **six thousand people:** On Lok, "About On Lok 30th Street," OnLok.org.

159 **What immediately:** Author site visit.

159 **Grace Li:** Grace Li, interview by the author, April 2023.

159 **elderly nuns:** Matthew Artz, "On Lok Center Looks After Elderly Nuns," *East Bay Times,* December 2008.

Chapter 7: How Will I Die?

162   **children witnessed death:** Marilyn J. Field and Christine K. Cassel, eds., *Approaching Death: Improving Care at the End of Life* (Washington, DC: National Academies Press, 1997), chap. 2.

162   **dramatic drop:** Bernard Guyer et al., "Annual Summary of Vital Statistics: Trends in the Health of Americans During the 20th Century," *Pediatrics* 106, no. 6 (December 2000): 1307–17.

163   **lifespan jumped:** Elizabeth Arias, Brigham Bastian, Jiaquan Xu, and Betzaida Tejada-Vera, "U.S. State Life Tables, 2018," *National Vital Statistics Reports* 70, no. 1 (March 11, 2021).

163   **changing employment landscape:** Field and Cassel, *Approaching Death.*

163   **home deaths had dropped:** Field and Cassel, *Approaching Death.*

163   **emergency call system:** "9-1-1 Origin and History," NENA the 9-1-1 Association, NENA.org.

163   **every imminent death:** Peter T. Hetzle and Lydia S. Dugdale, "How Do Medicalization and Rescue Fantasy Prevent Healthy Dying?" *Journal of Ethics* 20, no. 8 (2018): e766–e773.

163   **"medicalized dying":** Hetzle and Dugdale, "How Do Medicalization."

164   **"the rich wisdom":** Kathryn Mannix, *With the End in Mind: Dying, Death and Wisdom in an Age of Denial* (New York: Little, Brown Spark, 2018); "About Kathryn," KathrynMannix.com; Kathryn Mannix, "IMHO dying is not as bad as you think," Twitter, April 3, 2018.

164   **results of surveys:** Cheryl Lampkin, *End of Life Survey: Thoughts and Attitudes on Death and Dying*, AARP Research, April 2019.

164   **want to talk about death:** Brian Carpenter, interview on *Speaking of Psychology* podcast, Episode 51, December 2017; Nancy L. Schoenborn, "Older Adults' Preferences for Discussing Long-Term Life Expectancy: Results from a National Survey," *Annals of Family Medicine* 16, no. 6 (2018): 530–37; Andrea Lambert South and Jessica Elton, "Contradictions and Promise for End-of-Life Communication Among Family and Friends: Death over Dinner Conversations," *Behavioral Sciences* 7, no. 2 (2017): 24.

164   **feeling most prepared:** Levy and David, *Second Half of Life Study.*

164   **Attitudes and preferences:** Elise C. Carey, Michael J. Sadighian, and Rebecca L. Sudore, *Cultural Aspects of Palliative Care*, UptoDate, 2019.

164   **die suddenly:** Alyssa LaFaro, "Without Warning: Why Do People Drop Dead?" *Endeavors*, February 16, 2017.

164   **"external" causes:** Meredith S. Shiels et al., "Leading Causes of Death in the US During the Covid-19 Pandemic, March 2020 to October 2021," *JAMA Internal Medicine* 182, no. 8 (2022): 883–86.

164   **die of heart disease:** National Center for Health Statistics, "Older Persons' Health," CDC.gov, June 30, 2023.

164   **into our mid-seventies:** Our World in Data, "Causes of Deaths for People Who Were 70 Years and Older, World, 2019," OurWorldinData.org, 2019.

164   **deaths from drug:** Ellen A. Kramarow and Betzaida Tejada-Vera, "Drug Overdose Deaths in Adults Aged 65 and Over: United States, 2000–2020," National Center for Health Statistics, Data Brief no. 455, November 2022; Ellen A. Kramarow and Betzaida Tejada-Vera, "Alcohol-induced Deaths in Adults Aged 65 and Over: United States, 2019 and 2020," *NCHS Health E-Stats*, November 2022.

164 **likely to use drugs:** Maryann Mason et al., "Disparities by Sex and Race and Ethnicity in Death Rates Due to Opioid Overdose Among Adults 55 Years or Older, 1999 to 2019," *JAMA Network Open* 5, no. 1 (January 11, 2022): e2142982; National Institute on Drug Abuse, "Substance Use in Older Adults DrugFacts," NIDA.NIH.gov, July 9, 2020.

165 **want to die at home:** Liz Hamel, Bryan Wu, and Mollyann Brodie, "Views and Experiences with End-of-Life Medical Care in the U.S.," KFF, April 27, 2017; Gene Emery, "Home Is Now the Most Common Place of Death in the U.S.," Reuters, December 11, 2019.

165 **such as Taiwanese:** Shao-Yi Cheng et al., "A Cross-Cultural Study on Behaviors When Death Is Approaching in East Asian Countries: What Are the Physician-Perceived Common Beliefs and Practices?" *Medicine* 94, no. 39 (September 2015): e1573.

165 **Hmong culture:** Youhung Her-Xiong and Tracy Schroepfer, "Walking in Two Worlds: Hmong End of Life Beliefs and Rituals," *Journal of Social Work in End-of-Life and Palliative Care* 14, no. 4 (2018): 291–314; Stanford Medicine Ethnogeriatrics, "End-of-Life Care: Care of the Dying Person," Geriatrics.stanford.edu; Deborah Helsel, Kao Shoua Thao, and Robin Whitney, "Their Last Breath: Death and Dying in a Hmong American Community," *Journal of Hospice and Palliative Nursing* 22, no. 1 (2020): 68–74.

165 **Hindu tradition:** UMass Chan Medical School, Lamar Soutter Library, "Cultural Approaches to Pediatric Palliative Care in Central Massachusetts: Hinduism" (subject guide), LibraryGuides.umassmed.edu; Sujatha Shanmugasundaram, Margaret O'Connor, and Ken Sellick, "Culturally Competent Care at the End of Life: A Hindu Perspective," *End of Life Care* 4, no. 1 (2010): 26–31.

165 **Diane Meier:** Diane Meier, interview by the author, July 26, 2021.

166 **one in three Medicare beneficiaries:** Jonathan Rauch, "The Hospital Is No Place for the Elderly," *Atlantic*, December 2013.

166 **most hazardous area:** Stijn Blot et al., "Healthcare-Associated Infections in Adult Intensive Care Unit Patients: Changes in Epidemiology, Diagnosis, Prevention and Contributions of New Technologies, " *Intensive Critical Care Nursing* 70 (2022): 103227.

166 **ICUs limit visitors:** Vincent Liu et al., "Visitation Policies and Practices in US ICUs," *Critical Care* 17, no. 2 (April 2013).

166 **seven times higher:** Alison Kodjak, "Dying in a Hospital Means More Procedures, Tests and Costs," *Shots Health News*, June 15, 2016; Nick Stepro, "The Final Year. Where and How We Die," *Arcadia*, June 1, 2016.

167 **home deaths jumped:** Emery, "Home the Most Common Place"; Haider Warraich, *Modern Death: How Medicine Changed the End of Life* (New York: St. Martin's Press, 2017), 312: Advisory Board, "More People Are Dying at Home Than in Hospitals. Is That a Good Thing?," Advisory.com, December 2019; Sarah H. Cross and Haider J. Warraich, "Changes in the Place of Death in the United States" (correspondence), *New England Journal of Medicine*, December 12, 2019.

167 **growth of hospice programs:** Emery, "Home the Most Common Place"; Sarah H. Cross and Haider J. Warraich, "More Americans Are Dying at Home. Is That a Good Thing?" *STAT*, December 11, 2019; Kieran L. Quinn et al., "Association Between Palliative Care and Death at Home in Adults with Heart Failure," *Journal of the American Heart Association* 9, no. 5 (February 19, 2020).

167 **expanding access:** Cross and Warraich, "More Americans Dying at Home."

167 **Cicely Saunders:** "Dame Cicely Saunders, Founder of the Modern Hospice Movement, Dies," *BMJ* (July 18, 2005).

168 **spread to the United States:** National Hospice and Palliative Care Organization, "History of Hospice," NHPCO.org.

168 **conversation about the end:** Elisabeth Kübler-Ross, *On Death and Dying* (New York: Collier Books, 1970).

168 **first hospice facility:** Andi Rierden, "A Calling for Care of the Terminally Ill," *New York Times,* April 19, 1998.

168 **team-based care:** National Institute on Aging, "What Are Palliative Care and Hospice Care?," NIA.NIH.gov, May 14, 2021.

168 **not traditionally paid for:** NIA, "What Are Palliative and Hospice Care?"

168 **Most hospice services:** National Hospice and Palliative Care Organization, *NHPCO Facts and Figures Report,* NHPCO.org, December 2022.

168 **"hospice houses":** For in-patient hospice settings, see Medicare, "Hospice Care," Medicare.gov.

169 **doctor must certify:** Medicare, "Hospice Care"; Centers for Medicare and Medicaid Services, "Medicare Hospice Benefits Facts," DGSMedicare.com, December 2014; Shea Corti, "Medicare Coverage of Hospice" (blogpost), SHIPHelp.org, May 27, 2022.

169 **benefits can vary:** Hospice Foundation of America, "Paying for Hospice Care," Hospice Foundation.org, November 1, 2023.

169 **around-the-clock care:** Sarah Creed, interview by the author, September 22, 2022.

169 **day-to-day caregiving:** National Institute on Aging, "Frequently Asked Questions About Hospice Care," NIA.NIH.gov, February 8, 2021.

169 **does *not* pay for:** Compassus, "What Is Hospice Respite Care?" Compassus.com.

169 **less than eighteen days:** NHPCO, *Facts and Figures 2022.*

170 **Sarah Creed:** Creed interview.

170 **palliative care:** NIA, "What Are Palliative and Hospice Care?"; Get Palliative Care, "Disease Types and Palliative Care," GetPalliativeCare.org.

171 **focuses on quality of life:** Diane E. Meier, "Defining Palliative Care," (YouTube video), CAPC Palliative, February 5, 2015.

171 **day of diagnosis:** Amy Goodman, "Palliative Care Pioneer Dr. Diane Meier on How People Struggle with Serious, Sometimes Terminal, Illness," Mount Sinai, April 8, 2010.

171 **help patients understand:** Goodman, "Palliative Care Pioneer."

171 **Diane Meier:** Meier interview.

172 **Center to Advance Palliative Care:** Center to Advance Palliative Care, CAPC.org.

172 **dying from the underlying:** Pekka Vartiainen et al., "Worse Health-Related Quality of Life, Impaired Functioning and Psychiatric Comorbidities Are Associated with Excess Mortality in Patients with Severe Chronic Pain," *European Journal of Pain* 26, no. 5 (2022): 1135–46; Kathryn A. Fisher et al., "Prevalence and Risk Factors of Depressive Symptoms in a Canadian Palliative Home Care Population: A Cross-Sectional Study," *BMC Palliative Care* 13, no. 1 (2014): 1–13; Gene R. Pesola and Habibul Ahsan, "Dyspnea as an Independent Predictor of Mortality," *Clinical Respiratory Journal* 10, no. 2 (2016): 142–52; Lingxiao Chen et al., "Association of Chronic Musculoskeletal Pain with Mortality Among UK Adults: A Population-Based Cohort Study with Mediation Analysis," *EClinicalMedicine* 42 (2021): 101202; Zachary Zimmer and Sara Rubin, "Life Expectancy with and Without Pain in the US Elderly Population," *Journals of Gerontology: Series A, Biomedical Sciences and Medical Sciences* 71, no. 9 (2016): 1171–76; Katherine D. Sborov et al., "Acute Pain Consult and Management Is Associated with Improved

Mortality in Rib Fracture Patients," *Regional Anesthesia and Pain Medicine* 47, no. 10 (2022): 643–48.

173 **more than tripling:** Center to Advance Palliative Care, "Growth of Palliative Care in U.S. Hospitals: 2022 Snapshot (2000–2020)," CAPC.org.

173 **less depressed:** Jennifer S. Ternel et al., "Early Palliative Care for Patients with Metastatic Non-Small-Cell Lung Cancer," *New England Journal of Medicine* 363 (August 19, 2010): 733–42.

173 **spent fewer days:** Ternel et al., "Early Palliative Care."

173 **far lower costs:** Stacie T. Pinderhughes et al., "Expanding Palliative Medicine Across Care Settings: One Health System Experience," *Journal of Palliative Medicine* 21, no. 9 (2018): 1272–77.

173 **fewer ER visits:** R. Sean Morrison et al., "Health Affairs at the Intersection of Health, Health Care and Policy," *Health Affairs* 30, no. 3 (2011): 454–63; Jennifer L. Boen, "Palliative Care Is Not Just for Hospice Patients," *Next Avenue*, July 20, 2016; Rebecca McAteer and Caroline Wellberry, "Palliative Care: Benefits, Barriers, and Best Practices," *American Family Physician* 88, no. 12 (2013): 807–13; Nita Khandelwal et al., "Estimating the Effect of Palliative Care Interventions and Advance Care Planning on ICU Utilization: A Systematic Review," *Critical Care Medicine* 43, no. 5 (May 2015): 1102–11; Mary Hua et al., "Association Between the Implementation of Hospital-Based Palliative Care and Use of Intensive Care During Terminal Hospitalizations," *JAMA Network Open* 3, no. 1 (January 3, 2020).

173 **implications for hospice referral:** University of Chicago Medicine, "Doctors Overestimate Survival Times for Terminal Patients," UChicagoMedicine.org, February 17, 2000; Nicola White et al., "A Systematic Review of Predictions of Survival in Palliative Care: How Accurate Are Clinicians and Who Are the Experts?" *PLoS One* 11, no. 8 (August 25, 2016): e0161407; Jo Cavallo, "Understanding Oncologists' Perceptions About Palliative Care and the Barriers Preventing Its Use: A Conversation with Ajeet Gajra, MD, MBBS, FACP," *ASCO Post*, May 25, 2022.

174 **higher chance of curability:** Kah Poh Lah et al., "Association of Prognostic Understanding with Health Care Use Among Older Adults with Advanced Cancer: A Secondary Analysis of a Cluster Randomized Clinical Trial," *JAMA Network Open* 5, no. 2 (2022): e220018.

174 **medical school and residency:** Jessica M. Schmit et al., "Perspectives on Death and Dying: A Study of Resident Comfort with End-of-Life Care," *BMC Medical Education* 16, no. 297 (2016).

174 **politically devisive:** JoNel Aleccia, "Docs Bill Medicare for End-of-Life Advice as 'Death Panel' Fears Reemerge," *KFF Health News*, February 15, 2017.

174 **35 percent of Black:** Katherine A. Ornstein et al., "Evaluation of Racial Disparities in Hospice Use and End-of-Life Treatment Intensify in the REGARDS Cohort," *JAMA Network Open* 3 no. 8 (2020): e2014639.

174 **in their final months:** Ornstein et. al., "Evaluation of Racial Disparities."

174 **may have less trust:** Otis Webb Brawley and Paul Goldberg, *How We Do Harm: A Doctor Breaks Ranks About Being Sick in America* (New York: St. Martin's Griffin, 2012), 29–30.

174 **forgoing life-sustaining:** Ornstein et al., "Evaluation of Racial Disparities."

174 **less convenient access:** Rural Health Information Hub, "Rural Hospice and Palliative Care," RuralHealthInfo.org; Daniel S. Gardner et al., "Racial and Ethnic Dispar-

ities in Palliative Care: A Systematic Scoping Review," *Families in Society: The Journal of Contemporary Social Services* 99, no. 4 (October 29, 2018).

175 **never heard of palliative care:** J. Nicholas Dionne-Odom, Katherine A. Ornstein, and Erin E. Kent, "What Do Family Caregivers Know About Palliative Care? Results from a National Survey," *Palliative Support Care* 17, no. 6 (December 2019): 643–49.

175 **same as hospice:** Dionne-Odom et al., "What do Family Caregivers Know?"

175 **survey of oncologists:** Cavallo, "Understanding Oncologists' Perceptions."

176 **not enough doctors trained:** Boen, "Palliative Care Not Just for Hospice Patients."

176 **which classes they wanted:** Katie Williams, interview by the author, September 1, 2022.

177 **sixty volunteers:** Kiwi Kawhena Karapu and Whakawhirinaki Kaitiaki, "We Make Coffins that Cost Less," Kiwi Coffin Club Charitable Trust Rotorua, Kiwi Coffin Club; Shauni James, "Coffin Club Rotorua Founder Katie Williams Celebrated for Her Work with the Club," *Rotorua Daily Post*, April 21, 2022.

177 **"People can't afford":** James, "Coffin Club Rotorua Founder."

177 **"How splendid":** "We Did It Our Way," Coffin Club Rotorua, Katie Williams, 2014.

177 **"good death":** Emily A. Meier et al., "Defining a Good Death (Successful Dying): Literature Review and a Call for Research and Public Dialogue," *American Journal of Geriatric Psychiatry* 24, no. 4 (2016): 261–71.

178 **Such a death:** Amy Callahan-Lesher, *The Phenomenon of a Good Death*, National Institutes of Health, February 2011.

178 **feel cheated or guilty:** Cole Imperi, "The Problem with American Deathwork and the Concept of a 'Good' Death," ColeImperi.com, December 2018.

178 **their definitions:** Geoffrey Scarre, "Can There Be a Good Death?" *Journal of Evaluation in Clinical Practice* 18, no. 5 (September 21, 2012): 1082–86; Field and Cassel, *Approaching Death*; Meghan McDarby, "Culturally Diverse Communities and Palliative and End-of-Life Care," American Psychological Association, 2010.

178 **Deborah Kado:** Deborah Kado, interview by the author, December 3, 2021.

178 **restrictive visitation rules:** Al Baker, "New Law Gives Gay Partners Visiting Rights in Hospitals," *New York Times*, October 2, 2004.

179 **kept them up to date:** Chithra R. Perumalswami, James F. Burke, and Lesli E. Skolarus, "Older Adults' Experiences with Advance Care Planning," National Poll on Healthy Aging, University of Michigan Institute for Health Care Policy and Innovation, April 6, 2021; Rachel Lustbader, "Caring.com's 2023 Wills Survey Finds That 1 in 4 Americans See a Greater Need for an Estate Plan Due to Inflation," Caring.com, 2023.

179 **State laws vary:** American Bar Association, "Living Wills, Health Care Proxies, and Advance Health Care Directives," AmericanBar.org.

179 **living will specifies:** Johns Hopkins Medicine, "Advance Directives," HopkinsMedicine.org.

179 **designate a trusted person:** ABA, "Living Wills."

180 **proxy has broader power:** Hopkins Medicine, "Advance Directives."

180 **Patient Self-Determination Act:** Daniela J. Lamas, "When Faced with Death, People Often Change Their Minds," *New York Times*, January 3, 2022; K. Kelley, "The Patient Self-Determination Act: A Matter of Life and Death," *Physician Assistant* 19, no. 3 (March 1, 1995): 53–56, 59–60.

180 **had a living will:** Jeffrey M. Jones, "Prevalence of Living Wills in U.S. Up Slightly,"

Gallup, June 22, 2020; Danielle Christina Funk, Alvin H. Moss, and Atticus Speis, "How COVID-19 Changed Advance Care Planning: Insights from the Virginia Center for End-of-Life Care," *Journal of Pain and Symptom Management* 60, no. 6 (December 2020): E5–E9; Catherine L. Auriemma et al., "Competition of Advance Directives and Documented Care Preferences During the Coronavirus Disease 2019 (COVID-19) Pandemic," *JAMA Network Open* 3, no. 7 (2020).

180 **don't influence medical decisions:** Ryan D. McMahon, Ismael Tellez, and Rebecca L. Sudore, "Deconstructing the Complexities of Advance Care Planning Outcomes: What Do We Know and Where Do We Go? A Scoping Review," *Journal of American Geriatrics Society* 60, no. 1 (2021): 234–44; R. Sean Morrison, Diane E. Meier, and Robert M. Arnold, "What's Wrong with Advance Care Planning?" *Journal of the American Medical Association* (October 8, 2021); Geronimo Jimenez et al., "Overview of System Reviews of Advance Care Planning: Summary of Evidence and Global Lessons," *Journal of Pain and Symptom Management* 56, no. 3 (September 2018): 436–59; Sangeeta C. Ahluwalia et al., "A Systematic Review in Support of the National Consensus Project Clinical Practice Guidelines for Quality Palliative Care," *Journal of Pain and Symptom Management* 56, no. 6 (December 2018): 831–70; McMahon, Tellez, and Sudore, "Deconstructing the Complexities."

181 **recognized in another state:** Charles Sabatino, "Can My Advance Directives Travel Across State Lines? An Essay on Portability," *Bifocal, the Journal of the ABA Commission on Law and Aging* 38, no. 1 (September 2016).

181 **change our minds:** Terri R. Fried et al., "Stages of Change for the Component Behaviors of Advance Care Planning," *Journal of the American Geriatrics Society* 58, no. 12 (December 9, 2010): 2329–36.

182 **Five Wishes:** Five Wishes, "Five Wishes," FiveWishes.org. The Five Wishes cover: (1) the person I want to make care decisions for me when I can't; (2) the kind of medical treatment I want or don't want; (3) how comfortable I want to be; (4) how I want people to treat me; and (5) what I want for my loved ones to know.

182 **all but four states:** Five Wishes, "Five Wishes in My State," FiveWishes.org.

182 **as they near death:** MaryJo Prince-Pail, "Understanding the Meaning of Social Well-Being at the End of Life," *Oncology Nursing Forum* 35, no. 3 (May 2008): 365–71.

183 **A living trust:** MetLife, "Living Trust vs. Will: What's the Difference?," MetLife.com, November 3, 2022.

183 **instructions for allocating:** Kerry Hannon, "Estate Planning in the Time of the Coronavirus Pandemic," AARP, April 29, 2020.

183 **arrangements complex:** Martin Shenkman, "Estate Planning for the Modern Family: What to Do When You're Not the Cleavers," *Forbes*, October 1, 2019.

183 **only one in three:** Lustbader, "Caring.com's 2023 Wills Survey."

183 **low-cost and even free:** Lustbader, "Caring.com's 2023 Wills Survey."

184 **long-term wealth:** Astrid Andre, "Can Estate Planning Be Used to Help Preserve Economic Assets in Low-Income Communities?," Shelterforce, March 1, 2019.

184 **delegates important decisions:** Andre, "Can Estate Planning Be Used."

184 **likelihood of having a will:** Lustbader, "Caring.com's 2023 Wills Survey."

184 **racial disparities in estate planning:** Neil Bhutta, Andrew C. Chang, Lisa J. Dettling, and Joanne W. Hsu, "Disparities in Wealth by Race and Ethnicity in the 2019 Survey of Consumer Finances," Board of Governors of the Federal Reserve System, September 28, 2020.

184 **homeownership figures:** Carey L. Biron, "Will Power: Could Property Inheritance Help Close the U.S. 'Wealth Gap?,'" Reuters, November 12, 2019.

185 **cost of an adult funeral:** John Egan, "How Much Does a Funeral Cost?" *Forbes*, October 21, 2022; National Funeral Directors Association, "Statistics," NFDA.org.

185 **plots for caskets:** Geoff Williams, "Funeral Costs to Plan For," *US News & World Report*, July 14, 2023.

185 **"green burials":** Rachel Fritts, "'Green' Burials Are Slowly Gaining Ground Among Environmentalists," *ScienceNews*, March 2, 2021.

185 **opt for cremation:** Markian Hawryluk, "Death Is Anything but a Dying Business as Private Equity Cashes In," *KFF Health News*, September 22, 2022.

185 **amazingly creative:** Dignity Funeral Directors, "What to Do with Cremation Ashes," DignityFunerals.co.uk; Ruth Asawa, "The Faces of Ruth Asawa," RuthAsawa.com, July 6, 2022.

185 **legal to scatter ashes:** U.S. Environmental Protection Agency, "Burial at Sea," EPA.gov.

186 **may not get our money back:** AARP, "Funeral Scams," AARP.org, November 30, 2020.

186 **Medical aid in dying:** David Nowels, Gregg Vanderkieft, and Jennifer Moore Ballantine, "Medical Aid in Dying," *American Family Physician* 97, no. 5 (2018): 339–43.

186 **74 percent of adults:** Jones, "Prevalence of Living Wills."

186 **ten U.S. states:** Thaddeus Mason Pope, "Medical Aid in Dying: Key Variations Among U.S. State Laws," *Journal of Health and Life Sciences Law* 14, no. 1(2020): 25–29.

186 **more than one doctor:** Paula Span, "Aid in Dying Soon Will Be Available to More Americans. Few Will Choose It," *New York Times*, July 8, 2019; Physicians News Network, "Will Hospitals, Physicians Opt Out of Assisted Suicide?" PhysiciansNews Network.com, May 23, 2016.

186 **Data from several states:** California Department of Public Health, *California End of Life Option Act 2021 Data Report*, CDPH.ca.gov, July 2022; Office of the Chief State Medical Examiner, *New Jersey Medical Aid in Dying for the Terminally Ill Act 2020 Data Summary*, OCSME.nj.gov, 2021.

186 **most common diagnosis:** CDPH, *California End of Life Option Act*; OCSME, *New Jersey Medical Aid in Dying for the Terminally Ill Act.*

186 **just 577 patients:** California Department of Public Health, *California End of Life Option Act 2017 Data Report*, CDPH.ca.gov, June 2018.

187 **support giving others:** Span, "Aid in Dying."

187 **point to the challenge:** Huong Q. Nguyen et al., "Characterizing Kaiser Permanente Southern California's Experience with the California End of Life Option Act in the First Year of Implementation," *JAMA Internal Medicine* 178 no. 3 (March 2018): 417–21.

187 **argues that it is incompatible:** American Medical Association, Code of Medical Ethics, "Physician-Assisted Suicide," Code-Medical-Ethics.ama-assn.org.

187 **religious groups oppose:** Pew Research Center, "Religious Groups' Views on End-of-Life Issues," PewResearch.org, November 21, 2013; Pew Research Center, "Views on End-of-Life Medical Treatments," PewResearch.org, November 21, 2013.

187 **disability rights groups worry:** National Council on Disability, *The Danger of Assisted Suicide Law: Part of the Bioethics and Disability Series*, NCD.gov, October 9, 2019.

187 **won't feel that death:** Rebecca Cokley, "Why the 'Choice' for Assisted Suicide Is No Choice for Disabled People," *Medium*, March 13, 2021.

187 **highest rates of death by suicide:** Centers for Disease Control and Prevention, "Complete Fatal Injury Data and Visualization," Web-Based Injury Statistics Query and Reporting System (WISQARS), CDC.gov.

187 **men in their teens:** National Institute of Mental Health, "Suicide," NIMH.NIH. gov.

187 **high rates among older people:** American Association for Marriage and Family Therapy, "Suicide in the Elderly," AAMFT.org; Institute on Aging, "The Difference Between Elder Suicide and Dying with Dignity: Why Some Older Adults Want to Die," IOAging.org, November 30, 2015.

187 **buffer against risk:** Conwell Yeates, Kimberly Van Orden, and Eric D. Caine, "Suicide in Older Adults," *Psychiatric Clinics of North America* 34, no. 2 (June 2011): 451–68; Kevin Caruso, "Elderly Suicide," Suicide.org.

188 **Friendship Line:** Institute on Aging, "Friendship Line," IOAging.org,

188 **Chester Nimitz, Jr.:** Lewis M. Cohen, "Deaths with Dignity," *Slate*, June 6, 2013; National Museum of the Pacific War, "Admiral Chester W. Nimitz," PacificWarMuseum.org; Sara Rimer, "With Suicide, an Admiral Keeps Command Until the End," *New York Times*, January 12, 2002.

188 **Betsy:** Betsy Van Dorn, interview by the author, July 24, 2022.

189 **ending life support:** Jones, "Prevalence of Living Wills."

190 **care related to:** National Institute on Aging, "Providing Care and Comfort at the End of Life," NIA.NIH.gov, November 17, 2022.

190 **align with their values:** Patricia A. Bomba, Marian Kemp, and Judith S. Black, "POLST: An Improvement over Traditional Advance Directives," *Cleveland Clinic Journal of Medicine* 79, no. 7 (July 2012): 457–64; Charles P. Sabatino, "Eight Advance Care Planning Lessons That Took Me Thirty Years to Learn," *Bifocal, the Journal of the ABA Commission on Law and Aging* 34, no. 6 (July 1, 2013): 115–19.

190 **Sarah Creed:** Sarah Creed, interview by the author, September 22, 2022.

191 **Lark:** Lark, interview by the author, January 12, 2023.

192 **eleven million widows:** U.S. Census Bureau, "Widowhood," Census.gov, 2022.

192 **lost a spouse:** Benjamin Gurrentz and Yeris Mayol-Garcia, "Marriage, Divorce, Widowhood Remain Prevalent Among Older Populations," U.S. Census Bureau, April 22, 2021.

192 **huge amount of their time:** Gretchen Livingston, "On Average, Older Adults Spend Over Half Their Waking Hours Alone," Pew Research Center, July 3, 2019.

192 **"widowhood effect":** J. Robin Moon et al., "Short- and Long-Term Associations Between Widowhood and Mortality in the United States: Longitudinal Analyses," *Journal of Public Health* 36, no. 3 (September 2014): 382–89.

192 **caring for someone at the end:** Katherine Ornstein et al., "A National Profile of End-of-Life Caregiving in the United States," *Health Affairs* 36, no. 7 (July 2017).

192 **survivor's heart muscle:** National Council on Aging, "The Widowhood Effect: How to Survive the Loss of a Spouse," NCOA.org, August 24, 2021.

193 **help in the aftermath:** NCOA, "Widowhood Effect."

193 **first two years:** Jialu L. Streeter, "Gender Differences in Widowhood in the Short-Run and Long-Run: Financial, Emotional, and Mental Wellbeing," *Journal of the Economics of Ageing* 17 (2020): 100258.

193 **Widowers tend to:** Streeter, "Gender Differences in Widowhood."

193 **may lack access:** Patricia Amend, "Eight Common Estate Planning Mistakes," AARP, January 20, 2023.

193 **survive their spouse:** Kathleen M. Rehl, "Recent Widows Need Financial Guidance After a Spouse's Death," CNBC, March 6, 2020.

193 **objective review:** Rehl, "Recent Widows."

193 **survey of seventy thousand widows:** Sarah Wilcox et al., "The Effects of Widowhood on Physical and Mental Health, Health Behaviors, and Health Outcomes: The Women's Health Initiative," *Health Psychology* 22, no. 5 (2003): 513–22.

193 **interviewed three years later:** Wilcox et al., "Effects of Widowhood."

Chapter 8: A Better Second Fifty

195 **spends more per person:** Matthew McGough et al., "How Does Health Spending in the U.S. Compare to Other Countries?," *Health System Tracker*, February 9, 2023.

195 **200,000 fewer of us:** Frances Stead Sellers et al., "Compare Your Life Expectancy with Others Around the World," *Washington Post*, October 3, 2023.

195 **into their eighties:** Author's calculations from U.S. Census Bureau, "How Has Our Nation's Population Changed?" Census.gov, 2023.

196 **did not cover the cost:** Thomas R. Oliver, Philip R. Lee, and Helene L. Lipton, "A Political History of Medicare and Prescription Drug Coverage," *Milbank Quarterly* 82, no. 2 (June 2004): 283–354.

196 **per-person growth:** Margot Sanger-Katz, Alicia Parlapiano, and John Katz, "A Huge Threat to the U.S. Budget Has Receded. and No One Is Sure Why," *New York Times*, September 5, 2023; Phillip L. Swagel to Sen. Sheldon Whitehouse, "Re: CBO's Projections of Federal Health Care Spending," CBO.gov, March 17, 2023.

196 **more than one hundred:** FP Analytics and AARP, *Planning for Aging Societies: An Analysis of Governmental Plans for Healthy Aging from Around the World*, AARP International, 2023.

196 **Some U.S. states:** FP Analytics and AARP, *Planning for Aging Societies.*

197 **"a California for all":** California Department of Aging, "Master Plan for Aging," MPA.aging.ca.gov.

197 **Fernando Torres-Gill:** Fernando Torres-Gill, interview by the author, March 11, 2023.

197 **assistant secretary on aging:** UCLA Luskin School of Public Affairs, "Fernando Torres-Gil," Luskin.UCLA.edu.

197 **developed polio:** Patricia Lombard, "Wilshire Resident Fernando Torres-Gil, Polio Survivor on World Polio Day," *Larchmont Buzz*, October 23, 2020.

198 **twenty-three strategies:** Scan Foundation, "Brief Overview of California's Master Plan for Aging," ScanFoundation, January 14, 2021.

198 **reducing co-payments:** Calif. Dept. of Aging, "Master Plan for Aging."

198 **state mandates:** Center for Health Care Strategies, "The Unexpected Benefits of a State Multisector Plan for Aging: Lessons from California," CHCS.org, April 2022.

199 **in Singapore:** Debra Whitman and Lina Walker, "Singapore: An Island Nation with a Big Vision for Aging," AARP International, October 1, 2020.

199 **Global Roadmap on Healthy Longevity:** National Academy of Medicine, "The Global Roadmap for Healthy Longevity," NAM.edu.

200 **Ageism is the belief:** World Health Organization, "Ageing: Ageism," WHO.int, March 18, 2021.

200 **age discrimination in employment:** AARP International, "The Longevity Economy Outlook," AARPInternational.org, 2019.

200 **4 percent larger:** AARP and *Economist* Intelligence Unit, *The Economic Impact of Age Discrimination: How Discriminating Against Older Workers Could Cost the U.S. Economy $850 Billion*, AARP.org, 2018.

200 **costs of age discrimination:** Organization for Economic Cooperation and Development, *Promoting an Age-Inclusive Workforce. Living, Learning and Earning Longer*, OECD.org, December 16, 2020.

200 **Supreme Court ruling:** *Babb v. Wilkie*, 589 U.S. (2020); Erich Wagner, "Supreme Court Makes It Easier for Feds to Prove Age Discrimination," *Government Executive*, April 6, 2020; *Gross v. FBL Financial Services*, 557 U.S. (2009).

201 **their health declining:** Stephanie E. Rogers et al., "Discrimination in Healthcare Settings Is Associated with Disability in Older Adults: Health and Retirement Study, 2008–2012," *Journal of General Internal Medicine* 30, no. 10 (2015): 1413–20.

201 **ageist prejudices:** Todd D. Nelson, "Reducing Ageism: Which Interventions Work?" *American Journal of Public Health* 109, no. 8 (August 2019): 1066–67.

201 **shed the myths:** Jo Ann Jenkins, *Disrupt Aging: A Bold New Path to Living Your Best Life at Every Age* (New York: PublicAffairs, 2016), 36–43.

201 **3.5 million years:** Thomas A. LaVeist, Darrell Gaskin, and Patrick Richard, "Estimating the Economic Burden of Racial Health Inequalities in the United States," *International Journal of Health Services* 41, no. 2 (April 1, 2011): 231–38; Ani Turner, *The Business Case for Racial Equity: A Strategy for Growth*, W.K. Kellogg Foundation, 2018.

201 **ten million fewer jobs:** AARP and *Economist* Impact, *Our Collective Future: The Economic Impact of Unequal Life Expectancy*, AARP.org, 2022.

201 **continue to fall:** Steven H. Woolf and Laudan Aron, eds., *U.S. Health in International Perspective: Shorter Lives, Poorer Health* (Washington, DC: National Academies Press, 2013).

202 **ensuring equal treatment:** Brian D. Smedley, Adrienne Y. Stith, and Alan R. Nelson, eds., *Unequal Treatment: Confronting Racial and Ethnic Disparities in Health Care* (Washington, DC: National Academies Press, 2003).

202 **women and men rises:** George Institute for Global Health, "Greater Gender Equality Helps Both Women and Men Live Longer," GeorgeInstitute.org, June 3, 2023.

202 **put off visits to doctors:** Cleveland Clinic, "Men Will Do Almost Anything to Avoid Going to the Doctor" (press release), My.ClevelandClinic.org, September 4, 2019.

202 **MENtion It!:** Cleveland Clinic, "MENtion It: The Importance of Men's Health," *Health Essentials Newsletter*, September 1, 2019.

202 **death toll among men:** David Brooks, "The Crisis of Men and Boys," *New York Times*, September 29, 2022.

202 **Low-quality education:** Yenee Soh et al., "State-Level Indicators of Childhood Educational Quality and Incident Dementia in Older Black and White Adults," *Journal of the American Medical Association* 80, no. 4 (February 13, 2023): 352–59.

203 **diploma or less**: U.S. Census Bureau, "Census Bureau Releases New Educational Attainment Data," Press Release no. CB23-TPS.21, Census.gov, February 16, 2022.

203 **closing the health gap:** Steven H. Woolf et al., "Giving Everyone the Health of the Educated: An Examination of Whether Social Change Would Save More Lives Than Medical Advances," *American Journal of Public Health* 97, no. 4 (April 1, 2007): 679–83.

203 **the longest lived:** Anne Case and Angus Deaton, *Accounting for the Widening Mortality Gap Between American Adults With and Without a BA*, Brookings, September 27, 2023.

203 **"If you have a college":** Jennifer Karas Montez, interview by the author, September 7, 2022.

203 **the more education:** Jennifer Karas Montez, Mark D. Hayward, and Anna Zajacova, "Educational Disparities in Adult Health: US States as Institutional Actors on the Association," *Socius* 5 (March 11, 2019).

203 **make college unaffordable:** Emily DeRuy, "Measuring College (Un)affordability," *Atlantic,* March 23, 2017; Lori Trawinski, Susanna Montezemolo, and Alicia Williams, *The Student Loan Debt Threat: An Intergenerational Problem,* AARP Public Policy Institute, May 14, 2019.

203 **isn't worth the cost:** Douglas Belkin, "Americans Are Losing Faith in College Education, WSJ-NORC Poll Finds," *Wall Street Journal,* March 31, 2023.

203 **declining enrollment:** National Student Clearinghouse, "Spring 2023: Current Term Enrollment," StudentClearinghouse.org, May 24, 2023.

203 **401(K)ids accounts:** Sarah Godlewski, "State Treasurer Sarah Godlewski: Public Hearing on 401(K)ids Is a Step Toward Making Investment Accounts for Every Wisconsin Child a Reality," Office of the State Treasurer, State of Wisconsin, March 2, 2022.

203 **increase financial resources:** Madeline Brown, Ofronama Biu, Catherine Harvey, and Trina R. Shanks, "The State of Baby Bonds," Urban Institute, February 2, 2023; Jim Huang et al., "Asset Building and Child Development: A Model for Inclusive Child Development Accounts," *Journal of the Social Sciences* 7, no. 3 (August 2021) 176-95.

204 **Tennessee Promise:** Tennessee Promise, "About," TN.gov.

204 **removing requirements:** Intelligent, "34% of Companies Eliminated College Degree Requirement to Increase Number of Applicants in the Past Year," Intelligent.com, January 30, 2023; Anne Case and Angus Deaton, "Without a College Degree, Life in America Is Staggeringly Shorter," *New York Times,* October 3, 2023.

204 **innovative models:** Debra Whitman, Marc Freedman, and Jim Emerman, "Social Security Lifelong Learning Benefits," *Public Policy and Aging Report* 28, supp. 1 (2018): S55–S63; Stacy Rapacon, "Free or Cheap College Courses for Older Adults in All 50 States," AARP, February 5, 2020.

205 **prenatal and infant care:** America's Health Rankings, "2020 Annual Report, International Comparison," AmericasHealthRankings.org, 2021; Eunice Kennedy Shriver National Institute of Child Health and Human Development, "Are There Ways to Reduce the Risk of Infant Mortality?" NICHD.NIH.gov, October 29, 2021.

205 **list of policy solutions:** Kathleen Mullan Harris, Malay K. Majmundar, and Tara Becker, eds., *High and Rising Mortality Rates Among Working-Age Adults* (Washington, DC: National Academies Press, 2021).

205 **poverty doesn't result:** Kenneth Nelson and Johan Fritzell, "Welfare States and Population Health: The Role of Minimum Income Benefits for Mortality," *Social Science and Medicine* 112 (2014): 63–71.

205 **replaces less:** Organization for Economic Cooperation and Development, *Pensions at a Glance 2021,* OECD-ilibrary.org.

205 **antipoverty spending:** Jason Beckfield and Clare Bambra, "Shorter Lives in Stingier States: Social Policy Shortcomings Help Explain the US Mortality Disadvantage," *Social Science and Medicine* 171 (2016): 30–38.

205 **nine-year gap:** National Center for Health Statistics, "Life Expectancy at Birth by State" (press release), CDC.gov, August 24, 2022.

205 **strong policies:** Jennifer Karas Montez, Mark D. Hayward, and Douglass A. Wolf, "Do U.S. States' Socioeconomic and Policy Contexts Shape Adult Disability?" *Social Science Medicine* 178 (2017): 115–26.

205 **Beaufort County:** Erwin Tan, Angela Houghton, and Justin Ladner, *How Geography, Race, and Ethnicity Affect Life Expectancy at 50—Report 2: National Level Analysis,* AARP Thought Leadership, 2023.

206 **most important factors:** Sarah Galvani-Townsend, Isabel Martinez, and Abhishek Pandey, "Is Life Expectancy Higher in Countries and Territories with Publicly Funded Health Care? Global Analysis of Health Care Access and the Social Determinants of Health," *Journal of Global Health* 12 (November 12, 2022): 04091.

206 **those with chronic conditions:** Amelia Whitman et al., *Addressing Social Determinants of Health: Examples of Successful Evidence-Based Strategies and Current Federal Efforts,* Report HP-2022-12, Assistant Secretary for Planning and Evaluation, U.S. Department of Health and Human Services, April 1, 2022.

206 **Meals on Wheels:** Meals on Wheels, "The Escalating Issue of Senior Hunger: 2023 National Snapshot (fact sheet), MealsonWheelsAmerica.org, September 2023.

206 *six years more*: Sarah Forrester et al., "Racial Differences in Weathering and its Associations with Psychosocial Stress: The CARDIA Study," *SSM-Population Health* 7 (2019).

206 **older black Americans:** Vicki A. Freedman and Brenda C. Spillman, "Active Life Expectancy in the Older US Population, 1982–2011: Differences Between Blacks and Whites Persisted," *Health Affairs* 35, no. 8 (2016): 1351–58; Cynthia G. Colen, Patrick M. Krueger, and Bethany L. Boettner, "Do Rising Tides Lift All Boats? Racial Disparities in Health Across the Lifecourse Among Middle-Class African-Americans and Whites," *SSM-Population Health* 6 (December 2018): 125–35.

207 **"Health in All Policies":** Centers for Disease Control and Prevention, "Health in All Policies," CDC.gov, June 9, 2016.

207 **Ministers for Loneliness:** United Kingdom, "Government's Work on Tackling Loneliness," Gov.uk, June 21, 2023.

207 **"epidemic" of loneliness:** U.S. Surgeon General Vivek H. Murthy, *Our Epidemic of Loneliness and Isolation: The U.S. Surgeon General's Advisory on Healing Effects of Social Connection and Community,* Office of the U.S. Surgeon General, 2023.

207 **average sixty-year-old:** Author's calculations from World Health Organization, "Healthy Life Expectancy (HALE)," WHO.int, 2020.

208 **Affordable Care Act:** Chiquita Brooks-LaSure and Ellen Montz, "Inflation Reduction Act Tax Credits Improve Coverage Affordability for Middle-Income Americans," Centers for Medicare and Medicaid Services, August 10, 2022; Rachel Garfield, Kendal Orgera, and Anthony Damico, "The Uninsured and the ACA: A Primer—Key Facts About Health Insurance and the Uninsured Amidst Changes to the Affordable Care Act," KFF, January 25, 2019.

208 **still uninsured:** Jane Sung and Olivia Dean, *Policy Options to Improve Older Adults' Health Insurance Affordability: a Series Overview.* AARP Public Policy Institute, November 15, 2023.

208 **fifteen thousand preventable:** Sarah Miller, Norman Johnson, and Laura R. Wherry, *Medicaid and Mortality: New Evidence from Linked Survey and Administrative Data,* National Bureau of Economic Research, Working Paper no. 26081, July 2019.

208 **Expanding access:** Rachel Schwab, Rachel Swindle, and Justin Giovannelli, "State-

Based Marketplace Outreach Strategies for Boosting Health Plan Enrollment of the Uninsured" (issue brief), Commonwealth Fund, October 25, 2022.

208 **all important components:** Dan G. Blazer, Sarah Domnitz, and Catharyn T. Liverman, eds., *Hearing Health Care for Adults: Priorities for Improving Access and Affordability* (Washington, DC: National Academies Press, 2016); Institute of Medicine, *Advancing Oral Health in America* (Washington, DC: National Academies Press, 2011); Annalyn Welp, R. Brian Woodbury, Margaret A. McCoy, and Steven M. Teutsch, eds., *Making Eye Health a Population Health Imperative: Vision for Tomorrow* (Washington, DC: National Academies Press, 2017).

208 **untreated tooth decay:** Centers for Disease Control and Prevention, "Older Adult Oral Health," CDC.gov, May 5, 2021.

208 **poor oral health:** Centers for Disease Control and Prevention, "Oral Health Conditions," CDC.gov, September 20, 2023; Tamanna Tiwari et al., "Association Between Mental Health and Oral Health Status and Care Utilization," *Frontiers in Oral Health* 2 (February 2022): 732882.

208 **untreated hearing loss:** Nicholas S. Reed et al., "Trends in Health Care Costs and Utilization Associated with Untreated Hearing Loss over 10 Years," *JAMA Otolaryngology– Head and Neck Surgery* 145, no. 1 (2019): 27–34.

208 **Vision loss:** Welp, Woodbury, McCoy, and Teutsch, *Making Eye Health.*

209 **help offset:** Amber Willink et al., "Dental, Vision, and Hearing Services: Access, Spending, and Coverage for Medicare Beneficiaries," *Health Affairs* 39, no. 2 (February 2020): 297–304.

209 **only 5 percent:** Organization for Economic Cooperation and Development, "Health Expenditure and Financing" (chart), Stats.OECD.org.

209 **greater use of primary care:** Cost Growth Target Advisory Committee, "Evidence for Primary Care Investments Reducing Total Cost of Care," Oregon.gov, July 2022.

209 **more equitable distribution:** Barbara Starfield, Leiyu Shi, and James Macinko, "Contribution of Primary Care to Health Systems and Health," *Milbank Quarterly* 83, no. 3 (2005): 457–502.

209 **Oregon, an assessment:** Portland State University, *Implementation of Oregon's PCPCH Program: Exemplary Practice and Program Findings,* Oregon.gov, September 2016.

209 **long-standing relationship:** Molly FitzGerald, Munira Z. Gunja, and Roosa Tikkanen, "Primary Care in High-Income Countries: How the United States Compares," Commonwealth Fund, March 2022.

209 **have a heart attack:** Neil K. Mehta, Leah R. Abrams, and Mikko Myrskyla, "US Life Expectancy Stalls Due to Cardiovascular Disease, Not Drug Deaths," *Proceedings of the National Academy of Sciences* 117, no. 3 (2020): 6998–7000.

209 **preventive services:** Centers for Disease Control and Prevention, AARP, and American Medical Association, *Promoting Preventive Services for Adults 50–64: Community and Clinical Partnerships,* CDC.gov, May 31, 2016.

210 **first in obesity:** Woolf and Aron, *U.S. Health in International Perspective*; ProCon/*Encyclopaedia Britannica,* "Global Obesity Levels," ProCon.org, March 27, 2020.

210 **One in five deaths:** Ryan K. Masters et al., "The Impact of Obesity on US Mortality Levels: The Importance of Age and Cohort Factors in Population Estimates," *American Journal of Public Health* 103, no. 10 (2013): 1895–901.

210 **recommended weight:** Samuel H. Preston, "Deadweight?: The Influence of Obesity on Longevity," *New England Journal of Medicine* 352, no. 11 (March 17, 2005): 1135–37.

210   **up to eight:** Medicare, "Counseling to Prevent Tobacco Use & Tobacco-Caused Disease," Medicare.gov.

210   **severe shortage:** Association of American Medical Colleges, *The Complexities of Physician Supply and Demand: Projections from 2019 to 2034*, AAMC.org, June 2021; Lisa M. Haddad, Pavan Annamaraju, and Tammy J. Toney-Butler, "Nursing Shortage," StatPearls, February 13, 2023.

210   **number of geriatricians:** American Geriatrics Society, "Geriatrics Workforce by the Numbers," AmericanGeriatrics.org, 2023; Paula E. Lester, T. S. Dharmarajan, and Eleanor Weinstein, "The Looming Geriatrician Shortage: Ramifications and Solutions," *Journal of Aging and Health* 32, no. 9 (2020): 1052–62.

210   **lowest-paid medical specialties:** Lester, Dharmarajan, and Weinstein, "Looming Geriatrician Shortage."

210   **Programs that promote:** Ariadne A. Meiboom et al., "Why Medical Students Do Not Choose a Career in Geriatrics: A Systematic Review," *BMC Medical Education* 15 (2015): 1–9; Shahidullah, "Why the US Health Care System."

210   **we should emphasize:** Kevin T. Foley and Clare C. Luz, "Retooling the Health Care Workforce for an Aging America: A Current Perspective," *Gerontologist* 61, no. 4 (2021): 487–96.

211   **Geriatrics Workforce Enhancement Program:** American Geriatrics Society, "GWEP Coordinating Center," AmericanGeriatrics.org, 2023.

211   **Increasing funding:** Foley and Luz, "Retooling the Health Care Workforce."

211   **$38 trillion:** Andrew J. Scott, Martin Ellison, and David A. Sinclair, "The Economic Value of Targeting Aging," *Nature Aging* 1 (2021): 616–23.

212   **projected to reach:** Alzheimer's Association, *2023 Alzheimer's Disease Facts and Figures*, Alz.org, 2023; Kumar B. Rajan et al., "Population Estimate of People with Clinical Alzheimer's Disease and Mild Cognitive Impairment in the United States (2020-2060)," *Alzheimer's and Dementia* 17, no. 12 (2021): 1966–75.

212   **14 percent:** Centers for Disease Control and Prevention, "New Estimates of Americans with Alzheimer's Disease and Related Dementias Show Racial and Ethnic Disparities," CDC.gov, September 20, 2018.

212   **cost per person:** National Academies of Sciences, Engineering, and Medicine, Reducing the Impact of Dementia in America: A Decadal Survey of the Behavioral and Social Sciences (Washington, DC: National Academies Press, 2021), chap. 7; Julie Zissimopoulos, Eileen Crimmins, and Patrick St. Clair, "The Value of Delaying Alzheimer's Disease Onset," *Forum for Health Economics Policy* 18, no. 1 (November 4, 2014): 25–39.

212   **$290 billion:** Alzheimer's Association, *2019 Alzheimer's Facts and Figures*.

212   **save $145 billion:** Super, Ahula, and Proff, *Reducing Cost and Risk of Dementia*.

212   **Alzheimer's disease risk study:** Jae Jeong Yang et al., "Association of Healthy Lifestyles with Risk of Alzheimer Disease and Related Dementias in Low-Income Black and White Americans," *Neurology* 99, no. 9 (2022): e944–e953.

213   **National Plan to Address Alzheimer's Disease:** U.S. Department of Health and Human Services, Office of the Assistant Secretary for Planning and Evaluation, National Plan to Address Alzheimer's Disease: 2021 Update, ASPE.HHS.gov, December 27, 2021.

213   **new goal:** ASPE, National Plan to Address Alzheimer's.

213   **increased nearly eightfold:** Alzheimer's Association, "Research Funding," Alz.org.

213 **majority of people:** Halima Amjad et al., "Underdiagnosis of Dementia: An Observational Study of Patterns in Diagnosis and Awareness in US Older Adults," *Journal of General Internal Medicine* 33, no. 7 (2018): 131–38.

213 **1.5 percent of those:** Sumit Agarwal, Sanjay Basu, and Bruce E. Landon, "The Underuse of Medicare's Prevention and Coordination Codes in Primary Care: A Cross-Sectional and Modeling Study," *Annals of Internal Medicine* 175, no. 8 (2022): 1100–8.

214 **GUIDE Model:** Rosalyn Carter Institute for Caregivers, "Guiding the GUIDE Model Toward Stronger Caregiver Supports" ATIAdvisory.org, September 2023; Centers for Medicare and Medicaid Services, "Improved Dementia Experience (GUIDE) Model," CMS.gov, 2023.

215 **working longer:** Jonathan Yoe, "Why Are Older People Working Longer?" *Monthly Labor Review,* July 2019.

215 **either have a job:** U.S. Bureau of Labor Statistics, "The Employment Situation—October 2023," News Release no. USDL-23-2318, BLS.gov, November 3, 2023.

215 **employers benefit:** Aon Hewitt, *A Business Case for Workers Age 50+: A Look at the Value of Experience,* AARP Research, April 2015.

215 **more age diversity:** OECD, Promoting an Age-Inclusive Workforce; Eric Larson, "New Research: Diversity + Inclusion = Better Decision Making at Work," *Forbes,* September 21, 2017.

216 **ninety thousand hours:** Jessica Pryce-Jones, *Happiness at Work: Maximizing Your Psychological Capital for Success* (Hoboken, NJ: Wiley, 2010).

216 **workers know their shifts:** Lisa F. Berkman, Beth C. Truesdale, and Alexandra Mitukiewicz, "What Is the Way Forward? American Policy and Working Longer," in *Overtime: America's Aging Workforce and the Future of Longer Working,* ed. Lisa F. Berkman and Beth C. Truesdale (New York: Oxford University Press, 2022).

216 **productive lives:** Centers for Disease Control and Prevention, "Increase Productivity," CDC.gov, December 4, 2015.

216 **state job-training programs:** Carl E. Van Horn, Kathy Krepcio, and Maria Heidkamp, *Improving Education and Training for Older Workers,* AARP Public Policy Institute, March 2015.

217 **make grants available:** Van Horn, Krepcio, and Heidkamp, *Improving Education and Training.*

217 **care for a family member:** Susan C. Reinhard et al., *Valuing the Invaluable: 2023 Update, Strengthening Supports for Family Caregivers,* AARP Public Policy Institute, March 2023.

217 **state family leave laws:** Jeremy Nobel et al., *Supporting Caregivers in the Workplace: A Practical Guide for Employers,* Northeast Business Group Solutions Center and AARP Family Caregiving, 2017.

217 **poverty rates falling:** Gary Burtless, "Working Longer in an Age of Rising Economic Inequality," in *Overtime: America's Aging Workforce and the Future of Longer Working,* ed. Lisa F. Berkman and Beth C. Truesdale (New York: Oxford University Press, 2022).

218 **has begun rising:** Emily A. Shrider and John Creamer, *Poverty in the United States: 2022,* Current Population Reports no. P60-280, Census.gov, September 2023; John Creamer, Emily A. Shrider, Kalee Burns, and Frances Chen, *Poverty in the United States: 2021,* Current Population Reports no. P60-277, U.S. Census Bureau, September 2022.

218 **options frequently discussed:** Social Security Administration, "Office of the Chief Actuary's Estimates of Individual Changes Modifying Social Security," SSA.gov.

218 **bipartisan initiatives:** SSA, "Office of the Chief Actuary's Estimates."

218 **hard to wait:** National Academy of Social Insurance, "Older Workers in Physically Challenging Jobs Need Stronger Social Insurance Supports," NASI.org, September 2023.

219 **must wait years:** Social Security Administration, "Outcomes of Applications for Disability Benefits," *Annual Statistical Report on the Social Security Disability Insurance Program, 2021*, SSA.gov, 2021.

219 **bottom third:** OECD, *Pensions at a Glance 2021*.

219 **our peer countries:** U.S. Government Accountability Office, *Retirement Security: Recent Efforts by Other Countries to Expand Plan Coverage and Facilitate Savings*, GAO-22-105102, GAO.gov, August 29, 2022; David John, Gary Koenig, and Marissa Malta, *Payroll Deduction Retirement Programs Build Economic Security*, AARP Public Policy Institute, July 2022.

219 **have nothing saved:** Neil Bhutta et al., "Changes in U.S. Family Finances from 2016 to 2019: Evidence from the Survey of Consumer Finances," *Federal Reserve Bulletin* 106, no. 5 (September 2020).

219 **reduced tax revenue:** John Scott and Andrew Blevins, "State Automated Retirement Programs Would Reduce Taxpayer Burden from Insufficient Savings," Pew Trusts, June 2, 2023.

219 **Saving through paychecks:** John, Koenig, and Malta, *Payroll Deduction Retirement Programs*.

219 **creating retirement savings:** Georgetown University Center for Retirement Initiatives, "State Programs 2023: More Programs Are Open and Enrolling Workers, Smaller Sates Actively Explore Partnership Opportunities, while Other States Continue to Introduce Legislative Proposals," CRI.Georgetown.edu, 2023.

219 **conservative and liberal:** Mark Iwry and David C. John, "The Automatic IRA at 15: Helping Americans Build Retirement Security," Brookings, February 12, 2021.

220 **financial shock:** PEW Charitable Trusts, "How Do Families Cope with Financial Shocks?" (issue brief), PEWTrusts.org, October 28, 2015.

220 **offset accessibility investments:** Shannon Guzman, Janet Viveiros, and Emily Salomon, *Expanding Implementation of Universal Design and Visitability Features in the Housing Stock*, AARP Public Policy Institute, July 2017.

220 **CAPABLE:** Brendan Flinn and Susan Reinhard, *CAPABLE: A Model of Empowering Older Adults to Remain Independent*, AARP Public Policy Institute, 2022.

220 **range of housing types:** Melissa Stanton, ed., *Discovering and Developing Missing Middle Housing*, AARP Livable Communities, 2022.

221 **new zoning:** Julie Grant, Shannon Guzman, and Rodney Harrell, *Accessory Dwelling Units: A Step by Step Guide to Design and Development*, AARP, 2019.

221 **separate living spaces:** Grant, Guzman, and Harrell, *Accessory Dwelling Units*.

221 **program in Ireland:** Stephanie Firestone and Esther Greenhouse, *Rightsizing in Place: Ava Housing, Ireland*, AARP Equity by Design, 2021.

221 **spend more than a third:** Linda M. Couch, "Falling Short: Federal Housing Assistance Is Failing Older Adults," *Generations Journal*, Summer 2020.

221 **living in homeless shelters:** Joint Center for Housing Studies of Harvard University, *Housing America's Older Adults: Meeting the Needs of an Aging Population*, JCHS.Harvard.edu, 2014.

222 **in rural areas:** U.S. Department of Agriculture, "Multifamily Housing Rental Assis-

tance," Rd.Usda.gov; U.S. Department of Housing and Urban Development, "Section 202 Supportive Housing for the Elderly Program," HUD.gov.

222 **750 communities:** AARP Livable Communities, "The Member List," AARP.org, 2023.

222 **live at home:** Super, Ahuja, and Proff, "Reducing Cost and Risk of Dementia."

222 **Neighbors and community:** Ruth A. Hackett et al., "Social Engagement Before and After Dementia Diagnosis in the English Longitudinal Study of Ageing," *PLoS One* 14, no. 8 (2019): e0220195.

222 **programs that encourage:** Frye Art Museum, "Arts Engagement for Adults Living with Dementia," FryeMuseum.org; Norman Burns, "The Memory Café: Creating a Museum Program for People with Dementia," American Alliance of Museums Blog, July 17, 2019; Museum of Modern Art, "meetme: The MoMA Alzheimer's Project," MoMA.org.

223 **WA Cares:** WA Cares Fund, "About the WA Cares Fund," WACaresFund.wa.gov.

223 **Several other states:** Mark Miller, "States Try Easing the Burden of Long-Term Care's High Cost," *New York Times*, June 16, 2023.

223 **pay only for nursing home:** Edem Hado and Brendan Flinn, *Home and Community-Based Services for Older Adults*, AARP Public Policy Institute, November 2021.

223 **half of U.S. states:** Susan Reinhard et al., *Innovation and Opportunity: A State Scorecard on Long-Term Services and Supports for Older Adults, People with Physical Disabilities, and Family Caregivers*, AARP Public Policy Institute, September 2023.

223 **more than twice as much:** Medicaid and CHIP Payment and Access Commission, "Estimates of Nursing Facility Payments Relative to Costs" (issue brief), MACPAC.gov, January 2023.

224 **dignified quality of life:** David Dayen, "An Interview with Ai-jen Poo," *American Prospect*, October 21, 2020.

224 **National Strategy to Support Family Caregivers:** Administration for Community Living, *2022 National Strategy to Support Family Caregivers*, ACL.gov, May 1, 2023.

225 **one in five Medicare dollars:** Ian Duncan et al., "Medicare Cost at End of Life," *American Journal of Hospice and Palliative Care* 36, no. 8 (August 2019): 705–10.

225 **well-designed hospice:** Elrycc Berkman, Tim Doyle, and Ryan Brancati, *Palliative Care in Medicaid Costing Out the Benefit: Actuarial Analysis of Medicaid Experience*, National Academy for State Health Policy, December 17, 2022.

225 **"concurrent care":** Bernard J. Wolfson, "Shift in Child Hospice Care Is a Lifeline for Parents Seeking a Measure of Comfort and Hope," *KFF Health News*, September 22, 2022.

225 **requiring clinicians:** Quan Vega et al., "Place of Death from Cancer in US States With vs. Without Palliative Care Laws," *JAMA Network Open* 6, no. 6 (2023): e2317247.

226 **save $1.2 billion:** Diane E. Meier, "Increased Access to Palliative Care and Hospice Services: Opportunities to Improve Value in Health Care," *Milbank Quarterly* 89, no. 3 (2011): 343–80.

226 **expanding coverage:** Sam Teshale and Wendy Fox-Grage, "Emerging State Innovations in Developing a Medicaid Community-Based Palliative Care Benefit," National Academy for State Health Policy, August 2022.

226 **California, Hawaii:** Michael Ollove, "Why Some Patients Aren't Getting Palliative Care," *Stateline*, July 10, 2017.

226 **rates of death by suicide:** CDC, "Complete Fatal Injury Data."

226 **twelve million older people:** Beth Carter, Claire Noel-Miller, and Olivia Dean, "New

Funding Package Will Improve Access to Care for Older Adults with Depression," AARP Blogs, March 21, 2023.

226 **biggest risk factor:** American Association for Marriage and Family Therapy, "Suicide in the Elderly," AAMFT.org; Carter, Noel-Miller, and Dean, "New Funding Package."

226 **screened for depression:** Centers for Medicare and Medicaid Services, "Depression Disparities in Medicare Fee-for-Service Beneficiaries," CMS.gov, February 2021.

227 **were never asked:** Carter, Noel-Miller, and Dean, "New Funding Package."

226 **Mental Health Parity and Addiction Equity Act:** Centers for Medicare and Medicaid Services, "The Mental Health Parity and Addiction Equity Act (MHPAEA)," CMS. gov, September 6, 2023.

227 **limit the number of days:** Carter, Noel-Miller, and Dean, "New Funding Package."

228 **struggle at every stage:** U.S. Department of Health and Human Services, Office of Diseases Prevention and Health Promotion, "Poverty," Healthy People 2030, Health. gov; Richard G. Rogers et al., "Dying Young in the United States: What's Driving High Death Rates Among Americans Under Age 25 and What Can Be Done?," *Population Bulletin* 76, no. 2 (2022).

228 **certain advantages:** Stephen Crystal, Dennis G. Shea, and Adriana M. Reyes, "Cumulative Advantage, Cumulative Disadvantage, and Evolving Patterns of Late-Life Inequality," *Gerontologist* 57 no. 5 (October 1, 2017): 910–20.

229 **Joe Manchin:** AARP States, "AARP WV, Senator Manchin Speak Out About Need for Lower Rx Drug Prices," States.AARP.org.

230 **does not have to wait:** ALS Association, "ALS Advocacy Pays Off with Enormous Win Ending SSDI Waiting Period" (blogpost), als.gov, December 8, 2020.

INDEX